THE PHILOSOPHY OF PRAXIS

International Library of Social and Political Thought

General Editor: István Mészáros

Lukács:	THE YOUNG HEGEL
Vázquez:	THE PHILOSOPHY OF PRAXIS
Davidson:	GRAMSCI: AN INTELLECTUAL BIOGRAPHY
E.P. Thompson:	WILLIAM MORRIS
Mészáros:	BEYOND CAPITAL
Constantino:	NEO-COLONIAL IDENTITY AND COUNTER-CONSCIOUSNESS

The Philosophy of Praxis

BY

ADOLFO SÁNCHEZ VÁZQUEZ

translated by Mike Gonzalez

MERLIN PRESS: LONDON
HUMANITIES PRESS: NEW JERSEY

Copyright © 1977 English Translation The Merlin Press

All rights reserved

First published in Great Britain in 1977 by The Merlin Press
2/4 West Ferry Rd., London E.14

First published in the United States of America
by Humanities Press Inc.
Atlantic Highlands, N.J. 07716

Copyright © 1966 by Adolfo Sánchez Vázquez

Translation Copyright © Merlin Press

Library of Congress Cataloging in Publication Data
Sánchez Vázquez, Adolfo, 1915—
The philosophy of praxis.

Translation of Filosofia de la praxis.
Bibliography: p.
Includes index.
1. Practice (Philosophy) I. Title.

B831.3.S313   1976   146'.4   76-23235
ISBN 0-391-00650-9

Printed in Great Britain
by Whitstable Litho Ltd., Whitstable, Kent.

Contents

INTRODUCTION 1

From ordinary consciousness to the philosophical consciousness of praxis 1

A note on terminology 1

The ordinary consciousness of praxis 2

Towards a history of the philosophical consciousness of praxis 10

Towards a full vindication of human praxis 23

Marxist polemics on praxis 30

Praxis as a central philosophical category 31

PART I: PHILOSOPHICAL SOURCES OF THE STUDY OF PRAXIS 40

Ch. 1: The conception of praxis in Hegel 40

The theoretical activism of German Idealism 40

The Hegelian concept of labour before *The Phenomenology of Mind* 46

Human Labour in the *Phenomenology* 51

Practice as a practical idealism in the *Science of Logic* 57

Summary of the Hegelian concept of praxis 64

Ch. II: The conception of praxis in Feuerbach 70

The critique of religion 70

The relations of subject and object	72
Theoretical and religious behaviour	76
Theory and religion	78
Anthropology and religion	81
Religion and practice	82
What is praxis for Feuerbach?	84
Summary of the Feuerbachian concept of praxis	88
Ch. III: The conception of praxis in Marx	92
Theoretical and practical necessity of a philosophy of praxis	92
Philosophy and action	97
The revolution and the historical mission of the proletariat	99
Productive praxis as alienated labour	104
The transformation of man and the world	107
Man and nature: the anthropological character of natural science	111
Praxis and knowledge: the "Theses on Feuerbach"	115
Praxis as the basis for knowledge (Thesis I)	117
Praxis as a criterion of truth (Thesis II)	120
Revolutionary praxis as the unity of the change in man and the change in circumstances (Thesis III)	122
From the interpretation of the world to its transformation (Thesis XI)	125
Praxis in "The German Ideology"	127
Production in History and in social life	128
Necessity for revolutionary praxis	129
The materialist conception of history and the theory of praxis	131

The problem of the transition from theory to action	134
Marxism as a philosophy of praxis	137

PART II: SOME PHILOSOPHICAL PROBLEMS OF PRAXIS — 148

Ch. IV: What is praxis — 149

Activity and praxis	149
The adaptation of acts to ends	150
Practical activity	155
Forms of praxis	156
Theoretical activity	161
Philosophy and praxis	163

Ch. V: Unity of theory and practice — 169

The "common sense" point of view: pragmatism	169
Practice as the foundation of theory	172
Science and production	173
Unity of theory and revolutionary praxis	178
Praxis as the end of theory	186
Praxis and the comprehension of praxis	188
Praxis as a criterion of truth	190
The relative autonomy of theory	191
Practice as subjective and objective activity	193

Ch. VI: Creative and reiterative praxis — 199

Levels of praxis	199

Creative praxis	200
Revolution as creative praxis	204
Artistic creation	206
Reiterative or imitative praxis	209
Bureaucratised praxis	211
Reiterative praxis in human labour	214
Supremacy and decline of the hand	218
Imitative praxis in art	223

Ch. VII: Spontaneous and reflective praxis	228
Consciousness in the practical process	228
Practical consciousness and the consciousness of praxis	229
The new levels of praxis	230
The spontaneous and the reflective in revolutionary praxis	232
The historical mission of the proletariat in our time	234
Flashes of consciousness and class consciousness	237
From spontaneous to reflective praxis	238
The Leninist conception of socialist consciousness	239
Marxism as a philosophy of the proletariat	241
Marxism as science and ideology	243
The Intellectual and the proletariat	247
The Party as a "collective intellectual"	253

Ch. VIII: Praxis, Reason and History	259
Intentional praxis	259

Intention and result	260
Intentional praxis in art	262
Intentional praxis in social life	263
Unintentional praxis	265
Men, the subjects of history	267
Individuality and sociality	270
Unintentional products of an intentional praxis	271
Historical rationality and teleology	273
The rationality of actual history	275
The universal rationality of history	278
The universal and structural rationality of history	280
The rationality of changing social structures	283
Unintentional historical products	286
The duality of individual praxis	287
From intentional praxis to a common, intentional praxis	290
Interests and social structure	293
Limits of an intentional, collective praxis	295
Subjectivism and voluntarism in intentional, historical praxis	297
The subjective factor and objective rationality	299
Rationality and purpose in historical praxis	301
Ch. IX: Praxis and violence	305
Violence as a human attribute	305
Violence in productive and artistic praxis	306
Violence in social praxis	308

Violence and counter-violence	310
Potential violence and violence in the act	311
Revolution and violence	312
The historical necessity of violence	313
Non-violence	316
The consciousness of non-violence	318
The apologia for violence	319
Objective elements of violence	319
Men and the instruments of violence	324
Non-violent social praxis	325
The violence that negates itself	327
Towards the exclusion of violence	328
Conclusion	331
APPENDICES:	
One	338
Two	352
Bibliography	371
Index	381

Prologue

It is now five years since this study first appeared. Since then, important events have occurred in the realm of practice, and particularly of social, revolutionary praxis. And things have not stood still in the field of Marxist theory either. Despite the serious obstacles that lay in the way, the years of sclerosis and dogmatism have been progressively overcome both in theory and practice. This volume was and continues to be a contribution to that process of overcoming, a process which is in any event irreversible. But there has been a cost, as new scientific-positivist and abstract humanist versions of Marxism make their appearance.

Having reflected on the theoretical and practical developments of the last few years, I would reaffirm still the underlying conception of the present work—Marxism as a philosophy of praxis. I continue to believe that Marxism is above all a philosophy of praxis and not a new philosophical praxis. Marxism must certainly be constituted as a science, as distinct from an ideology or an utopia—but that must be derived from its character as practice, *from, through* and *in* praxis. The very fate of Marxism as a theory (as a new theoretical arm of the revolution) depends upon the role accorded to praxis within it.

This reaffirmation of the original conception of the book leads me to the conclusion that the shape, structure and basic perspective of the work should remain as originally written. This does not mean that the text cannot or should not be changed in part or as a whole; on the contrary, the theoretical and practical developments of recent years make it necessary to introduce a whole number of modifications and additions. Unfortunately, the urgency of the need to prepare this second edition, combined with a lack of time, has made it impossible for that substantial revision to be carried out. The first edition has been out of print for a year, and it is clearly necessary to prepare this second edition with maximum speed. Thus, there are few changes in this, second, edition.

I wish to take this opportunity to thank those critics and scholars who have devoted their attention to this work. The number of seminars and round table discussions the book has provoked bear witness to the interest of scholars. As far as the critics are concerned, the many reviews and commentaries to which this volume has given rise have, whether through convergence or divergences, in agreement or in disagreement, given the author a valuable stock of suggestions which will prove most useful in his future work.

To all of them, and to the reading public for their enthusiastic reception of this study, my sincere thanks.

Adolfo Sanchez Vazquez

Mexico City, August 1972.

Introduction

From ordinary consciousness to the philosophical consciousness of praxis

A note on terminology
   The Ancient Greeks used the word praxis (πρᾶσις) to denote action itself. In English only the word *practice* is in common usage, while *praxis* has a more limited philosophical status[1]. The latter has been used throughout this study, however, with a specific purpose in view: to free the concept of practice from the limited meaning it normally has of practical human activity in a restricted and pejorative utilitarian sense in expressions like "a practical man", "practical results" etc. If we are to elaborate a philosophical concept of practical actitity, it must first be freed from the associations that it has in everyday language; hence the use throughout of the term praxis which, despite its etymological links with "practice" does not necessarily carry with it the same semantic undertones.
   On the other hand, the use of the word *praxis* should not be taken to imply an acceptance of its original meaning; the Greeks perceived action as an end in itself rather than as an act producing or creating an object distinct from its agent and from the activity itself. For Aristotle moral action was praxis, insofar as it engendered nothing outside itself; the activity of the artisan, on the other hand, which produces something that exists independently of the agent of that activity, is not regarded as praxis. Action which generates an object external to the subject or his acts is called *poiesis* (ποιησις,)–literally the act of production or manufacture. In this sense, the artisan's work is *poetic* rather than *practical.* Rigorous attention to the original Greek meanings, in fact, would demand the use of poiesis rather than praxis, and the philosophy whose basic concepts we are now seeking to clarify

would be called "the philosophy of poiesis". Poiesis is still preserved, however, in the root of words like poetry, poetic, etc; "Poetry" in fact still retains a special meaning so restricted as to make its use to designate practical activity in broad terms, inappropriate. So *praxis* will be used throughout the study to designate that human activity which produces objects, but stressing at the same time that this activity is not seen in the narrow utilitarian sense that belongs to the term *practice* in common usage.

The ordinary consciousness of praxis

Praxis, then, is the central category of the philosophy which is not merely an interpretation of the world, but also a guide to its transformation; that is, Marxism. Yet the philosophical consciousness of praxis does have other antecedents in the past; nor does the philosophy of Marx represent its most complete expression. Having gone beyond German Idealism, Marxism represents the most developed consciousness as well as its most profound link with actual praxis. It leaves the Idealist consciousness behind, and travels even further from the immediate or ingenuous standpoint of ordinary consciousness.

The Marxist conception of praxis in no sense implies a return to prephilosophical attitudes nor to the standpoint of vulgar or metaphysical materialist philosophy, which was still tied to ordinary consciousness and which preceded the more developed expositions of Idealist philosophy (in Kant, Fichte and Hegel). The Marxist conception of praxis, then, does not represent a return to the past, but an advance, an overcoming, the negation and assimilation in a dialectical sense of traditional materialism and of Idealism. This implies, of course, that both had an essential contribution to make to the development of Marxism, particularly as far as praxis was concerned, though Idealism did present human practical activity in an abstract and mystified form.

The Idealist conception was a necessary stage in the development of a true philosophy of praxis understood not only as the activity of consciousness, whether human or superhuman, but as the material activity of social man. The fact of overcoming that conception, moreover, did not in any sense entail a return to pre-Idealist conceptions, nor the restoration of the immediate, ingenuous standpoint of ordinary consciousness. Philosophical Idealism could not be overcome by a dose of "common sense", but only by another philosophical theory whose materialist character would enable it to go even further than Idealism beyond ordinary consciousness. Such a philosophy must not only offer a theoretical explanation of a reality, the reality of praxis, but must also show under what circumstances the transition from theory to practice is possible in a way that leaves intact their intimate unity.

The historical fact that Marxism has been, and still is in some instances, reduced to the old materialism fertilised by dialectics on the one hand, or a materialist metaphysics which is little more than an inverted Idealism, on the other, is a result of the deliberate omission or rejection by some commentators of the centrality of the category of praxis (not only interpreting the world, but changing it)[2]. The explanation is to be found in the failure to analyse the dual and apparently contradictory significance of German Idealism for the development of Marxism as a philosophy of reconciliation (interpretation) on the one hand, and a philosophy of activity on the other. Marxism, it is true, is the result of a radical break with Idealism; yet it owes to Idealism a significant debt.

The Hegelian deformations of Marxism and the mechanistic, scientific or neopositivist interpretations of Marx's work are equally guilty of misrepresenting the true sense of praxis as the actual, objective material activity of men who are practical, *social,* beings *in* and *through* praxis. These false perspectives cannot be overcome, however, by retreating to the standpoint of ordinary consciousness, thereby elevating that standpoint to the consciousness of praxis *par excellence.* The implication would be that ordinary men, because they live in a practical utilitarian world, or within the realm of immediate needs and the acts which can satisfy those needs, are closer to a true conception of praxis than the philosophers whose existence in the realm of abstractions and mediations enables them to perceive praxis as best only in an abstract and idealistic way. That seems to be the significance of the suggestion that the only way to escape the speculative excesses of Idealism is to return to ordinary consciousness. The problem is that in this, as in every other sphere of knowledge, the essence is not given directly or immediately in appearance; day to day practice serves to conceal that essence rather than reveal it. It is true that speculative, Idealist philosophy, and that of Hegel in particular, presented the essence of praxis in a mystified form; but we cannot conclude from that that ordinary consciousness is closer to a true conception of praxis than philosophical consciousness, even in its Idealist, Hegelian form.

Idealist philosophical consciousness surpasses the immediate, abstract and unilateral point of view of ordinary consciousness, a true consciousness of praxis can in turn only be achieved by overcoming the restricted and mystified standpoint of Idealist consciousness, rather than by returning to a prior, prephilosophical state. In this sense, the abolition of the standpoint of ordinary consciousness as well as a dialectical negation of the mystified consciousness of praxis are necessary preconditions of the development of an objective, scientific perspective upon man's practical activity. Only in this way can thought and action be united in consciousness. And only when the framework of ordinary consciousness is transcended can the philosophical consciousness of praxis and the elevation of reiterative, spontaneous everyday praxis to a higher, creative, level be achieved. Hence Lenin's assertion that "without revolutionary theory, there can be no revolutionary movement."[3] The theory of revolutionary praxis requires that the instinctive and spontaneous point of view of ordinary proletarian consciousness be overcome, and that for both theoretical and practical reasons, it be countered by a correct understanding of praxis.

Here as elsewhere, the natural everyday attitude coexists with a philosophical attitude that has emerged through time; that must be the point of departure for a philosophical conception of praxis. This natural attitude regards practical activity as a simple datum that requires no explanation, and sees its relationship with the world of practical acts and objects as direct and immediate; it regards the links between that world and itself as occurring on an atheoretical plane. It feels no urgent need to tear away the veil of prejudices, mental habits and commonplaces on to which it projects its practical acts, for the links with the world of practice are affirmed to exist without reference to the theory or pursuit of contemplation whose only purpose can be to divert it from the pressing need to satisfy the practical and immediate needs of daily life[4]. It would, however, be little more than frivolous to accept unquestioningly what the average man thinks of himself, or how his consciousness perceives itself. Clearly, he does not live in an absolutely atheoretical world; he is a historical and social being, immersed in a network of social relations and rooted in a given historical soil. The day to day character of his life, as well as the vision that he has of his own practical activity, are historically and socially determined, and his consciousness nourished by an accumulation of ideas, values, judgments and prejudices of all kinds. He is never called upon to confront a naked fact, for each fact is assimilated by him into an ideologically determined perspective generated by the particular social and historical conditions of his daily life. So his attitude towards praxis entails a consciousness of the practical fact, its assimilation into a perspective governed by certain ideological principles. His consciousness of praxis is shot through with

ideas that are present in the very air he breathes; in many cases, that consciousness represents the unconscious adoption of points of view which had originally arisen as reflections upon the practical fact. Thus the ordinary consciousness of praxis has a theoretical basis, even where it degrades or dismisses theory.

The average man is in general unable to recognise the social and class dimensions of activity; when he judges the individual activity of the revolutionary to be fruitless, foolish or irresponsible, and asserts that such behaviour can never lead to the transformation of the world in its present state, he is explicitly devaluing the activity of men in the social field and making himself party to that school of thought that disregards the active role of men in transforming society. By its deprecatory and negative attitude towards revolutionary activity, ordinary consciousness walks hand in hand with those contemporary philosophies, many of which originate in the pessimistic irrationalism of Schopenhauer, that reject the transforming possibilities of human action, deny the socio-historical reality and rob both history and human action of any and all significance. The primitive philosophical thesis reappears in ordinary consciousness; yet there remain even in this elemental form theoretical elements of what had once been a reflective philosophical theory. Nevertheless, the obscure and distant echo of an unconsciously adopted philosophical thesis is not sufficient for there to persist any theoretical aspects in this attitude to praxis; for the crucial moment of a conscious linking up of consciousness and its object is absent. The average man, it is true, stands in a direct and immediate relation to things, and that relation cannot fail to be conscious; but he does not separate or stress practice as his proper object in such a way that that separation occurs first of all in consciousness as a theoretical attitude, or an object of thought. Ordinary consciousness thinks practical acts, but it does not see praxis, the act of transforming society, as its proper object; it does not, nor can it produce a theory of praxis.

On the other hand, ordinary men do seem to have some idea of praxis, albeit in an obscure and restricted sense; but that idea will remain tied to practice until they step outside the everyday plane and raise the idea to that level of reflection whose highest expression is philosophical consciousness. How can ordinary consciousness free itself from this ingenuous, spontaneous conception? The answer to this question will require an analysis of praxis at a whole number of different levels, but it can be stated at the outset that ordinary consciousness can never nurture a true revolutionary praxis until it has made that transition through reflective consciousness to a philosophy of praxis.

In what forms has the philosophical consciousness of praxis presented itself historically? And under what conditions does the ordinary consciousness which must be abandoned if man is to be able to transform his world in a creative, revolutionary way, emerge and come to coexist with that philosophical consciousness?

The ordinary man regards himself as the authentic practical man par excellence, living and acting in a practical way. In his world not only do things exist *in themselves,* but they exist primarily in terms of their practical significance, to the extent that they satisfy the immediate necessities of daily life. That practical significance, however, appears to him as an immanent quality of things, which occurs independently of the human actions that confer such a significance upon them. Things are not only known in themselves, irrespective of their relation to human activity of any kind (the standpoint of ingenuous realism), but they are also significant in themselves, disregarding the fact that because they have a practical significance practical acts and objects exist only *for* and *through* men. The characteristic of ordinary consciousness is that it regards the practical world as a world of things and meanings *in themselves.* And together with this objectivism which disregards the human, subjective aspect, and maintains the separation between the practical object and the subject, ordinary consciousness, perhaps unwittingly, reduces the practical to a single utilitarian dimension, whereby a practical action or object is one which has material utility or which produces profit or advantage; that which lacks that direct or immediate utility, is impractical, and thus lies beyond the limits of the practical world thus defined. In this respect ordinary consciousness and the standpoint of capitalist theories of economics and production coincide in their interpretation of artistic creation, for example. For ordinary consciousness what is productive is by definition practical; from the point of view of capitalist production the practical is defined as whatever produces new value or surplus value[5].

The attempt to satisfy the "practical" aspirations of ordinary man sometimes leads to an effort by those in power to deform, emasculate or drain his political consciousness, with the apparent object of integrating him into political life, but in fact on condition that he restrict himself exclusively to its "practical" aspects, that is politics as a career. When the content of politics is reduced to its "practical", productive aspects, it can evidently only retain a negative significance for those who, because they are marginal to this integrative process, fail to see any dimension to politics outside this "practical" aspect, other than romanticism, idealism or Utopia. The attempt to satisfy the "practical" aspirations of ordinary men can also take another form, much favoured by those in power, whose object is to suppress any awakening of a clear political consciousness, however slight, and to maintain ordinary people in a totally apolitical state. This depoliticisation, moreover, creates an immense vacuum in the consciousness of the people which is of use to the ruling class to the extent that it can be filled with acts, prejudices, habits, cliches and concerns which ultimately contribute to the maintenance of the established social order. The apoliticism of large sectors of society leads to their exclusion from the process of solving fundamental economic, social and political problems; in this way the stage is left clear for a minority to assume these tasks and to carry them out in accordance with their own particular class or group interests. Both "practical politics" and the kind of "apoliticism" that is encouraged and sustained for "practical" reasons, satisfy the aspirations and interests of ordinary, "practical" people; but what this means in fact is that they separate them from any real political activity and particularly from revolutionary praxis. In this sense both "practical politics" and "practical" apoliticism are elements of bourgeois ideology, above all the ideology of a bourgeoisie in power whose politics have lost all their attraction for the oppressed or the exploited classes.

In a world governed by immediate practical necessities, in the practical-utilitarian sense, not only do art and politics, particularly revolutionary politics, come to be seen as unproductive or impractical activities par excellence since they produce only aesthetic pleasure on the one hand and (often) hunger, misery and persecution on the other, and therefore make no contribution to the satisfaction of immediate personal needs; theoretical activity, too, appears to ordinary consciousness as a parasitic activity which has little relevance to immediate practical necessity; the theoreticians and philosophers who speculate and theorise yet offer no practical contribution, are spurned by ordinary men because their activity does not result in any useful product. Like Thales' servant twenty five centuries ago, the ordinary man is always ready to deride the philosopher who lives absorbed in a speculative heaven, but cannot avoid stumbling over objects in the world of everyday things. For ordinary consciousness life is a "practical" affair, not in the sense in which Marx used the term, but in a strictly utilitarian sense[6]. But ordinary consciousness does not recognise this as a limitation; on the contrary it regards it as being endowed with a self-sufficient power, as an activity that can forge its own way forward with no need for external support; the ordinary man sees no need for a theoretical activity which can only, in his view, be a diversion from the real purpose. Ordinary consciousness always has before it the image of a "practical" man who exists in a world of "practical" necessities, objects and acts that impose themselves on him in a perfectly natural way; he cannot opt out of that world unless he is willing to stumble and fall like the theoreticians and the philosophers.

For ordinary men, practice is sufficient unto itself; it needs no broader basis or support. That seems self-evident in their view, and does not create any problem for them. They know, or believe they know what is required with respect to their own demands, for practice itself offers a repertoire of solutions. Any problems that do arise, therefore, can only be the result of a speculation that fails to take into account these demands and their solution. Practice speaks for itself. Thus ordinary men regard themselves as practical beings who have no need of theories; problems are solved in practice itself or in reliving past practice in the form we call experience. Thought and action, theory and practice, therefore, are separate realms. Theoretical activity, that is, impractical or unproductive and useless activity par excellence, becomes increasingly alien to them, for they do not see reflected in it what they regard as their true practical-utilitarian nature.

Assuming that this is a fair picture of the ordinary man, and without losing sight of the fact that he is a historical man whose daily life is inseparable from the social structure that sets the frontiers of that life, it is clear that he does retain some notion of praxis, however limited and false it may be. He has a consciousness of praxis forged in a spontaneous and unreflecting way yet in a degraded, crude and simplistic form it retains certain theoretical and ideological elements. He is conscious, for example, of the conscious character of his practical acts; he knows that his practical activity is not simply mechanical or instinctive, but that it demands the intervention of his consciousness. Yet as far as the actual content and significance of his acts, that is as far as a consciousness of praxis is concerned, he never gets beyond the utilitarian, individual and self-sufficient (atheoretical) notion of it which was discussed earlier.

The average man, immersed as he is in a world of everyday concerns and necessities, never reaches a genuine consciousness of praxis that might enable him to surpass the narrow frontiers of his practical activity and see certain aspects of his activity (work, politics etc.) in their whole anthropological, cognitive and social dimension. In other words, he rarely succeeds in recognising the extent to which he, through his practical activity, is contributing to the writing of the history which is the process through which men form and create themselves; nor is he able to understand the extent to which praxis requires theory, or the degree to which his own practical activity forms part of a total human and social praxis such that his individual actions imply those of others, and in turn those of others reflect his own activity. In that sense ordinary consciousness cannot overcome the utilitarian and individualistic conception of praxis without at the same time negating itself. For ordinary consciousness there exist both objects that have a given significance (a simply utilitarian one) and the act of producing and consuming them; so long as it remains on this atheoretical level of everyday life, however, ordinary consciousness must always fail to recognise the actual human significance of those acts and objects. For that is only available to consciousness that can grasp the content of praxis in its social and historical totality integral to which are both the specific forms adopted by the praxis (labour, art, politics, medicine, education, etc.) and its particular manifestations in the activities of specific individuals or groups, as well as their varied products. Historically it is possible to trace the development of that perspective from the ingenuous, empirical conception of praxis to the philosophical consciousness that finds expression, though not yet a complete or absolute expression, in Marxism. That philosophical consciousness is not casually arrived at, nor is it the result of an immanent internal development in human thought; it can only be achieved in a given historical moment, when practical material activity (praxis) itself has reached a point in its development where men can no longer continue to act upon and change the world creatively, that is in a revolutionary way, without first gaining a true philosophical consciousness of praxis. It is the history of actual praxis itself that makes such a level of consciousness imperative at a certain stage of its development, though that stage can only be reached in turn when the necessary theoretical premises have been allowed to mature through the history of ideas.

It could be said that a true conception of praxis presupposes the whole history of man as a practical, social being, and the whole history of philosophy. It is for this reason that ordinary consciousness, caught within the frontiers of its own spontaneous and unreflective conception of practical activity, could never rise to a true philosophical conception of praxis.

Towards a history of the philosophical consciousness of praxis

For centuries the philosophers seemed fully to merit the attitude of suspicion and scorn on the part of ordinary people typified by the servant of the Ionian philosopher, Thales, for far from trying to explain praxis in its true human dimension, they simply turned their back on the problem. Of course the attitude of the Ancient philosophers had scientific and social roots which prevented them from recognising its true significance. So in Ancient Greece, where Western philosophy originated, philosophers persistently ignored or rejected the practical world because they regarded that world as having only a practical-utilitarian character; in that respect, they shared the perspective of ordinary consciousness. They considered practical material activity, and labour in particular, to be unworthy of free men and the proper province of slaves. Contemplative, intellectual activity, on the other hand, was much extolled. The Ancient Greeks were concerned primarily with the domain of the human universe, with the transformation of social matter, of man, and with the creation and development of that specific social, human reality that was so much an innovation in the Ancient world—the *polis*. The *polis* was the highest expression of the process of man's conscious transformation as a social being or "political animal"; the transformation of things, of Nature, occupied only a secondary place, for productive material praxis was of little interest to the Greeks, since they did not acknowledge any link between that praxis and what they regarded as the principal human enterprise—the transformation of the human universe. Even if they had been interested in establishing man's dominion over nature, it was for them inconceivable that it could be achieved through the practical transformation of things, of matter; man's direct and immediate relation to material things through praxis, simply enslaves and demeans him. The idea that man makes and elevates himself as a human being as a direct result of his practical activity, his labour, which transforms the material world is one that was alien to the Greek world. For the Ancients, the process of man's development moved in the opposite direction, liberating him from all practical, material activity, from practice, and isolating him in the realm of theory.

It is in Plato and Aristotle that this conception has its most developed expression. In the work of Plato theoretical life, the contemplation of essences *(bios theoretikos),* acquires a new primacy and a new metaphysical status. Life, properly speaking, was contemplation. The full life could only be achieved by liberating men from every obstacle in the empirical world to the contemplation of perfect, immutable and eternal ideas. These obstacles originate in the senses, in the attachment of man as a physical being to things, to matter, and his subjection to practical concerns. Plato isolates theory from practical activity, that is from those activities that cannot dispense with material things; according to Plutarch, this led him to consider the application of geometry to practical tasks humiliating, and even to deprecate those arts like painting and sculpture which, like craft and manual labour, tied man to a close relationship with matter. Aristotle, too, echoes his master's scorn for physical work, and his assertion of the superiority of theory. For Aristotle, practical material activity had no human significance: "A state with an ideal constitution... cannot have its citizens living the life of mechanics or shopkeepers, which is ignoble and inimical to goodness. Nor can it have them engaged in farming; leisure is a necessity, both for growth in goodness and for the pursuit of political activities".[7] The most human, authentic and valuable kind of life is a theoretical life in which men dedicate themselves to "thought of the best object"[8]. At this higher level, where man exists as a rational being, theory is adequate to itself and does not need to be applied or subordinated to practice. Clearly, Aristotle shares Plato's scorn for all material practical activity, understood as the transformation of material things through human labour.

Productive material praxis (labour) makes man a slave to matter, to things; that is why it was considered unworthy of free men in the slave-owning society of Greece. Since it was subject to matter, productive activity was deemed to be worthy only of slaves; free men must live in leisure, as philosophers or as politicians, and devote themselves to contemplation and political activity, to contact with ideas and to the conscious regulation of the acts of men in their capacity as citizens of the *polis*. Physical activity, because of its servile and demeaning character, was to be left in the hands of slaves.

In the ancient world, theory never lost its supremacy, however important a role political activity might fulfil. Plato and Aristotle, for example, recognised the legitimacy of political praxis, but always saw it as subordinate to theoretical life. Plato did recognise, however, that theory had to be practical, that thought and action would have to maintain a unity which was located in the realm of politics. That unity is maintained by allowing ideas to become practical in themselves; theory becomes practical, according to Plato, not only because it represents a knowledge whereby man can liberate himself from enslavement to matter, maintain and defend his human condition and realise himself as a human being, but also because theory shapes practice in the fullest sense, so that the former ceases to be pure knowledge and fulfils a social and political function. Ultimately theory and practice, philosophy and politics merge in the person of the philosopher king. Plato admits the possibility that worthwhile activity can take place in the field of politics, but only insofar as it is totally impregnated by theory in a relation in which theory is always given primacy. This means that the political praxis of men has no function other than to let itself be moulded by theory, although theory receives nothing in return from praxis. Theory is not dependent on praxis; the philosopher is in no way subservient to the *polis*. Theory must impose itself upon practice; only in this sense can it have practical content. Plato's attitude to political and social praxis, as a theory that is itself praxis, or as praxis adapted to theory, simply prefigures future Utopian conceptions of the transformation and organisation of society. He admits that theory can become practice, and even accepts the possibility of political praxis, but only to the extent that this implies the application of the absolute principles set out in his theory. Praxis, therefore, must be philosophical; its value derives from its rational theoretical content. So the Platonic unity of theory and practice simply represents the dissolution of praxis in theory.

Aristotle, too, acknowledged the legitimacy of political praxis, but regarded it as inferior to theoretical life. Unlike Plato, however, he no longer expected political activity to adjust itself to the absolute principles laid down by theory. The political circumstances of his time led him to conclude that the unity of theory and practice was impossible and impracticable, and therefore that it was no longer feasible to insist that theory should govern practice. That which Plato had aspired to keep together in ideal terms, had now been divided by life itself. The philosophers could not be kings, nor the kings philosophers. The Platonic distinction between these two lives and their respective types of reason, has to be accepted; but it must be recognised at the same time that they are not exclusive but that they can merge and complement one another once their differences and hierarchies have been recognised. Theory in the Platonic sense, had shown itself, by Aristotle's time, to be impracticable because of its refusal to acknowledge any practical activity unless it was governed by theory. The exigencies of real life in Aristotle's time had shown that political activities could no longer be guided by the absolute principles of theoretical reason. The conclusion was that theory must renounce practice, and practice must in turn become independent of theory. Both would continue to exist, but on separate planes. This did not mean, however, that political activity was essentially irrational; it had a rational content, but of a different order, for the reason that inspires it, which is practical reason, has as its object not pure essence but human acts. Thought, when it is linked to action, has not the capacity to "receive what is essential and what is intelligible"[9], but is an inferior, practical, intelligence. At this level, Aristotle takes into account the nature of actual, empirical States, and accepts a theory of political praxis which is the art of directing public affairs in practice. Nonetheless, and despite the existence of a political praxis, material productive activity is still separate from theory and remains not only alien to human essence, but opposed to it. For both Plato and Aristotle it is still the case that man's authentic realisation can only be achieved in theoretical life. The denial of a relation, or a possible link, between theory and productive material praxis, stems from the Greek conception of man as the rational and theoretical being par excellence. This conception, which was central to the ruling ideology of Greek society, stemmed from the social conditions of ancient cities in which the impotence of the mode of production based on slavery coupled with the capacity of a servile labour force to satisfy all the practical needs of the *polis* led to a debasement of the value of human labour, which appeared as a routine and demeaning activity whose product alone was of importance. And the value of the product itself stemmed not so much from the subjective activity to which it gave material form, as from its use value, that is its ability to satisfy the needs of another.

In Greece, work was seen as a function of the product, and the product in its turn as a function of its utility or capacity to satisfy a concrete human need. Exchange value, or the value of a commodity in relation to other commodities where all are regarded as equivalent expressions of general human labour[10], is of no interest; use value was the only criterion of value. Aristotle did, it is true, perceive the need to stabilise commodity production in order that they could be exchanged, but as Marx points out, he could never discover how these relations of equality might be assessed[11].

In *Das Kapital*, Marx is at pains to point out that the writers of the ancient world saw no significance in quantity and exchange value, but held exclusively to notions of quality and use value. The product was judged in terms of the concrete necessity which it was to satisfy and of the use to which it could be put by another; it was never considered either as a commodity or as a product of human activity, of labour. Both productive activity and the object produced exist by virtue of a necessity external to the artisan; the product and its producer remain in an external relation to one another, and while the product accrues value in accordance with its usefulness for someone other than the producer himself, the latter and his labour are deprecated as merely servile. In this way the artisan is twice a slave; enslaved both by the alien need that he serves, and by the matter that he transforms. Greek society, therefore, regarded production, or the transformation of nature as inferior to the self-transformation of man, or of the citizen of the *polis*. Intellectual work, on the other hand, which was considered to be the highest form of human labour, was the proper realm of the class of free men. Theoretical activity and practical productive labour stood in an antagonistic relation characterised by the superiority of the spiritual over the practical and the primacy of theoretical over practical life. It was the province of free men to devote themselves to free activities, while the slaves dedicated themselves to the activities appropriate to their station which, because of the contact with material things which they entailed, actually represented a negation of human labour.

The social division of labour, therefore, served to emphasise the gulf between contemplation and action, and equated human nature with theoretical activity only. The primacy attributed to free activity, and the deprecation of physical labour, simply confirmed the social division between free men and slaves. The hostility of Greek society towards manual labour was also extended to all those activities which necessarily entailed some contact with matter; hence the practical applications of a science like geometry, technical pursuits, surgery, and those artistic activities which, like painting and sculpture, which could not avoid some contact with material substances, were held in equal disdain. Plato, for example, considered it demeaning for geometry to be applied to practical problems, and established within a single science a clear distinction between 'learned', theoretical science and a vulgar, inferior experimental science *(Philebo 56d)*. According to Plutarch, Archimedes spurned the practical application of the science of mechanics, while Aristotle *(Proteptikos* frag 5) used the example of geometers and carpenters to show that theory and practice had different areas of application. So, although certain material activities were deemed worthy of respect particularly in the area of art[12], the Greeks generally maintained throughout their scornful attitude toward productive labour and the mechanical arts.

The philosophical consciousness of praxis in ancient slave-owning societies corresponded, therefore, to the interest of the ruling class in maintaining a negative conception of the relationship between theoretical and practical productive labour. And although political praxis is accepted, it is regarded as subordinate to theory since it is not, as Aristotle points out, inspired by theoretical reason, but by practice. In this way, the primacy of theory, and of human activity properly speaking, could be maintained. There were some in Ancient Greece, however, who disagreed with this disdainful attitude towards productive labour and the mechanical arts. Hesiod, for example, in *The works and the days* (302-313) accords to human labour a significance beyond its narrow utilitarian sense; in his judgment labour, because it produces wealth, has a redemptive character, pleasing the gods and granting independence and dignity. The Sophists, who declared their opposition to slavery, held similar opinions. Antiphon proclaimed, for example, that all men are by nature equal, including barbarians and Greeks. In his view, the pressing need for labour arises from the fact that "goodness can never come by itself, but is always accompanied by pain and trials". Plato himself *([Carmides]* 163 a,d) has left evidence of the high value ascribed to labour by Prodic, another Sophist, and the cynic Antisthenes is recorded as having taken a similar position, in a fragment collected by Diogenes Laertius (VI 2). It could be sustained, on the other hand, that the radical separation between theory and practice, or between science and its practical-mechanical applications characteristic of Ancient Greece, had never taken root at all in Ionia. The unity of science and technology which had occurred in the industrial and commercial cities of Ionia, found expression in the attitudes and nature of the *sophos* or Ionian sage. In contrast to the attitude of disdain prevalent in Athens, the mechanical arts did undergo some development in other Greek cities. It was the material conditions of life in Ancient Greece which was characterised by a slave-holding mode of production, which determined the rupture between theory and practice, held back technical progress and "blocked" that progress both socially and ideologically, in part as a result of its negative attitude towards productive physical labour[13].

The philosophical consciousness of praxis underwent radical changes during the Renaissance, changes associated with the names of Leonardo, Giordano Bruno and Francis Bacon among others. In this new philosophical perspective, man ceased to be regarded as a merely theoretical animal, and became instead the active subject, builder and creator of the world. Human dignity was vindicated, in their view, not only in contemplation but also in action; man is a creature of reason, but he is also a creature of volition. Reason allows him to understand nature and his will, illuminated by reason, to dominate and modify nature. The knowledge and transformation of nature began thus to be evaluated in terms of the economic interests of the bourgeoisie and the nascent capitalist mode of production. The power and future development of this social class were clearly linked to the practical, material transformation of the world, and to the progress of science and technology which would in turn be conditioned by that transformation of nature. Scientific knowledge was now no longer regarded as an activity valid in itself, which is degraded when it is applied to practical-mechanical problems; it was now to be put at the service of capitalist production and be driven forward by it. In this way, the nascent capitalist relations of production contributed directly to the development of a science and a technology which would in their turn fortify the new mode of production[14]. This entailed a new attitude towards those activities linked to the transformation of nature, which now no longer fell to the slaves, as they had in Greece, but to free men. As a result the actions of men and disinterested contemplation were now deemed equally worthy of appreciation; now not only art and war, but all those activities which had previously been regarded as inferior because of their material contact, were now considered worthy and noble. Furthermore, the producer is now worthy of attention as well as his product, and the latter acquires value precisely because it is the work of a human being. Gionnozzo Manetti, for example, proudly states in his *Dignitate et excelentia hominis:* "They are ours; what we have before us as are human things, made by men: houses, castles and cities and all the infinity of buildings scattered over the surface of the Earth"[15]. This idea of man as an active being is reasserted by the most eminent representatives of Renaissance humanism, Pico della Mirandola, Leon Bautista Alberti etc. The social position of the artisan, and of the artist too, was thus elevated.

The Renaissance vindication of practical human activities, however, was still limited in character, for it was determined by the need to dominate and transform nature by first understanding it. Man, it is true, has need of practical, transforming activity; but the practical man was not the be all and the end all, nor was it practice that revealed his human condition in the deepest sense. The exaltation of man as an active being did not, in other words, imply that contemplation ceased to occupy a privileged place; it was still regarded as superior to practical work and in particular to manual labour. Certainly work was no longer rejected as being a servile pursuit; no writer suggested that mere contact with matter was degrading. Far from enslaving him, it was generally accepted that it was a necessary condition of man's liberty. By that time the opposition between practical and theoretical activity, or between intellectual and physical labour, which had been maintained for class reasons throughout the ancient and the medieval world, had by now been reduced to a simple opposition between servile humiliating activities on the one hand, and free, elevated activity on the other. Yet although the distance between these two forms of activity was no longer so great, nor was physical labour any longer defined as the negation of human nature, it was still the case that the virtue of such activity lay in the fact that it prepared or preceded that properly human state of contemplation. Indeed contemplation still retained such a high status that Leonardo felt bound to rescue it from its previous bad name and proclaim it as a science, announcing to all and sundry that its principles had nothing to do with manual activities. So important was it to distinguish the artist from the artisan that Leonardo raised art to the level of a science so that the artists should be seen to be on a par with the contemplators or investigators of nature. Thus he was careful, for example, to distinguish between the principles of painting and other manual activities which fell within the purview of the artisan: "The scientific and true principles of painting... are understood by the mind alone and entail no manual operation; and they constitute the science of painting which remains in the mind of its contemplators; and from it is then born the actual creation, which is far superior in dignity to the contemplation or science which precedes it"[16].

As far as human labour was concerned, its value lay not in itself but in the degree to which it facilitated progress towards contemplation. That, for example, was the view of Bruno and of Thomas More. In *The expulsion of the glorious beast,* Bruno condemned leisure and extolled labour. In the Golden Age, he says, men lived a life of leisure free from worries and fatigue, yet they were no happier than the beasts and stupidity was master over all. In the age of labour, on the other hand, spurred by poverty and by necessity, men had discovered the arts and invented industry and had thus been able to triumph over nature. Labour had thus enabled man to raise himself above bestiality, and approach that truly human condition which culminated in the contemplation of God. It prepared the way for man to raise himself with heroic fury and rational impulse to the disinterested contemplation of divine being. In his *Utopia,* Thomas More accepted and exalted labour as an unpleasant necessity from which man would have to free himself if he was to devote himself to those higher tasks, like spiritual contemplation, which were man's proper pursuits.

There were, nonetheless, Renaissance thinkers who did not acknowledge the privileged role of theoretical activity. Bartolomeo Sacchi, for example, in *De optime cive* and Matteo Palmieri in *Della vita civile,* stressed that speculation isolates man, turns him into an egoist and removes him from the tasks which redound to the public good. Although Renaissance thought generally recognised the value and dignity of human labour, it continued to assign a higher place to contemplation than to practical activity. Moreover, the active, creative and constructive activity that was deemed worthy of Renaissance man appeared as the special province of exceptional, privileged personalities who had risen above the mass of subjects engaged in simple physical or mechanical activities. It was one thing to produce useful objects, and quite another to create works of art[17], for art, like politics, was the product of exceptional people who retained control over their own acts and who never invested the full extent of their powers in any one object. Giordano Bruno, for example, considered that labour made possible the existence of a small group of wise men and contemplative heroes, for the contemplation of God was not within the reach of every man. In his *Utopia,* More extended the obligation to work to every member of the community, with the exception of a handful of citizens whose exemption allowed them to devote all their energies to science and speculation. It is Campanella, in his *City of the sun,* who makes the most vigorous effort to overcome the opposition between physical and intellectual work, between contemplation and productive material praxis. He rejected the conception of work as a necessary precondition for a privileged few to raise themselves to the elevated state of contemplation; work, in his view, was available to all in equal measure, so that every citizen could go on to dedicate himself to specifically spiritual tasks. Thus contemplation would lose its privileged place, and would cease to be the province of a few. Campanella was clearly aware of the opposition between physical and intellectual work and of the division of society into antagonistic classes. Thus if true humanity and genuine human freedom were reserved to a few, it followed that the rest lived without liberty and in a condition that denied their humanity.

As a whole, the Renaissance philosophical consciousness of praxis relegated practical productive material activity to an inferior level. Other forms of activity certainly existed, like art and politics, but they shared with contemplation the exceptional character which restricted their availability to the mass of inferior, practical, subjects like artisans, mechanics, agricultural workers etc. Yet the unity of theory and practice can only be achieved in these special activities, as Leonardo, Alberti and Machiavelli continually stressed. Leonardo gave primacy to theory over practice: "The man who devotes himself to practice without regard to science," he argues, "is like a pilot who embarks on a voyage without rudder or compass... Science is the captain, and practice the crew". Machiavelli, on the other hand, put theory at the service of praxis and gave their unity a strongly pragmatic flavour.

Machiavelli's political theory was not simply the description or generalisation of a political praxis, but also an attempt to adapt and direct that praxis in the interests of the incipient Italian bourgeoisie. The theory expounded in *The Prince* reflected the peculiar situation that Italy was living through in the 15th and 16th centuries, an Italy divided into a series of states which were sliding into decadence as a result of their fragmentation. The solution offered by Machiavelli required the abandonment of medieval political conceptions and the establishment of a strong, centralised State under the firm leadership of the prince; to this end he set out in his most famous essay what he regarded as the most efficient political means for the achievement of this objective. Religion and morality, on the other hand, were to remain separate from, and subordinated to politics since ultimately it was politics that would determine their frontiers. As far as an efficient governor was concerned, his most important characteristics were, according to Machiavelli, his capacity and power to make decisions that would ensure the maintenance of power, together with a refusal to be weakened in this resolve by the need to employ violent, cruel or devious methods. Machiavelli recognised that in the actual historical situations of which he had experience, politics was not the sphere of ideals or of abstract moral principles, but of interests. The prince acted on behalf of the general interests of a bourgeoisie in need of a strong, centralised power. Having set out the concrete historical objectives, like national unity and a strong State, which best corresponded to those social interests, everything would then depend upon the courage and astuteness of the prince, on his correct understanding of the situation and of the particular and conflicting interests at work within it, on his knowledge of human psychology and on his familiarity and ability to use those means which must be employed to achieve those ends. Machiavelli could tolerate a crime, but not an error; thus political praxis required a theory, a political science based on knowledge of the facts, but which would not limit itself to a description and justification of those facts, since it would also set out the possibilities of moving beyond them. Whether or not his interpretation was simplistic or crude, this was the theory which Machiavelli put at the service of the nascent Italian bourgeoisie, as a contribution to their concrete political praxis.

The rising bourgeoisie also had a pressing need to transform nature and develop both the productive forces and the science and technology associated with them; in this respect, the Industrial Revolution of the 18th century was a decisive turning-point[18], for in response to those class interests and to the exigencies of production, human labour and technology were accorded an ever greater value, although there was no parallel evaluation of the worker nor of the human significance of his activity. Francis Bacon, Descartes, the Encyclopedists and the English economists all testified to the progressive raising of the consciousness of productive praxis. In response to social needs and determinations, it had become imperative to dominate nature through production, science and technology and take possession of the natural world, to overcome the spontaneous forces of nature and subordinate them to human purpose. For Bacon practice, in the sense of experiment or experimental scientific activity, would make this possible. The power of man over nature would be affirmed through a knowledge nourished by experience. For Descartes, too, reason was useful in itself because it could provide knowledge that aided practice, allowing man to dominate nature and become master of his world. It is in this sense that he argued, in the *Discourse on method,* that philosophy must be practical: "... in place of that speculative philosophy which is taught in the schools, we can achieve a practical one by means of which, by ascertaining the force and action of fire, air, the stars, the heavenly bodies and the skies, of all the physical things that surround us, as distinctly as we know the various trades of our artisans, we can apply them, in the same way, to all the uses for which they are fit, and thus make ourselves, as it were, the lords and masters of nature"[19]. Now, although Bacon's empirical conception was to give way to Descartes' rational-idealist conception of praxis, both regarded theoretical activity as the real source of man's power. It was they who maintained through the 16th and 17th centuries, the value of the transformation of nature, of production under the guidance of science and theory; yet the value of that transformation was still assessed in utilitarian terms rather than in the light of the transformation, at once positive and negative, that occurred in man as a result of that process. Labour and its products were still evaluated, then, without reference to the subject of the process—the producer, or the worker.

The Encyclopedists also set great store by technology, the mechanical arts and human industry; they regarded technology as the manifest form of the unity of theory and practice. "It is difficult, if not impossible," affirms the entry under 'Technology', "to drive practice very far without speculation, and vice versa..." They saw men affirming themselves in ways both practical and theoretical which merged in the labour and technology which they commended so highly. The French thinkers of the Enlightenment, therefore, sought to affirm in various ways the positive qualities of human culture, science, technology and labour. Only Jean-Jacques Rousseau refused to add his voice to the general chorus. For him the centuries of human progress in the field of culture and technology, and the growth of man's power over nature had failed to achieve a positive balance. He set man's much-vaunted progress against the consequences that it had had for him, and reached the following conclusion: that the transformation of nature had only served to transform man in a negative way. Rousseau had perceived for the first time the relationship between the transformation of nature, as theoretical and practical culture, and the transformation of man. For Rousseau's conclusion was that the human social praxis that transforms the natural and the human reality through labour, technology, art and politics, had yielded only a negative result; historically, it had done little more than degrade and vilify man. Rousseau's views stood in radical contrast to those of his enlightened contemporaries, just as his analysis of human labour clashed directly with the English economists writing in his own century. In one sense, Rousseau seems to lag behind them all, yet in another his assertion of the relative negativity of human productive praxis was well in advance of his own time; many of his ideas, in fact, were to be developed much later by Marx[20].

Towards a full vindication of human praxis

The Classical economists (Adam Smith, Ricardo etc.) also eulogised the material praxis which they observed in bourgeois society; indeed they elevated that praxis to the general category of productive praxis. It is to their credit that they recognised in human labour the source of all material wealth and value. Both Marx and Engels, however, emphasised the merits and the limitations of this conception of labour-value, which the classical economists, because of their class perspective, were never able to carry through to its ultimate conclusions.

English political economy, classical German philosophy and French socialism are the three pillars on which Marxism was built (Lenin: *Three sources and three integral parts of Marxism*). Marx and Engels, for example, read and criticised the classical economists at an early stage of their development, first Engels in his "Outlines of a critique of political economy"[21] and a little later Marx who, as a result of reading Engels' study, turned to economics for the first time in the autumn of 1843, and left as the fruit of his reading a series of notebooks published for the first time in 1932 under the title *Economic studies (Extracts)*[22]. Immediately afterwards he wrote what was to be the first draft of a work based on those earlier notes; this work was never published during his lifetime, and is known today under the title used by its editors in 1932 as *The economic and philosophical manuscripts of 1844*[23]. In it he embarked upon a critique of classical political economy which was to culminate in the works of his mature years, *Grundrisse der Kritik des politischen Oekonomie* (published for the first time in Moscow in 1939), *Das Kapital* and *Theorien über den Mehrwert*[24].

The core of Marx's critique can be summarised thus: the economists dissociated the worker from the concrete man that he is, and saw man exclusively as *homo oeconomicus*[25]. Yet they never succeeded in establishing the relation between the transformation of nature and the transformation of man that occurs as a result of the modification of natural reality by human labour. The concept of praxis, limited to the material activity which transforms the natural reality, was therefore reduced to an economic concept. If philosophical consciousness was to arrive at a full vindication of praxis in its totality as man's essential province, it would first be necessary to discover the human character of material praxis, of labour, for until then that character had been deemed to rest exclusively in theoretical activity or in certain privileged areas of human activity like art and politics. The philosophers of the Renaissance had already recognised, to a limited degree, that man is an active, creative being; the Classical economists, for their part, acknowledged the central importance of human labour. The full vindication of praxis, however, had to take a further step whose point of departure would be that creative human activity must be seen as productive material practice i.e. as praxis.

German Idealist philosophy, and Hegel in particular, represented a decisive step in this direction. Feuerbach reacted against the Idealist conception and by trying to reduce Hegelian Spirit to a human measure, prepared the way for the problem of praxis to be firmly located on human terrain where Marx and Engels were to elaborate their conception of man as an active, creative, *practical* being who transforms the world not only in his consciousness, but also in practice, in reality. Not only does the transformation of nature cease to be separated in this way, from the transformation of man, but it becomes a necessary precondition of that transformation. Production e.g. productive material praxis, is not only the basis of man's dominion over nature, but also of his domination of his own nature. Production and society, or production and history, therefore, form an indissoluble unity. It was this conception of praxis that Marx outlined for the first time in his *Theses on Feuerbach,* and which was to become the central category of his thought. The problems of knowledge, history, society and being itself must be seen in the light of praxis, for as Marx says in his Second Thesis on Feuerbach, the reality or unreality of thought is a scholastic question marginal to practice. The fundamental problems of philosophy have to be posed in their relation to practical human activity, which is central not only from the anthropological standpoint, because man is what he is *in* and *through* praxis, but also from the standpoint of history (since history is the history of human praxis), cognition (since praxis is the basis and the end of knowledge, as well as its sole criterion of truth) and ontology (since the problem of the relation between man and nature, or between thought and being, cannot be resolved without reference to practice).

The first part of the present volume is concerned with the development of the concept of praxis through that phase of the history of ideas marked by a movement away from the philosophical consciousness of praxis and culminating in a view of praxis as human material activity that transforms the natural and social world. The landmarks in that movement are Hegel, Feuerbach and Marx. Hegel merits detailed study, but this should not be taken to mean that Fichte, whose thought revolved around the problem of man's creative activity, did not make an equally significant contribution to the debate. The point is that Hegel summarised, absorbed and raised to a higher level all the elements of Fichte's philosophy of action, indeed Hegel constitutes the cornerstone of the whole German Idealist movement[26]. Similarly the fact that we have singled out Hegel, Feuerbach and Marx alone, does not imply the exclusion, on our part, of the relevance to the discussion of work in other fields like economics (in the doctrines of the English political economists) and sociology (in particular of Saint-Simon). Clearly Hegel owed a considerable debt to the English economists, whose theories he was later to synthesise and transcend, as Lukács[27] and Marx himself were to point out. But it was Marx's critique of English political economy which was to show most clearly and fundamentally to what extent they had both added to and obstructed the development of a theory of praxis. As far as Saint-Simon is concerned, some recent commentators have exaggerated his influence on Marx[28]; nevertheless, it is undeniable that some elements of his doctrine were incorporated into the conception of praxis: the idea of society as "production", that is, as individual and collective effort, the social reality producing itself. This production, or *social praxis* to use Marx's terminology, encounters obstacles which are the result of the predominance of private property, money and the State. Saint-Simon believed that only socialism could eliminate these obstacles. The mode of its attainment, however, is not revolutionary social praxis, as it is in Marx, but persuasion and love. This failure to link productive practice (the transformation of nature through human labour) and revolutionary practice (the transformation of society through the actions of men) as two inseparable elements of a total social praxis, however, calls seriously into question the Saintsimonian antecedents of the philosophy of praxis.

The work of Marx fused elements derived from Feuerbach, Hegel, the English economists and contemporary socialist doctrines. On the basis of actual practices (productive, revolutionary, scientific, artistic etc.), he raised these several elements into a superior synthesis from which there emerged the Marxist conception of praxis, a conception which was not merely an aggregation of disparate elements, but a new totality in which they took on new forms and implications.

This conception of praxis should, perhaps, have disappeared when after the death of Marx and Engels, the Second International rejected the practical, revolutionary transformation of society, and sought to reduce the struggles of the proletariat to a struggle for reforms within the capitalist system, leaving intact the structures and fundamental contradictions of that system. The great social-democratic theorists like Bernstein, Kampffmeyer and Vorlander aspired to bury praxis and substitute ethical for scientific socialism by reducing the latter to a mere interpretation with no real or practical significance. Bernstein and the other social democratic theorists of the turn of the century reinterpreted Marx and Engels' materialist conception of history either in a fatalistic or in a vulgar economistic sense, in order to find in them a justification for their deviation towards idealistic or ethical socialism. Social development was in turn conceived in an evolutionary sense, turning the doctrine of class struggle on its head and leading to the rejection of social revolution. This ethical, reformist version of Marxism necessarily meant in practice the abandonment of revolutionary class struggle on the part of the proletariat, and at the theoretical level, the denial of praxis as a central category of Marxism.

It is, therefore, to Plekhanov's credit that he stood in the path of this reformist, fatalist interpretation of Marxism, and insisted that according to the fundamental principles of historical materialism, history is the work of man, and practical human activity the key to social development[29]. It was Lenin above all, however, who was to restore the practical revolutionary aspect of Marxism to its central role, not by opposing it to an objective, scientific interpretation of reality, but precisely by basing his activity on just such an interpretation. While Bernstein and the others separated theory and practice by asserting that the socialist movement had no need of theories[30], Lenin reasserted Marx and Engels' conception of the unity of theory and practice, of socialism and science, and thus returned praxis to its proper place. "Marxism," said Lenin, "differs from all other socialist theories in the remarkable way it combines a complete scientific sobriety in the analysis of the objective state of affairs and the objective course of evolution, with the most emphatic recognition of the revolutionary energy, revolutionary creative genius, and revolutionary initiative of the masses and also, of course, of individuals, groups, organizations and parties that are able to discover and achieve contact with one or another class"[31].

Lenin the political activist and the philosopher, achieved the unity of thought and action which Marx had anticipated throughout his work. Lenin had opposed the leadership of the Second International by underlining time and again the role of the practical revolutionary activity of men, the subjective factor, as a decisive element in the transformation of the economic, social and political reality. He had been careful to point out at the same time, however, that this subjective factor could only be decisive when it had become integral to the movement of objective factors (social and economic forces, social reality as a totality whose contradictions had to be distinguished, specified and overcome). In the course of that revolutionary praxis, however, or in the process of preparing and directing it, there emerged a series of theoretical problems on whose solution the very outcome of revolutionary praxis could well depend. To that end, Lenin wrote a series of theoretical articles and rejoinders whose object was to resolve the problems of theory that presented themselves in the course of revolutionary praxis. In 1894, for example, his essay "Who are 'the friends of the people'?"[32] set out to criticise the terrorism of the populists and show that, in contrast to the subjectivism of non-Marxist sociologists, society developed according to objective laws; in 1902, in "What is to be done?"[33], he analysed the essential nature of revolutionary theory and the role of the Party as well as the fusion of theory with the workers' movement, rejecting both economism and the cult of the spontaneous, economic struggle of the proletariat. In 1909, in "Materialism and empirio-criticism"[34], Lenin rebuffed those who were trying to revise Marxism from a subjective-idealist point of view, and by developing the Marxist view of the role of practice in the acquisition of knowledge, was able to assert that "the point of view of life, of practice, should be first and fundamental in the theory of knowledge"[35]. And in 1914, on the eve of the First World War, Lenin began to read, annotate and reflect upon Hegel's *Science of Logic*[36], with the aim of clarifying and enriching his conception of knowledge, of the dialectic and of the role of practice.[37] Lenin's life offers countless more examples of the man of action whose search for truth stemmed from the necessity for its realisation, that is, in order to guide practical activity in more correct and effective directions, or of the theorist who not only aspired to interpret, to think out the truth, but to give action firm roots in a knowledge of reality and of the actual conditions in which human activity was carried out, as well as in a theory of knowledge and of action itself.

Lenin's theoretical work can be characterised as a theory of concrete social praxis, given form in the October Revolution; the aim of the theory was to clarify in historical terms the actual subjective and objective conditions in which that revolution took place. It was, therefore, to the actual revolutionary transformation of society in the specific national and international conditions in which that first socialist revolution occurred, that he contributed with his theoretical writings. He was later to develop a theory of the transition to socialism specifically designed to clarify the nature of that process in the internal and external conditions characteristic of post-revolutionary Russia. Insofar as his interpretations were correct, he contributed directly to the transformation of reality and to the greater efficacy of its corresponding social praxis—the building of socialism. Not only did Lenin bring new elements to bear on the development of a theory of actual practice related to the concrete problems of building socialism in a given country. He contributed also to the refurbishment of a theory of praxis (with its characteristic elements of the primacy of the practical and the unity of theory and practice) which was to re-establish, after long years of deformation and revision, the true theoretical and practical dimensions of Marxism.

There clearly will not be space here to follow through the later historical development of the concept of praxis as it was theoretically expounded by Marx and elaborated in action by Lenin. Very few studies of its unfolding are available; yet it is difficult to conceive of how any commentator could deny the centrality of the concept to Marxism, unless his object is to extirpate from scientific socialism its revolutionary heart.[38] None of the great Marxist theorists of the past have denied its significance, though it is equally true to say that they have often neglected its key significance in Marxism-Leninism, a neglect due in large part to a failure on their part to take account of the many and varied new forms offered by actual practice.

Marxist polemics on praxis

Most Marxists derive their ideas about praxis from the *Theses on Feuerbach;* occasional reservations about Marx's earlier works, and disagreements about the significance of the work in the evolution of Marx's thought[39] notwithstanding, there is general acceptance of Marx's notion of praxis particularly as expressed in Theses 1, 2 and 11. Nonetheless, there have been significant differences of interpretation, which have been all the more profound given the central place occupied by the concept of praxis in Marxism. The polemics have taken different forms at different times: the problem of the relations between thought and being, for example, and the debate about the ideas of Bukharin in the nineteen twenties in which Hermann Duncker, Lukács, Korsch and Fogarasi took a prominent part, and to which years later Gramsci was to add his voice when he submitted their ideas to a radical critique from the standpoint of "the philosophy of praxis"[40]; Gramsci's own philosophy, and particularly his concept of praxis, have been submitted in recent years to a new critique by Louis Althusser, who has himself elucidated new positions on the question of praxis[41]. Kolakowski, Adam Schaff[42] and Karel Kosik underlined the weaknesses of the simplistic definitions of praxis[43]; Rutkevich and Gaidukov on the one hand, and Davydova and Eles on the other, have elaborated sharply contrasting interpretations of the concept[44], which in turn was the motive of serious divergences between the German Marxists[45]. The debate has turned upon a number of common problems: the significance of praxis for Marxism, its definition as a concept, the relations between theory and practice, the forms adopted by praxis etc. The present work constitutes an attempt to define more precisely the concept of praxis and to delimit more clearly the relation of theory to practice. Similarly, we have in the second part carried the study into less familiar areas particularly in the discussion of the levels of praxis, and in the study of the relation of praxis to violence, an important question that has barely been touched upon since Engels discussed "The theory of violence and power" in the second part of his *Anti-Dühring*. The lacunae are all the more serious in view of the fact that praxis is the fundamental category, if not the central category distinguishing Marxism from all previous philosophies. To understand Marxism, therefore, we must be aware of the nature and role of the concept of praxis, and this in turn will depend on whether Marxism is regarded as just one more philosophy, an interpretation of the world which inverted Idealism in order to set materialism upright, but preserving at the same time the concept of dialectic divested of the mystifications it had carried in Idealism; or whether it is acknowledged as a philosophy of revolutionary action whose objective is to transform the world, and in which the Idealist form of praxis was inverted in order that the practical, objective activity of men as concrete, socio-historical beings could come to occupy a central place. These two versions of Marxism lead to very different explanations of the radical change of direction in the history of philosophy which is represented by Marxism. In the first case, Marxism is merely a single step from one (Idealist) interpretation of the world to another (materialist) one; this would set Marxism itself within the frontiers of that philosophy which Marx had criticised in the first part of his Eleventh Thesis on Feuerbach ("The philosophers have interpreted the world in various ways"). In the second case, there is movement from philosophy as interpretation to philosophy as a theory of the transformation of the real world, which justifies the second half of the Eleventh Thesis ("the point is to change it"). Broadly, it is the latter perspective that informs the present work.

Praxis as a central philosophical category

This study is in two parts. The first seeks to analyse the basis and unfolding of the second perspective discussed above through the work of Hegel, Feuerbach and Marx. Part Two attempts, through a more precise definition of praxis, to shed light on the relations between theory and praxis in such a way that each retains its specificity. This leads to an analysis of the various levels of praxis in order to determine which form most fully realises the truly human dimension, and is closely tied to the concept of creation and in the social field, to the peculiar form of creative, transforming activity which is the revolution. Within the context of man's capacity to inaugurate a new reality there emerges, however, the problem of determining the role of violence in the process of transformation, since violence would seem at first sight to be the very negation of man's creative being. These are the problems posed by the transition from an ordinary consciousness to a philosophical consciousness of praxis. What is clear is that there exist today the necessary historical and practical preconditions for the development of a profound and authentic philosophical consciousness of praxis.

The fundamental contradictions of contemporary capitalist society have reached the point where man can only resolve them and ensure a genuinely human future for himself by acting in a creative, revolutionary way. That demands a theoretical clarification of his social practice and the regulation of his actions as the subject of history; and that in its turn requires a true consciousness of praxis. Clearly there is an imperious need for Marxists to discuss these questions openly and without prejudice, to take account of contributions to the debate which might come from other fields of philosophical analysis[46], and to render more systematic and precise a discussion of praxis which has until now been almost entirely restricted to the cognitive aspect, that is, to practice as the basis of knowledge and the criterion of truth. Bearing in mind that Marxism is a philosophy of praxis and not simply a new version of pragmatism, and taking into account that Marxism has emerged historically as the scientific theory of the revolutionary praxis of the proletariat, it is clear that the cognitive framework is simply inadequate to the task. Elsewhere, praxis has been misrepresented in the light of a subjective and voluntaristic notion of class, set aside under the influence of mechanistic determinism, or relegated to a secondary role in obedience to some cold, doctrinaire attitude. Clearly it must be restored to the central place given to it by Marx and Engels from the *Theses on Feuerbach* and *The German ideology* onwards.

This is, of course, not the first time that Marxism has been characterised by the rubric "the philosophy of praxis"; Gramsci's definition of Marxism in these terms is well known. He did not use this phrase, as some interpreters have suggested, simply in order to avoid the prison censor, for whether or not such a circumstantial motive existed, Gramsci used the denomination in order to clarify his understanding of what Marxism meant. It enabled him to distinguish Marxism both from mechanistic materialism on the one hand, and from speculative philosophy which was divorced from actual history and from practical human activity (and particularly politics), on the other. Further, it was a means of stressing the role in actual history of the subjective factor, of the revolutionary consciousness and activity of the proletariat under the leadership of their party; in this he was reacting against a prevalent "lazy" Marxism which used objective factors and the development of productive forces to justify a rejection or postponement of revolutionary activity which was translated into the crudest kind of opportunist reformism. This explains why, well before he wrote the Prison Notebooks, he should have given one of his essays the incomprehensible (for a Marxist) title of "The Revolution against *Capital*"[48], with reference to the Russian Revolution. Although we would not wish to justify the title, it is understandable if we take into account Gramsci's purpose in underlining the role of practical revolutionary activity at a time when most of the leaders of European social-democracy had dismissed it altogether. This legitimate preoccupation, however, led him to underestimate the determinant role of objective factors which the opportunists had converted into absolutes; on the other hand, his advocacy of the role of the subjective factor led him to convert theory into a simple expression of political praxis, or "pure historicity"[49], thus weakening its scientific character and rendering it as an ideological-historical expression[50]. Marxism cannot be reduced to a mere ideology, nor can its scientific character be simply overlooked; the correct interpretation of the complex relations of theory and practice which would justly allow Marxism to be designated a "philosophy of praxis", have their source in the indissoluble unity of the science and the ideology of the proletariat, that is, as a theory both historically conditioned and scientifically based.

Our persistent references to Marxism as a philosophy of praxis, then, do not imply that we share Gramsci's view; nor does it, on the other hand, mean that we underestimate Gramsci's contribution to the fight against the mechanistic deformations of Marxism. The point is to rescue the category of praxis from the distortions it has suffered, and restore to it the richness of meaning with which Marx invested it; that is the objective of the present work.

Notes
1   The Oxford English Dictionary characterises *praxis* as an alien term. In Italian, by comparison, 'prassi' and 'practica' are distinct terms; French and Russian each use a single word to cover all meanings, while German uses only 'praxis'.

2   K. Marx: *Theses on Feuerbach* in *The German Ideology* (Lawrence & Wishart, London, 1965): p.653 [hereafter referred to as *Theses on Feuerbach*].

3   V.I. Lenin: "What is to be done?" in *Collected Works* [hereafter referred to as *Works*], English edition, Moscow and London, 1961-4, Volume 5, p.369.

4   The theme of the daily life and consciousness of the ordinary man has merited special attention from contemporary bourgeois philosophy, especially Husserl, and later Jaspers, Ortega y Gasset, Heidegger and others. Despite Marx's extremely valuable discussion of the subject, however, there have been virtually no Marxist studies in this field; this is why Karel Kosik's essays on the problems of daily life and related questions are of especial importance: Cf. Karel Kosik *Dialektika konkretinho* (Prague 1963). See also Lukács' characterisation of ordinary thinking in the first chapter of his *Die Eigenart des Ästhetischen*, Ästhetik Teil, I. Halbband, s.33-78.

5   Cf: in this respect chapter 6 ("Productivity and non-productivity of artistic labour") and the essay on the fate of art under capitalism in my study of Marx's aesthetic ideas: *Art and Society:* (Merlin Press, 1974).

6   "All social life is essentially *practical*"–*Theses on Feuerbach, ed.cit.* p.653.

7   Aristotle: *Politics:* (Trans. E. Barker, OUP, 1946) IX, p.301 (1328 b).

8   Aristotle: *Metaphysics:* (Trans. W.D. Ross) Revised edition (OUP, 1953) Volume 2, p.373 (1072 b).

9   *Ibid:* vol. 2, p.373 (1072 b).

10 Marx: *Capital* Vol. 1 pp.73-4. [*Capital* in 3 volumes published by Lawrence and Wishart/Progress Publishers: London/Moscow: Vol. I (1965): vol II, (1967) Vol. III (1972) Hereafter referred as *Capital:* Vol.].

11 "There was, however, an important fact which prevented Aristotle from seeing that, to attribute value to commodities is merely a mode of expressing all labour as equal human labour, and consequently as a labour of equal quality. Greek society was founded upon slavery, and had, therefore, for its natural basis, the inequality of men and their labour-powers... The brilliancy of Aristotle's genius is proven by this alone, that he discovered, in the expression of the value of commodities, a relation of equality". *Capital* Vol. I pp.59-60.

12 Arnold Hauser has this to say in this respect: "The ancient world, impelled to bridge the contradiction between this contempt for manual work and its high estimation of art as a vehicle for religion and propaganda, finds the solution in a conceptual separation of the work of art from the personality of the artist; it reveres the creation while despising the creator." Arnold Hauser: *Social history of literature and art:* (Routledge and Kegan Paul, London, 1951–2 volumes) vol 1 p.125.

13 Cf: the following studies on this subject: V. de Magalhaes-Vilhena:

"Progrès technique et blocage social dans le cité antique" in *La pensée*, Paris 1962, no.102, pp.103-120. Also Benjamin Farrington: *Greek science:* (Penguin, Harmondsworth, 1961).

14   J.D. Bernal, in his admirable study of the birth of modern science *Science in history*, clearly emphasises these mutual relations: "The movements of capitalism and science are related, though much too intimately for that relationship to be expressed in simple terms of cause and effect. It can, however, be said that at the beginning of the period the economic factor was dominant. It was the conditions of the rise of capitalism that made that of experimental science possible and necessary. Towards the end of the period the reverse effect was beginning to be felt. The practical successes of science were already contributing to the next great technical advance–the Industrial Revolution". J.D. Bernal: *Science in history:* (Penguin, Harmondsworth, 1969–4 volumes) vol. 2 p.374.

15   Quoted in F. Battaglia: *Filosofia del trabajo:* (Madrid 1955) p.79. [Original *Filosofia del lavoro:* Bologna 1951].

16   Quoted in J.D. Bernal: *op.cit.:* vol. 2 p.391.

17   Cf: A. Hauser: *op.cit.:* vol. 1 pp.326-330.

18   Cf: J.D. Bernal: *op.cit.:* vol. 2 Ch. 8–"Antecedents and consequences of the Industrial Revolution".

19   R. Descartes: *Discourse on method:* (Penguin, Harmondsworth, 1960) p.84.

20   A more detailed exposition may be found in our essay "The philosophy of Rousseau and the ideology of Independence" included in the volume *Rousseau en Mexico* (Grijalbo, Mexico, 1969) pp.40-69. There we add: "Rousseau brilliantly perceived a problem still more immediate and concrete: how is it that the human faculty for self-perfection, so positive in itself, that has created culture and technology, should have turned against man, corrupting and estranging him. Rousseau contested the bourgeois rationalist saintliness of the Enlightenment; he saw culture degrading man and bringing him finally to the pitiful state in which he presently found himself. Rousseau had seen that culture was not an end in itself, but should be at the service of man; when it is emptied of its human content, therefore, its so-called progress is little less than tragic for man".

21   F. Engels: "Outlines of a critique of political economy" in *Engels* (Penguin, Harmondsworth, 1967–selection by W.O. Henderson).

22   There is no English edition. They may be found in the original in the Marx and Engels *Complete Works*, published from 1932 onwards in Moscow, under the general editorship of Riazanov and known by the rubric MEGA (I,3).

23   Marx: *Economic and philosophical manuscripts of 1844:* (Trans. M. Milligan, Lawrence and Wishart, London, 3rd edition 1967) [hereafter referred to as Marx: *1844 MSS*].

24   Marx: *Theories of surplus value:* (Lawrence and Wishart, London/ Moscow: 2 volumes so far, I (1964), II (1968).

25 Marx: *1844 MSS:* pp.23-27, pp.46-48 and especially the section "Estranged labour" pp.64-78. On the "homo economicus" cf: K. Kosik: *op.cit:* pp.105-115.

26 On Fichtean idealism as a philosophy of action see R. Garaudy: *Karl Marx:* (Ed. Seghers, Paris, 1964) pp.39-55, though in the author's view Garaudy exaggerates when he attributes to Fichte a concept of practice which is only found in Marx, and in an idealised, mystified form in Hegel. Althusser also refers, in *For Marx* (Penguin, Harmondsworth 1969) p.35 and pp.223-4, to a young Kantian-Fichtean Marx, corresponding to his brief sojourn at the *Rheinische Zeitung* (1842), but he does not link Marx to Fichte through the concept of practice, or praxis.

27 G. Lukács, *The Young Hegel,* (Merlin Press, London, 1975).

28 For example, in those sections of his study of the sociology of Marx which George Gurvitch devotes to an analysis of the relations between the thought of Saint-Simon and that of Marx. Cf: G. Gurvitch: "La sociologie de Karl Marx" in *La vocation actuelle de la sociologie* (2nd edition, vol. 2, PUF, Paris, 1963) pp.235-240.

29 Cf: those essays devoted by Plekhanov to the defence of Marxism against the revisionists of the late 19th and 20th centuries in his *Selected philosophical notes* published in Russian: Moscow 1956: vol. 2.

30 "The socialist movement does not depend on any theory". E. Bernstein: *Zur Geschichte und Theorie des Sozialismus:* (Berlin, 1901) S. 297.

31 Lenin: *Works:* vol. 13, p.36.

32 Lenin: *Works:* vol. 1.

33 Lenin: *Works:* vol. 5.

34 Lenin: *Works:* vol. 14.

35 Lenin: *Works:* vol. 14, p.142.

36 Cf: the notes and commentaries by Lenin collected under the title of *Philosophical Notebooks* in his *Works* volume 38, and in particular the "Conspectus of Hegel's book *The Science of Logic*" (pp.85-238), which we shall deal with at greater length in the chapter on Hegel.

37 Lenin underlines time and again the decisive role of practice in the process of cognition: "From the living perception to abstract thought, *and from this practice:* such is the dialectical path of the cognition of truth, of the cognition of the objective reality" (*Works:* vol. 38, p.171). And later: "The practice of man and of mankind is the test, the criterion of the objectivity of cognition" (*Ibid* p.211) *"Practice is higher than (theoretical) knowledge,* because it has not only the dignity of universality, but also of immediate actuality" (*Ibid:* p.213) etc.

38 See the Bibliography Section for a list of some Marxist studies in which the problem of praxis has been more or less directly and systematically discussed.

39 See in this respect the eleven essays published as "Sur le jeune Marx" (*Recherches internationales,* no. 19, 1960), and the analysis of them by

Althusser in the section of his *For Marx* (Harmondsworth 1969) which bears the same title. N.I. Lapin has discussed both bourgeois and Marxist approaches to the question of the "young Marx" in his *The struggle for the ideological inheritance of the young Marx*, published in Moscow, in Russian, in 1962.

40 See the studies by A. Zanardo, L. Gruppi and A. Sabetti in *Studi Gramsciani* (Rome, Ed. Riuniti, 1958) and also Gramsci's own critique of Bukharin's *Historical materialism* in his *Historical materialism and the philosophy of Benedetto Croce:* (in Gramsci: *Opere:* (Einaudi, Turin, 1948)). Vol. 2, pp.119-168.

41 For his critique of Gramsci see *Reading Capital* (NLB, London, 1970) pp. 120 ff., and for his own position on the question see the essays "On the materialist dialectic" in *For Marx*, pp.161-218, and "Theory, theoretical practice and theoretical formation" in *Casa de las Americas:* Havana: no. 34.

42 L. Kolakowski: "Karl Marx and the Classical definition of truth" in *Studia Filosoficne,* Warsaw, 2/11/1959; and Adam Schaff "The true face of the young Marx" in *Recherches internationales,* no. 19, 1960.

43 The majority of popular works on Marxism reduce praxis to a cognitive category. For Kosik, however, it has a deeper dimension: "Praxis penetrates and determines man in his totality", providing "the basis of a possible ontology" [whose] "most essential feature is the creation of a socio-human reality". *Dialektika Conkretinho, ed. cit.*

44 Eles and Davydova define praxis as "the infinite living process of change and transformation" and see the dialectic as the generalisation of the theory of praxis. "The materialist dialectic", they say, "is the science of the transformation of the natural world into a human world: it is the theory of the revolutionary transformation of man himself". (*Voprosy filosofii,* no. 9, 1965, p.15).

45 The *Deutsche Zeitschrift für Philosophie* carried, in 1961-2, a long polemic on the problem. It centred on an article by G. Klaus and D. Wittich called "Zu eigenen Fragen der Verhaltnisses von Praxis und Erkenntnis" (*D/Z Ph,* no. 11, 1961), in which the authors acknowledged theoretical activity as a legitimate form of praxis. Although writers like Klotz, Muller, Thom and Kreschnak took opposing positions in the course of the polemic, the discussion took as its starting-point throughout the concept of praxis as a cognitive category and never overcame the framework of the relations between praxis and knowledge.

46 There are very few works which deal specifically with the category of praxis from a non-Marxist point of view. Whatever the criticisms that might be levelled against Sartre's interpretation, his *Critique de la raison dialectique* is far superior to any non- or anti-Marxist literature on the subject. See Bibliography, Section B, for those writers who have dealt with praxis from a perspective alien, if not hostile, to Marxism.

47 Cf: in particular Gramsci's *Historical materialism and the philosophy of*

B. Croce, ed. cit.
48 Published in *Il grido del popolo* (Turin) 5th January 1918, and reproduced in *Rinascita*, XIV, no. 4, April 1957.
49 Gramsci: *Historical materialism...: Loc cit.* pp. 34-6.
50 Since subjectivism is, at the outset, incompatible with science, this underestimation of the importance of the objective factors has often resulted in a tendency to set aside the scientific character of Marxism; the consequences may be observed in the practice as well as the related theory of many Marxist-Leninist parties. In this respect the title of the collective work *Reading Capital* (London 1970) is itself significant as a contrast to Gramsci's essay cited above. The writers of *Reading Capital* are in fact returning the attention of Marxists to the determinant role of objective factors like the mechanism and structures of capitalist relations of production, and analysing them with the conceptual rigour and objectivity demanded by the scientific character of Marxism. The concern of its authors (Althusser, Balibar and Etablet) to reassert these aspects is as legitimate and praiseworthy as was Gramsci's in his time: but there is a price that has to be paid. The defence by these Marxist scholars of the scientific character of Marxism has led them to relegate the subjective factor at work in praxis to a minor role, and thus to forget that, while Marxism is a science, or precisely because it is one, it remains fundamentally a philosophy of the transformation of the world. The price is, therefore, too high as well as unnecessary. The legitimate concern of Althusser and his colleagues to rescue the science of Marxism need not entail the elimination of subjective factors, nor the elevation of the objective factor into the true subject of history. We shall return to this point in the course of the present study.

PART ONE

PHILOSOPHICAL SOURCES OF THE STUDY OR PRAXIS

I. Philosophical Sources of the Study of Praxis

1. The Conception of Praxis in Hegel

Although German Idealism was concerned with activity, it restricted its attention to the activity of the consciousness of the Spirit. Particularly in the form developed in Hegel's work, it was a philosophy of absolute action (or knowledge), and as such opened the way to a Marxist philosophy of praxis whose point of departure was a radical inversion of the Hegelian perspective.

The theoretical activism of German Idealism
    In German Idealism, the liberty and sovereignty of consciousness were made manifest through its activity, since the principle of liberty and autonomy was the source of its action. The various historical forms adopted by this philosophical movement simply served to reimpose that principle, although each form sought to give it a firmer foundation than the last. Hegel saw and acknowledged the centrality of that principle to a movement whose fundamental unity he also recognised.
    It was Kant who, by basing his theory of knowledge on the subject rather than the object, had laid the bases of the Idealist movement; consciousness provided the supreme basis of both knowledge and morality. And by making the subject, an abstract subject marginal to history, the axis of knowledge and morality, Kant carried through his "Copernican revolution". Yet by accepting at the same time the existence of a "thing-in-itself" outside the ambit of the cognate consciousness and the presence of a God that set limits upon the sovereignty of moral consciousness, Kant also limited the development of the free activity of the subject. Hegel, on the other hand, while giving credit for having established that the source of activity and of freedom lay in the subject, in consciousness, reproached him for having accepted a new dualism which weakened and restricted the

impact of the principle which Kant had established and which was to provide the point of departure for all modern German philosophy. Hegel characterised the Idealist movement that had culminated in his own philosophy as well as its problems and limitations, in the following global sense: "What is manifested in Germany through this philosophy is the absolute concept that thinks of itself and returns to itself; in this way everything that is essential must fall within the confines of self-consciousness. The Idealism that reclaims for self-consciousness all the moment of the in-itself still involves a contradiction, however, for it persists in distinguishing this in-itself from itself."[1] By separating the "thing-in-itself" from the activity of the subject, Kant accepted limits that could only be overcome by discarding Kantian dualism and formalism, that is, by eliminating the "thing-in-itself" and deriving both its form and its content from consciousness itself. Hegel extended his critique of Kant to Fichte and Schelling too, since they had all failed to carry the principle enunciated by Kant to its logical conclusion.

The Fichtean ego acknowledged no limits other than those it imposed upon itself; everything stems from the ego. Thus that which is unconditioned is presented as its own condition. The ego is activity, but if there is to be any possibility of actual activity, it must suppose an object for its action, an aggregate of resistances (the Non-Ego) which is to be overcome. In Hegel's view, the Fichtean attempt to transcend Kantian dualism by deriving the whole world of consciousness from the ego failed because the Non-ego remained an element of the consciousness. For the consciousness can accept nothing alien to itself, since to do so would imply, as it did in Kant, setting limits to free and unconditionally active consciousness. Having reduced the Non-ego to the Ego, therefore, Fichte was unable to accept any other source of the activity of consciousness, and ultimately retreated into subjectivism.[2] Hegel asserted that Fichte had never transcended subjective idealism; since his ego was individual, not universal, it could only be a finite consciousness or an idealism of the finite. The solution, he concluded, lay in an objective or absolute idealism. Before Hegel could embark on the elaboration of a solution in these terms, however, Schelling published his own heroic attempt to overcome both Kantian dualism and Fichteian subjectivism, and restore the principle of the absolute activity of consciousness. Schelling's approach was closest to Hegel's own, in that he sought to establish the identity of spirit and nature, of subject and object, in the Absolute, or in Absolute reason, in which contraries merged in a synthesis from which could be derived the multiple determinations of both nature and human consciousness. Hegel regarded this identity as little more than unity in indifference, "the night in which all the cats are black"; it was not a true identity, but a new dualism, the unity of the world at the level of "absolute identity" and its diversity at the level of reality. Schelling too had failed, in Hegel's view, to arrive at a satisfactory explanation of the development of the Absolute, or of how unity emerged from diversity. What most irritated Hegel, however, was Schelling's assertion that it was possible to reach the Absolute through an exceptional act of *intellectual intuition,* for Hegel firmly believed that the knowledge or self-knowledge of the Absolute was an ongoing process in which there was no insurmountable gulf between ordinary and philosophical consciousness, since through the unfolding of that process consciousness could be raised from its lowest level—sensual certainty—to Absolute Knowledge.[3]

German Idealist philosophy was founded upon the activity of consciousness or of Spirit. Yet Hegel saw that his spiritual activism was related to the actual, concrete, historical conditions of the time both inside and outside Germany. Theoretical, spiritual activity was given primacy in Germany at a time (the end of the eighteenth century and the beginning of the nineteenth) when the theoretical depth and richness of German philosophy stood in sharp contrast to a notable absence of practical revolutionary activity in that country. This poverty in the field of practice is all the more patent if we compare it to the great revolutionary events that France was experiencing during the same period. In 1789, the replacement of the old regime by a new bourgeois order became a question of practice, whilst in Germany it was, and remained until well after Hegel's death, a *theoretical* problem only. Whereas the French had passed from theory to practice, the Germans remained caught in the field of theory.

Hegel was acutely conscious of this divorce between theory and action, and with this in mind posed the question which Marx was later to take up again in his *Introduction to Hegel's critique of the philosophy of right* in 1843.[4] Hegel began by admitting that a single principle lay behind both the actual, practical revolution that had taken place in France and the "revolution of the Kantian system which would transcend it": the principle of the freedom of the will elucidated by Kantian philosophy. "There is nothing alien to my will; nothing can be imposed upon me by dint of authority... *Among the Germans this was never more than a passive theory; the French, on the other hand, have striven to realise it in practice. Two questions* arise therefrom: why did this principle of liberty never become anything other than a formal principle? And why did the French seek to realise it in practice, but not the Germans?"[5]

Hegel considered that, while both the French and the Germans had tried to assert the Kantian principle of the freedom of the will, only the French had attempted to put it into practice. Why the difference? "It might be suggested," Hegel replies, "that the French are hotheads *(ils ont la tête près du bonnet)*. But there is a deeper reason. In Germany, the world and reality opposed the formal principle of philosophy. The needs of the spirit are internally satisfied. The Germans only behaved in a passive way at this time because they were reconciled to reality."[6] This reconciliation was in turn the result of the fact that "the Protestants had already carried out their revolution with the Reformation".[7] At this point Hegel's philosophy itself shows a conciliatory face towards reality, excluding for Germany the need for the kind of revolutionary changes that had taken place in France by asserting that they had already taken place on a spiritual level in Germany as a result of the Reformation, which had made real, practical revolution unnecessary. Henceforward, it would simply be a matter of carrying further the tasks initiated by the Reformation by emphasising the activity of the consciousness, of Spirit. The German Idealist philosophers as a whole made a virtue of necessity by putting the transformation of consciousness on a par with a practical revolution of the kind that had taken place in France. Heine said, for example, that if the French had beheaded a king, Kant's *Critique of pure reason* had decapitated God.[8] Fichte, for his part, had unhesitatingly drawn a parallel between the French Revolution and his doctrine of the Ego by affirming that both had been founded, one on a theoretical, the other on a practical level, on the principle of the autonomy of the will and the sovereignty of reason in man.[9]

Clearly, then, the German Idealist philosophers, and Hegel in particular, were conscious of the disproportion between theory and practice, and were at pains to relate this activism of the consciousness to real historical circumstances like the Reformation. Marx, however, was to explain this disproportion between theory and practice, between the richness of German philosophy and the poverty of German revolutionary practice by reference to the importance in the economic and political spheres of a weak bourgeoisie which was neither willing nor able to carry out a true revolution in the backward economic and political conditions of Germany. Germany was in a real sense an anachronism, which explained its contemporaneity in the field of thought and its backwardness in the field of action.[10]

This theoretical activism, determined by the poverty of actual praxis, found its theoretical justification in an Idealist movement that vindicated the activity of the consciousness, of the Spirit, and ultimately raised it to the unconditional and absolute plane on which it was located by Hegel. Unlike Kant, Fichte and Schelling, there was nothing in his philosophy to limit or condition the absolute activity and sovereignty of the Spirit which reveals itself both in the spiritual world whose highest expressions are art, religion and philosophy, and in human nature or human history. Hegel did not separate the spirit and the world, subject and object, as had those among his predecessors who had been incapable of reaching the point of view of "absolute identity" whose achievement, for Hegel, required an explanation of the world and therefore of the spirit, which entailed a process of spiritual self-knowledge both as far as the subject and as the object are concerned. Obviously the subject, the Spirit, cannot immediately achieve this full self-knowledge, that is "absolute knowledge"; it must first pass through a number of stages expounded by Hegel in his *Phenomenology of Mind* at the end of which the spirit recognises itself as subject and all subject-object dualisms, of the consciousness of the object and the object of consciousness, disappear. Thus the history of the Spirit is the history of the men who are its bearers. As Marx points out, this spiritual history does not present concrete human experience in its actual, historical form, but as a moment or manifestation of the development of the Spirit.[11] Hegel, then, reduced everything to a phenomenology of spiritual activity of which practical material activity, human labour, was simply a manifestation.[12] Although labour does appear in a mystified form in Hegel's writing, however, it must be recognised that in integrating practical material activity into his philosophy, Hegel had gone much further than any of his predecessors.

Praxis is conceived in his philosophy, then, as the absolute and universal activity of the Spirit; in this respect, he did no more than carry Kant's Idealist principles to their ultimate conclusions. Yet it embraced at the same time a conception of the activity of the Spirit in the specific form of practical, human activity, or labour, and to this extent he opened the way to a true, non-mystified, conception of praxis which Marx was to formulate once he had submitted Hegelian Idealist philosophy, and its doctrine of labour in particular, to a broad critique.

Hegel's was the first philosophical study in depth of human praxis as a transforming activity which produces material objects. In this sense, he distinguished himself from his immediate (Idealist) predecessors who had restricted practice to a special aspect of the activity of consciousness, which was a fundamentally moral activity. Kant, for example, had opposed practice and speculation, or what was proper to consciousness, and argued that "what it is possible to achieve through liberty is what is meant by morality". Kant also accepted another sphere or tendency which originated in consciousness and in which the latter acted in a free and disinterested way—art—which he contrasted to craft, or inferior practical activity; the latter he called "mercenary art", describing it as an occupation which is disagreeable in itself, and whose only attraction lies in its effect (profit). Furthermore, men can be forced to engage in this kind of inferior activity.[13] Kant, therefore, did not regard practical material activity like labour as a field of action appropriate to free men; only 'practice' in a restricted (moral) sense, and in certain cases art, were worthy activities in this sense; and both were activities of consciousness. Fichte, by contrast, gave action a moral sense or, in other terms, gave his ethics an active character. In this interpretation, the Ego acquires metaphysical overtones, since it can only be ethically realised by creating an objective world, a Non-Ego, on which its very existence must ultimately depend. Hegel went far beyond either Kant or Fichte[14] and for the first time integrated human labour into the concept of practical activity; his knowledge of English political economy, the most advanced economic science of his time, was an important element of that change. Yet although he much enriched the content of labour which had always been a merely economic category for Adam Smith and the other Classical economists, he never transcended his general conception of activity as the activity of the Spirit. This should not lead us to underestimate, however, the considerable contribution which Hegel's reading of the economists, and of Adam Smith in particular, made to the development of his philosophy. As Georg Lukács has pointed out, "Among all the German philosophers, Hegel had the deepest and most complete understanding of the nature of the French Revolution and the Napoleonic period. He was also the only German thinker of his time to devote himself seriously to studying the problems resulting from the Industrial Revolution which was then taking place in England, and the only one to relate the problems of Classical English economics to the problems of philosophy and dialectics."[15] In that light, we can now move on to consider the principal stages of development of the Hegelian conception of praxis and its concrete manifestation in the form of human labour.

The Hegelian concept of labour before 'The Phenomenology of Mind'

The theme of practice, and of labour in particular had emerged in Hegel's writings on philosophy well before the publication of the *Phenomenology of Mind* in 1807; it had been discussed in his *Systemfragment* (1800), in the *System of morality* (1802) and in the two courses on *Realphilosophie* (1803-4 and 1805-6). Later, in the *Phenomenology of Mind* it was to be integrated into the active universal process whose ultimate subject was the Spirit, and finally given a key place in the system elaborated in the *Science of Logic* (1812-1816). In the pages that follow, we shall consider Hegel's philosophical treatment of praxis as material activity in those works which most clearly correspond to the three stages in his philosophical evolution.

In the second part of his *Systemfragment*,[16] Hegel considered labour for the first time in the context of a concern with religion which characterised the work of his youth, written during the so-called

Frankfurt period (1797-1800). Hegel believed at the time that religious life offered a possibility of overcoming what he called positivity or dead objectivity. This category was central to Hegel's early philosophy; it was always used in a negative sense and variously expressed what was external, opposed to or given in relation to creative freedom, or in other words that which had lost its significance as a product of creative human activity and become an inert or reified object. If man was to become reintegrated into the original unity or totality from which his sins had separated him, it was imperative to overcome or transcend that state of dead objectivity. Hegel went on to examine the relations between men and objects in this light, distinguishing between the normal relations of economic life, in which the object is destroyed in order to be consumed, and the truly religious relation which is the result of an act of sacrifice whereby the object is destroyed with no specific end in view to justify that destruction. In the first case, destruction has a utilitarian purpose; in the second, it is a purposeless destruction, or destruction for its own sake. The utilitarian destruction of the object does not require its total destruction,[17] so that its objectivity is not actually negated in this relation; the subject simply passes from one objectivity to another. Through sacrifice, or the non-utilitarian destruction of the object, on the other hand, the subject is able to overcome dead or inert objectivity, and thus transcend its own particularity in order to become integrated into the movement of infinite life.

Clearly, Hegel was operating at this time within a conception of labour as merely utilitarian activity. This is not surprising if one takes into account that, according to his biographer Rosenkranz and the hypotheses of Lukács, Hegel was already familiar with the work of Adam Smith. Thus the activity which was man's proper province was not practice, the utilitarian destruction of objects, however necessary it may have been, but the non-utilitarian practical activity which, however useless it may seem from the point of view of everyday need, did have a very clear purpose at the religious level. Hegel regarded labour in the first sense as a normal element of everyday economic relations; if he emphasised it, therefore, it was simply in order to underline the superiority of the relation based upon sacrifice, the religious relation.

With the *System of morality* (1802), Hegel abandoned his previous concern with religion, and turned his attention to the relations between ethics, economy and society, examining in this light the practical activity of men not only in a moral sense, but also in terms of the concrete content which it acquired in social life. He still did not go beyond his earlier definition of labour as utilitarian destruction, but he now saw it at the same time as a peculiar relation between men and objects in which the subjective and the objective, the particular and the general, merged through the use of tools. For the tool was subjective insofar as it was prepared and used by the worker himself, but also objective in the sense that it was "objectively orientated towards the object of labour..."[18] And with respect to the unity of the particular and the general, Hegel added: "... through tools the subjectivity of work is raised to the level of the universal; anyone can imitate it and work in the same fashion; to that extent it is the constant rule of work."[19] Here Hegel had already touched on the theme of the relations between subject and object, of objectification in the practical world of labour. His analysis, however, was only to overcome its unsatisfactory, abstract character and develop in new, creative ways in *The Phenomenology of Mind*. Before considering his major works, however, we should consider the conception of labour which Hegel elaborated in his two lecture courses on the philosophy of reality *(Realphilosophie)*[20], in which he made significant departures from his earlier conception of labour. Although labour is there no less a practical, utilitarian activity, it did acquire a new dimension which anticipated the central thesis of the *Phenomenology;* that man's production is a process of self-production through labour.

In the first course of *Realphilosophie*, Hegel considered labour in relation to desire and to the object of labour. Natural animal desire is directed at the object in order to destroy it; thus both the desire and the object desired are immediately negated, the first because it has been satisfied, the second because it has been destroyed. The two elements of the relation can only remain if the natural quality of desire is transcended and its relation with the object mediated through a third term; it was labour that was to provide that mediation. Through labour, the object was rescued from destruction, or rather it was both destroyed and preserved at the same time. In the same way natural desire now became human desire by making possible a relation between the two terms which had been negated in the earlier relation, based on natural desire alone. So labour not only provided the basis for the transformation of desire, but also showed itself to have a social character as a consequence of its simultaneous relation to both necessity and desire. Labour, in this sense, was the mediate satisfaction of need, not an immediate instinctive satisfaction. Man does not work in order to make immediate use of the product of his labour; the actual satisfaction of need is set aside in favour of an ideal and possible satisfaction. In this way, labour acquires an abstract, universal character. In working for himself, and in order to satisfy a need, man exchanges the satisfaction of his own needs for the satisfaction of the needs of others; to the extent that he satisfies a totality of needs, he works for everyone. This in turn entails the division of labour. Hegel, like the English economists, stressed the material benefits of the division of labour, arguing that it increased the amount of wealth produced; yet he recognised that this division also had negative consequences, particularly in respect of automated labour, insofar as it implied the limitation of the capacity of the individual worker and the growing degradation of his consciousness. As individual labour is linked to an infinite aggregation of needs, those links become increasingly unconscious.

As Lukács showed, Hegel had by this stage (1802) assimilated the key concepts of English political economy: labour as a source of wealth, the division of labour as a mode of increasing the amount of wealth produced, its negative consequences from the worker's point of view etc. Hegel did not simply repeat, however, the conclusions of the English economists. He did not simply regard labour as a source of wealth whose acquisition brought negative consequences for the worker (although, as Marx said, the English economists acknowledge those consequences in the most cynical way); he saw that labour also allowed man to overcome the natural quality of desire, and as a result to install himself on a human plane, because it was the mode of satisfying both an immediate, individual need and an abstract, universal labour which satisfied the needs of all. With the division of labour and the concretion of the universal abstract of the tool in the machine, however, labour had come to affect the worker in a negative way, undermining and confusing his self-consciousness, degrading his skills and turning the connection between individual labour and the infinite mass of needs into a casual relation which lay outside his control. Hegel did not draw a veil over the negative consequences of labour; yet he could not go very much further than the English economists, because he was not aware of the social, class roots of that negativity. Had he made *that* connection, Hegel would have dissolved into Marx.

In the second course of lectures, Hegel returned to the basic ideas expounded in the first part of the *Realphilosophie*. Man transcended merely natural life when labour mediated between the desire and its satisfaction; the activity of labour developed, in its turn, through tools produced by labour, which mediated between man and the object. "Man makes tools because he is rational; they are the first manifestation of his *will*. This will, however, is still abstract will, the pride of a people in its tools".[21] The relation between the will and its manifestation in tools demonstrated, in Lukács view, that Hegel had now surpassed the conception of will dominant in the ethics of Fichte and Kant. The peculiar characteristic of the will, in this respect, is that it develops as activity, and provides its own content by affirming itself. In this way it ceases to be a formal and empty potentiality, and can now be applied in reality. For when Hegel referred to abstract will, and regarded tools as the mode whereby that will made itself manifest, he was not, of course, referring to an empty, pure will devoid of content, but to will which must act, that is, a will which must provide itself with a content for its activity. In brief, abstract will had ceased to be, for Hegel, "pure will" in the Kantian sense.[22]

Since it is a relation between man and nature, labour represents the mediated satisfaction of desire. The object is not destroyed, but its form is changed. Because the form of the object, but not the object itself, is destroyed, it receives a form which it had never possessed in itself. Labour, then, is a process of formation and transformation. Man negates the immediate quality of the natural object, but unlike the animal that destroys, consumes the object in order to satisfy its immediate desire, man transforms it; he can only transform it, however, to the degree that he understands its laws, respects its legality and adapts himself to them. If man makes tools because he is a rational being, then his use of them must also be rational; he makes tools in accordance with the nature of the object, so that he can change its form and provide it with a new form. This whole transformation is based upon a capacity to adapt to the legality of the object; this capacity constitutes the "astuteness of reason" which is embodied in the tool which represents an adjustment to the laws of nature the better to transform it.

In this second course of lectures, Hegel reemphasised the increasing separation of human from natural need, and the progressively more abstract and universal interdependence of human needs and human labour consequent upon the introduction of machines and the establishment of the division of labour. This had a series of negative consequences closely linked, as the English economists had seen, to the growing division and mechanisation of labour. In *Realphilosophie II* Hegel enumerated those negative consequences in terms akin to those employed later by Marx, in the *1844 Manuscripts,* to describe the characteristics of estranged labour: "the very act of labour becomes completely mechanical or responds to a simple determination"; "man becomes increasingly *mechanical,* sordid and spiritless as a result of the abstraction of labour"; "a) in labour I render myself *immediately* a thing, a form, that is being. b) In the same way, I deprive myself of a being that is my own, make of it a being that is alien to me and then find myself trapped within this latter being".

Hegel, therefore, had pointed to both the positive and the negative aspects of labour, although he never arrived at the root of its negativity nor perceived how it could regain its value for man's formation. In this sense he remained within the framework of modern political economy, which in any event was not to be overcome until much later. Nevertheless, the conception of labour as a philosophical, or rather anthropological category whose content included more than a merely economic element, was developed well before the publication of the *Phenomenology,* as the analysis of the *Realphilosophie* has shown. Thus material productive praxis was, by 1803, already an integral part of his concept of man.

Human labour in the 'Phenomenology'

What, then, does the *Phenomenology* add to the concept of material productive praxis or human labour already elaborated in the *Realphilosophie?* Broadly, it progressed along two axes: it enriched the concept of labour, emphasising its positive role in the formation of man, and it integrated labour into the universal process of the self-knowledge of the Absolute, so that human labour, practical material activity, was rendered as a manifestation of the development of the self-knowing Spirit. In the end, material praxis was thus reduced to a form of spiritual activity.

The process is described in the *Phenomenology* as "the science of the experience of consciousness";[23] it occurs both in knowledge and in its objects, and as a result consciousness becomes consciousness of the Absolute, or self-consciousness, which is the identity of subject and object. The *Phenomenology* traces the progress of consciousness from the point at which it sees itself divided into consciousness of the object and object of consciousness, to its final moment, Absolute Knowledge, in which all objectification and all alienation is overcome because the consciousness has come to recognise the subjective, spiritual nature of all those objects which, until then, had appeared before it as something objective or alien. Thus the subject-object dualism is finally transcended, as is the dualism of the object of consciousness and the consciousness of the object: subject and object become one.

This self-consciousness, the consequence of these various *moments of consciousness,* can only occur in real individuals, in men. The Absolute achieves full self-consciousness, true awareness of its spiritual nature, only in and through human consciousness. In this respect its phenomenological itinerary has a concrete-historical basis; the history of the relations between human consciousness and the world of real objects becomes, therefore, the history of the Spirit of which man is the bearer. Thus human actions, including practical material activity, are simply spiritual activities and as such, are an integral part of the spiritual history of the Absolute even when men are not conscious of the fact that real history is in the end the process whereby the Spirit arrives at self-knowledge.

In revealing the movement of consciousness from immediate, empirical, individual knowledge to the philosophical consciousness (Absolute Knowledge) in which the Spirit becomes fully aware that all is Spirit, that real history is no more than the history of the Spirit, or that every subject is object, Hegel simply underlined the fact that self-consciousness, self-knowledge, was a stage in that process. For self-conciousness is consciousness of oneself; but consciousness cannot remain within the singularity. *"Self-consciousness can only be realised"*, Hegel argued, *"in another self-consciousness"*.[24] As long as desire is desire for one thing only, that singularity cannot be transcended; it must first become the object of another desire. Self-consciousness "is only such to the extent that it is recognised as such".[25] A man only satisfies his *human* desire when another man acknowledges its human value. In other words, man is only human insofar as he relates to other men. Human essence cannot exist in an isolated individual, for the individual is only such as one member of a community of men. In this necessary transition from individual consciousness to a plurality of consciousness Hegel reveals, albeit in an idealistic form, the *social* nature of man. The individual is not sufficient unto himself; he cannot remain enclosed in his individual subjectivity unless he is prepared to renounce his human nature. Only socially can he be considered to be a human individual.

Desire, then, is the desire to be recognised. If every consciousness seeks that recognition, the result will be a conflict between them, since their mutual recognition presupposes a mutual exclusion. Thus the action born of desire is converted into a struggle, and the desire for recognition leads to a struggle to the death.[26] If the struggle were to end in the suppression of all those who reject my recognition, death would rob me of victory, since there would be no one left to recognise the victor. Victory must ensure recognition by way of allowing the vanquished to live in exchange for recognition of the victor and their renunciation of their own right to recognition. This relation of domination on the one hand and subservience on the other, is what Hegel describes as the relation of master and slave.[27] Yet Hegel does not present this life and death struggle between master and slave, oppressor and oppressed, as an actual fact of history whose source is to be found in actual, concrete contradictions, but in a timeless and abstract form corresponding to the progress of the Spirit towards a full self-recognition. The concrete historical fact is mystified and converted into a mystical struggle for recognition independent of the actual material interests in conflict which, in historical terms, have been the real causes of war. It is thus possible to offer an ideological justification of slavery.[28] According to Hegel, it is the master who carries the struggle forward at the risk of his own life. The slave, on the other hand, fearful of death, retreats from the struggle and renounces recognition. By risking his natural, biological life, then, the master stands on a human plane, which the slave cannot attain.

The master's superiority, however, is not simply spiritual; it is also an actual material superiority. Once he has won recognition as pure self-consciousness, he puts the slave at his service and makes actual material use of him by obliging him to work on his behalf. The slave's fear of death, which held him back from risking his life in the struggle, has led him to a situation in which he must work; labour, therefore, is slavery, dependence on the master. As a real, practical activity, however, this dependence involves the transformation of nature and the creation of a product. The subjective is made objective in the product and thus in turn creates a world of its own. The product of the slave's labour ceases to exist *in itself* and comes to exist *for itself*, and he can be recognised in the products that he has created. Thus, by transforming nature, the slave comes to recognise his own nature. The recognition of the self in its products is the self-consciousness of the human being. The slave can therefore liberate himself from his own (enslaved) nature by liberating himself, through labour, from external nature.

The master on the other hand, does not create products, and therefore transforms neither nature, nor himself. So while the slave does raise himself as a human being, and gains consciousness of his liberty in the labour process, the master cannot develop in this way. The slave can raise his consciousness of liberty, but he cannot realise that liberty; he can only liberate himself at the level of the ideal. Indeed the philosophies that emerged after the collapse of the Ancient World were an expression of this consciousness of liberty which could only be realised at the spiritual level.

Labour, practical material activity, appears then as part of the process whereby the subject (Spirit) raises itself to the level of full self-consciousness. The superiority of the slave over the master in this respect derives from the fact that he has been inserted into that movement, while the master remains marginal to it. By infusing things with the forms of his spirit, the slave ensures the development of the Spirit; but as Marx pointed out, this stemmed from Hegel's conception of labour as spiritual labour, an activity through which the Spirit, of which man is the bearer, recognises itself in things. The positive aspect of labour is obvious, since by forming things it forms and forges man himself. No man can exist in leisure, marginally to labour; the master is proof of this in a negative way, and the slave in a positive sense. Indeed Marx argued that the great merit of Hegel's work was that it had placed so much emphasis on the positive facets of labour.[29] Its major limitation, on the other hand, lay in Marx's view in his failure to point to its negative aspects in the concrete form in which they appear in estranged labour.[30]

Thus practical material activity was shown to have an extra dimension which no one had previously recognised; through it, man was seen to form and produce himself. Yet Hegel's need to merge this real process into the general movement of the Spirit led to a mystification of the real, historical relations between master and slave, and to a deformation of the true relations between human consciousness and practical, human activity. In the end, the cause of the struggle between oppressors and oppressed, between masters and slaves, is spiritual; the struggle for recognition subsumed the class war. In this way the real motor of the struggle disappears, and violence is seen to have its source not in real contradictions, but simply in every man's human (spiritual) desire to be recognised in terms of his own human worth. Yet violence does contribute to the maintenance of slavery; external, not internal, submission is the result of an actual correlation of forces which favours the oppressor. It is not therefore, as Hegel maintained, the fear of death or a submissive spirit which leads to slavery.

Hegel undoubtedly did highlight the positive aspects of labour; equally, he recognised that labour, insofar as it was the embodiment of a dependent situation in which the worker was enslaved, was an external labour carried out under the threat of force. Yet in the *Phenomenology of Mind,* in contrast to his earlier work, Hegel idealised labour to the point where could see in it (alienated labour) the very source of the worker's self-conciousness, of his human value, of what Marxists were later to call his class consciousness. Hegel ceded to labour the virtue of raising the consciousness of the worker to the consciousness of his liberty and his human value. This he presented as the consciousness of the worker who sees himself as a creative being, even under conditions of violence and oppression, whose subjective activity takes on an objective form in the products of his labour, such that a new world emerges bearing his stamp. Certainly this humanisation of the product and the concomitant humanisation of the subject occur throughout actual history. The fact that it does occur objectively does not, however, in any sense imply necessarily that it exists for the subject, for the worker,[31] for whom it is only possible to reach this level of consciousness as a result of a long theoretical and practical struggle against exploitation, at the end of which the oppressed, in this case the worker, rises to consciousness of his alienation and at the same time to a consciousness of his liberty— which for Hegel means a consciousness of his creative nature. But Hegel fails to recognise in the *Phenomenology* that it is inseparable from a consciousness of his alienation. In our view, Hegel analyses the situation as if the worker in a regime of servitude and exploitation could achieve consciousness of his liberty without first becoming conscious of his alienation. He emphasises the role of labour, of practical activity, in raising the consciousness of the worker or the slave to the level of consciousness of liberty; yet he ignores the role of social praxis and of the struggle against oppression itself. For him, liberation is a matter of consciousness; it is not imposed by the real, effective struggle. The struggle is only significant in terms of the master's domination and the slave's submission; yet it does not liberate man. It can free labour, but only on the spiritual level. The slave, in other words, is free insofar as he recognises his own human value in his work, and to the extent that this value is recognised as his in another world, in God. The key to domination and to liberation, therefore, lay in the recognition of human value which occurred on the spiritual plane. The real, material contradictions which led to struggle, the reasons for the master's triumph and the liberation of the slave, were all located at the level of Spirit. This ideal liberation can coexist with the most concrete forms of oppression and exploitation; in this respect, Hegelian

Idealism shares many of the characteristics of redemptive philosophies like Stoicism and Christianity. In this sense it was possible for a man who was spiritually free to continue to live in chains.[32]

Marx, in the *1844 Manuscripts*, was at pains to stress the significance of the Hegelian conception of labour, whose central element was the discovery of the role of productive material praxis in the formation and liberation of man. Yet Hegel had submerged that material praxis in spitirual praxis, and made of this spiritualised labour the basis of human liberty understood as no more than the *consciousness* of liberty. The slave who had lost his human condition not as a result of an objective material process, but as a result of a subjective renunciation stemming from the fear of death, may now recover his human value precisely by virtue of his objective position as a producer in society; his labour enables him to recognise himself as human in his products, and to claim recognition from others in the spiritual sphere of a divine world. If Hegel overestimated the subjective element (the fear of death) in the loss of humanity, he lays exclusive stress in the process of its recovery on the objective element of production, where this is always seen as spiritualised production. In the final analysis, the subject of this dialectic of master and slave is always the consciousness; thus material praxis, human labour, in the end serves only to raise the self-consciousness of the Absolute to new, and higher, levels.

Practice as a practical idealism in the "Science of Logic"

Hegel was to return to the problem of practice in his *Science of Logic*, particularly in the second chapter of the concluding section, in which he analyses the Idea of the Good. Here he considered practice as a practical idea whose synthesis with the theoretical yielded the absolute idea.

In the *Phenomenology*, practice had appeared as a stage in the phenomenalisation of the Spirit, the movement whereby consciousness reaches the point of recognising the identity of subject and object. The task of the *Logic* is to systematically, if not historically, elucidate this identity; the truths encountered or whose foundation lay in history were to receive a systematic, abstract exposition in the *Logic*. Whereas in the *Phenomenology* practice (human labour) appears as a stage in the coming into being of consciousness which culminates in the identity of subject and object, in the *Logic* practice (as a practical idea) is presented as part of a logical process of a concretion of categories, which leads from the poorer category of pure being, to the richest in content and concretion, which is the Absolute Idea. Practice (the practical idea), therefore is simply one determinant of a process from abstract to concrete which culminates, as a result of an internal, logical necessity, in the latter category. Thus practice forms part of that vast logical canvas on to which the whole universe is embroidered, the totality with all its concretions. The praxis *historicised* in the *Phenomenology,* as a phase in the history of the spirit, now appeared in *logical form,* as a step in the movement of reason which is manifest in the movement of those categories which together constitute a concrete and rational reality.

Productive material praxis is presented in the *Phenomenology* as a human activity, for man is the bearer of Spirit. Its role in the formation of man is therefore already clear, even though it is presented in a mystified form within the context of spiritualised production. That is why Marx was able to make the *Phenomenology* the point of departure for his analysis of the anthropological significance of labour, even though Hegel had regarded it as the work of the Spirit in the history of consciousness. In *The Science of Logic,*[33] practice was no longer presented explicitly as human activity, but as a category-phase in the logical, rational development of the Idea; as a result, the anthropological significance of labour becomes much more difficult to discern. Nevertheless Lenin, in his notes on the *Logic,* did reveal its continuing presence by translating into anthropological terms what Hegel had expressed in an abstract, speculative way.[34] Where Hegel speaks of "the concept", Lenin rendered it as "man".[35] At this point, and without losing sight of the connection between the *Practical Idea* and human practice (however much it is mystified by Hegel), it is the logico-ontological fate of praxis in Hegelian logic that claims our attention.

Since it is a logical category, practical activity is rendered as determination of the Idea, that is, as a practical idea. "The idea", according to Hegel, "is the *adequate Notion,* which is objectively *true* or the *true as such.* When anything whatever possesses truth, it possesses it through its Idea, or *something possesses truth only in so far as it is Idea*".[36] This truth, whose most complete form is the Absolute Idea, is arrived at by way of consciousness; in this mode of cognition, the idea arrives at truth, that is at the adaptation of the object to the concept. In neither analytic nor synthetic knowledge is the concept capable of realisation in terms of its unity with itself, that is with its reality. "Hence in this cognition the Idea still falls short of truth on account of the inadequacy of the subject matter to the subjective Notion".[37] The transition from analytic and synthetic knowledge to the knowledge of truth, occurs through the Idea of the Good. Hegel suggested and counterposed two types of relation between the concept and the objective world which arise as a result of this movement of the Idea towards the knowledge of truth. In one case, the state of the real world is not called into question; in the other, the world is not acceptable as it is, and there exists an aspiration to transform it in accordance with an end. These two tendencies, otherwise theory and practice, are counterposed by Hegel in the following terms: "In the theoretical idea, the subjective Notion, as the *Universal that lacks any determination* of its own, stands opposed to the objective world from which it takes to itself a determinate content and filling. But in the practical Idea it is as actual that it confronts the actual; the certainty of itself which the subject possesses in being determined in and for itself is a certainty of its own actuality and the *non-actuality* of the world".[38]

This difficult passage may be interpreted in the following way: in the theoretical relation, the subject faces the object passively; as it lacks determination, it takes its determination from the object itself. Far from being negated, therefore, the object comes to determine the subject. In the practical relation, on the other hand, the determinant role passes from object to subject; the subject confronts the world as non-reality in the sense that its objectivity determines the activity of the subject. Having said this, Hegel goes on to develop further his earlier conception of the practical idea: "It is not only the world's otherness as an abstract universality that is a nullity for the subject, but the world's individuality and the determinations of its individuality. The subject has here vindicated *objectivity* for itself; its immanent determinateness is the objective, for it is the universality that is just as much absolutely determined; the formerly objective world, on the contrary, is now only something posited, something *immediately* determined in various ways, but because it is only immediately determined, "the unity of the Notion is lacking in it and it is, by itself, a nullity".[39]

Lenin tried, in a footnote, to summarise Hegel's conception in this passage: "Man's consciousness not only reflects the objective world, but creates it".[40] At first sight, Lenin's interpretation might appear to violate Hegel's text; but it does not if we take into account that Lenin was reading Hegel's text from an anthropological standpoint. Consciousness certainly meant for Hegel universal consciousness, spirit or idea; but we already know from the *Phenomenology* that, because man is the bearer of Spirit, there had to exist some relation between spiritual history and real history, or between spiritual and material activity. Thus it was legitimate for Lenin to replace Hegel's "consciousness" with "man's consciousness". Lenin's understanding of the concept, which was so close to Marx's own in the *1844 Manuscripts,* was further clarified in another comment or note to the text, in which he summarised the argument in a slightly different way. "The notion (=man), as subjective, again presupposes an otherness which is in itself (=nature independent of man). This notion (=man) is the *impulse* to realise itself, to give itself objectivity in the objective world through itself, and to realise (fulfil) itself."[41]

Subject and object, subjective and objective world are therefore the terms of both the practical relation and the theoretical idea. In the latter, however, the subject accepts the objectivity given and takes the world as it is as its measure, whereas in the former it does not accept any such norm and feels the impulse to give itself objectivity in this objective world that is, in Lenin's words, "the otherness which is in itself (=nature independent of man)". The subject, man, feels the impulse to self-realisation, to create an objectivity for itself and thence to create itself for itself; and this impulse is not something external to the subject, because it is also his *self*-realisation, his *self*-fulfilment. Lenin underlines the anthropological content of this notion in his summary of Hegel's text: "The world does not satisfy man, who decides to change it through his activity".[42] What can be learned, therefore, with the aid of Lenin's anthropological key, from Hegel's Practical Idea is a notion of practice as the transformation by man of a world with which he is dissatisfied. This interpretation, on the other hand, could well lead us to forget that Hegel inserted the Practical Idea into a movement which culminated in the Absolute Idea. It is in this light that, in Hegel's view, praxis makes it possible for man to give himself objectivity in the objective world and to realise himself in this way. In the final analysis, man could hardly nullify material praxis without at the same time renouncing the possibility of self-realisation; but in terms of the Hegelian perspective, praxis is no more than one stage in the logical development of the Idea, which itself had to be nullified or transcended if the next, higher, stage, in which material praxis was transcended in spiritual activity itself, were to be capable of realisation.

It is into this framework that Hegel introduces the Idea of the Good. But what is the Good? Traditionally, it had been understood in an ethical sense, but it should by now be clear that Hegel's conception of praxis does not carry the moral implication characteristic of the concept of practice in earlier Idealist philosophers who had never gone beyond a simple opposition to theory. Even if Hegel did give it an abstract and mystified form, its content is far richer and deeper than the narrow ethical understanding of it typical of previous German Idealist philosophy. If practice can be taken in a Hegelian sense to mean transformation, however, it was not in the sense of a transformation of nature and society, but simply a moral transformation.

What, then, was the Idea of the Good for Hegel? In the *Logic*, he defines it in this way: "This determinateness, contained in the Notion and in the likeness of the Notion, and including within it the demand for an individual, external actuality, is the *Good*".[43] It is a demand for an external reality and an end to be realised; it is to give itself objectivity through nullifying the determinations of the external world, and "to give itself reality in the form of an external actuality".[44] None of this is meaningful, however, unless practice is understood not in the narrow sense of moral activity, but as an activity which permits a new objectivity to emerge by overcoming the determinations of the objective world. That, at least, is Lenin's interpretation. He argues, correctly in our view, that "the 'good' is a 'demand of external actuality' i.e. by the 'good' is understood man's *practice* = the demand also of *external* actuality".[45] Hegel, too, defines the good as "an end to be realised", and in this sense the following passage from the *Logic* would seem to justify the interpretation of the good as practice, or human practice in anthropological terms.

> "Hence the activity of the end is not directed against itself in order to adopt and appropriate a given determination [which is precisely what happens with knowledge, with the theoretical idea]; *on the contrary, it is in order to posit its own determination and by sublating the determination of the external world to give itself reality in the form of external actuality*".[46]

The good, then, is practice itself, albeit in the abstract mystified form corresponding to Hegel's Idealist philosophy.[47] The Good appears as the requirement to locate its own determination, which it already possesses, in the external world. In fact the idea already has objectivity in itself; but that objectivity must take the form of an external reality in order to actualise the content that the idea already possesses in itself. In this sense, the Good has primacy over the idea of knowing, "for (as Hegel says) not only does it possess the dignity of the universal, but also that of absolute reality"; not only is it objective in itself, but it also realises that objectivity as a result of its impulse to self-fulfilment. Lenin echoed Hegel's thesis, once divested of its Idealist character, when he said, "*Practice is higher than theoretical knowledge, for it has not only the dignity of universality, but also of immediate reality*".[48] Hegel's affirmation of the superiority of the idea of the Good over the theoretical idea implies the primacy of praxis, since praxis, unlike knowledge, contains reality. But in Hegel, the movement of the Idea did not stop there; the Good reveals its limitations and demonstrates at the same time the need to proceed to a new stage, that of the Absolute Idea, in which the idea achieves its full truth and reality. Those limitations, however, are the limitations imposed by practice itself. The Good is an impulse to self-realisation and has still to be realised. If the realised end yields the full truth of the Idea, that is its complete adjustment to reality, then this tendency to self-realisation can only become the Absolute Idea when it is fully realised; for there persists an imbalance between the idea and the reality. This is Hegel's understanding of the finite and limited character of the content of the practical idea. The Good is absolute and has a value in and for itself, but in its encounter with reality this original impulse becomes a particular end, with a given finite content; it is not a fully realised end, but an end in the process of being fulfilled during which it is exposed to obstacles and difficulties and even prevented from unfolding further. "Thus, the good remains an *ought-to-be;* it is *in* and *for* itself, but *being,* as the ultimate abstract immediacy, remains also confronting it in the form of a *not-being*".[49]

So the Good remains in a state of ought-to-be, that is in process of realisation; to it may be counterposed a realised, complete Good which, at this level of the dialectic of the idea "is simply an abstract postulate".[50] The realisation of the good is always finite, unfinished, in a state of ought-to-be, and the idea of a complete Good remains an "abstract postulate"; in this way, practice itself reveals its finite and limited character. Having demonstrated the superiority of practice over the theoretical idea, of action over knowledge, then, Hegel goes on to show that praxis is incapable of establishing or achieving the full adaptation of ideas to reality, that is a complete realisation. The reality that had existed prior to practice as "null-in-itself", insofar as it was a reality that had to be transformed, now presents itself as an insurmountable limit. Practical activity and the objective world are thus counterposed, but even here reality emerges also as a limit that cannot be overcome by the practical idea, obliging it to fall back upon itself. What, then, is lacking in the practical idea? As revealed by a reality that cannot be transcended, it is "the moment of consciousness proper itself",[51] that is theory itself, that is missing. While theory regards the objectivity as a reality that exists independently of subjective action, the practical idea sees reality as both null in itself and a limit incapable of being overcome. Reality is null to the extent that it is moulded by an original impulse; but it is at the same time a determining limit upon the realisation of the Good.

Hegel attempted to overcome this limitation on the idea not by falling back on an absolute activism which would have implied the absolute negation of reality and would have brought him back to a Fichteian conception of practical activity, but by negating and absorbing the end that is realised and the reality formed by that end into a superior synthesis. Thus, having accepted the notion of the transformation of reality, Hegel now declared it to be finite and limited. Having demonstrated the superiority of the practical idea, Hegel then went on to negate the practical idea as such, as an impulse to transform reality. The practical idea must itself possess consciousness; its vision of itself should return to itself and the theoretical and practical unite, because only thus could each overcome its unilateral character. This synthesis is the Absolute Idea. Cognition is reaffirmed in conjunction with the practical idea; the end no longer recognises any limits upon itself, and reality in its turn, becomes the realised end. The idea thus comes to exist as an immediate reality, which is found in cognition as a truly existent objectivity. Practical activity, reabsorbed into the process of the Idea, would thus have lost its external character, since the Absolute Idea is the synthesis of subject and object, of reason and reality.

Summary of the Hegelian conception of praxis

Hegelian praxis, whether as human labour (in the *Phenomenology*) or as a practical idea (in the *Logic*), is no more than a stage in the process of self-consciousness of the Absolute. The conception of praxis revealed in his early works (those written during the Jena period) probably remained closer to its real significance; in his system, however, of which the *Phenomenology* and the *Logic* form part, his philosophy was in the end nothing more than the philosophy of the Absolute or, to be more precise, the philosophy of the knowledge and the consciousness of itself which the Absolute possesses; to this extent it was an absolute theory in which praxis itself found its basis. In the final analysis, Hegelian praxis is a theoretical praxis which finds its true foundation, its real nature and its end in the theoretical movement of the Absolute itself.

Yet in both the *Phenomenology* and the *Logic* Hegel revealed, although in a speculative, Idealist form, important aspects of actual concrete praxis: human praxis. In order to arrive at true, human, material praxis, it would first be necessary to invert Hegel's abstract, spiritual, theoretical praxis of the Absolute in two related ways. 1) In order to make real subjects the subject of praxis, where in Hegel that subject had been the Absolute; in other words, to pass from the Absolute to the human level. And 2) having humanised it in this way, to replace the spiritual, theoretical content of Hegelian praxis with an actual, concrete and real content. It was Feuerbach who took the first step, and Marx who took the second; and it is they who are the objects of the remaining two chapters in this first part.

Notes

1 G.W. Hegel: *Lessons in the history of philosophy.*
2 The Rumanian Marxist K.I. Gulian explains Fichte's idealism in terms of his ethicism: "The objective world exists so that the Ego may realise itself on the ethical level. Even the influence and action of the object upon the subject is, for Fichte, no more than an appearance of objectivity ... If the Ego is not to encounter any external limitations on its free activity, reality must be a creation of the Ego; so the frontiers of the Ego are the frontiers of itself. Thus individualism and subjectivism are given a theoretical justification. In other terms, that individualism is explained as a necessary expression of the protest against the political and spiritual tyranny which characterised the historical period during which the feudal personality was being finally annihilated and the ideological struggle against it gaining strength". (K.I. Gulian: *Metoda si sistema la Hegel:* Bucharest 1957: Russian edition, Moscow, 1962, pp. 236-8). With reference to the relation between the philosophy of Fichte and his time, see R. Garaudy: *Dieu est mort:* (P.U.F., Paris, 1962: pp. 140-2 and 151) and also Herbert Lindner: "Fichtes Humanismus der Tat" in *Deutsche Zeitschrift zur Philosophie,* Berlin, no. 4, vol. X, 1962.
3 On the philosophy of Kant, Fichte and Schelling, as stages in the German Idealist movement which culminates in Hegel, see Part 2, chapters 1, 2 and 3 of Garaudy's *Dieu est mort (ed. cit.)* and the corresponding sections of Gulian's study. As far as the relation of Hegel's philosophy (especially in the period up to and including Jena—1803-7) to earlier representatives of German Idealism, is concerned, Georg Lukács offers a detailed study of the Idealist movement in his *Young Hegel.*
4 According to Marx: "In politics, the Germans have *thought* what other nations have *done.* Germany was their *theoretical conscience.* The abstract and presumptive character of its thinking was in step with the partial and stunted character of their actuality". (Marx: *Introduction to a critique of Hegel's philosophy of right:* edited by Joseph O'Malley: Cambridge University Press, 1970: p. 137) [Hereafter referred to as Marx:*Critique of Hegel*].
5 Hegel: *Lectures on the philosophy of history:* Bohn, London, 1857: trans. J. Sibree.
6 *Ibid.* p. 463.
7 *Ibid.* p. 464. Although he does not quote from Hegel, Marx obviously had his words in mind when he wrote: "Even from the historical point of view, theoretical emancipation has a specific, practical importance for Germany. Germany's revolutionary past is precisely theoretical: it is the Reformation.

As at that time it was a monk, so now it is the philosopher in whose brain the revolution begins". (Marx: *Critique of Hegel:* pp. 137-8)

8 "The *Critique of pure reason* was the axe that in Germany decapitated the God of the Deists", wrote Heine, adding with an ironic air of superiority, "No doubt you Frenchmen have been benign and moderate in comparison with us Germans. You were only able to kill a king, and yet afterwards you raised Cain and made the whole world tremble. In fact any comparison between Robespierre and Kant would do Kant a great injustice". (H. Heine: *Germany*).

9 "My system", writes Fichte, "is the first system of liberty. Just as France has liberated mankind from its physical chains, my system has liberated it from the yoke of the *thing in itself,* of external influences. Its first principles make man an autonomous being". (Letter to Baggesen, quoted in Garaudy: *Dieu est mort: (ed. cit.:* p. 141).

10 Marx: *Critique of Hegel:* p. 134-5.

11 Marx: *1844 MSS:* pp. 140-2.

12 *Ibid.* p. 143.

13 Kant: *Critique of judgment.*

14 Gulian *(op. cit.)* refers to Fichte's "ethicism" and his "ethics of action": "The whole metaphysics of Fichte's subjective idealism, in which the Ego creates the Non-Ego (the objective reality) is the logical consequence of his ethicism". For this reason it seems appropriate to speak of Fichte's moral-metaphysical sense, or of his metaphysical ethicism. In developing his notion of the metaphysical content of action, however, Fichte went beyond Kant and opened the way to the philosophy of Hegel. In our view, however, he was never close enough to Hegel or Marx for his concept of praxis to cover or include the practical creative activity of men. This is why Garaudy seems to us to be guilty of exaggeration in regarding Fichte as a sort of Hegel, or even a Marx, *avant la lettre;* for example, when he asserts that "the notion of praxis to which Marx was to give a concrete, historical, social and material significance was indisputably of Fichtean origin". (Garaudy: *Karl Marx:* Ed. Seghers, Paris, 1964: p. 41). Or again: "In the end, Fichte's conception of praxis, despite his Kantian vocabulary and his Idealism, represents the dedication of the whole man to a collective effort to make history, transform nature and build society". (*Ibid.* p. 51).

15 Lukács: *Young Hegel: ed. cit.* p. xxvi.

16 The *Systemfragment* comprises two folios, which are all that remains of forty seven of which it was originally composed. The 8th and 47th Folios have survived, and form pages 346-8 of the volume *Hegels Theologische Jugendschriften* published in Tubingen in 1907 by Herman Nohl.

17 Hegel did not refer explicitly to labour in the *Systemfragment,* but only to the utilitarian destruction of the object. He might have made more explicit reference to it in other parts of the manuscript, now lost, in

describing useful destruction directed to a particular end, as he did later in his *System of morality:* (Cf: Lukács: *Young Hegel: ed. cit.* p. 173.
18   Hegel: *System of morality:* Jena 1802: Quoted in Lukács: *Young Hegel: ed. cit.:* p. 173.
19   *Ibid.* p. 220.
20   The first course of lectures is devoted to the dialectic of consciousness whose content is immediately linked to the act in which consciousness of it is formed. The development of consciousness, insofar as it is a theoretical process, is presented in the form of memory and language, the earliest forms of the subject-object synthesis. The theoretical process gives way to the practical process in which the synthesis is realised in the form of desire, human desire, and more concretely, in the form of labour. Consciousness continues to develop towards its highest expression, which is the "Spirit of the people" *(Volksgeist).*

The second course is given over to the dialectic of the Spirit as it progresses through the phases of objective Spirit, real Spirit and Constitution. Here labour appears linked to the first phase, in which the will seeks to actualise itself or find a content of its own.

Hegel's two courses on the philosophy of reality prefigure the progress of consciousness understood as a process of overcoming the subject-object opposition, which he was later to elaborate in the *Phenomenology.* Both courses of lectures were published under the title *Jenenser Realphilosophie* (J. Hoffmeister, Leipzig, Meiner, 1931-2) in two volumes.
21   *Realphilosophie II:* p. 197.
22   Lukács maintained that "when he calls that manifestation of the will abstract, he means that it is the starting point from which he will move towards the broader and more complex problems of society, the problem of the social division of labour etc., whose concretion he sees in the totality of those activities". (Lukács: *Young Hegel: ed. cit.).*
23   Hegel specifies the meaning of experience thus: "This *dialectical* movement that consciousness carries through within itself, both in its knowledge and in its object, is what we shall call experience insofar as there emerges in it and for it a new object". (Hegel: *Phenomenology of Mind:* p. 142).
24   Hegel: *Ibid.* p. 229.
25   *Ibid.* p. 211.
26   "Only by risking one's life", writes Hegel, "is liberty maintained and proof given that the essence of self-consciousness is not *being,* not the immediate mode of self-consciousness, nor does it entail submerging the self as life expands. For nothing occurs in consciousness that is not in turn a stage that will be overcome in its development. Self-consciousness is pure *being for itself.* The individual who has not risked his life can certainly be recognised as a *person,* yet this does not mean that he has arrived at the true recognition of independent self-consciousness. Every

68 The Philosophy of Praxis

man, therefore, tends when he risks his life to bring the life of the other into jeopardy, for the other is worth only as much as he himself is worth..." (Hegel: *Ibid.* p. 233).

27 On the concept of recognition and the life and death struggle of master and slave in the *Phenomenology,* see the lucid and penetrating study by the Vietnamese philosopher Tranc-Duc-Thao: "Le 'noyau rationnel' dans la dialectique hégelienne" In *La pensée,* Paris, no. 119, 1965, pp. 3-23.

28 "The interpretation of the power of the master as a power founded on the courage shown in combat, is no more than a pretext invented by the dominant class in order to justify its oppression". (Tranc-Duc-Thao: *loc. cit.* p. 15).

29 "The outstanding thing in Hegel's *Phenomenology* and its outcome-that is, the dialectic of negativity as the moving and generating principle—is thus first that Hegel conceives the self-genesis of man as a process... he thus grasps the essence of *labour* and comprehends objective man—true, because real man—as the outcome of man's own labour". (Marx: *1844 MSS:* p. 140).

30 "Hegel grasps labour as the essence of man-as man's essence in the act of proving itself: he sees only the positive, not the negative side of labour. Labour is man's coming-to-be, for himself, within alienation or as alienated man". (Marx: *1844 MSS:* pp. 140-1).

31 "The *consciousness of the worker,* as Hegel presents it, is not the authentic consciousness of the worker in the experience of production." (Tranc-Duc-Thao: *loc. cit.* p. 19).

32 "Given the *Spiritualism* of such an 'ideal' liberty, the regime of oppression and exploitation can perpetuate itself in the *sordid materialism* of actual relations" (Tranc-Duc-Thao: *Ibid:* p. 23).

33 Hegel's *Science of Logic:* (Trans. A.V. Miller, Allen and Unwin/Humanities Press: London/New York: 1969) [Hereafter referred to as Hegel: *Logic*] p. 72.

34 See Lenin's notes, summaries and comments on the *Science of Logic,* first published in 1929-30 in volumes 9 and 12 of the *Leninski Sborniki* (Complete Works) together with other notes and commentaries written during the same period stemming both from a reading of Hegel's other works, and from studies of Aristotle, Lasalle, Abel Rey, Dietzgen, Plekhanov et. al. In 1933 they were published in a separate volume entitled *Philosophical notebooks,* by which title they are still known. In the English edition of the *Collected Works* they occupy the whole of volume 38, and include the essay "Conspectus of Hegel's book 'The Science of Logic' ".

35 Lenin: *Works:* Vol. 38, pp. 212-214 (Cf: note 41 below).
36 Hegel: *Logic:* p. 755.
37 *Ibid.* p. 817.
38 *Ibid.* p. 818.
39 *Ibid.* p. 818.

40	Lenin: *Works:* Vol. 38, p. 212.
41	*Ibid.* p. 212.
42	*Ibid.* p. 213.
43	Hegel: *Logic:* p. 818.
44	*Ibid.* p. 819.
45	Lenin: *Works:* Vol. 38, p. 213.
46	Hegel: *Logic:* p. 819.
47	Our interpretation of the Idea of the Good as practice going beyond the narrow meaning of activity contrasts with the interpretation sustained by Gulian, according to whom neither Hegel nor the German Idealist philosophers were able to transcend that narrow moral significance: "The German Idealist philosophers, Kant to a greater extent and others, like Hegel, to a lesser, do not include in their definition of practical activity either the transformation of nature (technology) or the transformation of society (politics), but limit themselves to moral self-perfection." "In his analysis of the Idea of the Good, that is of man's ethical relations with life, Hegel never went further than to establish a general difference between *ethical* and *theoretical* relations." (Gulian: *op. cit.:* Russian edition, vol. 2, p. 665). Had Hegel gone no further than this, Lenin's anthropological reading would lack meaning and the whole procedure of standing Hegel on his head, which Marx carried out, would have been quite pointless. As far as practice is concerned, there can be no doubt that Hegel had taken actual, objective practice into account in analysing the transformation of nature and of society; but by integrating it into an ideal process in which (as Marx pointed out) real labour in production was dissolved into spiritual labour, Hegel mystified and inverted that notion of practice. If Hegel had not surpassed the German Idealist conception of practice; if he had not gone further, even though he inverted and deformed real labour as he did so, Marx would not have found in Hegel anything more than he could already have found in the work of Kant, and the task of extracting the rational core from his philosophy in general and from his conception of praxis, of human labour in particular, would have been purposeless.
48	Lenin: *Works:* Vol. 38, p. 213.
49	Hegel: *Logic:* p. 820.
50	*Ibid.* p. 820.
51	*Ibid.* p. 821.

II. The conception of praxis in Feuerbach

The critique of religion

Feuerbach's critique of religion and its application to Hegel's whole Idealist philosophy, represented the displacement of the Absolute (God or the Idea) by actual man, who in Feuerbach's analysis was no longer merely a predicate of Spirit, but a real entity, a true subject who, while he continues to be nature, is also spirit. And precisely because he is a real entity endowed with reason, will and emotions, he reacts to the precariousness of his own existence by creating a God into whom he projects his aspiration to eternity and perfection. The core of the critique of religion which Feuerbach elaborates in *The essence of Christianity*[1] may be summarised in the following way.

God does not exist in and for himself, that is as a subject, but rather as an object that is ultimately a human predicate. Man objectifies himself in that object which is himself, his essence given objective form. Since man is not conscious that the object of religion, God, is his own product, and furthermore fails to recognise himself in God, the relation between the subject and the object adopts the form of alienation. God is man's essence idealised and set outside man. If Hegel saw God in man to the extent that he regarded actual history simply as the history of God, Feuerbach saw man in God insofar as God was, albeit in an inverted form, the consciousness that man has of himself. God as an ideal being embodies that generic perfection that the individual cannot himself achieve. In other words, God is a form of man. This concentration of perfect attributes in the religious object, however, which is realised by actual men carried with it negative consequences for them. Not only does God present himself to man as something alien, given that man is not conscious that what he has before him is one of his own products, and not only does man fail to recognise himself in God, but he also directly impoverishes himself as a human being to the extent that the object that he has created is enriched as a result of the attributes of perfection with which man has endowed him. There are here present, then, the three conditions which characterise all alienated relations, not only the religious alienation to which Feuerbach addressed himself, but also the economic alienation analysed by Marx in the *1844 Manuscripts.* These conditions are: a) the subject is active and creates the object through his own activity; b) although the object is his product, the subject does not recognise himself in it, but sees it as alien, as other; c) the object thus acquires a power that it does not possess in itself and turns against man, dominating and converting him into its own predicate.

Since religious alienation occurs in consciousness, it must be expunged from consciousness when the subject, real man, becomes conscious of his actual nature, of his condition as subject, and recognises in himself the attributes he had transferred to the object of his creation. This, broadly speaking, is the core of Feuerbach's critique of religion.[2]

By making actual man the subject and showing God or the Idea as a human practice, Feuerbach struck at the anthropological roots of both religion and Hegelian Idealism. Having laid the bases of his method in *The essence of Christianity,* Feuerbach extended it to a critique of Hegel's Idealism both in his *Provisional theses for a reform of philosophy* and in the *Principles of a philosophy of the future,* both of which appeared in 1843.[3] Just as religion transfers the human essence to God, so speculative, Idealist philosophy transferred the essence of man and nature to the Absolute Idea which in turn became a subject while man and nature were reduced to the status of predicates of that Idea. Thus his analysis of both speculative philosophy and religion aimed at reestablishing the true relations between subject and object (predicate). "The method we have employed in our critique of speculative philosophy in general is the same as that employed in our critique of religion. We have only to make the predicate a subject, and convert the subject into an object or principle; we have only to *invert* speculative philosophy in other words, and we shall arrive at the pure unadulterated truth".[4] Furthermore, Feuerbach argued, "we shall never abandon theology until we have abandoned the philosophy of Hegel",[5] for "the essence of theology is the essence of man made transcendent, projected outside man; the essence of Hegel's *Logic* is transcendental thought, man's thought *placed outside man*".[6]

Having exposed the anthropological roots of theology and of Idealist philosophy (or speculative theology), the place of praxis again becomes problematic. In religion, God is the true active, creative being, while man is such only by derivation; in speculative, Hegelian philosophy, the Absolute is universal and absolute spiritual activity and material praxis is no more than one of its transitory phases. Now if man takes the place of God, and if the Absolute is his creation, what is now the role of praxis as human activity understood not merely as spiritual activity but as material practice?

The relations of subject and object

Feuerbach expounds his theory of the relations of subject and object in the Introduction to *The essence of Christianity* and in its twelfth chapter ("The meaning of creation in Judaism"). There he provides the basis for a discussion of the Feuerbachian conception of praxis and its relation to theory. In considering that conception, however, we shall take into account Marx's penetrating critique formulated in his *Theses on Feuerbach*, in which he reproaches Feuerbach with having a) only grasped the thing in the form of an object of contemplation; b) failed to conceive human activity as sensual, subjective activity, as practice; c) considered theoretical behaviour as truly human behaviour; and d) grasped the meaning of practice only in its sullied, Judaic form.[7] The question is whether Marx is justified in suggesting that Feuerbach, like the old materialists, had effectively ignored practice, or rather had followed the Idealists in ignoring any activity not arising specifically from consciousness. It should be emphasised that all activity, whether real or ideal, material or spiritual, practical or theoretical, implies a certain subject-object correlation such that the object cannot remain absolutely in itself, without reference to its relations with the subject. Because it is activity, then, practice also implies a relation in which the object exists only to the extent that it is the real product of the actual, sensual activity to which Marx referred and which he believed Feuerbach had omitted from his analysis. For in Marx's sense, the object could not be grasped simply as an object of contemplation existing in and for itself, and abstracted from the subject; it had to be grasped subjectively, as an objectification of the subject. It was Marx's contention that Feuerbach had ignored that crucial aspect; and it is a valid critique insofar as Feuerbach did follow the Idealists in failing to recognise the anthropological and cognitive significance of practice. On the other hand Feuerbach, like the Idealists, *did* recognise the active side of the subject; although he saw it as activity of the consciousness, he acknowledged that consciousness creates an object to which it accords a reality in itself, where in fact it only has the reality of a product of consciousness. In this sense, we can say that in *The essence of Christianity* Feuerbach elaborated a theory of the deforming, alienating activity of consciousness, rather than of a formative, creative activity in the Kantian Idealist sense. He recognised that the subject is activity, but the activity he had in mind was the activity of the consciousness. Unlike the Idealists, however, he regarded the object as one term of an inverted, deformed relation between subject and object. For Feuerbach the object is grasped in a normal, truly human, that is, a theoretical relation, as the object of contemplation. In this respect, Marx's first thesis on Feuerbach ("Only theoretical behaviour is considered to be authentically human"), is seen to be fully justified.

Feuerbach examined the subject-object relation as a relation between the subject as conscious being, and the object of his consciousness. Man as conscious subject cannot, therefore, dispense with a world of objects; he is conscious of objects. Man cannot exist without the objects of his consciousness; or as Feuerbach put it, "Man is nothing without an object".[8] Thus the subject has a dependent relation to the object; but the question is to what extent it is a correlation in the sense that the object depends on, or is constituted by, the subject himself. Feuerbach did make a distinction between what he called the sensual object *(Sinliche Gegenstand)* and the object of religion. The first is categorically "external to man" and is "of itself indifferent, independent of the soul and of intellectual power". The object of religion, on the other hand, cannot exist outside human consciousness, for there is no way of distinguishing whether it is something other than what it is for me. "I cannot know whether God is something else himself or for himself, than he is for me;

what he is to me, is to me all that he is."[9]

Throughout *The essence of Christianity*, it is the relation between the subject and the object of religion that concerns Feuerbach; therefore his conclusions in respect of this relation cannot simply be extended, as Rodolfo Mondolfo does, to cover all subject-object relations.[10] For by extending what might be called a theory of religious knowledge to objects in general, the characteristics of the religious relation—that is, the alienated relation between subject and object—are taken to be features of all relations between consciousness and its object. What emerges from such an analysis is not a conception of the object in abstract separation from the subject, which was Feuerbach's standpoint, but a subject and an object in indissoluble unity not only in the religious relation but in cognitive relations in general. This leads Mondolfo to affirm without reservation that "... despite the fact that Feuerbach applied to religion in particular the theory that made man the measure of all things and all realities, there can be no doubt that it represented for him a general theory of consciousness itself."[11] Feuerbach's distinction between the sensual object existing outside man and his consciousness, and the religious object that exists only *in* man, as a product of his consciousness, is sufficient evidence of Mondolfo's misreading of Feuerbach.

Clearly, however, Feuerbach did stress that it was impossible to distinguish between the object in itself and the object as it is for me; but he said it of the object of religion, which is in fact not independent of the subject, since it is neither external nor indifferent to him. It is his product, a product of his consciousness. Clearly, too, Marx's critique of Feuerbach in the First Thesis was not concerned with this type of object. Nevertheless, Feuerbach did derive his study of the relations between the subject and the religious object, which is the fundamental element of his work, from a theory of consciousness which would seem to run against our own position, in the sense that it presented the relation between the subject and the object of religion as little more than a special and extreme case of the subject-object relation in general. This apparent contradiction deserves further consideration.

Feuerbach distinguished between consciousness of the object and self-consciousness; at the same time he set them in relation to one another by pointing out that consciousness of the object always reveals some element of self-consciousness.

> "In the object which he contemplates, man becomes acquainted with himself; consciousness of the objective is the self-consciousness of man. We know man by the object, by his conception of what is external to himself; this object is his manifested nature, his true objective *ego*. And this is true not merely of spiritual but also of conscious objects. Even the objects which are the most remote from man . . . are revelations of human nature . . . That he sees them, and so sees them, is an evidence of his own nature."[12]

What Feuerbach means here is that whatever the existence of the object in itself, it is an object for me, for my senses, my reason, my feelings or my will, which is evidence of my sensuous, rational, affective or volitional nature. The attitude of the subject to the object oscillates between two extremes; on the one hand, a total subjectivisation of the object (establishing an absolute distinction between the *in itself* and the *for itself*, to the point that the object is only such for me, and what it is for me is taken to be its being in itself), and on the other, a type of relation set out by Feuerbach in which only the object is taken into consideration, and where the subject goes so far as to discount his own presence in order to distinguish "the object from the impressions that it produces on his feelings, regarding it in and by itself without reference to human personality."[13] So the analysis of subject-object relations introduces two possible modes of behaviour, the one subjective, in which the object exists only as a product of the subject, the other objective, in which the subject attempts to grasp the object in itself, independently of any relation he may have with it. In the radical form that it adopts in religion, the first is incompatible with the second, which is the standpoint of authentic understanding. Clearly Marx's critique of Feuerbach in the first Thesis, is directed at the merely contemplative or theoretical conception of the subject-object relation. Before relating that critique to Marx's understanding of the Feuerbachian conception of praxis, however, it will be necessary to examine these two types of relation in more detail.

76 The Philosophy of Praxis

Theoretical and religious behaviour

The characteristic of the religious relation with the object is that, unlike relations with sensual objects, the distinction between consciousness of the object and self-consciousness disappears: "the consciousness of God is self-consciousness."[14] As Feuerbach had already pointed out, this self-consciousness manifested itself both in the religious object, and in sensual objects. What characterises religion is precisely the fact that its object cannot be understood without reference to its human connection. Because of that distinction between the consciousness of the object and self-consciousness, that which has a relative character in non-religious relations, has, in the religious relation, an unrestricted nature. "Here may be applied without any reservation the proposition: the object of any subject is nothing else than the subject's own nature taken objectively."[15] In religion, obviously, man is not conscious of that lack of distinction; to the believer, God is not himself. He is not aware that his consciousness of God is his own self-consciousness, indirectly; that it is his objectified essence in an unrestricted form. He is unaware that the essence of the object is his own subjective essence: "The distinction between object and thought, between God in himself and God for himself, is a sceptical and therefore an irreligious one."[16] It follows that for Feuerbach, the unrestricted subject-object relation, because both its terms contain the same human essence, is only possible in the sphere of religion. The religious object, in this sense, has no content of its own; all its determinations are human ones introduced into the object but without the limitations which they retain in sensual relations. In these words, Feuerbach asserted the true, or anthropological essence of religion: "Man is the beginning, the middle and the end of religion."[17] Since God is man's nature given objective form so that its content is wholly human, the religious consciousness that presents him as if he were a distinct, super-human being constitutes the false, or theological essence of religion. "The secret essence of religion is the unity of human and divine; its form, that is its conscious manifest nature, is the difference between these two natures. God is human nature, but consciousness represents him as a distinct, other being."[18] The resulting false consciousness of the divine is therefore false consciousness of the human. God emerges when the subject posits himself as a distinct and alien being. The source of his alienation lies in the failure to recognise himself in an object that is his own product and through which he gives his nature objective form. If alienation is the result of false consciousness, therefore, it can only be overcome by consciousness itself, in recognising the subject in the object and the disappearance of the distinction between the consciousness of God and the consciousness of man. When man sees that the religious object is an illusory entity, a simple projection of the subject, and realises that God is himself and that the superhuman being is an objectification of himself, he will be able to recuperate all that he had yielded up to that illusory being and recover his human nature. God's role would then pass completely to man, and history itself would undergo a decisive change. There is no being more absolute and divine than man himself: *"Homo domini Deus est"*,[19] man is God because man is God for man.

Religious behaviour, therefore, is not properly human; quite the contrary. Two questions arise from this: are theoretical and practical behaviour opposed to one another in the same way? And does Feuerbach find human nature in theory, in practice or in a cult of man that is no more than a new form of religion?

It will be recalled that, according to Marx, "Feuerbach, in *The essence of Christianity,* regards the theoretical attitude as the only genuinely human attitude . . ."[20] This assertion seems to be confirmed by Feuerbach's suggestion that self-consciousness defines what is properly human and is the source of decisive historical changes, not through the subterfuge imposed upon him by religion which sustains the distinction between the consciousness of God and the consciousness of man, but as an absolute, direct consciousness of human nature. Man is only authentically himself when he behaves *theoretically* towards himself. This behaviour in turn makes it possible for man to overcome alienation and recuperate his human nature. Whilst in religious behaviour the consciousness of God deforms and falsifies man's self-consciousness and makes God an object in itself rather than a human or humanised object, in theoretical behaviour God is revealed as human predicate and ceases to be an object in itself; this in turn makes it possible for a human consciousness of a self in and for itself to emerge and develop. Hence Marx's assertion that

Feuerbach regards only theoretical behaviour as authentically human, as opposed to the religious behaviour defined by Feuerbach as the false consciousness of human essence which converts a human product into a superhuman being. Feuerbach's closing thesis ("man is God for man") seems to suggest, however, that theoretical behaviour strictly speaking, not only as man's direct relation to himself consequent upon a true consciousness of his essence, but also as a relation to sensual object and other men outside himself, does not necessarily exhaust all the possibilities of authentic human behaviour. Clearly it is important to understand exactly what Feuerbach meant by theory, by the relations between theory and religion and between theory and praxis, if we are to avoid the erroneous attribution to Feuerbach of the concept of the unity of theory and praxis which Marx was, in fact, the first to develop. Mondolfo, for example, says that "if theory is disinterested activity, it is not for this reason opposed to praxis, as it is to egoism"[21]; later he refers to "the inseparability of praxis and theory", and to "the impossible suggestion that praxis possesses the actual, concrete reality when it is separated from and indeed opposed to theory."[22]

Theory and religion

What, then, does Feuerbach understand by theory, and in what sense does he oppose the theoretical to the religious point of view? The question, in other words, is to what extent Marx's comment to the effect that in *The essence of Christianity* "practice is only grasped and given shape in sullied form," is justified. In the theoretical relation, according to Feuerbach, the subject grasps the object in itself, setting aside all subjective determinations; it represents man failing to recognise himself. "Theory begins with a contemplation of the heavens," says Feuerbach. "The first philosophers were astronomers. It is the heavens that admonish man of his destination and remind him that he is destined not merely to action, but also to contemplation."[23] Theory, then, begins by ignoring actual, human interests: theory is contemplation. It is a matter for the understanding which is itself indifferent, natural and objective: "the understanding knows nothing of the sufferings of the heart... it has no desires, no passions, no wants and for that reason, no deficiencies and weaknesses, as the heart has."[24] It can contradict our deepest feelings and inclinations: "Only by and in the understanding has man the power of abstraction from himself, from his subjective being—of exalting himself to general ideas and relations . . ."[25] The understanding grasps the object in itself without reference to man; thus for Feuerbach, the intellectual characteristically submerges himself in nature. He thinks neither of himself nor of his own salvation, but of what is outside himself; and this is precisely the opposite of the religious attitude. "The Christians scorned the pagan philosophers, because instead of thinking of themselves, of their own salvation, they had thought only of things out of themselves. The Christian thinks only of himself."[26]

The understanding, and theory and contemplation too, are characteristically egalitarian; this is the result of its worship of the object, of the universe, rather than of God, or man through God, which is the province of religion. "By the understanding an insect is contemplated with as much enthusiasm as the image of God-man. The understanding is the absolute indifference and identity of all things and beings."[27] Feuerbach means by this that for theory all things exist at the same level and all are at the same distance from the understanding. And as Feuerbach suggests, this is equally true of man: ". . . the understanding also affirms the nature of man, but it is his objective nature, which has reference to the object for the sake of the object, and the manifestation of which is science."[28] But if man is God for man, the egalitarian understanding that puts men and insects on the same level must appear, in Feuerbach's eyes, as a restraint upon that self-consciousness which is inverted or rendered indirectly in religion. Theoretical behaviour would entail the destruction of the religious illusion; yet man cannot cease to try to satisfy those heartfelt needs which he had tried to allay through the religious illusion. So when theory is set against religion, that authentic, secret anthropological essence of religion remains unsatisfied. Theory is an objective, not a subjective activity; it does not disturb objects in their objectivity—that is, unlike religion or practice it does not submit them to the subject. "The stand-point of theory is the stand-point of harmony with the world."[29] It is only the religious, or the practical relation that undermines that harmony to the benefit of the subject. Theory does not disturb the object because it is indifferent to it, since it is not concerned to concentrate man's attention upon himself, but upon an object outside himself. Feuerbach exemplifies this double relation by contrasting paganism and Christianity in chapter XVI of *The Essence* . . . The Ancient Greeks contemplated nature theoretically and forgot themselves; and for the pagans too, the theoretical, contemplative attitude involved setting limitations upon their subjectivity. The religious attitude of the Christians turned them in upon themselves, separated them from the world of things which was scorned precisely because it represented a restraint upon their subjectivity. The pagan standpoint is the theoretical objective standpoint; that of the Christians, the subjective, religious point of view. And not only are these two positions distinct; they are in fact contradictory. Furthermore, their very opposition denotes an absence in which consciousness, far from striving for truth, is cast into "the night" which symbolised Feuerbach's conception of the relations between God and religion, and theory: "God, the night of theory," "the night, mother of religion." His earlier writing had offered a similar statement of his conception: "Theory in its most original and general sense, that of objective contemplation and experience, of the intellect, of science."[30]

God is the object of religion not theory, of the heart, not the understanding. For religion ignores theory and thus separates the heart from the understanding. So it is evidence not of knowledge. but of non-knowledge; it is "the explanation of the inexplicable." While religion seeks to satisfy a heartfelt need and excludes things in themselves from its consideration, theory, on the other hand, seeks those things in themselves and maintains them all at the same distance. By contrast, religion rejects this rational egalitarianism and applies a human measure to things, for God is not located at the same distance as man, nor is man himself on the same level as things. Religion shows, in a secret, hidden way, that not everything is equidistant; while the understanding regards everything from an equally remote standpoint, the measure of religion is love, which springs from the heart. Feuerbach believed religion and reason to be mutually exclusive. God is *loved* above all, so that the love of man is derivative.[31] Once the true, anthropological essence of religion is discovered, however, and it is revealed that God is man himself and man is God, the supreme being, then human love becomes the highest law. It is a love that knows no bounds, not even those of faith; it is love of man for the sake of man.

Thus Feuerbach counterposed reason, the understanding, and the heart, and set theory above religion by demonstrating *theoretically* that religion is simply a false and illusory form of human consciousness. For man's true essence is not theological, but anthropological. He showed further that religion can only satisfy the needs of the heart by sacrificing reason and the theory that sustains a distinction between God and man; it functions by concealing the fact that the human consciousness of God is nothing more than self-consciousness of man himself.

Anthropology and religion

Theory destroys the false, theological essence of man by providing him with an authentic self-consciousness; his anthropological essence, on the other hand, which had been concealed by religion, remains to him. Man replaces God, and himself becomes the supreme being; the love of man ceases to be derived and becomes an original and absolute love.[32] So theory is not only opposed to religion; it also allows man's true anthropological essence to emerge by undermining the false, theological standpoint of religion. Yet the understanding is not opposed to the needs of the heart; indeed it makes it possible for the heart's needs, and particularly its need for human love to be satisfied now openly and authentically. Thus the theoretical standpoint is ultimately reconciled with the religious point of view, and the understanding need no longer stand in opposition to the heart. Having destroyed man's false consciousness (his consciousness of God) the way lies open for the needs of the heart to be satisfied not through love of God, but through an unstinted love for man.

Feuerbach repeatedly stressed that his negative, critical attitude towards the religious relation was neither absolute nor was it aimed at the destruction of religion itself, but only of that illusory religion which falsified man's consciousness. Two years after the publication of *The essence of Christianity*, in his prologue to the second edition, Feuerbach said: "If my work is negative, irreligious, atheistic, let it be remembered that atheism—at least in the sense of this work—is the secret of religion itself, not indeed on the surface, but fundamentally, not in intention or according to its own supposition, but in its heart, in its essence, believes in nothing else than the truth and divinity of human nature."[33] Feuerbach's anthropology is incompatible with theology, but not with religion. His concept of man excludes God, but not the religious relation. Once free of theology, the religious relation became compatible once again with the theoretical point of view. Not only are reason and the heart not mutually exclusive, but they can indeed be reconciled. The relation with object is not simply theoretical, but emotional as well; at all events, it is a matter for consciousness.

Feuerbach's conjugation of the subjective and the objective, the religious and the theoretical, the rational and the emotional points of view, is less than convincing. Although his theoretical standpoint allowed him to destroy the religious illusion that made God the subject and the actual human relation a new predicate, he continued to maintain a religious point of view, rendering man divine and making the love of man for man a timeless and abstract relation between human beings by removing them from the concrete world in which they live. His conception of man becomes a new abstraction, as Stirner indicated.[34] Marx, even in his early work,[35] and Engels in *Ludwig Feuerbach and the end of classical German philosophy* provided a similar critique. Engels said, for example, that Feuerbach "himself never contrives to escape from the realm of abstraction, for which he has a deadly hatred, into that of living reality . . . But from the abstract man of Feuerbach one arrives at real living men only when one considers them as participants in history. And that is what Feuerbach resisted."[36] The point is that Feuerbach, by making man a theoretico-religious being, failed to take into account the practical dimension of his existence, as is revealed by a study of his conception of the relations between religion and practice and between theory and praxis.

Religion and practice

Feuerbach's view of the relations of religion and practice is ambiguous: sometimes he referred to human activity in a general sense, so that its content cannot be assimilated into the concept of human practical, material activity, but at other times he spoke directly of practice and the practical point of view. In referring to human activity in general, Feuerbach maintained that religion denies man as an active being; yet that negation, if we take into account the anthropological essence of religion, can only be apparent. If God is the active being par excellence on the one hand, and the objective essence of man on the other, then his activity is nothing more than human activity—"he who makes God act humanly, declares human activity to be divine."[37] Human activity is transferred to God, and thus man ceases to be, in appearance at least an active being, or rather his activity comes to have its source, its impulse, outside man. "For the very reason that he regards activity as objective, goodness only as an object, he necessarily receives the impulse, the motive, not from himself but from this object." [38] Activity belongs originally to God and not to man, yet it is man that makes God act. God apparently works for and through himself and in and for me at the same time; he is the origin of my acts. But there is no such being; it is man who acts and is the origin of his own actions. By transferring his activity to God and denying it to himself "he who thus defines God, only in appearance denies human activity, in fact making it the highest, the most real activity."[39] When man transfers his own attributes to God, he does so unconscious that he is transferring them to an illusory being produced by him; in this way he both enriches God with his own attributes, and impoverishes his own human essence. This process is a characteristic feature of religious alienation and necessarily entails in its turn man's passivity before God. God is active as a result of man's initiative; yet the deformed relation between the subject (real man) and an unreal, apparently active God, presents the unreal as the determinant of the real. Divine activity, on the other hand, is unlimited: it can transform water into wine, revive the dead, cure the incurable and so on. Faced with such an infinite active capacity, man has no need to act; it is sufficient to have faith in that omnipotent divinity, and await the result of its actions. The manifestation of the relations between an all-powerful God and passive man is "the miraculous power (that) realizes human wishes in a moment, without any hindrance."[40] Feuerbach emphasised in his analysis that that power was the negation of man's activity, in that it relieved him of the need to act. Because God acts on his behalf, human activity is surrendered to a superhuman, illusory, God.

The opposition that Feuerbach established between divine and human activity could be interpreted to lead to an affirmation of *praxis*, in that as a result of eliminating religious alienation, man will be able to reconquer his true essence as an active producer: "By restoring to man his reality, the concrete actuality of the subject-object relation is recaptured; only in this way can *praxis*, understood as productive activity, be realised."[41] Feuerbach, however, never understood practice as productive, material activity in the way that Hegel, however ideally or abstractly, had approached the concept. Indeed he never went beyond the conception which characterised all the German Idealists with the exception of Hegel, and which identified praxis with moral activity. In fact, at the same time as he referred to the anthropological character of divine activity, he reemphasised the moral content of that activity. He regarded "God as an active being, and not only so, but as morally active and morally critical, as a being who loves, works, and rewards good, punishes, rejects and condemns evil . . . God acts that man may be happy and good. God is the principle of my salvation, of my good dispositions and actions, consequently my own good principle and nature . . ."[42] Religion, therefore, is the negation of praxis insofar as praxis is practical moral activity. But this does not justify the suggestion that Feuerbach saw in the overcoming of religious alienation the vindication of praxis as a productive material activity.

What is praxis for Feuerbach?

If practice in the ethical Idealist sense of moral activity is not compatible with praxis properly speaking, what then is the significance of praxis for Feuerbach? Not only did he see no opposition between religion and praxis; he regarded "the standpoint of religion as the practical, that is subjective standpoint."[43] Here, practice is opposed to theory; where the theoretical standpoint considers the object in itself, without reference to man, the practical point of view necessarily links the object to the man whose heartfelt need that object satisfies. God, in turn, "is an object, a being who expresses the essence from the practical rather than the theoretical point of view."[44] Religion considers this object in relation to man, with its source not in reason but in feelings, the instinct for happiness, fear and hope, and the influence that these things can have on man. From a practical, subjective point of view, God acts upon the subject, and is therefore a practical, not a theoretical being who cannot be considered independently of the practical effect he has upon the subject. This contrast of practice and theory exposes the true Feuerbachian conception of praxis, as Marx outlined it: it is practice grasped and moulded in its more sordid manifestations. Marx, indeed, must have had to hand the twelfth chapter of *The essence of Christianity*, where Feuerbach elaborated most clearly his notion of praxis. There he argued that the practical relation with the world, as evidenced by the Judaic doctrine of Creation, was rooted in egoism. "The doctrine of the Creation in its characteristic significance, arises only on that standpoint when Man in practice makes Nature merely the servant of his will and needs."[45] Egoism led men to imagine an omnipotent God capable of bridging the abyss between desires and their realisation; in this sense, God is the egoistic will made divine, so that desires can be realised simply by wishing it so. The relation between the egoistic subject and Nature, therefore, cannot be a harmonious one that considers Nature in itself but does not seek to alter it; the only relation possible is a practical one which submits Nature to narrow, subjective, utilitarian needs. "When . . . man places himself only on the practical standpoint and looks at the world from thence, making the practical standpoint the theoretical one also, he is in disunion with Nature; he makes Nature the abject vassal of his selfish interest, of his practical egoism."[46]

So practice is not merely useful activity but utilitarian in its narrowest and most sordid sense; and it is this subjective, practical point of view which is the basis of Judaism and of religion in general. Among the Jews, egoism takes the form of a religion: "Utilism is the essential theory of Judaism... their principle, their God, is the most practical principle in the world (and) Nature a mere means towards achieving the end of egoism, a mere object of will."[47] Far from raising man to his full humanity, or humanising nature, its conception simply reveals the corrupt self-interest of the human subject. For Feuerbach, then, man can only affirm himself in practical behaviour at the level of arbitrary self-interest. By contrast, the theoretical standpoint represented that harmony with the world characteristic of the Greeks, whose contemplation of Nature he opposed to the egoistic point of view of the Israelites, which had robbed them of "their free, theoretical sense and instinct." While theory makes Nature an object of contemplation, practice makes of it an object of utility and profit. At one level, of course, "even the Israelites could not, as a man, withdraw for practical reasons from the contemplation and admiration of Nature." [49] Nevertheless, practice always retained its primacy.

In the end, Feuerbach failed to recognise the role of human praxis in any of its three fundamental manifestations:

a) *As productive activity,* transforming nature in the process of transforming man. Feuerbach did not perceive the role of production and human labour in social life. He considered practice only as an act of consumption responding to man's direct, natural needs.

b) *As the revolutionary activity* of men engaged in transforming their own social relations. Given that, for Feuerbach, man's alienation occurs at the level of consciousness, the means and methods with which to overcome that alienation must also be sought in consciousness; thus it is theoretical activity, rather than practical action, that is essential to that process. This is the reason why Feuerbach failed to move from theory to practical, revolutionary activity, despite the fact that his contemporaries the Young Hegelians had already acknowledged the failure of "the arm of criticism" to cope adequately with the actual, direct offensive of the Prussian State, and recognised the urgent need to develop practical, political action. Their notion of a synthesis of the German theoretical spirit and the practical spirit of the French gave expression to their disquiet, and the bilingual journal *Annales franco-allemandes* of 1844 provided a forum where the unity of theory and practice, philosophy and politics, could be developed. This particular conception of the unity of practice and revolutionary theory cannot have been totally unknown to Feuerbach; he himself had argued, in *Principles of the philosophy of the future,* that "if philosophy is to keep in step with *life* and with *man,* it must have *Franco-German blood.*" Yet Ruge and Marx himself had both failed to incorporate Feuerbach into the *Annales.* [50] Feuerbach had argued that the situation was still not ripe for action; in a letter to Ruge (June 20th, 1843) he wrote: "We cannot yet pass from theory to practice because we still lack a complete and fully developed theory." Feuerbach, in other words, remained at the level of a "human essence" lost or gained in and through consciousness, and without reference to the socio-historical reality; and theoretical activity, rather than dedication to practical revolutionary tasks, remained paramount.

c) *As social practice; as the basis of understanding*, since Feuerbach's narrow, utilitarian interpretation of practice prevented him from acknowledging that practice could provide a basis for knowledge. Having excluded practical activity from the subject-object relation, both terms stand in an external relation in which the first faces the second in a passive way, while the latter functions simply as an object of contemplation. And this faculty of knowledge or contemplation is given once and for all, and does not undergo changes whatever the development produced by social praxis itself in the subject or in the object of the cognitive relation.

In his theory of knowledge, Feuerbach stressed the role of sensation, yet never fell into vulgar empiricism or sensualism, since he regarded the senses as a point of departure from which, via reason, man could arrive at scientific knowledge. Both the activity of the senses and of reason, and the object of the subject's contemplation, however, develop without reference to the practical activity of men. Hence Marx and Engels' objection that "(Feuerbach) does not see how the world around him is not a thing given direct from all eternity, remaining ever the same, but the product of industry and of the state of society . . . Even this 'pure' natural science is provided with an aim, and with its material, only through trade and industry, through the sensuous activity of men."[51] As far as the criterion of truth is concerned, Feuerbach finds it in practice: "Whatever doubts remain to you in theory, will be resolved in practice," he said in *The philosophy of the future*. But what he means by 'practice' in this context is not material, human activity which transforms the world. The criterion of truth is practical only in the sense that it must be sought in human relations. "Concordance is the first element of truth... *species* its *ultima ratio*. If I think along generic lines, I will be able to think as man in general *is capable* of thinking, and thus as each man *should* think if he is interested in thinking normally, logically, and therefore truthfully. *Whatever concords with the essence of the species is true,* and whatever contradicts it, false. There is no other law of truth." This concept of truth as conformity with the essence of the species left a strong Idealist aftertaste. For if it was practical to think generically, and if conformity to the species is common to all, then we cannot properly speak of practice as the criterion of truth.

Summary of the Feuerbachian conception of praxis

Feuerbach's contemplative materialism is incompatible with a true philosophy of praxis. The critique to which he submitted Hegel left a negative, or rather uneven, balance as far as the conception of praxis was concerned. After Hegel's discovery of praxis, albeit in a speculative, mystified form, it may be asked what it gained as a result of Feuerbach's critique. On the one hand, it did represent a significant advance towards a true conception of praxis as actual, material, human activity; on the other, it had developed little as a result of Feuerbach's contribution. Overall, things had remained very much as before. On the one hand, man had now replaced Spirit as the true subject, and the absolute theoretical behaviour of the Spirit reduced to human behaviour, although still of a theoretical kind. On the other, in the course of this transition or radical new departure from the Universal Absolute to the human absolute, from Hegel's absolute theory to Feuerbach's human theory, the actual human practice which Hegel had considered in its mystified form (particularly in the *Phenomenology* and the *Logic*) had largely disappeared. So despite the movement from absolute to human, and the restrictions imposed upon the abstraction, Feuerbach's man remained an abstraction, as both Stirner and Engels pointed out. Thus despite its positive character, Feuerbach's conception of praxis necessarily remained on a level of abstraction which, in the last analysis, is the negation of true praxis.

Notes

1. See the Introduction to *The essence of Christianity:* (translated from the Second German edition by Marian Evans; John Chapman, London 1854) [Hereafter referred to as *Essence of Christianity*], and see also its first chapter "The essential nature of man".
2. The introduction to *Essence of Christianity* is followed by two sections called "The true or anthropological essence of religion" (Part I) and "The false, or theological, essence of religion" (Part II). The discovery in part I of the true essence of religion leads to the humanisation of God, or the deification of man. The discovery in part II of the false essence of religion demonstrates the incompatibility of theology and man, but not of true religion and true humanity, which can be reconciled once religious alienation has been overcome.
3. L. Feuerbach: *Vorlaufige Thesen zur Reform der Philosophie* (Provisional theses for the reform of philosophy) and *Grundsätze der Philosophie der Zukunft* (Principles for a philosophy of the future) are both included in L. Feuerbach: *Kleine Philosophische Schriften (1842-5)* (ed. Max Gustav Lange; Verlag Felix Meiner, Leipzig, 1950).
4. Feuerbach: *Vorlaufige Thesen...: ed. cit.* S.56.
5. *Ibid.* S.72.
6. *Ibid.* S. 58.
7. *Theses on Feuerbach:* pp. 651-2.
8. Feuerbach: *Essence of Christianity:* p. 4.
9. *Ibid.* p. 16.
10. See Rodolfo Mandolfo's study "Feuerbach y Marx" collected in *Marx y Marxismo. Estudios histórico-críticos* (Fondo de Cultura Económica, Mexico/Buenos Aires, 1960). Mondolfo, an Argentine Marxist philosopher, overestimates the influence of Feuerbach on Marx and consequently tends to obscure the line that divides them, particularly after 1845 (the year of the *Theses on Feuerbach*). According to Mondolfo, Marx never transcended the confines of Feuerbachian anthropology, or at least he never ceased to follow Feuerbach's thought despite occasional inconsistencies. Cf. also, on the same theme, a later work by Mondolfo: *El humanismo de Marx* (F.C.E., Mexico/Buenos Aires, 1964).
11. Mondolfo: *Marx y marxismo: ed. cit.* p. 31.
12. *Essence of Christianity:* p. 5.
13. *Ibid.* p. 34.
14. *Ibid.* p. 12.
15. *Ibid.* p. 12.
16. *Ibid.* p. 12.
17. *Ibid.* p. 183.
18. *Ibid.* p. 245.
19. *Ibid.* p. 275.
20. *Theses on Feuerbach:* p. 651.

90 The Philosophy of Praxis

21 Mondolfo: *Marx y marxismo: ed. cit.* p. 49.
22 *Ibid.* p. 50.
23 *Essence of Christianity:* p. 5.
24 *Ibid.* p. 33.
25 *Ibid.* p. 34.
26 *Ibid.* p. 45.
27 *Ibid.* p. 45.
28 *Ibid.* p. 45.
29 *Ibid.* p. 112.
30 *Ibid.* p. 185.
31 *Ibid.* p. 276.
32 *Ibid.* p. 276.
33 *Ibid.* p. viii.
34 In *The Ego and its Own* (1845), Stirner considered Feuerbach's man in general as a new abstraction, against which he set his own "Ego", the individual, subject to nothing and absolutely independent, recognising no moving force superior or transcendent to him, be it God, Humanity or Society. "Feuerbach affirms," wrote Stirner, "that it is sufficient to invert speculative philosophy in order to arrive at the truth pure and simple ... The contrary is the case; by transferring to man what until then had belonged to God, the tyranny of the sacred becomes the more onerous since thenceforth man is chained to his own essence."
35 "Feuerbach resolves the religious essence into the human essence. But the human essence is no abstraction inherent in each single individual. In its reality it is the essence of social relations." (*Theses on Feuerbach:* p. 652). Or again, "[Feuerbach] never arrives at the really existing active man but stops at the abstraction 'man' ..." (Marx & Engels: *The German Ideology: ed. cit.:* p. 58).
36 F. Engels: *Ludwig Feuerbach and the end of classical German philosophy* in Marx and Engels: *Selected Works* in 2 volumes: (Foreign Languages Publishing House, Moscow—English edition—1958). Vol. 2. p. 385.
37 *Essence of Christianity:* p. 29.
38 *Ibid.* p. 30.
39 *Ibid.* p. 28-9.
40 *Ibid.* p. 128.
41 Mondolfo: *Marx y marxismo: ed. cit.* p. 24.
42 *Essence of Christianity:* p. 28-9.
43 *Ibid.* p. 184.
44 *Ibid.* p. 185.
45 *Ibid.* p. 111.
46 *Ibid.* p. 112.
47 *Ibid.* p. 112, 113, 114.
48 *Ibid.* p. 117.
49 *Ibid.* p. 195.

50 On the *Annales,* and in particular on Feuerbach's relations with its founders see A. Cornu: *K. Marx and F. Engels:* (P.U.F., Paris, 1958). Vol. 2, pp.229-238: and Emile Bottigelli: "Les Annales Franco-Allemandes et l'opinion française" in *La pensée:* Paris: no. 110, 1963.
51 *The German Ideology: ed. cit.* pp. 57-58.

III. The Conception of Praxis in Marx

The conception of praxis in Marx

With Marx praxis, or the human activity aimed at transforming nature and society, came to occupy a central place; and philosophy became its consciousness, its theoretical foundation and its instrument. The relation between theory and praxis was, for Marx, both practical, insofar as theory is a guide to man's activity, particularly his revolutionary activity, and theoretical insofar as the relation is a conscious one.

Theoretical and practical necessity of a philosophy of praxis

All previous philosophies had had practical consequences independent, to a greater or lesser extent, of the intentions of the philosophers. In this sense, the relation between theory and practice is not theoretical even where it has a practical character, since its actual presentation and consequences in real life are not only not sought after, but are frequently rejected. Thus practice is often regarded with suspicion precisely because it can so often stain the purity of theory; that was certainly the attitude adopted by the Greeks and by the majority of pre-Hegelian Idealists. Thus the only philosophy that can posit the question of the relations between theory and practice is one which regards its own frontiers as limits to be transcended through a conscious link with practice, a process which obeys a double, and indissolubly connected theoretical and practical necessity.

Prior to Marx, it was German Idealism and Hegel in particular that represented the highest degree of consciousness of praxis. As we have seen, German Idealism was contemporaneous with the revolutionary movement which guaranteed full social and political hegemony to the bourgeoisie in France. Hegel himself could not but acknowledge the link between philosophy and the revolutionary reality of his time, but it was Marx who pointed out most clearly the relations between Idealist philosophy and contemporary revolutionary practice, although at the same time he set that relation against the background of a Germany whose historically anachronistic character made it unlikely that French developments would be reproduced there. Yet Marx also observed that "in politics the Germans have thought what other nations have done. Germany was their *theoretical conscience*."[1] Indeed Hegel himself had said that the actual revolution taking place in France had occurred in Germany at the level of thought; but a revolution that occurs at that level only leaves the concrete reality intact and in the end merely sanctions it. Although Hegel did pose the problem of the relations between philosophy and reality, his absolute Idealism was content to leave the world as it was, since in his judgment the mission of philosophy was to explain what is, but not to set in motion its actual transformation; in his own words (in *Lessons in the history of philosophy*), "the ultimate end and interest of philosophy is to reconcile thought, concept and reality."

The relation between theory and praxis can, of course, be conscious; yet even this need not imply practical consequences. The *critical* neo-Hegelians, for example, held this view, and saw their function in the transformation of concrete reality through the simple exercise of critical thought of a pure kind. Once again practical activity was submerged in theoretical activity. Ultimately their highly theoretical perspective was indistinguishable from an Idealism as absolute, if not more so, as Hegel's. Hegel himself had certainly recognised the richness and depth of the concept of praxis (in the form of human labour in the *Phenomenology* or of the Practical Idea in the *Logic*); indeed both Marx, in the *1844 Manuscripts* and Lenin (in his *Philosophical Notebooks*) were able, by demystifying the Hegelian conception, to find many and fruitful new possibilities in the concept. On the other hand, there can be little doubt that Hegel dismissed the notion of a self-sustaining practice, regarding it throughout as one moment in the self-consciousness of the Spirit, and one theoretical step in the development of a theory of the Absolute. The problem is that the closed, absolutely theoretical nature of his concept ends by immobilising reality itself. The system strangles the method. And that is the source of a contradiction underlined in the first instance by the Young Hegelians, and later by Marx and

Engels, between a Spirit that moves and unfolds itself, yet at the same time turns in upon itself to the extent that it ends by accepting reality as it is.[2] For Hegel, of course, there could be no such contradiction, since truth occurred only as a closed totality; the Spirit *is* what it *must be*. Being contains all its own determinations; the dice are cast. What maladjustments there are occur in the consciousness that the Spirit has of itself, of *its* reality which is the whole of reality. Whether it is a question of philosophy, of history or of socio-economic relations, the cards are already down. Thus the philosopher's mission, insofar as he is the bearer of the Spirit, is to understand, and justify, all that is. Hegel's own summation of his philosophy is presented in his famous aphorism, "Minerva's owl takes flight only at dusk." It is in this sense that Hegel's philosophy is incompatible with a true philosophy of praxis, of action, of the revolutionary transformation of reality. German Idealism is the philosophy of the activity *of the consciousness*. Hegel's philosophy, therefore, by carrying this activity, or knowledge, to the level of the absolute, becomes the philosophy of absolute action at the level of thought and thus of absolute reconciliation with reality as it is.

The Hegelian Left set out to break with this principle of conciliation, and to make a philosophy practical in the sense that it would have a contribution to make to the transformation of the world, of reality, and in particular of the contemporary reality of their own nation. This transforming zeal was directed, above all, at the twin pillars of German society—Church and State; it is not surprising, therefore, that it should have been the philosophy of religion (through David Strauss and Bruno Bauer) and the problems of politics (through Arnold Ruge in particular) that occupied the central role in their discussions in the years following the death of Hegel.[3] And their reflections on religion and politics had a practical end in view; where Hegel had refused to meddle with reality, they aspired to change it. This practical function of philosophy took the form of a constant and profound critique of the irrational aspects of reality, and of the frozen, irrational institutions like the Christian Church or the Prussian State, which simply served to detain the development of a Spirit which could only obtain temporary shape or embodiment in any given concrete, historical reality. The Young Hegelians believed that a confrontation of reality and reason, together with the exposure of the irrational aspects of reality resulting from their critique, would restore the movement of the Spirit. In this sense, the demand that philosophy take on a practical significance should be seen in the light of their conviction that a critical philosophy could, by the power of ideas alone, transform the world. Their notion of transforming activity, then, still turned on the belief in a theoretical activity capable of transforming reality.

It was the political reality of the Prussian State whose concrete actions were finally to reveal how inoperable and ultimately how inactive was this theoretical activity. The contracts between the presumed omnipotence of this activity and its actual ineffectiveness, posed as a matter of urgency the transition from theoretical activity (which never transcended its theoretical status and thus could never become a genuine praxis) to practical activity. And it is against the background of the problems that presented themselves to the Young Hegelians for solution that the evolution of Marx's thought must be understood. For it was Marx who resolved the contradiction and elaborated a philosophy of praxis which was no longer theoretical praxis, but a real activity designed to transform the world.[4] What was required was not a theory whose praxis was limited to a critique of a reality which would then transform itself, nor a philosophy of action which would restrict itself to elaborating the objectives of practical action, philosophies like those of Cieszkowski and Hess, which were little more than a new form of Utopianism.

The transition to a genuine philosophy of praxis which transcended these false conceptions was, therefore, a result of the necessity of changing the world in practice. At the same time, the restricted and impotent character of the Young Hegelians' notion of theoretical practice was clearly established. A genuine philosophy of praxis could only be developed on the basis of an intimate conjugation of theoretical and practical factors. The theoretical factors stemmed from the fact that such a philosophy had as its starting-point German Idealism itself; although it had emerged from a radical break with speculative philosophy, it still had inherited its very basis from that philosophy which, albeit in an idealist form, had given to man the consciousness of his creative power to change the world. The practical factors, on the other hand, stemmed from the productive and socio-political human activity which put to the test the value and application of the theory itself. In this respect, Marx's elaboration of the category of praxis, which began with the *Theses on Feuerbach* and which was to become the central category of his philosophy, is at once a theoretical and a practical process.

Marx began his philosophical development as a Hegelian. Thus his point of departure was a speculative conception of the world, and from there he progressed beyond the confines of the Left Hegelians to arrive finally at a fully elaborated philosophy of praxis. Several theoretical elements intervene in the process: a critique and assimilation of other theories (Hegelian philosophy, through the Young Hegelians and Feuerbach; the theories of the English economists; socialist doctrines and the ideas of the Utopian socialists). And practical factors, too, influenced the development of the theory; the reality of capitalist economies, the condition of the English working class and the living experience of political and revolutionary struggle, all of which he assimilated in large part from the work of Engels.[5]

The problem is to determine at what point Marxism began to assert itself as such; that is, at what moment it began to be a theory clarifying praxis and providing a basis and a guide for practical, revolutionary transformation. Some commentators regard Marx's *Critique of Hegel's philosophy of right* (1843) as the turning-point, because it is there that Marx emphasised for the first time not only the mystificatory character of political philosophy, but its idealism in general. Others lay stress upon the Introduction to the *Critique,* written a little later, in which Marx formulated the notion of an alliance between philosophy and the proletariat whose world-historical mission was there set out for the first time. Similarly, a number of scholars see Marx's discovery in the *1844 Manuscripts* of human labour as an essential dimension of man, even though in bourgeois society it only exists in an estranged form, as the moment of greatest significance. Still others point to *The German Ideology* of 1845 as the work in which Marxism originated, since Marx first formulated there the laws of correspondence between productive forces and the relations of production, laws whose most rigorous expression is found in his now famous Prologue of 1859 to the *Contribution to a critique of political economy,* and through which material productive praxis was shown in its full socio-historical dimension, providing a basis for the materialist conception of history. Or did Marxism embark on its own road with the *Theses on Feuerbach,* written at almost the same time as *The German Ideology,* in which the transformation of the world was presented as the fundamental challenge for philosophy? Finally, there are many who find that radical change of direction in *The Communist Manifesto,* where Marx set out clearly and explicitly the theory of the revolutionary action of the proletariat whose task it is to carry through that transformation.[6]

In our judgment, no one work can be singled out as representing a definitive break with previous work. Marx's work should be seen as a process that is both continuous and discontinuous, of which each work forms a part, and which culminates in *The Communist Manifesto* where the foundations are laid for the meeting of thought and action. Marxism can only be said to exist as a philosophy of praxis after the publication of *The Communist Manifesto,* though not, of course, in a complete or finished sense, since praxis is in essence infinite, and the process of its theoretical clarification endless. Perhaps it would be more accurate to say that Marxism becomes a philosophy of praxis with the *Manifesto,* where a process with no foreseeable end is set in motion. The *Manifesto* ties together many of the loose strands which gave the philosophy of praxis its profile. In summary, Marx does pose the problem of the relation of theory and practice in his early work, and begins there to lay the basis for a philosophical category of praxis.

Philosophy and action

In his first work, Marx approaches the problem of the relations between philosophy and action within the framework set out by the Young Hegelians, who had concluded that if reality was to be changed, philosophy could not be a theoretical instrument for its conservation or rationalisation, but only an element in its transformation. In these terms, philosophy had to depart from a critique of reality designed to give impetus to that transformation. Since the critique did not succeed in transforming reality, however, it became necessary to establish a new kind of link between philosophy and reality, or between thought and action, which would entail a change in the mission, and in the very content of philosophy. Clearly philosophy cannot change reality simply by offering a critique of it: it must itself be realised, and that in turn would imply its disappearance. That, in any event, was Marx's perspective during the eighteen forties, when he set out its most precise formulation in his *Introduction to a critique of Hegel's philosophy of right*, originally published in the *Annales*. This interpretation, however, gave rise in its turn to a new series of questions and problems to be resolved. How can philosophy be realised? In what sense can it come to be the unity of theory and practice? What is this praxis so intimately linked to philosophy?

In the first place, Marx defines his own understanding of the relations between philosophy and reality in opposition to two prevalent misconceptions of his time which he calls the practical political party and the theoretical political party.[7] Both were theoretical expressions of the German liberalism of his time, the first crystallising among the "Young Germany" movement, a liberal-romantic movement which flourished between 1831 and 1835, and which opposed reactionary Romanticism and the Prussian State. The second was represented by the Left Hegelians. The representatives of the *practical political party*, concerned to transform actual reality in a direct and immediate way, deny philosophy; in this respect Marx found himself in agreement with them. On the other hand, they failed to see that philosophy could not be denied so long as it remained mere speculative philosophy, and was not realised. The members of Young Germany put all their weight behind practice and none behind theory, for they understood the negation of philosophy to mean withdrawal from theory and total devotion to practice.

The second current, the *theoretical political party*, denied practice in the name of philosophy, or rather believed that theory was of itself praxis. Theory won all their attention, and practice none, for they rejected the necessity of denying philosophy, in the belief that it could become practical and be realised as philosophy. Marx saw, however, that philosophy could never emerge from its own ambit and be realised while it remained mere speculation.

In both cases, then, there exists an absolute separation between philosophy and the world; in the first case, the world is believed to change without philosophy, in the second philosophy tries to change reality which remains as it is, however, because philosophy does not become integrated into reality. In both cases, praxis, the link between philosophy and reality, is absent. Yet only through praxis is philosophy realised, does it become practical and negate its own pure character, while at the same time reality becomes theoretical in the sense that it becomes impregnated with philosophy. Thus the transition from philosophy to reality requires the mediation of praxis. In the specific conditions of Germany at this time, philosophy meant politics or a political critique of the speculative philosophy of law and the State which in turn had a direct bearing upon the reality of contemporary Germany. But if, in contrast to the beliefs of the Young Hegelians, reality could not be changed by the critique alone without the mediation of practice, how could it become practice and level its direct assault upon reality? Marx posed the problem for the first time in 1843, and concluded that "the weapon of criticism cannot replace the criticism of weapons ... theory becomes a material force once it seizes the masses ... once it becomes radical."[8] So the theory that cannot by itself transform the real world becomes practice when it takes root in the consciousness of men. These then are the obstacles and preconditions for the concept to become practice; the theory by itself is inoperable and cannot replace action. But it can become an effective power, a "material power", when it is accepted by men.

The revolution and the historical mission of the proletariat

The passage from philosophy to reality requires the mediation of men; yet up to this point Marx had spoken only of their consciousness. Clearly the acceptance by men of a given theory is an essential precondition for a transformation, but it is still not the activity that can carry it out. Two questions, then, demanded resolution. First, what type of theory should be accepted and pass then into reality itself. Secondly, it is necessary to say what kind of concrete men can make the critique their own and convert it into action, into revolutionary praxis. In the first place, the critique must be radical. In the second, it is the role of the working class to realise philosophy and mediate between it and reality in the light of a given historical situation.

The critique must be radical if it is to take root. "To be radical," Marx said, "is to grasp matters at the root. For man the root is man himself."[9] Such a critique must respond to a radical necessity by taking man as its focus. "Theory will only be realised in a people in so far as it is the realisation of their needs."[10] Such a critique began with Feuerbach, whose analysis provided man with the possibility of a genuine self-consciousness. The critique of religion—"the prerequisite of every critique" according to Marx[11] —was a radical critique at the level of theory; the transition to a practical critique, in its turn, was the prerequisite of revolution, in which the radical critique, "praxis . . . at the level of principles"[12], is raised to a human level. Praxis, then, is the revolution, or a radical critique that passes from the theoretical to the practical plane in response to radical human needs. We might summarise Marx's analysis of the relations between theory and praxis in this way; a) theory is inoperable in itself because it cannot be realised; b) its efficacy is conditioned by the existence of a radical necessity expressed as a radical critique which makes the acceptance and adoption of that theory possible. That radical necessity provides the foundation both of the theory that is its theoretical expression and of the necessary transition from theory to praxis at the level of principles; that is, to Revolution or the total emancipation of men.

The transition from theory to practice or from radical critique to radical praxis is conditioned by a given historical situation; the Germany of Marx's time, for example, whose politically anachronistic character together with the fact that it had not lived through the phase of political emancipation already experienced by other nations, found itself facing the historical necessity of overcoming its own limitations, as well as those of other nations, through a radical revolution.[13] In this anachronistic situation, Marx said, it is not the radical revolution that is Utopian, but a simply political one.[14] As he was later to say, the only revolution possible in Germany was not the bourgeois, but the proletarian, socialist revolution. The transition is also determined by the existence of a social class, the proletariat, whose liberation is conditional upon the liberation of mankind as a whole. The world-historical mission of the proletariat does not have an 'a priori' or providential basis (as Marx and Engels made clear in *The Holy Family*, "the proletarians are not gods")[15]; its source is the concrete position occupied by that class in production in bourgeois society. The proletariat is historically destined to liberate itself through a radical revolution that entails its own negation and suppression as a class and the affirmation of a universal humanity.

In this way, Marx affirmed that the proletariat could not liberate itself without first passing from theory to praxis. Theory alone cannot liberate the proletariat, nor can its social existence alone guarantee that liberation. The class must first become aware of its situation, of its radical needs and of the necessity and conditions of its liberation. This consciousness is philosophy, or rather it is their philosophy; philosophy and the proletariat stand in an indissoluble unity. "Just as philosophy finds its material weapons in the proletariat, so the proletariat finds its spiritual weapons in philosophy." [16] Without the proletariat, philosophy can never transcend its own frontiers; it can only be realised when it is linked to the class as its instrument, its material weapon, and hence takes root in reality. On the other hand, the proletariat cannot liberate itself without philosophy, the spiritual and theoretical weapon of its liberation. In this relation the two terms condition one another; the realisation of the one entails the abolition of the other. "Philosophy cannot be actualised without the abolition *(Aufhebung)* of the proletariat; the proletariat cannot be abolished without the actualisation of philosophy."[17]

In 1843 Marx was not in a position to develop any further the question of the mission of the proletariat. It would first be necessary for him to analyse in greater detail the economic and social structure of bourgeois society and to uncover the true conditions and motive forces of its historical development. By establishing a link between philosophy and the proletariat, and perceiving that their realisation was a single process, Marx had posited for the first time the unity of theory (philosophy) and praxis (the revolutionary activity of the proletariat). Yet this concept of praxis had obvious limitations; its key concepts of emancipation, or the "total redemption of humanity,"[18] radical necessity and radical revolution, were not yet completely free of an element of Feuerbachian anthropologism. The worker appeared as the negation of humanity rather than in relation to a given stage of development in society. But a genuinely scientific concept of the proletariat was still lacking, and this could only be based on an analysis of capitalist relations of production. For Marx in this period the world-historical mission of the proletariat derived not so much from its socio-economic position within bourgeois society as from a philosophical conception of the proletariat as the negation and embodiment of what is universally human, and from the specific and anachronistic situation of Germany in his time. Making a virtue of necessity, Marx maintained that Germany's very backwardness created favourable conditions for the fulfilment by the proletariat of their mission, where this would prove much less feasible in the socially and economically more advanced nations. So what Marx put forward at this time was a philosophical justification of that mission from a narrow, historical point of view rather than from a scientific, historical and objective standpoint. He was still not aware of the laws governing capitalist material relations, class relations in bourgeois society and the true nature and function of the bourgeois State. He had still to develop a conception of history which would provide a foundation for the necessity of proletarian revolution.

Despite this inadequate foundation, and despite the conceptual imprecision to which it gave rise, Marx had already seen that praxis is a real, concrete transforming activity of men, whose most radical form was the revolution. Equally, he recognised the indissoluble relations between praxis and theory, or the philosophy or theoretical expression of a radical necessity, rather than as knowledge of a reality; and he perceived too the role of those social forces whose consciousness and action could establish the unity of theory and praxis. Marx now had to move on to a new and more radical conception of revolutionary social praxis and a richer concept of the proletariat's role as subject of that praxis; and this in turn would lead him to an understanding of the implications of overcoming the negative aspects of the proletariat and thus of man himself. The form of praxis that marked the beginning of the process was precisely material production, human labour. To the extent that this development clarified not only the nature of social praxis and other non-material forms of production, but also the interpretation of history as man's self-production, this discovery was a crucial stage in the development of the philosophy of praxis. Revolutionary praxis, or the conscious and radical transformation of bourgeois society by the proletariat, must necessarily take as its starting-point consciousness of productive material praxis. Marx would not have advanced very far had he not provided the conception of praxis with a deeper and richer content in the *1844 Manuscripts;* for not only did his exposition of praxis as productive praxis or human labour enrich the *concept* of social praxis, but it also added new dimensions to social praxis itself.

In his writings prior to the *1844 Manuscripts,* Marx saw a close connection between philosophy and the revolutionary praxis whose subject was the proletariat, the class destined to carry out the revolution of existing society. The proletariat was the concentrated expression of the sufferings inflicted on men, whose impulse is to free itself in such a way that it brings about its own abolition as a class and liberates the whole of mankind. Yet Marx had still to explain the conditions and possibilities of that liberation; and that could not occur as long as he failed to see the proletariat in terms of the properly proletarian quality of existence as a producer participating in given social and economic relations. Until 1844 he continued to regard the worker as a suffering being who is destined to be free; thus he is the subject of revolutionary praxis, but only in a rather speculative and anthropological sense that he represented human suffering as a whole. Only in *Capital* was he to develop a scientific concept of the proletariat as a social class lacking the means of production and producing surplus value because it is forced to sell its labour in the form of a commodity. Until this moment, then, Marx regarded the proletarian as a revolutionary moved to struggle by the universal human character of his suffering. Nonetheless, in objective terms Marx recognised in the *1844 Manuscripts* that, before his revolutionary activity began to unfold, he was already an active being producing objects, as a result of which he contracted relations with other men which in turn had vital consequences for his own existence.

The *1844 Manuscripts,* then, clearly do mark a turning point.

Until then, he had seen the proletariat as the negation of human essence, rather than as an agent of production, and had seen that negation as the source of struggle and ultimately, of the emancipation of the class. It was precisely the need to elaborate upon the necessity for emancipation and the character of the corresponding revolutionary praxis, that led him to analyse the situation of the proletarian as a worker. For the existence of the proletariat is defined as existence in work, in production, which, as Marx might have said in 1843, is the location of human suffering. Having shown the proletariat to be the subject of revolutionary praxis, then, Marx went on to analyse its role in productive praxis. The connection between these two forms of praxis, moreover, was an intimate one in the peculiar conditions of a backward Germany, whose production had scarcely developed; this explains why Marx saw the worker as a revolutionary first, and only secondly as a producer. Yet it was this very need to provide revolutionary praxis with a firmer basis that led him on to examine the practical, material activity of the worker in a process of production in the light of its alienated, or estranged, character.

Productive praxis as alienated labour

Marx had learned from the 18th century English economists that human labour is the source of all value and all wealth. This is, of course, a subjective source; thus Engels, who was to introduce Marx to the field of political economy, was right to characterise Adam Smith as the Luther of economics,[19] since he passed from a consideration of wealth in its objective form, external to man, to a notion of wealth as the subjective product of human labour. If that is the case, however, why Marx asked himself in the *1844 Manuscripts,* if human labour is the source of all wealth, is the subject of that activity (the worker) always in such an unequal and disadvantageous position vis-a-vis the capitalist? Bourgeois economics, of course, had no use for such a question, since it regarded the worker only as a worker, a productive instrument and a source of wealth, but not as a human being as such. Marx's question related to the human essence of the worker which is negated or mutilated in production. Thus although the principle that human labour is the source of all value and wealth seems to imply a recognition of man, it in fact left man as a human being outside the process of production; "Under the semblance of recognising man, the political economy whose principle is labour is really no more than the consistent implementation of the denial of man . . ."[20] Political economy, with a frankness bordering on cynicism, made no attempt to deny this inhumanity; but the worker was only of interest to it insofar as his labour produced goods for profit. The negative consequences of labour were natural and required no explanation; thus the conditions of human, or rather inhuman existence of the worker in production were deemed insuperable. For bourgeois political economy, labour was merely an economic category producing commodities and wealth. Clearly the negative effects of labour on man, however, give it a much deeper significance than the simply economic (the production of wealth), for it affects the worker at the human level in a radical way. This contradiction moved Marx to consider further this human activity which consists in producing a particular type of object which is then appropriated by the non-worker, that is the capitalist.

Marx began by defining labour as the productive, material activity whereby the worker transforms nature and creates a world of objects. Yet it is an alienated activity with the same features as religious alienation as Feuerbach had defined it: the creation of an object in which the subject fails to recognise himself, and which appears to him as something alien and independent whose power, with which he had endowed it, now stands in opposition to him.[21] Unlike Feuerbach, however, Marx did not restrict that process to the realm of consciousness, but presented it as an actual and effective alienation arising in the concrete process of material production. At the same time Marx approached this alienation in various forms; in the act of production, but also with respect to nature, to man's species life and to his relations with other men.[22] And he also referred to that particular form of alienation whose subject is not the worker but the non-worker, who without participating directly in the productive process, appropriates the worker's product. Unlike the worker, his relation to production is theoretical and contemplative, in that he only establishes a relation with the product once it has been separated from the process of production itself.[23] And insofar as the object, the activity of the subject (labour) and the worker all exist outside the process of the objectification of essential human powers, the relation of the non-worker to each of these elements is purely external. Thus both the active and the passive relation to objects, both the theoretical and the practical relation to production, lead to the alienation of man. Marx's analysis of the situation of the worker as the human subject of productive, material praxis, in the *1844 Manuscripts,* led him to the conclusion that labour is the denial of humanity. His point of departure was the human essence that is negated by the actual, concrete existence of the worker; so productive activity is a form of praxis that on the one hand, creates a world of human or humanised objects, but on the other produces a world of objects in which man does not recognise himself, and which even turn against him. In this sense, it is alienated activity. Furthermore, Marx did not regard this praxis as simply a particular relation between the worker and the products of his labour, and between the worker and himself (that is alienation with regard to his activity insofar as he does not recognise himself in it), but also as a peculiar relationship between men whereby the worker and the non-worker (the capitalist) find themselves in an inseparable, yet opposed, relation in the production process.[24] Thus alienation characterises not only the relations between subject and object, but also between the worker and other men. For only human relations can have an alienated character: "Through estranged labour man not only engenders his relationship to the object and to the act of production as powers that are alien and hostile to him; he also engenders the relationship in which other men stand to his production and to his product and the relationship in which he stands to other men."[25] Later, Marx was to designate these relations understood as social, not intersubjective relations, as relations of production. Production does not only create objects; it also creates human, social relations. So the material production of objects is social production.

The result of the analysis of praxis as productive human activity is negative, involving the alienation of man from the products of his labour, his productive activity and from his fellow men Yet the concept of alienation which originated in Feuerbach opened the way in Marx's thought to the development of significant notions about the role of production and the relations contracted by men in production (the relations of production). Much of the *1844 Manuscripts* is devoted to expounding this opposition between alienated labour and man, between the worker and his human essence. Human labour, he affirmed, is the negation of man, particularly in the form it adopts in capitalist material production. It seems legitimate to suggest, furthermore, that Marx believed this characterisation of human labour as alienated activity to be applicable to the whole of history, so that, until the establishment of communism, human history is simply the history of the alienation of human beings in labour. Man does and has always lived, then, in an alienated condition, that is to say, denying himself and his essence. Since this negation appears as alienated labour throughout, it follows that labour has historically presented a universally negative character, and therefore has an absolutely negative character.

The transformation of man and the world

This negative conception would seem, however, to contradict Hegel's affirmation, which Marx underlined and approved, that man is a product of his own labour.[26] Labour not only produces objects and social relations of an alienated kind, but also produces man himself. Thus the labour that denies man on the one hand, affirms him on the other because he himself is produced by it. If human labour were absolutely negative, and represented a total loss of humanity, total degradation to the level of animal or thing, then it would be impossible to conceive of how it could produce man as such. It could be argued that Marx did speak of the loss of humanity, of the reification or bestialisation of existence which made an animal of man,[27] but this should be understood to mean a fall to the most ignominious human level, rather than a literal submergence in the ontological status of the animal or the object. Alienated man may not be conscious of the creative human sense of his activity, but he continues to be an active, conscious being. On an intimate level he remains human, even if his humanity is alienated and distorted. Man alone can become alienated because he is the product of his own doing, of his own labour; as the creator of his own being (as a historical being in other words), he is directly involved in the process of his self-production, of humanisation, even though within that process there exist a whole gamut of levels, the lowest of which is that of alienated, reified man.

To return to Marx, labour both affirms and denies man. In our view, however, this does not mean that labour is either pure affirmation or pure negation. Marx reproaches Hegel, for example, with his failure to take into account the negative aspect of labour, its alienation.[28] Yet that very reproach stems from the Hegelian conception of labour, expound in the *Phenomenology of Mind,* which Marx approved, to the effect that man is the product of his own labour. Now Marx made a key distinction between objectification and alienation, establishing a mutually dependent relation between them, which can explain this apparent contradiction.

> "The *real* active orientation of man to himself as a species being, or his manifestation as a real species being (i.e. as a human being), is only possible by his really bringing out of himself all the *powers* that are his as the *species* man—something which is only possible through the totality of man's actions, as the result of history—is only possible by man's treating these generic powers as objects; and this, to begin with, is again only possible in the form of estrangement."[29]

The following conclusions can be derived from this passage: man only manifests himself as a human being to the extent that he objectifies his essential, generic powers, but this objectification (material praxis, human labour) is only made possible by entering into a relation with others "through the collective activity of men." It is the behaviour of men with respect to those powers in their objective form, as if they were something strange or alien, which makes alienation possible. Man cannot be man as long as he remains entrenched in his subjectivity; he must give himself objective form. Yet he is present as a social being in that objectification, which is a necessary component of the process whereby man makes or produces himself as such, and retains his human status. He carries out that process through labour which is, in principle, an objectification of his own being, of his essential powers. Hegel had already shown, in the *Phenomenology,* how man humanises Nature and himself through his labour, raising himself as a conscious being above his own nature.[30]

In that sense, material objectification, that is production, is essential to man.

From the *1844 Manuscripts* onwards production begins to take on a special significance for Marx, resulting not only from its economic (the production of useful objects in order to satisfy human needs) but more fundamentally from its philosophical content in the sense that for Marx, production is the self-production or self-creation of man. The role of production set out for the first time in the *1844 Manuscripts* in the form of the economic-philosophical concept of alienated labour, was later to be elaborated into the fundamental premiss of all human history. For this reason the *Manuscripts* constitute a decisive contribution to the formation of Marx's thought, for it must be recognised that any discontinuity between the Marx of the *Manuscripts* and the later Marx does not represent a radical, absolute break, but rather points to a more fundamental unity or continuity. The notion of a break can only be sustained by ignoring those elements of the *Manuscripts* which were carried forward and developed in Marx's later work, and reducing its content to a mere extension of Feuerbach's theory of "human nature" to political economy, a theory from which, it is suggested, Marx departed in a radical and conscious way from *The German Ideology* onwards. Such an interpretation burns all the bridges between the two works, but leaves unanswered the question as to how, in that case, Marx was able to move (or rather leap) from the speculative or ideological Feuerbachian perspective of the *Manuscripts* to the new scientific method of the work of 1845. Nor can this leap be explained simply by stressing the importance of the replacement of the concept of alienation by the concept of praxis (human labour), as Cornu did. If on the other hand this concept of praxis is regarded as "the ultimate triumph of speculative consciousness," then it would have been present in the *Manuscripts*, albeit in an ambiguous and rather speculative form.[32] This radical discontinuity between Marx's work of 1844 and that of 1845 can only be sustained by ignoring the contribution made by the *Manuscripts* to the key concept of production. Yet in his early work, Marx had already begun to approach what was later to become the materialist foundation of history which necessarily presupposed an earlier conception of man as a practical being who, even in his alienation, forms himself through his own labour, that is, creates himself *in* and *through* production. Cornu based his assertion of the continuity of Marx's thought on an analysis of the role of the theory of alienation in the formation of the concept of praxis and later of a new conception of history.[33] The fundamental thesis of the *Manuscripts*—that man transforms himself and the world through labour—comes to be the key to the subsequent development of Marx's thought, that is to the development of his conception of human history as the fruit of the dialectical unfolding of productive forces and the social relations which men contract in production.

In the first instance, production is linked to need; man is the creature of his needs and produces in order to satisfy them. Animals, too, have needs and in a way produce. What differentiates the human from the animal relation, however, is the relation that operates in each case between need and production. In the animal, as Marx emphasised, the relation is direct, immediate and unilateral, and further the first term determines the second, since animals produce only under the pressure of their needs. In man, the relation is mediate, since production only satisfies needs in this case to the extent that the need has *lost* its immediate, physical character. Man satisfies his needs and liberates himself from them by overcoming them, that is by making them lose their merely natural, instinctive character to become specifically human. As Marx put it "the animal produces one-sidedly, whilst man produces universally. It produces only under the dominion of immediate physical need, whilst man produces even when he is free from physical need, and only truly produces in freedom therefrom."[34] Man, therefore, is not strictly speaking a creature of his needs, but a being who invents or creates his own needs. Production is the creation of a world of objects; but man alone can stimulate himself to produce through the creation, in an unending process, of new needs. Insofar as he creates his own needs in this way, man creates or produces himself; but this production has adopted the peculiar form of alienated labour. Nonetheless, man is a social being, and as such has never ceased to affirm and produce himself, despite the alienated form that his objectification has adopted historically. "We have before us the *objectified essential powers* of man in the form of *sensuous, alien, useful objects*, in the form of estrangement, displayed in *ordinary material industry...*"[35]

It is labour, or production, that raises man above external Nature and above his own nature; his self-production consists in overcoming his natural being. Historically, however, man has only been able to objectify himself and dominate Nature by entering into a dependent relation with other men; that is why the process of objectification entails the negativity of alienated labour. In this sense, we can say that Marx sees alienation as a necessary phase in the process of objectification which man must overcome, if he is to develop his true essence, when the necessary conditions are present.[36] Thus productive, material praxis requires that alienation and objectification be at once related and distinguished.

Man only exists and produces himself to the extent that he objectifies himself and produces a human world. This objectification however, necessarily, but not essentially, presents an alienated character. This is precisely why alienation can be overcome, but not so objectification, which is an essential, constituent aspect of human existence. For that reason production is essential and fundamental to social life. Thus material praxis, or productive activity, becomes an economic-philosophical category which, from the *Manuscripts* onwards, came to occupy a central place in Marx's philosophical thought. The problem of the relations between subject and object, in both an ontological and a cognitive sense, must be seen in that light.

Man and Nature: the anthropological character of natural science

In the *Manuscripts* the subject-object question was posed in terms of the relation between man and nature, whereas in the *Theses on Feuerbach* it is presented as a matter of the relations between object and subject. Marx reaches the same conclusion in both cases: the second term of the relation—nature or the object—does not exist for man outside his practical activity, and thus has for him an anthropological character. This anthropologisation of Nature and the object *in* and *through* practice, determines in its turn the anthropological characterisation of knowledge, that is, of the cognitive relation of subject and object. What, then, is the status of external

Nature and the object respectively, with regard to the central role of praxis in Marx's work of 1844 and 1845? Marx's conception of man, as we have seen, is that of a being who in essence needs to objectify himself in a practical, material way in order to produce a human world. Production, in this sense, functions in two ways: on the one hand, it allows man to project and objectify himself in a world of objects produced by his own labour; on the other, it enables him to integrate Nature into the world of men so that it loses its status as pure nature *in itself*, and becomes a humanised nature, or nature for man. Since Nature does not of itself possess an anthropological character, man must mould it to his human world by transforming it through his labour. "*Industry* is the *actual*, historical relation of nature, and therefore of natural science, to man." [37] Through industry, production or labour, nature is adapted to human ends, for "neither nature objectively nor nature subjectively is directly given in a form adequate to the human being." It is through human intervention that nature becomes humanised; hence Marx's assertion that "industry is the open book of man's essential powers." The development of production, of productive praxis represents, therefore, the increasing humanisation of nature. "Nature, too, taken abstractly, for itself, nature fixed in isolation from man, is *nothing* for man."[39] It might be suggested, of course, that this represents little more than a new Idealist version of the notion that "there is no object without a subject," or that it is a new version of idealism, "an idealism of praxis."

Man only exists in terms of his practical relation with nature; and that relation is unavoidable, so that nature presents itself to man either as the object and material of his activity, or as the result of that activity, that is as humanised nature. In these terms, it is simply an abstraction to refer to nature in itself, without reference to man and his activity. For nature in that case becomes nature *without* the human imprint, in other words the absence of what is human, of the presence of a non-humanised world. Such a nature could only occur in itself, and therefore in an external abstract relation to man, for nature exists for man only to the extent that it ceases to be pure nature, and enables him to transform and humanise it through his labour. Nature is *nothing* for man outside that relation; it only has meaning for him as the object, or product, of his activity. Outside that relation, nature is merely the immediate, mediated by man, a reality unintegrated into the human world. Marx accepts the existence, and even the priority of such an immediate nature on an ontological level; "the worker," he says, "can create nothing without *nature*, without the *sensuous external world*. It is the material on which his labour is manifested, in which it is active, from which and by means of which it produces."[40] But for man *actual* nature is the object or product of his activity, of his labour; unformed nature, untouched by men, is *nothing* but a pure, original nature which only remains so until he (man) integrates it into his world. "The nature which comes to be in human history—the genesis of human society—is man's *real* nature; hence nature as it comes to be through industry, even though in an *estranged* form, is true *anthropological* nature."[41] The ontological priority of nature is made manifest in the meaning that it comes to have for man; but the nature that man knows is no longer a pure, original nature-in-itself, but a nature integrated into his world through practice, in the form of humanised nature, either in the form of a product of his labour, or of the object of his activity. Thus man's knowledge of nature is anthropological knowledge.[42]

What, then, is the significance of the fact that for Marx the natural sciences are, in the final analysis, human sciences? In what way should this interpretation be understood? The point of departure is the anthropological basis of industry and productive praxis in general. "The history of *industry* and the *objective* essence of industry are the open book of *man's essential powers*,"[43] Marx argued, adding that industry had only been considered hitherto in terms of its external utility, rather than in terms of its capacity to embody and realise those essential human powers. The reality of those powers had always previously been sought outside industry, in politics, literature, or art. But even in alienated forms, man does unfold his powers in this world of useful objects; industry, therefore, must be seen in relation to man. What is the relation, however, between man and the scientific knowledge of nature? It, too, is an actual, historical relation, insofar as he acquires that knowledge through industry. There is not one basis for industry and another for science;

there do not exist two separate worlds; one practical, the other contemplative. Natural science penetrates human life by way of industry and as in the case of productive, material praxis, presents itself under a double aspect; it both humanises man (by emancipating him) and dehumanises him (by complementing his alienation). Hence Marx's contention that "Natural science has invaded and transformed human life all the more *practically* through the medium of industry; and has prepared human emancipation, however directly and much it had to consummate dehumanisation."[44]

Natural science, therefore, already has an anthropological character to the extent that it is at the service of man, has a practical influence on human life and contributes directly to human emancipation. Man acquires knowledge in order to transform nature in accordance with his needs. Marx stressed, however, that the anthropological character of natural science is a consequence both of its practical function and of its object.[45] Nature is certainly the object of natural science, not the nature-in-itself that exists ontologically prior to man, but nature integrated or in process of integration into the human world. There is a unity of man and nature a) insofar as nature is man (humanised nature) and b) insofar as man, *qua* natural human being, is also nature. In this sense, Marx asserts that man is the immediate object of natural science, just as nature is the immediate object of man. If the science of nature is the science of man, then the latter is in its turn natural science. Nature is not distinct from man (hence Marx's reference to "the social reality of nature") nor natural from human science. Their common anthropological character tends to lead towards their merging, though their fusion will only occur in the future: "Natural science will in time subsume under itself the science of man, just as the science of man will subsume under itself natural science; there will be *one* science."[46] What is meant here is that the process whereby man attains his *real* nature, raising himself above external and internal nature, and similarly the process through which original nature takes on an anthropological character, are historical processes resulting from the productive, material praxis of men. In the same way the process whereby natural science becomes a human science is also realised in time just as man comes to understand that nature, the object of science, is a humanised nature. The discovery of the anthropological character of natural science, its functions and its object was therefore contingent upon industry's conversion of original nature into anthropological nature. With time, the process of the growing humanisation of nature would culminate in the obliteration of the distinctions between natural and human sciences.

It could be argued, on the other hand, that even in modern times, when the progress of industry and technology has already humanised nature to a considerable degree, the division between natural and anthropological science remains as firm as ever, despite their common anthropological basis. Marx himself acknowledged that this division was contradictory in view of their common basis, but he did not go on to clarify the origin of that contradiction; nevertheless the explanation is implicit in Marx's analysis, if we take into account his contention that alienated labour arises also in the form of an alienated relation between man and nature by virtue of which, far from according man a means of affirming and objectifying his essential powers, that labour becomes as it is for the animals, a simple means of subsistence remaining alien to him. When nature fails to have an anthropological character for man, his knowledge of nature also loses its anthropological nature; man, absent in nature, is absent too from natural science. The division between man and nature in an alienated relation leads to a division between natural and human science. Only when the practical relation between man and nature adopts an authentically human character, a creative, productive, non-alienated praxis, will the conditions exist for the union of natural science and the science of man on a common anthropological basis.

Praxis and knowledge: the "Theses on Feuerbach"

His consideration of the relations between man and nature opened the way for Marx to advance, although he still carried with him an element of anthropologism, towards a conception that situated practical, human activity at its centre, and made his philosophy a true "philosophy of praxis." The essential features of that philosophy were already clearly apparent in the *Theses on Feuerbach* of 1845, where Marx developed further a concept of practice as the basis of the unity of man and nature, as well as of subject and object, which had already been implicit in the *Manuscripts*.[47] In the *Theses*, Marx formulated a conception of objectivity founded on praxis, and defined his philosophy as the philosophy of the transformation of the world. These elements were intimately linked, moreover, for if praxis or the practical relation of subject and object were made the basis and origin of all human relations, then on the level of knowledge that relation must provide the boundaries of praxis itself. The problem of objectivity, and of the existence or quasi-existence of objects, can only be posed in the context of praxis; in other words the central role of practical, transforming activity in every human relation could not fail to have profound consequences in the field of cognition. Praxis emerges as the basis (Thesis I), the criterion of truth (Thesis II) and the end of knowledge, and the opposition between idealism and metaphysical materialism, or between idealism and realism, takes a new turn. The intervention of praxis in the process of cognition entails the transcendence of the antithesis between idealism and materialism, between the conception of knowledge as the knowledge of objects produced or created by consciousness, and the conception that sees in knowledge nothing more than the ideal· reproduction of objects in themselves. When practice becomes the basis, the criterion of truth and the object of knowledge, and when praxis is given the decisive role in the cognition process, both previous positions become untenable. It was no longer possible to hold to an Idealist position on the theory of knowledge, nor to abide by a realist theory like that of traditional materialism which had done little more than elaborate upon the standpoint of ingenuous realism.

The introduction of praxis into the cognitive relation, however, does not necessarily lead to similar conclusions on the part of other interpreters of Marx. For some, the fact that praxis is a factor in our knowledge does not mean that we cannot know things in themselves. Others regard the admission of the decisive role of praxis as an indication that we can never know things in themselves, outside their relation to man, but only things humanised through praxis and integrated thus into the human world: Gramsci, for example, summarised this attitude when he said, "Matter, then, cannot be considered in itself, but as socially and historically organised by production, and natural science, in the same way, as in essence a historical category, a human relation."[48] Finally others, like Kosik, maintain that without praxis, or the creation of a socio-human reality, knowledge of reality is itself impossible.[49] It is instructive, however, that each of these positions purports to find a basis in the *Theses on Feuerbach*. Obviously there is a pressing need to return to Marx's text and try to establish its actual meaning which, to judge by the opposing interpretations to which it has given rise, is itself a matter of some doubt.

Praxis as the basis for knowledge: (Thesis I)
> "Thesis I: The chief defect of all hitherto existing materialism—that of Feuerbach included—is that the thing, reality, sensuousness is conceived only in the form of the *object* or of *contemplation,* but not as *human sensuous activity, practice,* not subjectively. Hence it happened that the *active* side, in contradistinction to materialism, was developed by idealism—but only abstractly, since, of course, idealism does not know real, sensuous activity as such. Feuerbach wants sensuous objects, really distinct from the thought objects, but he does not conceive human activity itself as *objective* activity. Hence, in *Das Wesen des Christenthums,* he regards the theoretical attitude as the only genuinely human attitude, while practice is conceived and fixed only in its dirty-judaical manifestation. Hence he does not grasp the significance of 'revolutionary', of practical-critical activity."[50]

This First Thesis counterposes the traditional materialist conception of the object and its cognitive relation to the subject to that of idealism. In negating both positions, Marx indicates both the necessity that they should be transcended as well as the plane on which this process can take place, that is a conception of human activity as real, objective, sensual activity, or practice.

Marx's point of departure in his critique of traditional materialism is the mode of grasping the object. In the original he used two words to designate that object—*Gegenstand* and *Objekt*—in order to distinguish between the object as theoretical and practical objectification *(Gegenstand)* on the one hand, and the object itself, external to man and his activity *(Objekt).* This latter is opposed to the subject, for it is a given, existing *in* and *for* itself, and not a human product; thus the form of relation between subject and object in this case is one in which the subject is passive and contemplative, restricting itself to receiving or reflecting reality. Here knowledge is simply the result of the actions of objects in the external world and their effects upon the sense organs. The object is *objectively* grasped, rather than *subjectively* as the product of practical activity. Subjectivity, or sensual human activity, practice, is here opposed to objectivity, or the existence of an object in itself which is given through contemplation. The theory which Marx attributed to traditional materialism and criticised in the First Thesis regarded knowledge as a vision or contemplation through which the sensuous image of the object is imprinted on our consciousness without reference to the cognitive subject; thus knowledge, in this sense, is knowledge of the object in itself. The characteristic passivity of the subject in traditional materialism needed, in Marx's view, to be replaced by a conception of reality and the object as human activity, or practice. The object of consciousness is a product of human activity and is apprehended as such, rather than as a mere object of contemplation. Marx's critique of traditional materialism, including that of Feuerbach, stemmed from his judgment that its perspective regarded reality and the object as the subject's 'other', something opposed to him, instead of considering it subjectively as the product of man's activity.[51]

Idealism, on the other hand, did see and develop the "active side", the subjective aspect of the cognitive process. The subject, in this perspective, did not grasp objects in themselves, but as products of his activity; that at least had been the conception of knowledge first enunciated by Kant. It was to Idealism's credit, in Marx's view, that it had underlined the active role of the subject within the subject-object relation; but Idealism had perceived that activity as activity of the thinking, conscious subject, and had not taken into account real, practical, sensuous activity. That is why Marx regarded that conception, too, as an abstraction. Obviously Marx recognised that the solution lay in transcending Idealism, and not in returning to the naive, contemplative position of realism which Idealism had set out to demolish. Like the Idealists, Marx conceived the object as the product of subjective activity; he understood it not in abstract terms, however, but as real, objective, material activity. Like the Idealists too, Marx saw knowledge in relation to this activity as knowledge of the products of practical activity which was inseparable from the thinking activity of consciousness, on which the Idealists had concentrated all their attention.

Marx's position therefore, constituted an overcoming of both the contemplative attitude of traditional materialism and the Idealist, speculative conception of activity. True activity is revolutionary, practical-critical activity, which is revolutionary because it transforms reality, and at the same time critical and practical, that is theoretico-practical, because theory is no longer conceived as mere contemplation but as a guide to action, while practice is action guided by theory. Criticism, or theory, cannot exist, therefore, without reference to practice.

In sum, the First Thesis on Feuerbach placed praxis at the root of knowledge, rejecting any possibility of cognition unrelated to man's practical activity, and denying too the possibility of true knowledge as the object was considered as a mere product of consciousness. Knowledge is knowledge of the objects integral to man's relations with the world or with nature; and that relation is the fruit of practical, human activity. Practice is the foundation and the limit of knowledge and of the humanised object that is its object because it is the product of action. Beyond that limit lies an external nature which has as yet not become the object of practical activity. As long as it remains within its immediate existence, it remains a thing in itself, external to man, though it is destined to become the object of human praxis and therefore an object of knowledge.

Marx does not deny the existence of a nature outside praxis or prior to history; the nature that actually exists for him, however, is given *in* and *through* practice. Outside that relation, nature is a thing in itself destined to become human. Thus Marx accepts the ontological priority of a nature outside praxis whose ambit is progressively reduced as it becomes humanised nature. In *The German Ideology* Marx sustained quite explicitly that praxis is the foundation of the world in which we develop, although this does not imply that he denied the existence of a nature prior to praxis.[52] Because it is the foundation of the actual world as we know it, praxis offers to science and to knowledge both its end and its object; all of which serves to reaffirm what Marx had said in the *Manuscripts* about the relations between man and nature. Though Marx conceived the object as the product of subjective activity, he did not deny in principle the existence of a reality absolutely independent of man, external to him, that is a reality in itself. But he denied the possibility that knowledge could be mere contemplation unrelated to practice. Knowledge exists only in practice as knowledge of objects integrated into practice and of a reality that has already lost or is in process of losing its immediate existence to become a reality mediated by man. This, then, is in our view the true significance of Thesis I, which conceives the object as the product of a human activity that is real, objective and sensuous—that is practice.

Praxis as a criterion of truth: (Thesis II)

Thesis II is significant because it reveals a new dimension of the role of practice in knowledge; it provides not only the object of knowledge, but also the criterion of its truth.

> "Thesis II: The question whether objective truth can be attributed to human thinking is not a question of theory but is a *practical* question. Man must prove the truth, that is, the reality and power, the this-sidedness of his thinking in practice. The dispute over the reality or non-reality of thinking which is isolated from practice is a purely *scholastic* question."[53]

This thesis follows directly from the first; if praxis is the foundation of knowledge, that is if man knows the world only to the extent that it is the product of his activity, and activity aimed at the transformation of the real world, it follows that the problem of objective truth, or whether our thought accords with those things existing prior to it, is not a problem that can be resolved theoretically, merely by setting our concept against the object in a theoretical way, or setting my thoughts against the thoughts of others. The foundation of truth, in other words, is to be found outside the sphere of knowledge itself. The thought must seek its truth outside itself, by taking a material form, the form of practical activity, in reality itself. We can only speak of its truth or falsehood in relation to the praxis impregnated by it; we can only judge a thought that is shaped and realised in praxis, for it is only in practice that the truth, the 'this-sidedness' of thought can be proven or demonstrated. Outside praxis it is nothing; truth does not exist in itself, in the realm of pure thought, but in practice. It is in the sense that Marx says that the debate around the truth or falseness (reality or unreality) of thought unrelated to practice, is a purely scholastic question.

But how can I affirm that practice proves the truth or falsehood of a theory? Although Marx never offered a solution to this question, an answer can be found in his conception of praxis as a real, material activity adapted to certain ends. The action designed to transform reality has a teleological character, but the ends to be realised are conditioned in their turn and are founded upon knowledge of the reality to be transformed. If the ends pursued are achieved through action, this means that the knowledge out of which those ends can be elaborated is true knowledge. In the end it is practice that submits our theoretical conclusions about things to the test; if we base our hope for the achievement of certain ends on a given judgment about reality, and those ends are not achieved, it follows that our judgment was false. At the same time we must be wary of interpreting this relation between truth and success, or falsehood and disaster, in a pragmatic way, as if truth or falseness were determined by success or failure. If a theory can be successfully applied, it is because it is true; the reverse, however, is not necessarily also true. Success does not constitute truth; it simply reveals the fact that thought can adequately reproduce reality.

The role of practice as a criterion of truth should not be understood to mean that practice provides a criterion of validity such that a simple reading of practice would yield all the necessary evidence for a criterion of truth. Practice does not speak for itself; practical facts must be analysed and interpreted, since they do not reveal their meaning to direct and immediate observation nor to intuitive apprehension. The criterion of truth may be found in practice, but it is only discovered within a properly theoretical relation with practice itself. In Thesis VIII, Marx points to the necessity for theory to intervene if the truth present in praxis is to be revealed, in these terms: "All mysteries which mislead theory into mysticism find their rational solution in human practice and in *the comprehension of this practice*."[54] Thus Thesis II and III establish a unity of theory and practice in a double movement; from theory to practice (Thesis II) and from practice to theory (Thesis

III). This conception of practice as the criterion of truth contrasts with both the Idealist conception of the criterion of validity of knowledge, whereby theory contains within itself the criterion of its own truth, and the empiricist conception according to which practice provides the criterion for judging the truth of theory in a direct and immediate way. Thus Marx provides us with a role for practice as the criterion of truth independent of the specific forms it might adopt in different sciences,[55] and irrespective of the restrictions on its applicability which prevent it from becoming an absolute criterion of truth.[56]

Revolutionary praxis as the unity of the change in men and the change in circumstances: (Thesis III)

Previous materialist conceptions had reduced the transformation of man to the level of an educative task in which one section of society educates another. By contrast Marx in Thesis III puts the accent on revolutionary praxis that transforms society.

"Thesis III: The materialist doctrine that men are products of circumstances and upbringing and that, therefore, changed men are products of changed circumstances and upbringing, forgets that it is men who change circumstances and that it is essential to educate the educator himself. Hence this doctrine necessarily arrives at dividing society into two parts, one of which is superior to society.

"The coincidence of the changing of circumstances and of human activity can be conceived and rationally understood only as revolutionising practice."[57]

Marx was clearly referring to the ideas about social transformation sustained by the enlightened materialists of the 18th century, which were carried on into the 19th by Feuerbach and the Utopian socialists. Man, they maintained, is a product of circumstances and environment; he is determined by them (as Voltaire said) but not necessarily so, since the influence of environment can be offset by education. The Enlightenment, and in particular the German philosophers of the Enlightenment like Goethe and Herder, regarded the transformation of mankind as a vast educative enterprise; this conception was based on the idea of man as a rational being, whose progress demanded the destruction of "prejudice" and the imposition of the dominion of reason. In order for man to progress, enter the age of reason and live in a world constructed according to rational principles, all that is required is that consciousness be illuminated by the light of reason. Education, then, allows man to pass from the realm of "shadows" and "superstition" into the realm of reason. To educate is to transform mankind. But the question remains as to who the educators shall be. They are the philosophers of the Enlightenment and the "enlightened despots" who heed the philosophers' counsels. As for the rest of society, it has simply to allow its consciousness to be moulded; in this way, man shall come to live as a rational being in accordance with his own nature.

This conception of the transformation of society rests on the idea of man as passive matter which can be moulded by the environment and by other men. There is activity in one part of society only, among the philosophers and the enlightened despots; that activity, on the other hand, is simply pedagogical, and is restricted to the influence that the educators may have over the educated. This idea underlines all those philosophies which regard the transformation of society as a matter of education. In the third Thesis, Marx develops a critique of this perspective on the following basis: a) Men are not only a product of circumstances; circumstances are, in their turn, products of man. In this way, Marx vindicates the conditioning of the environment by men, and with it his active role in relation to that environment. Circumstances condition men; but since circumstances do not exist outside man, they are themselves conditioned. b) The educators must also be educated. This constitutes an explicit rejection of the conception of a society divided into educators and educated, with the peculiarity that the former are excluded from the process of education. In this sense, the subject of educative activity (the minority) is found in one part of society, while its object, its passive product, (the majority) is located in another part. The transformation of mankind, seen as the education of mankind, rests with the educators who do not transform themselves, however, since their task is solely to transform others. It is the minority, then, who are the subjects of history; other human beings are simply inert material which they mould. In this light, Marx's assertion that the educators must also be educated signifies a rejection of the principle that the development of mankind is embodied in one part of society whose transformation of itself is never in question. That was the conception characteristic of the 18th century revolutionary bourgeoisie which saw itself as the source of historical development while denying any change or development of itself. In the task of social transformation, Marx says, men cannot be divided into active and passive groups; that is why the dualism of "educators and educated" is unacceptable. Marx replaces the idea of a transforming subject who himself stands outside change with the idea of a continuous praxis in which both subject and object are transformed. As Marx said elsewhere,[58] in transforming external nature, man transforms his own nature too; and the process is never completed. There can never, therefore, be educators who do not themselves need to be educated. c) The circumstances that modify men are at the same time modified by him; the educator must also be educated. It is man who changes circumstances, just as he changes himself at the same time. And this coincidence of change can only be understood, in Marx's view, as revolutionary practice. In the practical-revolutionary transformation of social relations man modifies circumstances and affirms his dominion over them, that is his capacity to respond to his conditioning by abolishing the circumstances that conditioned him. Since it is a matter of human circumstances, of social and economic relations, men are conscious of their transformation and of the results of that transformation; changes in circumstances cannot be separated from changes in man, just as the changes that occur in him as a result of his heightened consciousness cannot be separated from changes in his circumstances. This unity of circumstances and human activity, or rather of the transformation of circumstances and the self-transformation of men, can only be achieved *in* and *through* revolutionary practice.

Marx emphasised this unity in order to oppose both those Utopian conceptions which regarded education, or man's self-transformation, as sufficient to produce a radical change in man irrespective of the circumstances of his life, and the rigorous determination which sustained, on the other hand, that changes in man's circumstances would suffice for man to transform himself, without reference to the changes in his consciousness resulting from the labour of education.

He maintained, on the contrary, that the modification of circumstances and of men, and the consciousness of changes in the environment and in education, could only be achieved through practical revolutionary activity. In this way the praxis approached in the first two Theses primarily as a cognitive category now becomes a sociological category fixing the conditions for a real social transformation; the change in circumstances and the change in man himself, whose unity in turn defined revolutionary praxis.

From the interpretation of the world to its transformation: (Thesis XI)

Thesis XI emerges from this conception of revolutionary praxis as action on circumstances and consciousness carried out in unity. It provides a definition of the historical connection between philosophy and action, and of the characteristic relation of Marxism to practice, which represented a definitive break with all previous philosophy.

> "Thesis XI: The philosophers have only interpreted the world in various ways; the point, however, is to change it."[59]

The world, in this thesis, is spoken of in two ways; as the object of interpretation and as the object of man's practical activity, that is as the object of transformation. What, then, is or will be the relationship between philosophy and the world? Marx's answer in the famous Eleventh Thesis is that philosophy must relate to the world, to the extent that the world is the object of its action. This response is perfectly congruent with the earlier theses, and particularly with theses I and II (see above). If man knows the world to the extent that he acts upon it, there can be no knowledge outside this practical relation and philosophy cannot be severed from practice and reduced to mere contemplation or interpretation. Yet that is precisely what all previous philosophers had done; and though such philosophies could have practical consequences, they would always remain within the framework of an acceptance of the status quo and contribute, in the end, to its justification and maintenance. Hegel, whose philosophy was the most refined expression of this viewpoint, aspired only to explain what is, and rejected all and any attempts to point to its future development. The transformation of the world was not his concern; he was only concerned to reduce the world to the level of thought, that is to interpret it. And once his interpretation was complete, the world could not be modified, since to admit that possibility would have meant admitting that there are things that escape thought; given Hegel's key thesis of the identity of thought and being, however, such an unthought world must be an unreal world. For Hegel the world *was as it ought to be,* and there was no place in his philosophy for a reality that might become the object of transformation.

When it is the transformation of the world that is at issue, we must reject all philosophies whose practical consequences, at the level of pure theory, contribute to an acquiescence in the world as it is and oppose its transformation. According to Marx, the German Idealism culminating in Hegel and Feuerbach was just such a philosophy of interpretation, not simply because it was mere theory, but above all because, insofar as it was a theory reconciling reason and the world, it had practical consequences far beyond its merely theoretical frontiers. Interpretation alone is not transformation—"the philosophers have only *interpreted* the world," that is to say, they have accepted and sought to justify it, but have not contributed to its transformation. Marx never denied that all philosophies, even Idealism, formed part of reality, since they have practical consequences for that reality even though they remain at the level of theory. And in rejecting those acquiescent, interpretative philosophies that did not contribute to the transformation of the world, he did not dismiss every philosophy or theory; as he was concerned with the transformation of reality, however, he necessarily set aside interpretative theories in order to adopt a practical philosophy which did regard the world as the object of praxis. In this sense his is a theory of praxis, an interpretation of the world that makes its transformation possible.

Thesis XI does not entail the diminution of the role of theory, and even less its rejection or exclusion. Marx rejects those theories which are mere interpretations isolated from praxis, and support a view that accepts the world as it is. He did raise to the highest level that philosophy whose links with praxis put it directly at the service of an actual transformation. Such a theory carries out in that process a dual function; it offers a theoretical critique of those theories that justify the world as it is, and it sets out as the level of theory the conditions and possibilities of action. Thus neither theory nor practice are sufficient in themselves; both are necessary in a close unity. That, in the final analysis, is the import of the eleventh Thesis, which represents the point at which a rift occurred between Marx's thought and all previous philosophical thinking. Marxism appears there for the first time as a revolution in the question, object and function of philosophy, seeking not only to interpret the world, but also to transform it. And the interpretation required for the transformation of the world must be a scientific interpretation. Thus the transition from interpretation to transformation, or from thought to action, entails in its turn a theoretical revolution that Marxism had to carry out in relation to the revolutionary praxis of the proletariat; that is, the transition from Utopia or ideology to scientific socialism.[60] Any analysis of Marxism which ignores its scientific aspect, and regards it as mere interpretation, leaves it within the frontiers of a philosophy which Marx had criticised and denounced in his Eleventh Thesis on Feuerbach.

Praxis in "The German Ideology"

The transformation of theory from Utopia or ideology into a science is an indispensable condition of revolutionary praxis. That is why Marx took such pains to overcome the limitations of the anthropological, Utopian or ideological character of his early work, which included the *1844 Manuscripts. The German Ideology,* written by Marx and Engels in 1845, constitutes a decisive stage in the process of transforming socialism into a science. It is important to stress, however, that the change of direction which occurs in *The German Ideology,* and which is based on the elaboration of key concepts in the interpretation of history and the analysis of capitalist society, responded to the demands of praxis. Thus the foundations of the materialist conception of history must be seen in the light of their close connection with praxis; they are not merely a development in interpretation, for it was objective historical, social and economic conditions which provided the basis for the revolutionary actions of the proletariat. They did not conceive their task in terms of simply creating consciousness of an existing fact, but in terms of overthrowing and transforming the status quo. The attention paid by Marx and Engels in *The German Ideology* to the Young Hegelian movement and to contemporary German Idealist historiography, for example, derived directly from the exigencies of praxis. They recognised that actual, authentic activity could not develop so long as the illusory faith in the power of ideas persisted, and so long as those ideas stood apart from the actual socio-economic foundation; hence their recognition of the need to explain ideological formations, their origin, their function and the means for their overthrow. Clearly, as Marx says, "it is a matter of explaining the formation of ideas from material practice" and not of "explaining practice from the idea."[61] The Young Hegelians regarded criticism, or the action of ideas, as the motor of history; Marx, on the other hand, considered actual, effective action—the revolution—to be the motive force of historical development. "Not criticism but revolution is the driving force of history, also of religion, of philosophy and all other types of theory."[62]

Production in history and in social life

This analysis of the true nature and function of ideas sheds considerable light on the question of the area of the actual transformation of reality. For Marx, then, the destruction of "ideological illusions" was a necessary precondition for the elaboration of a theory of the revolutionary transformation of existing society. The establishment of the connection between those illusions and the real conditions of social life underlined in its turn the need to understand the real, material conditions which on the one hand form man and his ideas, and on the other must be transformed by his actual activity. As Marx and Engels put it, "circumstances make man just as much as men make circumstances."[63]

It was this analysis that led Marx to lay increasing stress upon the role of production in history and social life, thus enriching and developing the ideas which had been expounded for the first time in the *1844 Manuscripts*. It is his productive activity that distinguishes man from the animals; in this sense, production is not simply one feature of human existence, but an essential element of it. "Men can be distinguished from animals by consciousness, by religion or anything else you like. They themselves begin to distinguish themselves from animals as soon as they begin to *produce* their means of subsistence, a step which is conditioned by their physical organisation. By producing their means of subsistence men are indirectly producing their actual material life."[64] The role of production also explains the mode of being of individuals. "As individuals express their life, so they are. What they are, therefore, coincides with their production, both with *what* they produce and with *how* they produce. The nature of individuals thus depends on the material conditions determining their production."[65]

The role of production, then, is "the fundamental condition of all history," involving not only the production of material goods and the indispensable means for the satisfaction of human needs, but also man's production of himself and of his social life. Marx introduced into his analysis two linked key concepts of historical materialism: productive forces and the relations of production (which Marx still called "forms of intercourse"). Productive forces determine the relations of production which in their turn condition ideological formations and the nature of the State; this is fundamental to the materialist conception of history formulated by Marx for the first time in *The German Ideology*. "This conception of history (he says) depends on our ability to expound the real process of production, starting out from the material production of life itself, and to comprehend the form of intercourse connected with this and created by this mode of production (i.e. civil society in all its various stages), as the basis of all history; and to show it in its action as State, to explain all the different theoretical products and forms of consciousness, religion, philosophy, ethics etc."[66]

The necessity of revolutionary praxis

Despite the vagueness of his terminology, Marx characterises the relations of production, or the relations that men contract in the process of production, as social relations which develop in the same way as productive forces. Their dialectical development constitutes the fundamental element of human history, whose development implies the step from one set of productive forces and connected relations of production to another. Furthermore, it is an objective process occurring in a necessary way, independently of the will or intentions of particular individuals, in accordance with which the productive forces which develop under the dominion of social necessity gave rise to particular relations of production, or "forms of intercourse" which in their turn influence the progress of productive forces and so on through a complex dialectical progression. Where the relations of production present an obstacle to the growth of productive forces, a contradiction is produced which takes the form of class conflict. The sharpening of this contradiction makes necessary a revolution, which is the form assumed by the practical activity of certain men, in particular the proletariat, conditioned by a certain level of development of the productive forces of a society and the corresponding contradictions with the relations of production. Communism arises, in its turn, as a scientific not a Utopian solution, insofar as it arises in the context of social and historical conditions in which the revolutionary activity of the proletariat has a real, objective, historical foundation. "Communism is not for us a *State of affairs* which is to be established, an *ideal* to which reality (will) have to adjust itself. We call communism the *real* movement which abolishes the present state of things."[67]

The necessity for a revolutionary praxis which leads to this solution is no longer presented as the result of a contradiction between history and the true human essence, but of a contradiction between productive forces and the relations of production. The proletarian is no longer seen as the embodiment of human suffering in general, nor as the worker who denies his human essence in labour, but as a member of a social class whose role in production, and particularly in the more advanced forms of production, brings it into conflict with the ruling class. Thus when the proletariat becomes conscious of the necessity for revolution, it carries it out with the aim of abolishing the dominion of any one class by abolishing classes themselves. "The class making a revolution appears from the very start, if only because it is opposed to a *class,* not as a class but as the representative of the whole of society; it appears as the whole *mass* of society confronting the *one* ruling class."[68]

The materialist conception of history and the theory of praxis

The materialist conception of history and the theory of revolutionary praxis are both clearly expounded, and their fundamental concepts set out in *The German Ideology*. They were the two basic elements of a doctrine which Marx and Engels were to deepen and enrich thenceforth in all their subsequent work. Clearly the founders of Marxism saw them as inseparably linked, and based their unity on the four aspects which together summarised their conception of history. Since it would be difficult to formulate that conception with the same clarity and precision as Marx and Engels themselves, we quote the relevant passage in its entirety.

"1) In the development of productive forces there comes a stage when productive forces and means of intercourse are brought into being which, under the existing relationships, only cause mischief and are no longer productive but destructive forces (machinery and money); and connected with this a class is called forth which has to bear all the burdens of society without enjoying its advantages, which, ousted from society, is forced into the most decided antagonism to all other classes; a class which forms the majority of all members of society, and from which emanates the consciousness of the necessity of a fundamental revolution, the communist consciousness, which may, of course, arise among the other classes too through the contemplation of the situation of this class. 2) The conditions under which definite productive forces can be applied, are the conditions of the rule of a definite class of society, whose social power, deriving from its property, has its *practical*-idealistic expression in each case in the form of the State; and therefore, every revolutionary struggle is directed against a class which till then has been in power. 3) In all revolutions up till now the mode of activity always remained unscathed, and it was only a question of a different distribution of this activity, a new distribution of labour to other persons, whilst the communist revolution is directed against the preceding *mode* of activity, does away with *labour,* and abolishes the rule of all classes with the classes themselves, because it is carried through by the class which no longer counts as a class in society, is not recognised as a class, and is in itself the expression of the dissolution of all classes, nationalities etc. within present society; and 4) Both for the production on a mass scale of this communist consciousness, and for the success of the cause itself, the alteration of men on a mass scale is necessary, an alteration which can only take place in a practical movement, a *revolution;* this revolution is necessary, therefore, not only because the *ruling* class cannot be overthrown in any other way, but also because the class *overthrowing* it can only in a revolution succeed in ridding itself of all the muck of ages and become fitted to found society anew."[69]

The following points arise from the previous passage: 1) the objective and historical character of the contradiction between productive forces and the relations of production whose solution (the consonance of the relations of production with productive forces on the basis of the abolition of private property) can only be provided by a social class arising out of social development itself and with whose class interests is linked the consciousness of the necessity for this solution as well as the revolutionary struggle necessary to bring it about. 2) If the correspondence of the relations of production and productive forces is to be achieved, it will have to be preceded by a struggle against the ruling class and the social power, the State, which stems from its material power. 3) This proletarian revolution is distinct from all previous revolutions because it does not seek the abolition of one form of ownership of the means of production, but the abolition of private property in general, and therefore the abolition of all class rule. 4) The communist revolution means not only the transformation of political and economic relations but also the mass transformation of man, or the creation of a mass communist consciousness. The revolution is necessary not only in order to overthrow the ruling class but also because only in this way can the revolutionary class create a new society.

The central role given to labour in the formation of man in the

1844 Manuscripts was given further and more concrete foundation in *The German Ideology* in demonstrating the determinant role of production in human history and social life. The process of man's formation, which constitutes the fundamental content of history, is no longer presented as a contradiction between man and his essence, but between productive forces and the social relations engendered by them. Alienation, which in the *Manuscripts* appeared as the denial of the worker in labour, ceased to have such a central role as it began to be seen as the reification of social relations. Similarly the class antagonism expounded in the *Manuscripts* with a weak basis in the mode of appropriation of the product in alienated labour, was elaborated in *The German Ideology* as a necessary expression of the contradiction between productive forces and the relations of production.

Having established the fundamental role of productive praxis, the relations between that and other forms of praxis, including ideological activity, acquire growing significance. And by destroying the illusions sown in this field by ideology and Utopianism and formulating their materialist conception of history, Marx and Engels revealed in the structure of society, in the movement of history and in the contradiction between productive forces and the relations of production, the foundation of that revolutionary praxis which brings about the practical transformation of society. This praxis, furthermore, is neither adventuristic nor Utopian; as was underlined by the materialist interpretation of history in *The German Ideology,* the revolution is determined by real, objective structures and conditions. This revolutionary praxis is not, as was shown in the *Theses on Feuerbach,* purely practical activity, but the location of the unity of thought and action. In *The German Ideology,* the human history that conditions revolutionary praxis is the history of production, whereas in the *Theses* it is the rational character of that praxis that is emphasised, and thence the unity of theory and practice. It is not enough to define the conditions for revolutionary praxis, as the materialist conception of history had done; some indication of how that historically and socially conditioned praxis might become a reality was also required. The consciousness of the revolution that exists in potential at the very core of the social structure must pass into real, concrete revolution; similarly, a concrete theory of revolution is an indispensable element in the overthrow of existing social relations. As Lenin said, "without revolutionary theory there can be no revolutionary movement."[70] That theory was now to move from an analysis of the social structure that conditions the revolution, to a theory of the revolution itself. And theory was to contribute to and determine action by shedding light on its objectives, concrete possibilities, and participant social forces. Its concentration would also involve the clearing away of the obstacles facing the revolution and the factors tending to invalidate or detain it. In this sense only can theory fulfil the active, critical role which we have outlined above.

The problem of the transition from theory to action

Although theory now takes on this double task as theoretical criticism and the foundation of real acts, it does not cease to be theory; that is, it cannot become practical activity in itself. We have already pointed out that even those theories that seek only to interpret the world have practical consequences, insofar as they oppose or hinder the transformation of reality. On the other hand, a theory that aspires to guide practical action aimed at transforming the world, nevertheless remains theory until it is realised or given material form in action. It is necessary to pass from theory to action, yet theory itself cannot make that transition. Even when there exists a conscious unity of theory and praxis which is more than the connection that may be established between a theory and the practical consequences which it may spontaneously generate, there need not be a transition from one sphere to the other. Clearly a truly revolutionary theory cannot remain at the theoretical level; yet in order for it to become praxis, it must be overcome and take material form. The question of how theory is materialised, how it is given material form, and how it may be converted into actions which are part of a total praxis, is therefore urgently posed.

Marx was only able to answer these questions, however, when the need arose to transform the world through a practical revolution, when the revolution became a practical task rather than a theoretical one. The answer came in *The Communist Manifesto,* written when Marx and Engels had become involved in revolutionary activity, and had joined with others who, like themselves, sought to transform the world, and had organised themselves to that end in the Communist League. The *Manifesto* was written to order; in fact they were contracted to write it by the Central Committee of the League on the basis of a series of projects, circulars and questionnaires formulated and distributed by the League. It was a work directed at the proletariat by a group of men who looked to a revolution brought about by that class. It was a question, then, of theoretical work immediately linked to practical, revolutionary needs. It was a theoretical work designed to give guidance to the concrete revolution of the proletariat, based on an intimate knowledge of the social reality that was to be overthrown, and designed at the same time to provide a basis for the necessity for revolutionary change and for the historic mission of the proletariat within it. The *Manifesto* provides the theory of a revolution that its writers were working to bring about. It is theory insofar as it provides a basis for the proletarian revolution, and insofar as it is a critique of those false conceptions that contributed to preventing or inhibiting that revolution. In one sense, the *Manifesto* simply synthesises Marx's previous theoretical insights; but it is not just one more theory of revolution. It enriched the Marxist conception of praxis by adding to it a new element which had no precedent in Marx's work. In this respect it did mark a radical, qualitative advance, to a theory that was both a theory of revolution and a theory of its organisation. It provides, in other words, a theory of the transition from theory to praxis; at the same time it answers the question of how revolutionary theory can pass from the theoretical plane to the plane of action. The answer is that it occurs as a result of organising the efforts and activities of certain individuals, who are in this case the revolutionary workers. That organisation requires an organ that can hold together and direct these efforts in accordance with the ends formulated in revolutionary theory; hence the Party, which mediates between theory and praxis, bringing together a nucleus of the most conscious and dedicated representatives of the working class. On the one hand, the Party establishes an organic link between theory and practice; on the other, it links one sector of the working class with the class as a whole. Marx and Engels envisaged a Party that could represent the general and future interests, at every stage of its emancipation, of that class whose destiny it is to fulfil a world-historical mission which lies beyond the partial or transitory interests pursued or defended by the class. It is in this sense that "the communists have no interests separate and apart from the proletariat as a whole. They do not set up any sectarian principles of their own, by which to shape and mould the proletarian movement. The communists are distinguished from other working-class parties by this only: 1. In the national struggles of the proletarians of the different countries, they point out and bring to the fore the common interests of the entire proletariat, independently of all nationality. 2. In the various stages of development which the struggle of the working class against the bourgeoisie has to pass through, they always and everywhere represent the interests of the movement as a whole."[71]

The Party exists to defend the universal, over and above the national or particular, temporary interests of the working class. Its advantage over the rest of the working class and over other parties stems from the fact that it combines the most resolute and advanced detachments of the class, adding practical superiority to a theoretical superiority that is the result of its knowledge of the ends, development and results of the movement. "The Communists, therefore, are on the one hand, practically the most advanced and resolute section of the working class parties of every country, that section which pushes forward all others: on the other hand, they have over the great mass of the proletariat the advantage of clearly understanding the line of march, the conditions and the ultimate general results of the proletarian movement."[72] Further, "the theoretical conclusions of the Communists are in no way based on ideas or principles that have been invented, or discovered, by this or that would-be universal reformer. They merely express, in general terms, actual relations springing from an existing class struggle, from a historical movement going on under our very eyes."[73]

Revolutionary theory presupposes the existence of an actual class struggle and the historical development of society of which that struggle is the expression. The Party is not the invention of certain individuals, but a response to the need to pass from theory to action under the appropriate actual, historical conditions. The *Manifesto* represents the revolutionary theory of a social class preparing itself to transform society in a revolutionary way. In organising and leading the struggle, and in providing a mediation between theory and praxis, the Party overcomes the merely theoretical character of its theory and transposes it to the level of organisation, where the unity of thought and action can be realised. The *Manifesto* is the clearest demonstration that Marxism is a philosophy of praxis, of the revolutionary transformation of the world. And it is there that the various strands of Marx's mature conception meet and fuse for the first time:

a) The conception of the world-historical mission of the proletariat, the subject of revolutionary praxis.

b) The materialist conception of history that provides the historical foundation for this praxis.

c) The study of the socio-economic reality which constitutes its real, objective basis.

d) The conception of philosophy as a theory which must be realised, and as a guide to the transformation of the world which goes far beyond mere interpretation.

e) The indissoluble unity of theory and practice in revolutionary praxis.

f) The transition from revolutionary theory to praxis (or the actual realisation of this unity) carried forward by the activity of the Party which embodies the general interests of the class as a whole, and the future of its movement over and above the immediate demands posed in one period or phase of the struggle.[74]

Marxism as a philosophy of praxis

We have tried to show that the conception of praxis is central to Marx's thought, since it provides the starting-point for understanding both the activity of men, and knowledge itself. Man defines himself as a practical being; Marx's philosophy is a philosophy of the transformation of the world, that is the philosophy of human praxis. In the years since Marx first elaborated his theory, the reformists and crude materialists have coincided in suppressing its true content, representing it not as a philosophy which foresaw its own overcoming, but as a philosophy of purely practical content, to the extent that it became little more than a kind of voluntarism.

This misrepresentation of Marx's thought makes it necessary to examine some of the more fundamental questions, although it will not be possible in the present work to cover all the questions that arise from the philosophy of praxis. The conclusion that will tend to emerge from this analysis is that Marxism demands that praxis be situated, as in our view Marx intended it to be, at the very centre of his philosophy. Once Marx had recognised in the *Theses on Feuerbach,* the central role of the category of praxis, it became illegitimate to return in his name to philosophical positions which he had abandoned precisely as a result of his elaboration of this category. The object cannot be considered without reference to human subjectivity or human activity, as the metaphysical materialists in general, and the crude materialists, maintained, nor can the activity whose object it is be understood, in the Idealist manner, in terms of mere spiritual activity, whether or not what is involved is the activity of human consciousness. The relationship between Marxism and these two forms of philosophy is one of negation and transcendence. The contemplative materialists, for legitimate reasons, rejected the idea that the real world was a product of consciousness and stressed the concrete, material nature of both subject and object; the result, however, was that they put subject and object in an abstract and external relation to one another. To overcome this materialism, it was necessary to see that the material nature of matter in turn presupposes subjective activity. For its part Idealism did take account of the active side of the subject-object relation, and of subjective activity, but at the cost of ignoring the material, objective aspects of that activity. The frontiers of Idealism could not be surpassed unless the material nature of activity and its products were set beside the notion of subjective action. Insofar as Idealism was a philosophy of ideal activity carried out by a mystified man, Marxism did invert it; that is why Marx cannot be reduced to an anthropologised Hegel nor a historicised Feuerbach, for neither had ever overcome the limitations of a philosophy conceived as an interpretation of the world. Their common medium was theory, and the youthful Marx shared that medium until he transcended it in the *Theses on Feuerbach* and *The German Ideology.* It is in praxis that Hegel's absolute idealism and Feuerbach's anthropologism are inverted; and this entailed a radical change in Marxist theory, as expressed in the classic formulation of the transition from Utopian to scientific socialism. Marx recognised that the task of his theory was to lay the actual and historical basis for practical, human activity and to set out its conditions, limits and real possibilities. It is in this sense that Marxism has come to be a process as infinite as its object, a philosophy of actual, objective activity, or human praxis. This is what Engels meant when he said that the German proletariat had "inherited classical German philosophy." If Idealism had remained a philosophy of activity, Marxism was properly speaking a philosophy of true, practical, transforming activity, and the philosophical consciousness of that activity. Not only is it related to praxis, revealing its foundation, conditions and objectives, but it is also conscious of that relation and thus can provide a guide to action.

It is in this respect that we can refer to Marxism as having overcome previous philosophical consciousness, whether materialist or idealist, as well as that philosophical consciousness which in our day, and in the form of vulgar materialism or speculative Idealism, represents a return to the very positions that Marxism had transcended. This process of overcoming is the result of a synthesis transcending all previous philosophical attitudes; that is why Marxism cannot be interpreted as a regression to philosophies prior to Marx nor to the prephilosophical postures of ordinary consciousness or common sense. Ordinary, prephilosophical, consciousness saw neither the material quality nor the activity of the subject; indeed it never went beyond a vague, spontaneous consciousness of praxis which might have seemed on the surface to surpass traditional materialist consciousness, by focussing its attention on practice, but which in fact was concerned only with the sordid forms of activity which Feuerbach had scorned because they bore no relation to theoretical activity. Ordinary consciousness also seemed to have overcome the speculative, Idealist consciousness of praxis; yet it saw the world as comprising finished products, rather than the products of human activity, and by conceiving activity in this strictly utilitarian sense, grasped it in a way which distinguished it from all theory.

The failure to grasp the full significance of the concept of praxis can, in its turn, lead to a number of deformations of Marxism, for

example:
a) What might be called the empiricism of praxis or pre-Marxist materialism, continuing to regard subject and object in an external, abstract relation, and reducing praxis to a simple mode of verification between the thought of the subject and an object in itself, without reference to its practical relation with the world.
b) The idealism of praxis, in which practical activity is conceived in an absolute and subjective sense only, thus negating the priority of external nature.
c) The pragmatism of praxis, or the point of view of ordinary, prephilosophical consciousness which ignored both the intrinsic subject-object relation (the standpoint of *ingenuous realism*) and the activity of the subject in both a theoretical and practical sense. In this perspective, the external subject-object relation is felt to be compatible only with practical-utilitarian activity, which prefigures the pragmatist position rather than a true philosophy of praxis.

It is a misrepresentation of the fundamental role of praxis in the formation of Marxism to interpret the radical separation from traditional philosophy, and in particular that of Hegel and Feuerbach, as a mere theoretical or "epistemological" break. This latter concept, first used by Gaston Bachelard, was adopted by Louis Althusser to express the transformation of Marxism from a prescientific or ideological standpoint to a scientific analysis which, according to Althusser, corresponded to a clear division between Marx's early work and the writings of his mature years. "The 'epistemological break' divides Marx's thought into two long essential periods; the 'ideological period' before, and the scientific period after the break in 1845." [75] Without entering at this point into a discussion which has been the subject of the whole of this chapter, it is important to stress that the argument that characterises Marx's "first period" as Feuerbachian fails to recognise that it is Hegel who is the actual object of Marx's critique. It was Hegel who had taken interpretative philosophy to its ultimate conclusions; the neo-Hegelians merely exacerbated the problem by rejecting the content of Hegel's work which was valid despite the mystified form it had adopted in the master's writings. Feuerbach, broadly speaking, continued that perspective, despite his anthropologisation of God and the Idea, and Marx himself struggled with Hegel's conception until he finally surpassed it in 1845 with the *Theses* and *The German Ideology*. Thus the break that undoubtedly does occur has a genuine theoretical-practical character; it represents a transition from a merely interpretative philosophy to one aimed at the transformation of the world. The break, therefore, is not simply "epistemological", for although it does represent a break with Hegelian Idealism and Feuerbach's critique, Marxism breaks more significantly with the conclusions of interpretative philosophy, which is in the end not an interpretation of the world but an instrument whereby man can reconcile himself to that reality. In this sense, it contributes to blocking the possibility of its transformation, and becomes a philosophy justifying a reality which the Marxists wish to transform. And since it has real social roots Marxism, when it breaks with that philosophy, must not only expose its ideological origins but also contribute itself directly to the transformation of the reality that had given rise to such a conciliatory ideology. It is not simply a matter, then, of an epistemological break between ideas, or degrees or levels of knowledge, nor of a simple progression from error to truth, from ideology to science; the process itself entails the existence of a praxis that transforms reality. So Marx's break or rupture with traditional philosophy, and by extension with the stage in his own thought which was still more or less influenced by it, cannot be characterised in purely theoretical or epistemological terms. It is in essence a break whose origin is to be found in praxis, occurring when Marxism is able to assert itself as a theory of revolutionary praxis in particular, and of practical human activity in general. It is in this respect that Marxism can be said to be, essentially, "a philosophy of praxis."[76]

Notes

1 Marx: Introduction to *Contribution to a critique of Hegel's Philosophy of Right.* (Cambridge University Press, 1970) [Hereafter referred to as Marx: *Critique*] p.137.

2 F. Engels: *Ludwig Feuerbach and the end of classical German philosophy* in Marx/Engels: *Selected Works* (Foreign Languages Publishing House, Moscow—English edition—1958 in 2 volumes) [Hereafter referred to as S.W.]. Volume 2, pp.366-7.

3 On the Left Hegelians, their tendencies and principal representatives, and

the ideological and historical atmosphere in which they developed, see Auguste Cornu: *Karl Marx et Friedrich Engels* (P.U.F., Paris, 1955-1962, in 3 volumes). See also Volume 1, Book One ("The crisis of the first German Hegelianism (1818-1844)" in Mario Rossi's *Marx e la dialettica hegeliana* (ed. Riuniti, Rome, 1963; in 2 volumes). Cf: also Claudio Cesa "Figure e problemi della storiografia filosofica della sinistra hegeliana" in *Annali 1963* (Feltrinelli, Milan, 1964) pp.62-104.

4 On Marx's relations with the Left Hegelians, see A. Cornu: *op.cit.*: especially vol. 1, chapter 4, and volume 2, chapters 1 and 2. See also Volume 2, chapter 1 of Rossi: *op.cit.;* and Emile Bottigelli: "Karl Marx et la gauche hegelienne" in *Annali 1963: ed.cit.:* pp.9-32.

5 Engels' first essay on economics, "Outlines of a critique of political economy" (in *Engels:* ed. W.O. Henderson: Penguin, Harmondsworth, 1967) was published in 1844 in the *Deutsch-französische Jahrbücher,* and exercised a profound influence in the formation of Marx's thought, contributing to a large degree to the awakening of Marx's interest in economic problems. Marx himself was later to characterise Engels' essay as a brilliant outline of a critique of economic categories.

6 The problem of determining in which work or at what stage of his thought Marx broke with previous philosophy depends upon the question which is deemed to be the point of separation. It might be suggested that the definitive break came with Hegelian Idealist philosophy, insofar as it represented a mystification of the reality that was to be transformed; in that case the division would occur on the question of the philosophy of right and of the State, and Marx's *Critique* would be, as Galvano della Volpe asserts in his *Rousseau and Marx,* the key work, since it is there that Marx strips away the veils of idealism concealing the true reality and the actual material conditions of existence. His critique did expose reality to the eye; the point, however—as he was to put it later—was not to transform its mystifications, but to transform the reality itself. The break with previous philosophy that occurs at this point, then, is still not a radical one, since Marx had still not reached the point where he could envisage a philosophy that was both theory and guide to action.

If on the other hand, it is asserted that Marx broke with all ideology before going on to elaborate the theory of scientific socialism, the break would correspond to the replacement of an ideological mode of thought— that is an unreal, false, illusory mode of thought in accordance with his own class conditioning—by scientific thought, then it would be justifiable to regard *The German Ideology* as being impregnated with ideological elements. In that case the true, scientific conception of society, based on the discovery of the contradiction between productive forces and the relations of production, could only be elaborated once the cardinal principles of the materialist conception of history had been laid down. Yet what is decisive in the formation of Marxism is not a change of concepts, although if theory is to fulfil its function in the transformation of society, new concepts must necessarily emerge. But the break does not occur on the level of theory alone; it occurs in intimate connection with praxis, since it is both an element and a product of that praxis. The reduction of Marxism to a simple elaboration of new concepts, new theories, although that could be seen as the effect of the transition from Utopia to science, would lead back again to a scientific or neo-positivist interpretation of Marxism, ignoring the fact that Marxism arose as a scientific theory of the revolutionary praxis of the proletariat.

7   Marx: *Critique* (Introduction) pp.135-7.
8   *Ibid.* p. 137.
9   *Ibid.* p. 137.
10 *Ibid.* p. 138.
11 *Ibid.* p. 131.
12 *Ibid.* p. 137.
13 *Ibid.* pp. 138-9.
14 *Ibid.* p. 139.
15 "When socialist writers ascribe this historical role to the proletariat, it is not... because they consider the proletarians as gods... Its aim and historical action is irrevocably and obviously demonstrated in its own life situation as well as in the whole organisation of bourgeois society today." Marx/Engels: *The Holy Family:* (Lawrence and Wishart, London, 1957). pp.52-3.
16 Marx: *Critique:* p.142.
17 *Ibid.* p. 142.
18 *Ibid.* p. 142.
19 F. Engels: "Outline of a critique of political economy" in *Engels* (Harmondsworth, 1967); and K. Marx: *Economic and philosophical manuscripts of 1844:* Lawrence and Wishart, London, 1967) [Hereafter referred to as *1844 MSS*] pp.87-8.
20 *1844 MSS:* p.88.
21 Cf: in *1844 MSS* the manuscript entitled "Estranged labour", pp.64-78.
22 *1844 MSS:* pp. 70-71.
23 *Ibid.* p. 78.
24 *Ibid.* p. 74.
25 *Ibid.* p. 75.
26 "The outstanding thing in Hegel's Phenomenology (is) ... that he thus grasps the essence of *labour* and comprehends objective man—true, because real man—as the outcome of man's *own labour.*" In *1844 MSS:* p. 140.
27 *1844 MSS:* p. 69.
28 *1844 MSS:* pp. 140-141.
29 *Ibid.* p. 140.
30 Cf: the whole chapter entitled "Independence and subjection of self-

consciousness; mastery and serfdom" in *Phenomenology of the Spirit.*

31   L. Althusser: *For Marx:* (Penguin, Harmondsworth, 1969) pp. 43-48.

32   M. Godelier: "Political economy and philosophy" in *Rationality and irrationality in economics:* (New Left Books, London, 1972) pp. 107-111.

33   "The theory of alienation enabled Marx to develop a profound critique of the capitalist system from the point of view of alienated labour. Through it, Marx was able to move towards an increasingly clear and precise notion of the determinant role of labour in practical activity, and in the development of human life and history." (Cornu: *Marx and Engels: ed. cit.* See too Cornu's assessment of the general results of the *1844 MSS* in terms of the genesis of historical materialism in *The German Ideology.* "(In the *Manuscripts*)—he says—Marx overtook the most advanced bourgeois thought of his time, represented by Feuerbach's philosophy, and laid down the principles of historical materialism, the basis of proletarian revolutionary thought." (Cornu: "Le materialisme historique dans 'L'Idéologie Allmande'" in *Annali 1963: ed. cit.:* p. 58).

Mario Rossi reacts to the tendency to open up an abyss between a so-called ideological period in Marx's work, represented by the *1844 MSS,* and his later work, by saying that "only an inattentive and superficial reading of the *Manuscripts* could interpret them as a document attesting to the ideologism surviving in the young Marx." (Rossi: *op.cit.:* vol. 2 p.587). He recognises that there do remain some ideological elements; but at the same time he sees it as overcoming the limits of ideology. T.I. Oizerman also rejects the notion of a radical discontinuity between the *1844 MSS* and Marx's immediately subsequent work, and assesses the youthful work within the general evolution of Marx's thought. "The *Economic and philosophical manuscripts* do show the influence of Feuerbach's anthropologism; yet despite surviving elements of conceptions which Marx was later to overcome, and despite the persistence of some of the terminology of those conceptions, they constitute the original formulation of the basic theses of dialectical and historical materialism"; T.I. Oizerman: *Formirovanie filosofii marksisma* (Formation of the philosophy of Marxism): Moscow, 1962; p.304.

34   *1844 MSS:* pp. 71-2.
35   *Ibid.* p. 102.
36   *Ibid.* pp. 96-7.
37   *Ibid.* p. 103.
38   *Ibid.* p. 146.
39   *Ibid.* p. 156.
40   *Ibid.* p. 67.
41   *Ibid.* p. 103.
42   *Ibid.* p. 103-5.
43   *Ibid.* p. 103.

44 *1844 MSS:* p. 103.
45 The contention that natural science, because of its object, had an anthropological character was later to be abandoned by Marx in elaborating, from *The German Ideology* onwards, his doctrine of the ideological superstructure, in which he evidently does not include natural science.
46 *1844 MSS:* p. 103.
47 Praxis appeared in the *1844 MSS* as productive activity, concretely as alienated labour, or as the human transformation of nature even within the alienated relation of man and nature. In anticipation of a more profound conception of praxis which he was to elaborate in the *Theses on Feuerbach* and *The German Ideology*, the *Manuscripts* already contained references to practical revolutionary activity as necessary to the transformation, not of an idea, but of reality. "In order to abolish the *idea* of private property, the *idea* of communism is completely sufficient. It takes actual communist action to abolish *actual* private property." (*1844 MSS:* p.115). Marx also refers to the decisive role of practice in solving theoretical problems: ". . . it will be seen how the resolution of the *theoretical* antitheses is only possible *in a practical way*, by virtue of the practical energy of men. Their resolution is therefore by no means merely a problem of knowledge, but a *real* problem of life, which *philosophy* could not solve precisely because it conceived this problem as merely a *theoretical* one." (*1844 MSS:* p. 102).
48 A. Gramsci: *Historical materialism. . .: ed.cit.:* p. 160.
49 K. Kosik: *Dialektika Konkretinho:* (Prague, 1963). p. 157.
50 *Theses on Feuerbach:* p. 651.
51 What Marx does not explicitly say in the *Theses* is directly stated in this passage from *The German Ideology:* "(Feuerbach does not see how the sensuous world around him is, not a thing given direct from all eternity, remaining ever the same, but the product of industry and of the state of society; and indeed in the sense that it is an historical product, the result of the activity of a whole succession of generations, each standing on the shoulders of a previous one, developing its industry and its intercourse, modifying its social system according to its changed needs. Even the objects of the simplest 'sensuous certainty' are only given him through social development, industry and commercial intercourse." (Marx/Engels: *The German Ideology:* Lawrence and Wishart, London, 1965) [Hereafter referred to as *German Ideology*] p. 57.
52 ". . . where would natural science be without industry and commerce? Even this 'pure' natural science is provided with an aim, as with its material, only through trade and industry, through the sensuous activity of men." He adds ". . . it is this activity, this unceasing sensuous labour and creation, this production, the basis of the whole sensuous world." As far as external nature in itself is concerned, without reference to the practical activity of men, Marx and Engels say a little further on: "Of course, in all

this the priority of external nature remains unassailed. ... For that matter, nature, the nature that preceded human history is not by any means the nature which Feuerbach lives, not the nature which no longer exists anywhere (except perhaps in a few Australian coral-islands of recent origin) and which, therefore, does not exist for Feuerbach." (*German Ideology:* p. 58).

53 *Theses on Feuerbach:* p. 651.
54 *Ibid.* p. 653.
55 On the application of the criterion of practice to particular sciences, see M.N. Rutkevitch et. al.: *Praktika-kriterii istiny v nauke:* Moscow, 1960.
56 Having affirmed that the practical point of view should be "primarily and fundamentally the theory of knowledge," Lenin said in this regard that "we must not forget here that the criterion of practice can never, in any depth completely confirm or deny any human representation. This criterion is 'imprecise' enough for it to prevent men's knowledge from ever becoming anything 'absolute'. . .". (Lenin: *Materialism and empirio-criticism* in *Collected Works* [Hereafter *CW*] volume 14, pp. 142-3).
57 *Theses on Feuerbach:* p. 652.
58 Cf: Marx: *Capital* Volume I (Foreign Languages Publishing House, Moscow/London, 1965) p. 177-8.
59 *Theses on Feuerbach:* p. 653.
60 Throughout their life and work, Marx and Engels remained faithful to their conception of the necessity of transforming socialism from Utopia into science, in response to the demands of practice. Thus Engels, in his pamphlet of 1877 unequivocally entitled *From Utopian socialism to scientific socialism* characterises scientific socialism in a way that makes clear the theoretico-practical content of Marxism: "To thoroughly comprehend the historical conditions and thus the very nature of this act, to impart to the now oppressed proletarian class a full knowledge of the conditions and of the meaning of the momentous act it is called upon to accomplish (the proletarian revolution), this is the task of the theoretical expression of the proletarian movement, scientific socialism." (In *S.W.* vol. 2, p. 155).
61 *German Ideology:* p. 50.
62 *Ibid.* p. 50.
63 *Ibid.* p. 50.
64 *Ibid.* p. 31.
65 *Ibid.* p. 32.
66 *Ibid.* p. 49.
67 *Ibid.* p. 47.
68 *Ibid.* p. 62.
69 *Ibid.* pp. 85-6.
70 Lenin: *What is to be done?* in *CW* vol. 5, p. 369.
71 Marx and Engels: *The Communist Manifesto* in *S.W.* vol. 1, p. 46.
72 *Ibid.* p. 46.

73 *Ibid.* p. 46.
74 The doctrine of the party of the proletariat as a conscious, advanced and organised detachment of the working class was elaborated above all by Lenin (*What is to be done?* loc. cit.). Nevertheless the premisses of his conception of the party can be found in the *Communist Manifesto*. This is why the tendency to attribute to Marx himself the idea that the proletariat as class is sufficient unto itself, that is, it has no need of a party in order to conquer power, or the idea that he identifies class and party, are without foundation. The best refutation of all is not only the text of the *Manifesto* itself, to which we have referred above, but Marx's practical involvement in the International; this is underlined by Marx and Engels' proposal in September 1872 that an article should be included in the statutes of the International in the following terms: "Article 7A: In its struggle against the unified power of the possessing classes, the working class can only act as a class if it organises itself through a political party of its own, opposed to all the old parties created by the possessing classes. This organisation of the working class as a political party is necessary if we are to guarantee the triumph of the social revolution and the achievement of its final objective: the disappearance of all classes." (Marx/Engels: *Complete Works:* 2nd Russian edition, Moscow 1961, volume 18, p. 143).
75 L. Althusser: *For Marx: ed. cit.:* p. 34.
76 With respect to this characterisation of Marxism, the work of the Soviet philosophers, entitled "The materialist dialectic as theory of revolutionary praxis" in *Voprosy filosofii,* no. 9, Moscow 1965, seems to us to be outstanding. The authors argue that "the materialist dialectic is the science of the transformation of the natural world into the human world; it is the theory of the revolutionary transformation of the human world itself into a humanised world." (*loc. cit.* p.15): "Marxism converted philosophy into a real science reflecting the practical activity of men and this radically transformed not only the attitude of philosophy towards reality, but the very concept of reality" (*ibid.* p.15): "Marxism cannot be abstracted from practice as it is above all the theory of revolutionary praxis, which constitutes its very core." (*ibid.* p.16).

PART TWO

SOME PHILOSOPHICAL PROBLEMS OF PRAXIS

IV. What is praxis?

Praxis and activity

All praxis is activity, but not all activity is praxis. Marx himself made this point in recognising that unlike materialism, Idealism had acknowledged the active side of the subject-object relation, although he went on to criticise Idealism's failure to see this activity as praxis.[1] It is important, then, to distinguish between praxis as a specific form of activity, and others which are not praxis, even though they may be closely connected to it.

We understand by activity (or action) in general, the act or conjunction of acts through which an active subject (the agent) modifies a given material. This general characterisation does not specify either the type of agent (physical, biological or human) or the nature of the raw material on which it acts (physical body, living being, psychic entity or social institution), nor does it elaborate on the kind of acts (physical, psychic or social) that can lead to a transformation. The result, or product of activity can also emerge in various forms; it can be a new practical, concept, tool, artistic work or a whole new social system. In this broad sense, activity is opposed to passivity, and its sphere is not one of possibilities but of concrete realities. The agent labours, acts, rather than existing in the potentiality or disposition to work; its activity is not potential, but actual, occurring through a constituent act or set of acts. In the relations between the parts and the whole, it is activity that has the features of a concrete totality; various unarticulated or casually juxtaposed acts do not merit the designation of activity, until they are articulated or structured as elements of a whole, or of a total process which results in the modification of a given material. The result or product must be considered together with the agent, which it affects; the act or set of acts executed on a given material are translated into a product or result which is the material after its transformation by the agent.

This concept of activity is sufficiently broad to encompass on a physical level, for example, the nuclear relations of particles which cause the transformation of chemical compounds; on a psychic level, the sensual activity of men or animals, their instinctive reflexes etc.; on this instinctive plane, the activity can consist in a series of acts as complex as those involved in the construction of a nest by a bird, although for all its complexity it does not cease to be a simply biological, natural act. Man can also be the subject of biological or instinctive activities which are no more than simple, natural acts and which cannot, for that reason, be regarded as specifically human. Human activity properly speaking only occurs when actions designed to transform an object are initiated on the basis of an ideal result or end, and culminate in an actual, concrete result or product. In this case acts are not only casually determined by a previous determination (the past conditioned by the present), but by something that has yet no actual existence yet which nevertheless determines and regulates the various activities even before they yield a concrete result; the determination is not in the past, therefore, but in the future.

The adaptation of acts to ends

This mode of articulating and determining the different acts in the active process draws a radical distinction between specifically human activity and all other simple, natural activities. It is the intervention of consciousness that determines whether a particular activity is human; this implies that the result of that activity exists at two levels, and at different moments; as an ideal result and as a real product. The actual product sought exists in the first place in the ideal form, as a product of consciousness, and the various acts in the process are articulated or structured in accordance with the result as it was originally projected in the form of an ideal. It is this anticipation of the result that gives human activity its conscious character. However far the real result may be from its ideal anticipation, human activity characteristically strives to adapt the real product to its ideal form in an intentional way. This does not mean that result need necessarily be a mere duplication in reality of a preexistent ideal model; the adaptation may not be perfect, and in fact it may not resemble the original projection at all since it can often undergo radical changes in the process of realisation. Provided, however, that an ideal outcome or end was proposed at the outset, and that there exists an intention to adapt the result to an ideal outcome, we can speak of human activity, whether or not the reality actually moulds itself to the ideal.

The failure to compaginate intention and outcome is characteristically manifest in both individual and social activity. As long as men remain ignorant of the laws that govern the socio-economic process, the prosecution of different ends by the members of a society gives rise to a whole multitude of individual and group activities whose ends are counterposed, balanced or subordinated among themselves and do not in the end yield results that accord with their original intentions. The relations of production, for example, are relations that men contract independently of their will and consciousness; they are the unintentional products of the activity of men.[2] Historical progress will be characterised, by, among other things, the overcoming of the unintentional nature of those relations. The men who in the past unintentionally produced slavery, feudalism and capitalism, for example, are today proposing the destruction of capitalist relations of production and the implementation of socialism. Although human history offers many examples of results which are not the intention of anyone, they are still the unintentional social form adopted by the activity engaged in by individuals or social beings who act consciously. As Engels put it, in his letter to J. Bloch, written in September 1880:

"History is made in such a way that the final result always arises from conflicts between many individual wills, of which each again has been made what it is by a host of particular conditions of life. Thus there are innumerable intersecting forces, an infinite series of parallelograms of forces which give rise to one resultant—the historical event. This may again itself be viewed as the product of a power which works as a whole, *unconsciously* and without volition . . . This past history proceeds in the manner of a natural process and is essentially subject to the same laws of motion. But from the fact that individual wills . . . do not attain what they want, but are merged into a collective mean, a common resultant, it must not be concluded that their value is equal to zero. On the contrary, each contributes to the resultant and is to this degree involved in it."[3]

Human activity, then, is an activity adapted to ends which exist only as products of consciousness, the consciousness of men. All authentic human action demands consciousness of an end which is subordinated in the course of actual activity. The end is, in its turn, the expression of an attitude to reality on the part of the subject. By tracing out an end for myself, I adopt a certain attitude to that end. When a man decides to embark upon a journey, make a chair, paint a picture or transform a social regime, he starts from a given attitude to an actual, concrete situation. If man lived in complete harmony with the world, or were totally reconciled to it, he would not feel the need to deny reality at the level of the ideal, nor to construct in his consciousness a still non-existent reality. It is clearly contradictory to propose an end for oneself which has already been realised, or a result that has already been obtained; the end prefigures ideally what has yet to be achieved. Thus in proposing objectives for himself, man denies the concrete reality and affirms another which has yet to come into existence. Ends, however, are products of consciousness governing conscious activity, which is not the activity of pure consciousness but the actions of social men who cannot avoid the production of ends in any of the forms of activity, including practical, material activity, in which they engage.[4] Marx, for example, emphasised the role of ends in practical activity like labour: "At the end of every labour-process, we get a result which already existed *in the imagination of the labourer* at its commencement. He not only effects a change of form in the material on which he works, but he also realises a purpose of his own that gives the law to his *modus operandi,* and to which he must subordinate his will."[5]

In emphasising the role of the production of ends in the labour process, Marx also pointed to the role of the object "the material that Nature provides," on which that activity is executed. The transformation of material nature into products through labour could not occur without these material conditions, but at the same time Marx quite correctly stressed the fact that since labour is a specifically human activity, the purpose has a determinant role, and the character of a law in that process of material transformation. Thus the purpose, the end, prefigures the result of an actual activity which has ceased to be merely the pure activity of consciousness. As a result man does not stand in an external relation to his various acts and his products, like animals or simple organisms, but in an internal relation to them, since the purpose that governs his acts was established in his consciousness; thus those acts are subordinated to a law that to a certain extent governs the product. This dominion can never be absolute, however, since it is limited by the object of activity and by the means that must be employed in order to materialise the ends. Thus man, having anticipated the actual outcome in an ideal sense, can adapt his acts accordingly as elements of a totality governed by an end, a purpose. Thus however much they may resemble one another in appearance, the acts of men are distinct from those of animals because of this governing ideal prefiguration of an actual result. "A spider conducts operations that resemble those of a weaver, and the bee puts to shame many an architect in the construction of her cells. But what distinguished the worst architect from the best of bees is this, that the architect raises his structure in imagination before he erects it in reality."[6] Taking into account the *external* similarity between human and animal acts, it is the essential, integral role of the activity of consciousness that distinguishes specifically human activity, an activity that develops as the production of ends prefiguring in ideal terms the actual result. At the same time, such activity is manifested as the production of knowledge in the form of concepts, hypotheses, theories or laws through which man comes to know reality.

There are important differences, however, between cognitive and teleological activity: whilst the former has to do with the explanation of the immediate reality, the latter is referred to a future, and as yet non-existent reality. Similarly, whilst cognitive activity itself does not entail the demand for concrete action, teleological activity implies the demand for realisation, as the end becomes a motive for real action. Insofar as the end is the ideal anticipation of a real result, it is also the expression of a human need which can only be satisfied by the realisation of that projected outcome. Thus it is not simply an ideal anticipation of what is to come, but of something whose realisation is activity pursued; in this sense it provides a motive for action, and shapes our present activities in terms of the future. Man does not only anticipate the future at the teleological level, but by explaining and understanding the actual reality, on the basis of which he is able to foresee a future phase in his development which is not yet in sight. That is the legitimate function of scientific prediction, which anticipates ideally what does not yet exist in reality, though this anticipation does not necessarily mean that we desire its realisation, nor that we aspire to contribute to that realisation. In this sense, the future does not determine our acts; the ideal prefiguration of a reality-to-be-brought-into-being, unlike our ends or purposes, does not govern our actions as a law, any more than cognitive activity moves us necessarily to act in a certain way. These various activities of consciousness, of course, are not irrevocably separate; we do not pursue knowledge for its own sake, but in terms of an end or a series of ends whose first stage may be the search for the truth; the ends produced at the level of consciousness entail in their turn the demand for realisation among whose preconditions is included a cognitive activity without which those ends could never come to earth and be fulfilled. All ends presuppose some knowledge of the reality that they deny at the ideal level, because they are themselves indications of a certain level of knowledge. Thus the activity of consciousness which characterises all authentic human activity appears as an intimately linked process of elaborating ends and producing knowledge. If man always accepted the world as it is, and himself in his present state, he would never experience the desire to transform the world and transform himself at the same time. Our acts are informed by knowledge, just as our knowledge has its origins in activity. All human knowledge is integral to the infinite human task of transforming both external and internal nature. On the other hand, knowledge does not contribute directly or immediately to this practical activity; its role is at the level of the formulation of the ends to be pursued through that activity. The relation between thought and action therefore requires the purposive mediation of men. On the other hand, if ends are not to remain at the level of mere desires or illusions but lead to an enthusiastic pursuit of their realisation, or the transformation of a given material in order to produce a certain result, there must exist knowledge of the object, of the means or instruments necessary to transform the object and of the conditions that prevent or facilitate that realisation; hence the indissoluble unity of the cognitive and teleological activities of consciousness.

The activity of consciousness itself has what we might call a theoretical character, insofar as it alone cannot lead to the transformation of the natural or social reality. Theory in the broad sense, including both ends and the knowledge of those ends, is opposed in a relative way to practice. In a more restricted sense the domain of theory includes all the knowledge contributing to the unifying principle which articulates and systematises that knowledge, providing the framework for a given field of scientific enquiry. Both in the formulation of ends and in the production of knowledge, consciousness is restricted to its own frontiers; its activity cannot materialise or become objective. Thus although both these aspects are types of activity, they are not in any sense, objective activity, or praxis.

Practical activity

Like all *human* activity, the practical activity that takes the form of human labour, artistic creation or revolutionary praxis, is an activity adapted to ends whose fulfilment requires a level of cognitive activity. What is distinctive about practical activity, however, is the real objective character of the material on which it is executed, as well as of its results or product. In practical activity, the subject acts upon a material existing independently of his consciousness and of the various manipulative operations necessary for its transformation, a transformation that demands, above all in human labour, a series of physical, corporeal acts without which the alteration or abolition of those properties preventing the emergence of a new object with new properties, could not be carried out. As Marx said, in labour "(man) opposes himself to Nature as one of her own forces, setting in motion arms and legs, head and hands, the natural forces of his body, in order to appropriate Nature's production in a form adapted to his wants."[7] Finally the product of his activity in this sense is a material object which subsists independently of the process of its gestation and whose own substantive character is affirmed in the eyes of the subject; in other words, it takes on an existence independent of the subjective activity that created it. This, in our view, is what Marx means when he talks about "objective activity,"[8] or the real, objective character of the praxis that transforms the external world outside the consciousness and the very existence of the subject. Nature, society or real men are objects of that practical activity, whose purpose is the actual transformation of the natural and social world in order to satisfy a human need. The result is a new reality, which comes to exist independently of the concrete subject or subjects whose activity brought it into being; ultimately, however, it only continues to exist for and through man as a social being. Without this objective action executed on a natural or human reality outside the practical subject, we cannot properly speak of praxis, or of conscious material activity which creates an objective reality. For simple, subjective, psychic or merely spiritual activity, which does not result in an objective, material object, cannot be considered as praxis in the sense that we have defined.

Forms of praxis

When the raw material of practical activity changes, so do the forms of praxis executed upon it. The object of the subject's practical activity can be a) that which is given in Nature, or natural entities; b) products of a previous praxis which in their turn become the material for a new praxis in the form of prepared materials elaborated by the worker or the creative artist; c) the human element itself, whether it be society, as the material or object of political or revolutionary praxis, or concrete individuals. In some cases, then, the object of praxis is non-human matter; in others, it is man himself.

One of the fundamental forms of human praxis is practical productive activity, or labour, "(which) is in the first place, a process in which both man and Nature participate, and in which man of his own accord starts, regulates and controls the material reactions between himself and Nature."[9] By overcoming the resistance of the materials and forces of his nature through his labour, man creates a world of useful objects that satisfy his needs. Because he is a social being, however, the process can only occur in certain social conditions, and within the framework of the relations that men contract as the agent of production in this process; those relations Marx aptly called *the relations of production*.[10]

In the labour-process, man employs the appropriate tools or means to transform an object; insofar as he gives material form in this way, to a project or end, he can be said to objectify himself in his product. Through labour, man "appropriates Nature's productions in a form adapted to his own wants."[11] But he only does this to the extent that he gives himself objective form in them, impressing his own stamp upon the material he has worked. Marx in fact emphasised that this adaptation to ends is one of the essential features of the labour-process: "the simple factors that intervene in the labour-process are: activity *adjusted to an end,* that is, *work itself, its object* and *its means."*[12] This characterisation of labour process allows us to speak of objective conditions (human activity and the material conditions of labour) which are represented in reality both by the object of labour and by the means or tools employed in the transformation of the object. There is no absolute distinction between the two, however, since man transforms the object in a purposive way through the use of tools which he himself both manufactures and uses; in this sense, they "are specifically characteristic of the *human labour-process.*"[13] By establishing the connection between the objective conditions in which the labour-process occurs, and which takes form in the tools employed, and human labour, he presents the tool in a humanised form precisely because man makes and uses it himself. It should be stressed, however, that the process whereby tools become humanised is not abstract or anthropological, but a direct expression both of a relation between man and nature, and of the social conditions in which men produce (the relations of production). "The instruments of labour are not only the barometer indicating the development of the force of labour in man, but also the exponent of the social conditions in which he works." [14] As the instruments of labour are improved the relations between man and nature are modified also; in this sense, they provide a revealing indication of the development of man's labour power and of his dominion over Nature. The introduction of the machine, for example, raised and extended the mediating power of the instrument of labour, to the point where man became radically separated from the object of production. But whatever the nature of the instrument employed in the transformation of nature in accordance with given ends, it is ultimately man who makes and uses them, and it is therefore man himself who acts upon matter and transforms it according to his needs. The predominant role of the means of production which Marx indicated does not, therefore, eliminate concrete man from the process; on the contrary, it unequivocally establishes the central place of man as the subject of production, manifested through the purposive character of that activity, or production. In the final analysis, however, this simply serves to underline the material nature of the conditions in which the labour-process occurs, and the dominant role of the means of production within the process.[15]

Practical, material activity clearly has a teleological character; this does not mean, however, that we can go on to abstract the material nature of that activity. The object of labour and its material instruments, form the subjective activity of men who modify nature themselves through the use of their instruments of labour. For in labour "man sets in motion arms and legs, head and hands, the natural forces of his body."[16] Not only does man produce a humanised and human world of objects that satisfy human needs and whose very production depends upon the extent to which they give human ends and projects an objective form; man also produces, forms or transforms *himself* in productive praxis. "By thus acting on the external world," Marx says in *Capital*, "and changing it, he at the same time changes his own nature. He develops his slumbering powers and compels them to act in obedience to his sway."[17] In this sense, productive praxis is a fundamental form of human praxis.

There are other forms of praxis, however, which are equally worthy of attention. Just as human labour transforms matter and gives it a specifically human stamp, for example, art or creative production imposes a new form on matter, not in response to practical-utilitarian needs, but to a general human need for expression and objectification. The activity of the artist is not constrained by the demand that his product satisfy a given need, and thus he is able to carry to its ultimate consequences the process of humanisation (of matter) which occurs in a limited sense in human labour. Artistic praxis, in other words, enables human or humanised objects to be produced which raise to a higher level the human capacity for self-expression or objectification already partially manifest in the products of labour. The artistic work creates a new reality; and since man affirms himself as such by creating or humanising whatever he touches, artistic praxis, in enriching and widening an already humanised reality, is an essential form of praxis. For its sphere of action is the transformation of matter, and its aim the creation of a new form of object which satisfies a human need. Art is neither mere material production nor pure spiritual activity, its practical, transforming character, however, means that it is closer to human labour, particularly where that labour had not lost its creative aspect, than to purely spiritual activity.

The category of practical activity also embraces experimental scientific activity, whose object is to test and prove hypotheses and to satisfy the general needs of theoretical research. The experimental form allows the investigator to modify at will a material object or the conditions in which a given phenomenon occurs; the researcher reproduces in the laboratory phenomena which arise in the first place in a natural environment. The artificial context in which he reproduces them, however, enables him to eliminate those impurities and perturbations which affect them in the natural situation and which would render his work much more difficult. Experimental scientific activity, then, produces given phenomena with the aid of appropriate physical instruments, and therefore qualifies as praxis, or objective activity giving rise to a product or an actual, objective result. The immediate object of this type of praxis is theoretical; it is designed to test a theory, or at least some aspects of it, and in turn to facilitate the development of that theory. An experiment, in agronomy for example, may have practical consequences; but they are not the direct result of experimental activity, but of the theory tested and proven by that activity.

Experimentation, of course, is not exclusive to science; it is possible to speak of experiments in art, education, economics or society. In these cases, experiment is not directly or immediately at the service of theory, but responds to the exigencies of a specific form of praxis. The objective of artistic or educative experiment, for example, is to give added impetus to the corresponding practical activity, be it art or education. Whereas experimental scientific activity serves to strengthen and develop theory itself, and thus serves practical activity in a mediate way, experimentation in other fields contributes immediately to the corresponding form of praxis, and its results are applied directly in the appropriate practical sphere.

These, then, are the fundamental forms of praxis through which man acts more or less directly on a natural material, immediate nature or a mediated nature, or a material which has already been the object of practical activity and which now serves as material for new acts. We have still to consider that type of praxis in which man is both subject and object: that is, the praxis in which man acts upon himself. This type of activity has a number of modalities, and includes all the various activities aimed at transforming man as a social being, and hence to a transformation of his economic, social and political relations. And to the extent that the object of his activity is not an isolated individual but a social group or class, this activity can be considered to be social praxis. In a broad sense, of course, all practice has a social character, even when its immediate object is nature rather than man; man can only carry out his activity if he first contracts social relations (relations of production in the case of productive praxis etc.). Furthermore, the modification of the non-human object is translated in its turn into a transformation of the social being of man.

To a more limited extent, social praxis is also action on the part of certain social groups or classes to transform the organisation and alter the structure of society on the one hand, or to carry through certain changes through the medium of the State on the other; that is, political praxis. In the conditions of a society divided into antagonistic classes, political praxis involves the struggle between classes for the conquest of power, and for a society organised in accordance with the interests and needs of the members of the class. Politics is thus a practical activity to the extent that it is linked to a specific form of real organisation of the members of a class, in political institutions or organisations like the party, for example. Although political activity may bring with it a clash or conflict of ideas, projects, programmes etc., and whatever the influence exercised upon actual, concrete political action by the ideological struggle, the practical character of that activity derives in the first instance from the fact that there exist forms, means and methods of struggle that are real and effective; the proletariat, for example, realises its struggle through strikes, demonstrations, meetings and even the use of violent methods. In the end, political activity is aimed at the conquest, maintenance, leadership or control of concrete organs of power like the State; for power is the vital element in the transformation of society.

Political praxis pre-supposes the involvement of broad sectors of society; but it is not a matter of spontaneous activity, even though some groups or individuals may act in a spontaneous way. Political activity is carried forward in pursuit of ends which correspond to the radical interests of social classes. In each concrete situation, the realisation of those ends, and the method of obtaining them, are conditioned by the objective possibilities of reality itself. If political activity is to avoid adventurism and failure, it must take account of those possibilities and have its basis in a genuine knowledge of that reality and of the objective correlation of social forces within it. In this sense the struggle must be conscious, organised and have a clear orientation; hence the need for political parties, which formulate lines of action based on varying degrees of consciousness of the conditions, objectives and possibilities of struggle. The mode of achieving the transformation of the ideal into the real, that is of realising in practice the political line elaborated by the party, is presented in the form of strategy and tactics. The strategy sets out the tasks appropriate to a particular historical moment, while tactics determine the way in which the political line can be realised within a relatively short time scale. Thus in terms of the application of the political line, strategy and tactics correspond to the general and the particular. As a practical, transforming activity, political praxis achieves its highest expression in revolutionary praxis, the most advanced stage in the transformation of society. In class society, revolutionary activity brings about radical changes in the economic and social structure on which the ruling class had based its maintenance of power, replacing them with a new society. The principal agent of this transformation is the proletariat, organised in a conscious way under the leadership of a party devoted to raising its class consciousness, setting out clearly the objectives of its struggle, its strategy and its tactics, and organising and directing its forces in a material way.

Man affirms his practical nature through this transforming activity which enables him to act in and upon both external nature and his own nature. Revolutionary praxis and productive praxis, therefore, are the two essential dimensions of his practical being; and both these and the other specific forms of praxis in which he may engage, are particular concrete forms of a total human praxis through which man, as a conscious, social being, humanises both the world of objects and himself.

Theoretical activity

Theoretical activity as a whole, whether as ideology or as science, has historically only existed through and in relation to the practice which is its foundation, its objective and its criterion of truth. However close the relation between them, theoretical activity does not possess the features which we have defined as specific to praxis. In our view, then, theoretical activity cannot be considered to be a form of praxis. Although theoretical 'practice' may transform perceptions, representations and concepts, producing in this way specific products called hypotheses, theories, laws etc., none of them can of themselves transform reality as they do not fulfil the practical conditions as far as the relation to matter, to activity, or to the results of activity are concerned. Theoretical praxis, in other words, has no material, objective aspect; thus to consider theory as praxis involves a contradiction. For what is distinctive in theoretical activity, which may produce ends and knowledge, is the specific nature of its object, its medium and the results that stem from it. Its object, or material, are sensations or perceptions—psychic objects that have a subjective existence only—or concepts, theories, representations or hypotheses which have only an ideal existence. The immediate purpose of theory is to transform its material at the level of the ideal, not at the level of actuality, with the aim of producing theories that can explain an actual reality, or models that prefigure its future shape or development. Theoretical activity is essential, of course, to the extent that it provides knowledge indispensible to those who will transform reality, and insofar as it formulates ends or objectives which anticipate that transformation in an ideal sense; in both cases, however, the concrete reality remains intact. Theoretical activity can transform a hypothesis into a theory, or one theory into another more sophisticated and developed one; but these are ideal transformations, changes in our ideas about the world, but not of the world itself. "Ideas can never lead beyond an old world system but only beyond the ideas of the old world system. Ideas cannot *carry anything out* at all. In order to carry out ideas men are needed who dispose of a certain practical force."[19] The operations required to produce ends and knowledge are mental operations; abstraction, generalisation, deduction, synthesis, prediction etc., which although they demand a physical substratum (the functioning of a higher nervous system, for example) remain nonetheless subjective, psychic operations, whatever the objective consequences they may have. Further, the notion of theoretical praxis contradicts the critique formulated by Marx in the *Theses on Feuerbach.* Thesis I, for example, criticises Feuerbach precisely on the basis that he conceived the subject-object (or man-nature) relation as merely contemplative, or theoretical. In Marx's view that was the fundamental error of Feuerbachian philosophy, as well as of traditional materialism; and in this sense, Marx counterposed theoretical, or contemplative, and practical relations; philosophy as theory or interpretation, unconnected with practice, and a philosophy consciously linked to the transformation of the world. (Thesis XI). Clearly, then, Marx did not regard theory as a form of praxis, but saw them in fact as opposed to one another.

In his *Introduction to a critique of political economy,* Marx established a further distinction between concrete thought and concrete reality. Cognitive, theoretical activity or the production of knowledge, is a process which advances from the abstract to the concrete; the whole process is realised, however, at the level of thought, and consists of the spiritual reproduction of the real object in the form of concrete thought. Marx makes very clear that, in his view, this is an activity, or mode of production, which produces nothing; that is to say it does not transform reality.[20] An activity realised in the mind, and resulting only in mental products, but which does not transform matter objectively into a new form which persists independently of the active subject, cannot be included within the framework of the kind of practical activity which we have defined as *praxis.*[21] We could only sustain the notion of theoretical praxis by extending the concept of praxis to the point where all the specific differences between theory and activity in general disappeared. Insofar as theoretical activity in itself does not modify the world in a real sense, however, although it can modify our *ideas about* the world, it seems illegitimate to speak of theoretical praxis at all.

Philosophy and praxis

Philosophical activity transforms our conception of the world, of society or of man, but it cannot modify reality in any direct or immediate sense. But is this true of all philosophical activity, even when it conceives the world not only as an object of interpretation, but also of transformation? According to Marx's Eleventh Thesis on Feuerbach, philosophy can be divided from a historical point of view, into those schools which contented themselves with attempting to explain what exists and which culminate, as Hegel's philosophy demonstrated in an exemplary way, in a conciliation of thought and reality (philosophy as an acceptance of the world), and those which served the transformation of the world through their conscious links with revolutionary praxis (philosophy as a theoretical instrument or as a guide to the radical transformation of the human world by man himself). Would it not be possible, therefore, to consider this latter conception of philosophy as a form of praxis, which might be called theoretical praxis? For the alternative appears to be that all philosophies would have the same theoretical character, and Marx's distinction between these two types of philosophy would have little meaning. Clearly what is involved is a much clearer delimitation of what is meant by true praxis.

In the first place we must discard the notion that it is possible to speak of philosophical praxis simply because a philosophy has repercussions in practice. All the great philosophical doctrines have had some practical echo, in a more or less direct way, since whatever the philosopher's intentions, those doctrines always fulfilled a social function; this is true, for example, even of those philosophies, like German Idealism, which did not express the remotest hope of transforming the world. What, then, of the philosophical activity which has conscious links with praxis, and which explicitly sees its role as that of a theoretical instrument for the transformation of reality? Clearly, it is Marxism itself that is involved here. Does Marxism itself conform to the conceptual content of praxis as defined? In our judgment, philosophy can never be praxis in a direct or immediate sense, whether it is simply interpretative or seeks to contribute to the transformation of the world. Marxist philosophy, since it is necessarily a scientific interpretation of the world, responds to practical human needs on the one hand, and both expresses an existing practice and aspires to provide guidance for revolutionary praxis, on the other. This serves to emphasise the social and ideological function of a philosophy that can only be practical to the extent that it excludes Utopianism and transcends its purely ideological character in order to become a science. What distinguishes Marxism from the philosophical doctrines to which Marx alluded in the first part of his Eleventh Thesis, and from other socialist doctrines, is its scientific character; furthermore it is conceived as a philosophy in function of praxis, at the service of and integral to the actual, effective transformation of the world. In this sense, revolutionary praxis is the end of theory.

Here, too, it is clear that theory cannot of itself transform the world. It can *contribute* to its transformation, but to do this it must emerge from itself and be assimilated by those who will carry through the transformation of society through their concrete activity. There intervenes between theory and practical, transforming activity, the task of educating and raising consciousness, organising the material means and the concrete programmes of action, which constitute essential preconditions for effective activity. Theory, then, can be said to be practical to the extent that it materialises, through a series of mediations, what had previously existed only in an ideal form as knowledge of reality or as an ideal anticipation of its transformation. If theory of itself cannot change the world, however, its contribution to that change derives precisely from its *theoretical* character. It is the necessary (but insufficient) condition of possibility for the transition from theory to practice; the practical function of theoretical activity stems from a consideration of the interrelationship between cognitive and teleological elements in praxis itself. The role of a philosophy linked to praxis, and aspiring consciously to be realised, does not require that the strictly theoretical content should be discarded, but on the contrary that content should be developed to its fullest and richest degree. The movement from the Utopian socialist theory of Saint-Simon, Fourier or Owen, or from the Utopian communism of Moses Hess, to the scientific socialism of Marx and Engels, entails not only the elevation of its practical function but also of its theoretical content, with the particular characteristic that these two components are indissolubly linked.

The philosophy that sees itself as a theoretical instrument of praxis remains theory, and as such cannot transform the world. The point, however, is to carry out that transformation, so that theory must transcend its theoretical frontiers and strive to realise itself through the appropriate mediations. This aspect is vital if change is regarded as the priority; yet far from abolishing the theoretical content of philosophy, or reducing it to a mere ideological ingredient, it presupposes necessarily a scientific theory which can give direction to practical activity. Thus neither philosophical activity as such, nor the philosophy of praxis, as the theory of man's practical activity in its relation to Nature and to other men, can be regarded as praxis. The idea that a philosophy of praxis is itself a form of practical activity is, in our judgment, an Idealist conception incompatible with the true concept of praxis, and implies a return to philosophical standpoints like that of the Young Hegelians, which had already been criticised and surpassed by Marx precisely in order to clear the way for a philosophy that would provide an instrument and a guide to the transformation of reality. Philosophical activity, whether divorced from practice or consciously linked to it, as mere interpretation or theoretical instrument, cultivated by intellectuals of bourgeois or even proletarian origin, is always theoretical, intellectual activity. Neither the qualitative differences between philosophies, according to their essentially ideological or scientific character, nor the various functions fulfilled by one or another, are a sufficient basis for legitimising the notion of theoretical praxis.

Praxis presents itself as material, transforming activity adapted to specific ends. Anything else is merely theoretical activity, which never goes beyond the realm of pure spirit. On the other hand, praxis is never simply material activity; one of its conditions is the production of the ends and the knowledge that characterises theoretical activity. In the next chapter we shall try to delineate more precisely the boundaries between theory and practice.

Notes

1. *Theses on Feuerbach;* p.651.
2. Thus the fundamental contradictions of the capitalist mode of production are also unintentional. According to Maurice Godelier, "Though resulting from the actions of all the agents of the system and of the development of the system itself, it has never been anyone's conscious plan or the aim pursued by any individual." M. Godelier: *Rationality and irrationality in economics:* (New Left Books, London, 1972) pp. 80-81.
3. Marx/Engels: *S.W.:* Vol. 2, p. 489.
4. On finality as a specific category of human activity and its relation to causality, see A. Sanchez Vazquez: "Contribution a la dialectica de la finalidad y la causalidad" in *Anuario de filosofia:* (UNAM, Mexico), Year 1, pp. 56-64.
5. Marx: *Capital I:* p. 178.

What is Praxis? 167

6 *Ibid.* p. 177.
7 *Ibid.* p. 177.
8 *Theses on Feuerbach:* p. 651.
9 *Capital I:* p. 177.
10 Marx: *Preface to a contribution to a critique of political economy* in Marx/Engels: *S.W.:* Vol. 1, p. 362.
11 *Capital I:* p. 177.
12 *Ibid.* p. 178.
13 *Ibid.* p. 179.
14 *Ibid.* p. 180.
15 In analysing Marx's conception of the labour-process in *Capital,* Louis Althusser stresses the material nature of the conditions of the labour-process and the dominant role of the means of production in that process. In his view, the labour *process* is determined by those material conditions ("the labour process as a material mechanism is denominated by the physical laws of nature and technology"). In showing "the irreducible conditions of the labour process," Marx broke with the conception of "labour as the essence of man" and with the "idealism of labour" implied in this conception, typical of the *1844 MSS.* (Cf: "The object of Capital" in L. Althusser et. al.: *Reading Capital:* NLB London, 1970: pp. 144-9.)

Althusser is clearly right to oppose the "anthropological ideology of labour" and to stress the importance of the material conditions of labour, which leads him to lay particular stress on two of the constitutive elements of Marx's view of the process. His analysis completely omits, however, the third of those elements, namely activity adapted to an end, or labour properly speaking. It is this omission that allows him to counterpose the *1844 MSS* and *Capital* in a radical way, and to reduce the conception prevalent in the earlier work to an "idealism of labour" and that of the later writings to "a materialist conception of production." In our view, the significance of this third element of the labour-process, which appears in different ways in both works, is that it sustains a certain continuity between the two conceptions, although this does not affect their essential differences.

16 *Capital I:* p. 177.
17 *Ibid.* p. 177.
18 On the relations between art and labour, and the conception of the artistic work as creation, see A. Sanchez Vazquez: *Art and Society* (Merlin Press, 1974) particularly the sections "Art and Marxism today" and "Marx's ideas on the origins and nature of aesthetics."
19 Marx/Engels: *The Holy Family:* (Moscow/London, 1956), p. 185.
20 "The method of advancing from the abstract to the concrete is but a way of thinking by which the concrete is grasped and is reproduced in our mind as a concrete. It is by no means, however, the process itself which generates the concrete", Marx, *Contribution to a critique of political*

economy, Chicago 1904, pp. 293-4.

21 On occasions the expression 'praxis' or 'theoretical praxis' is employed to designate "a specific practice exercised on an appropriate object and leading to its own product, knowledge." (Althusser: *For Marx:* NLB London, 1969, p. 173). In this case it is presented as a specific form of practice in general, understood as "the process of transformation of a given nature (raw material) into useful products, a transformation which is carried out through determined human labour, and employing given means (of production)." (*Ibid.* p. 167). Theoretical practice understood in this way corresponds in large part, though not totally, given that it also includes the production of ends, to what we have called theoretical activity.

Althusser does not employ the expression in the Idealist sense, so firmly rejected by Marx, of the production of ideas which themselves transform reality. He is also at pains to stress the distinctive and irreplaceable character of theoretical practice" (cf: L. Althusser: "Theory, theoretical formation. Ideology and the ideological struggle" in *Casa de las Americas:* Havana, [no. 34: pp. 13-17). Nevertheless, the extension of the term 'practice' to cover every type of relation to or appropriation of the real world, including not only the theoretical or ideological relation, but also the ethical and the religious relation (*Reading Capital:* p. 62-3) leads him to deny the essential character of praxis, which Marx correctly underlined, as the real, effective and concrete transformation of a real object, in contrast to an "idealism of praxis," which reduces praxis to a theoretical or moral activity. Thus in our view, the use of the word "practice" where that objective transformation does not occur, only serves to confuse the issue, despite the time expended on distinguishing between its specific forms.

V. The unity of theory and practice

Theoretical activity, as we have already underlined, is not praxis; indeed so long as it remains purely theoretical it is to some extent a denial of praxis. For theory is neither realised, nor given shape, nor does it produce any actual changes; the products of consciousness must be materialised if the ideal transformation is to become concrete. While practical activity supposes effective action on and in the world, whose result is an actual transformation, theoretical activity only modifies our consciousness of the facts, our ideas about things, but not the things themselves. In this sense, we can speak of an opposition between theory and practice; change can only be the consequence of practical activity in the world, it is not enough to think about revolution.[1]

The "common-sense" point of view: pragmatism

The opposition between theory and practice, however, has a relative rather than an absolute character. It is only possible to see an opposition between them when their relations are placed on a false basis, either by totally divorcing practice from theory, or by rejecting the possibility of conscious links between them. The first is the characteristic conception of ordinary consciousness, where practice is considered in a strictly utilitarian sense absolutely counterposed to theory, to the degree that it becomes irrelevant, if not directly detrimental, to practice. Theoretical formulations are thus replaced by a "common sense" point of view which bends obligingly to the dictates or exigencies of a practice devoid of theoretical ingredients. These, in their turn, are substituted by a whole network of prejudices, outmoded truths, and in some cases by the superstitions of an irrational (magical or religious) conception of the world. Practice is sufficient unto itself and "common sense" adopts a passive and uncritical attitude towards it; "common sense" is no more than the sense of practice. As there is no disparity between "common sense" and practice, ordinary consciousness regards as incontestable the criteria which arise directly and immediately from practice. In this light, the intervention of theory in the practical process can only be seen as a hindrance; absolute priority belongs to practice precisely because it is not impregnated with theoretical elements. The "common sense point of view", then, can be summarised as "practicalist"; practice without, or with a minimum theoretical content.[2]

The history of philosophical thought contains another example of a conception of the relations between theory and practice which is little more than a refined version of the common sense point of view raised to the level of a philosophical doctrine: the pragmatist standpoint. The pragmatist conception of truth, for example, takes the fact that our knowledge is linked to practical needs, and deduces from that that what is true is quite simply what is useful. Thus pragmatism undermines the very foundation of knowledge, or the reproduction of reality in the cognitive consciousness (although we can only know or reproduce that reality at the level of ideals). Faithful to the common-sense point of view of the "man in the street", pragmatism reduces what is practical to what is useful, and ends by dissolving theory into utility.

Some adversaries of Marxism have insisted that the Marxist conception of truth is equally pragmatist. Although there has been no lack of Marxists who have conceived the relations between theory and practice in a pragmatic way, in the sense of using theory as a justification of practice rather than as a clarification or a guide for praxis which both gives it a sound basis and enriches its content, Marxism can only be identified with pragmatism by inverting its actual conception and criterion of truth, and its view of the nature of praxis itself. Pragmatism identifies truth with utility. Since Marxism does not regard knowledge as an end in itself, but as a human activity closely related to man's practical needs, which that knowledge serves more or less directly, it might be possible to confuse the Marxist thesis with the utilitarian thesis of the pragmatists. Man's activities, and man's knowledge, are constantly developing in accordance with his needs; the practical-social nature of his activities, moreover, might lead us to regard human knowledge in general, and the natural and exact sciences in particular, in utilitarian terms. This does not mean, however, that Marxism and pragmatism coincide in their view. According to William James, "What is true is what it is in our interests to believe"; truth is related to our beliefs, and furthermore to those of our beliefs which are most beneficial for us;

truth, in other words, is subordinated to individual interests. Truth, in other words, is not to be judged by the degree to which what we believe is consistent with the reality reproduced in consciousness, but to the extent that it corresponds to our interests, or to what it is to our benefit to believe.[3] When Marxism refers to the usefulness, or the practical-social function of science, on the other hand, it does so from the point of view of social utility, rather than narrow egoism. True knowledge is useful to the extent that on the basis of that knowledge, man is better able to transform reality. Truth entails a spiritual reproduction of reality that is not an inert reflection but an active process which Marx defined as the ascent from the abstract to the concrete *in* and *through* thought, and in close connection with social practice. Knowledge is useful to the degree that it is true, but it is not true to the extent that it is useful as the pragmatists maintained. For Marxism, utility is not the basis or essence of truth, but its consequence; the pragmatists, on the other hand, subordinated truth to utility, or the efficacy or success of the actions of men, conceived as subjective, individual acts rather than as objective, material, transforming activity. The difference between the Marxist and the pragmatist conception of truth determines the distinction between their respective criteria of truth. Marxism tests the truth by assessing to what degree it represents a spiritual reproduction of reality; pragmatism to prove that what is true is useful. Both, it is true, locate the law of truth in practice itself, but that apparent coincidence is given the lie by the very different understanding of practice characteristic of one and the other. In the one case, practice is simply individual, subjective action designed to satisfy individual interests; in the other, it is objective, transforming activity responding to social interests which consists, from the socio-historical point of view, not only in the production of a material reality, but in the creation and unfolding of a human world.

For pragmatism, success is the criterion of truth, or the efficacy of man's practical actions; for Marxism, it is practice conceived as a material, transforming, *social* activity. While the pragmatist finds truth revealed in success, in the harmony of thought with my interests, the Marxist looks to social practice, to the consistency of thought and reality, to reveal the truth or falseness of a theory. Marxism and pragmatism, in short, hold diametrically opposed positions on the question of the conception and criterion of truth, and above all in their mode of perceiving practice.[4] In the final analysis, pragmatism, like ordinary consciousness, makes utility the arbiter of practice.

In the history of philosophy, the relation of theory and practice takes on other forms, and is usually presented in more absolute terms, either because theory is regarded as so omnipotent that it conceives of itself as praxis (a position characteristic of Idealism and particularly the Young Hegelians) or because practice itself is dismissed as the mere application, or degradation, of theory (as the Ancient Greeks held). In both cases, the implication is that practice can offer theory nothing. Such an absolute position, however, is rare, and the discussion has usually proceeded in terms of the relative autonomy or dependence of theory and practice within the framework of their essential unity. The problem can be posed at two levels: a) on a socio-historical level, as particular forms of the behaviour of men as socio-historical beings, in their relation to nature and to society; b) in given practical activities like the production of a useful object, the creation of a work of art, the transformation of the State and the inauguration of new social relations.

Practice as the foundation of theory

Practice, then, determines the development and progress of knowledge, and theory and practice are interdependent. In Engels' terms: "Natural science, like philosophy, has hitherto entirely neglected the influence of men's activity on their thought; both know only nature on the one hand and thought on the other. But it is precisely *the alteration of nature by men,* not solely nature as such, which is the most essential and immediate basis of human thought, and it is in the measure that man has learned to change nature that his intelligence has increased."[5] Scientific-natural knowledge advances on a par with the process of the transformation of the natural world, since the practical relation that man establishes with the world through material production presents new demands that broaden the horizons of both the problems that men must face and the solutions they must find.

Knowledge of natural forces originates with the development of man's dominion over those forces in the early stages of material production. The pretheoretical, magical or narrowly empiricist conception of nature is associated with a narrow, limited practice devoid of theoretical elements. Such a limited practice, due to the low level of development of productive forces and, therefore, to man's limited dominion over them, could be realised without reference to scientific knowledge of them. At this level, men would not seek causal relations between phenomena, but would be content to attribute them to the action of supernatural forces. When the forces of nature are as yet not integrated into production, pretheoretical, empirical knowledge is sufficient for man's practical needs. Theoretical knowledge, and its indispensable logical categories of quality, quantity, space and causality, arose on the basis of empirical knowledge accumulated over the centuries.[6] This initial phase of human knowledge is linked to the need to build the first instruments of labour, and to the demands of primitive productive practices, like hunting, agriculture and herding. It was precisely in slave society that there occurred a social division of labour which gave added impetus to theoretical activity by ensuring for it a relative autonomy within the context of its close association with practical needs. In the conditions of slave society, there had already been a progressive development of productive forces, coupled with a perfection of the instruments of production which necessarily set theoretical tasks intimately related to productive activity. From then onwards, theoretical knowledge, and even the most advanced forms of scientific activity, have progressed in concert with the practical needs of man.[7]

Science and production

The relations between the techniques of production and science vary from one socio-economic formation to another, and change according to the character and object of the particular science. It can be established historically, however, that a low level of development of productive forces makes fewer demands of science, so that science itself develops at a slower and less decisive rate. In fact, those demands have only increased in rigour and extension in the modern age, as material production has increased consistently with the emergence of a new social class, the bourgeoisie, dedicated to the transformation of nature in its own interests. In these socio-historical conditions, the progress of natural-scientific knowledge, constituted as modern science, becomes a pressing practical and social necessity. The progress towards a firm and coherent scientific theory gains impetus, in its turn from experience, whether it be the direct experience of production or the organised and controlled experience of experimental activity.

One of the sciences to have derived most benefit from the exigencies of production is physics. Its birth as such is late; neither Ancient Greece nor the Middle Ages had accorded it independent status. The weak development of productive forces in Greek slave society and in feudal society restricted both the need and the potential for its development. In fact, it arose in response to the practical needs of modern industry, and received its earliest expression in the work of Galileo. The characteristic relation of theory and practice in physics, however, only became clear as the result of the development of another science, chemistry, at an even later stage, for it was first constituted as a science in the course of the 18th and 19th centuries. What had persisted until then was little more than an extension of the old alchemy, retaining all its fantastic and mystical apparatus; for this pseudo-science had been so linked to a practical, experimental activity devoid of theory, that it had lacked both theoretical significance and a practical character in the true sense. The adoption of principles and methods already discovered by modern physics in response to the exigencies of new areas of production, like metallurgy, the dyeing industry, the textile and pharmaceutical industries etc., gave powerful impetus to the development of the new science of chemistry. Indeed its close connections with industry have continued into our day, providing a guarantee of its continuing enrichment and progress. In general terms, then, the sciences that progress most rapidly are those whose development is an essential precondition of the technical progress demanded by production itself which serves as a necessary mediation between production and the sciences.

The links between mathematics and production are less direct, which might explain why, in Ancient Greece (the age of Euclidian geometry), mathematics should have been so far in advance of the simply speculative physics of Aristotle. Mathematics could only serve production directly when productive practice posed its problems in the form of technical exigencies linked only indirectly to production itself, through the mediation of that branch of science most directly linked to its technico-productive requirements. The demand for the development of new mathematical abstractions, therefore, came from physics rather than production itself. In its origins mathematics was directly linked to practical needs and to the world of things. Geometry was born in Egypt, as a result of the need to delimit the areas of land periodically covered by silt left by the waters of the Nile, while Euclidian geometry had as its premisses the direct observation of the geometric properties of actual bodies with which men had a more or less direct relationship. It was only later that geometric forms were abstracted from their content, and geometric properties expressed through abstract propositions which were later integrated into a single deductive system with the aid of formal logic. That was the Euclidian system of geometry. Thus the concepts of Euclidian geometry had their origin in the real objects upon which men executed their practical activity, and whose real properties were then submitted to a process of generalisation and abstraction. Engels, for example, offered a similar interpretation in his critique of the Idealist conception of the origins of Euclidian geometry: "The concepts of number and figure have not been derived from any source other than the world of reality... There must have been things which had shape and whose shapes were compared before anyone could arrive at the idea of figure. Pure mathematics deals with the space forms and quantity relations of the real world; that is, with material which is very real indeed... Before one came upon the idea of deducing the *form* of a cylinder from the rotation of the rectangle about one of its sides, a number of real rectangles and cylinders, however imperfect in form, must have been examined."[8] We cannot, however, apply Engels' conclusions about Euclidian geometry to the development of mathematical thought in general.[9] Theory does enjoy an autonomy which, although not absolute, is nevertheless sufficient to enable it to establish a direct relation with already existing theories, either by extension or by negation. Thus, while the observation of the geometric properties of real bodies as a result of practical need was the starting-point for Euclidian geometry, non-Euclidian geometry, as Toth observes, emerged as a true intellectual creation arising out of the negation of existing geometry.[10]

Mathematics, then, does not satisfy practical needs in a direct way, but in relation to the theoretical problems posed by physics, and on occasion of technology itself. The development of differential calculus, for example, was not unrelated to the need to develop new and more useful machinery; the elaboration of Fourier's series obeyed the need to study the thermic phenomena associated with the development of the steam engine; the study of complex variables and operational calculus was stimulated by the need to resolve problems posed by technical progress. The relations between mathematics and practical demands have been more direct at times: the great maritime discoveries of the Modern Age, for example, contributed directly to the development of trigonometry; the calculation of probabilities became a matter of urgency as English foreign trade extended in association with the growth of English colonialism, and therefore increased the commercial risks and losses involved. Thus, in ways both direct and indirect, the technical progress associated with production has provided a constant impetus to mathematics. Even today, the development of quantum physics has provided a new stimulus to mathematics, as physics has turned to it for means to describe and explain their discoveries. The experimental practice of physics throws up constant demands for new mathematical abstractions, and mathematics seeks to answer that call.[11]

At another level, the development of production is linked to the use of powerful sources of energy, the guarantee of which poses new questions for science both in the present and in the immediate future. The practical need to raise the level of consumption of energy, and the none too remote possibility that some sources of energy may soon be exhausted, poses the urgent task for science and technology of discovering new energy sources. This involves very complex theoretical and technical problems, like the achievement of a controlled thermonuclear reaction and the transformation of solar into electrical energy. In the field of agriculture, stock-rearing, and medicine, selection has become a priority, and has posed for biological science the need to grapple with the complex problems related to the discovery of the chemical processes of inheritance and reproduction.[12] And we are witnessing the birth of a series of new branches of science related to the penetration and assimilation of the cosmos (cosmic biology, cosmic medicine etc.). The framework of a new practical human activity, which we might call cosmic praxis, is now being developed, which will exercise an as yet unsuspected influence on the future development of science. The creation and development of cybernetics, the science of administering complex, dynamic processes, responds in large part to demands posed in the present moment by ever more complex technico-productive processes, by the increasingly uncontrollable interaction of greater and greater numbers of individuals engaged in economic and military activities, by the gigantic growth in the resources and material means brought into play by those activities etc., all of which has made it imperative to refine the techniques of management. This need could only be satisfied by the development of a new science, cybernetics, whose theoretical origins lay in mathematics and in logic. In the same way, specific branches of this new science have arisen as a result of the automation of production. In all these ways, contemporary practice constitutes a powerful source of the development of theory. To the extent that theory is linked to the practical needs of social man, practice in its broadest sense, and production in particular, provide the foundation of theoretical progress.

In our day, the links between science and production represent a specific form of the unity of theory and practice; production has been the cause of a vigorous scientific development, but at the same time the increase in productive forces would have been inconceivable without a corresponding progress in science. Science not only provides an external resource for production, but is also central to the productive process, refining its tools and its machines; thus theory takes an objective, material form in that process. Marx himself pointed to the unity of science and production, whereby the former necessarily intervenes in productive activity to the extent that it is given objective form in the instruments of labour created by man. "Nature builds no machines, no locomotives, railways, electric telegraphs, self-acting mules etc. These are products of human industry, natural material transformed into organs of the human will over nature, or of human participation in nature. They are *organs of the human brain, created by the human hand;* the power of knowledge, objectified."[13] Thus science, the theoretical form of knowledge about reality, intervenes directly in production as an ideal factor given objective, material form in the productive process. This, in our view, is the import of Marx's characterisation of science in these terms: "The development of fixed capital indicates to what degree general social knowledge has become a *direct force of production,* and to what degree, hence, the conditions of the process of social life, have come under the control of the general intellect, and have been transformed in accordance with it. To what degree the powers of social production have been produced not only in the form of knowledge, but also as immediate organs of social practice, of the real life process."[14]

When society reaches a certain stage in its development, not only does production come to determine science, but it becomes integrated into production itself as its spiritual power, or directly as a productive force. In this way theory and practice unite and become one.

Unity of theory and revolutionary praxis

What may validly be said about the relations between productive material practice and scientific activity is equally applicable in the field of social life, particularly with respect to the relationship between theory and revolutionary practice. Marx and Engels, for example, stressed in their theoretical writings the crucial role played by social practice in their conception and development. Their theory of revolution evolved in close relation to practical activity; as the revolutionary struggle of the proletariat broadened its scope and yielded new possibilities, new solutions were elaborated. This development, however, must be seen against the background of earlier doctrines, particularly those of Weitling or Blanqui who, while they advocated a radical transformation of society, were so divorced from actual practice that they remained vulnerable to Utopian and adventurist interpretations. In the *Communist Manifesto* of 1848, published some months before the European revolutions of that year, Marx and Engels expounded their theory of revolution in a mature and scientific way. In that work the authors argued that the proletarian revolution was the historically necessary culmination of the struggle between the proletariat and the bourgeoisie, the resolution of the antagonism between classes stemming from the fundamental contradictions between bourgeois relations of production and the development of productive forces. They reaffirmed the world-historical mission of the proletariat, and began to formulate its concrete revolutionary tasks—the creation of its own party and of its own political power, ensuring the means whereby it could exercise its historical mission.

Marx and Engels built their theory of the ends, tasks and means to success of the revolutionary struggle upon a variety of foundations. From *The German Ideology* onwards, the fruits of previous research into the conditions that explain the socio-historical necessity of revolution were added studies of the practical revolutionary struggle of the German, French and English working class against the bourgeoisie. The *Manifesto* reflected contemporary revolutionary praxis: to move too far beyond that praxis would have entailed the risk of falling into Utopianism. In his *State and Revolution,* Lenin stressed that Marx and Engels' doctrine of the State and the proletarian revolution laid considerable emphasis upon the links between theory and practice. In this sense, Lenin recognised that the theoretical limitations of the *Manifesto* had to be understood in terms of the insufficiency of the very practice on which it was based and of the necessity to await new contributions to the revolutionary activity of the working class that might provide solutions to problems that the authors of the *Manifesto* were unable to solve. The *Manifesto* was by no means the final expression of Marxist theory of the State and the proletarian revolution. Marx and Engels themselves continued to develop and elaborate upon it in the light of new experiences offered by the practical activity of the proletariat in the field of class struggle in general and its highest manifestation—revolutionary practice—in particular. Thus the bourgeois revolutions of 1848-9 in a number of European countries, in which the working class took an active part, were of considerable significance for the founders of Marxism, despite the defeats in which they ended. In *Revolution and Counter-revolution in Germany* (1851), *The class struggles in France* (1850) and *The 18th Brumaire of Louis Napoleon* (1852), Marx assessed the revolutionary experiences of 1848-51. In doing so, he was able to gauge the validity of the theory developed up to that time, and determine to what extent experience afforded opportunities to expand and enrich the theory. In fact the revolutionary movements of those years seemed to Marx and Engels to confirm the theoretical propositions of the *Manifesto*—the class struggle as the motor of history, the necessity for the revolutionary transformation of society, the class character of the State etc. Practice does not serve, however, merely to corroborate theory; it is its very basis, and its lessons can allow current limits to be surpassed as new facets and solutions are added to the corpus of revolutionary theory. The thesis of permanent revolution, and of the possibility of an uninterrupted transition from the bourgeois to the proletarian revolution when the first is carried to its furthest limits, emerged directly from the revolutionary experience of 1848-51. In Marx's view that experience had confirmed the need to expand his theses on the State, for it had shown that the assumption of power by the proletariat did not necessarily lead, as he had suggested in the *Manifesto,* to the establishment of its political authority. The machinery of the bourgeois State, that is its military-bureaucratic system, had to be destroyed. In his commentary on the corresponding passage in Marx's *18th Brumaire,* Lenin stressed the difference between an abstract presentation of the question of the State in the *Manifesto* and the concrete way in which it is discussed in the *18th Brumaire* which permitted Marx to derive a precise and practical conclusion: "All previous revolutions have perfected the State machine, whereas it must be broken, smashed."[15] Marx was only able to reach that conclusion, however, as a result of the historical experience of the revolutionary years of 1848-51. As Lenin put it, "it was not logical reasoning, but actual developments, the actual experience of 1848-51, that led to the matter being presented in this way."[16] What should *take the place* of the State apparatus was a different matter, and one on which experience had not uttered—nor could it yet have done so—its final word. Marx was not to find the solution until later, as Lenin said: "Experience had not yet provided material for dealing with this question, which history placed on the agenda later on, in 1871."[17]

In the meantime, Marx continued to make rigorous demands of his developing theory of revolution; clearly he did not consider that the task derived its momentum from an analysis of revolutionary practice. That analysis could only provide an adequate basis if it were set within a theory of the emergence and character of the appropriate social formation, that is, of capitalism. It is for that reason that in the years immediately following the revolutions of 1848-51, Marx and Engels devoted themselves above all to the study and analysis of those experiences, and discussed in particular the problems directly posed by them—class struggle, revolution, the State etc. During the next period, Marx turned his theoretical attention to the capitalist mode of production, whose fundamental contradictions necessarily led to revolution. The assessment of revolutionary practice had therefore served to clarify and provide a firmer basis for the theory of revolution. In his economic works—*Capital* and the preparatory writings of 1857-9—Marx moved on to consider scientifically the laws and structures of capitalist socio-economic formations. His analysis was apparently restricted to the capitalist mode of production and, in particular, to its fundamental concepts: commodity, value, abstract and concrete labour, surplus value. It was carried to a point, however, where its very scientific character was to distinguish *Capital* from the work of the Classical economists (like Adam Smith and Ricardo) and from all previous economic theories. There is a clear distinction as far as the questions and objects of analysis are concerned. If we are to understand how radical are the implications of that break, it is not sufficient simply to point to the scientific character of the analysis presented in *Capital;* for Marx had aspired in that work to lay a theoretical foundation for revolutionary praxis. The same concern that had led him to analyse the revolutionary experiences of 1848-51 was to lead him years later to investigate the fundamental laws and concepts of capitalist production. It is no coincidence that *Capital* should have opened with a profound analysis of commodity and ended with an analysis of social class, albeit that Marx could only devote to this latter aspect some twenty lines of a chapter that he was never able to complete.[18]

The revolutionary praxis of the proletariat cannot be theoretically elucidated nor directed in practice without reference to an accurate, objective and scientific appraisal of the conditions that render capitalist relations of production possible and necessary. It was this indispensable theoretical task that Marx set out to accomplish with *Capital*, his contribution to the real and effective transformation of capitalist society. For Marx, the object of laying bare the basic laws and concepts of capitalist production and exposing the antagonistic contradictions to which it gives rise, was to provide a scientific explanation for the necessity of the transition from capitalism to socialism. In his writings after the revolutionary period of 1848-51, Marx developed a theory that had grown out of the practice reflected and analysed in those works. With *Capital*, that theory, expressed in a scientific way, became the indispensable precondition of a new praxis.

In the final analysis, no reading of *Capital* can fail to recognise there a theory not only based upon the special productive practice of capitalism, but determined also by the necessity for a revolutionary praxis of the proletariat. The failure to take account of either aspect could lead us to drive a wedge between theory and practice, and thus ignore the fact that what was essential for Marx was that the revolutionary substitution of socialism for capitalism and the historical mission of the agent of that transformation—the proletariat—should rest on a scientific basis. Lenin's affirmation that there could be no possible revolutionary movement without revolutionary theory makes it clear that his concept of theory embraced not only the theoretical understanding of a given revolutionary praxis and the analysis and evaluation of the experience of it, but also a study of the objective conditions which, on one or another historical level, determine the possibility and necessity of that praxis. *Capital* exposes the transitory nature of the capitalist system and demonstrates the necessity for its substitution. It is for this reason that *Capital* is integral to the Marxist theory of revolution. Indeed Marx's own words (in the Preface to the second German edition) could be dialectically applied to his own work:

> "It is a scandal and an abomination to bourgeoisdom and its doctrinaire professors, because it includes in its comprehension and affirmative recognition of the existing state of things, at the same time also, the recognition of the negation of that state, of its inevitable breaking up; because it regards every historically developed social form as a fluid movement, and therefore takes into account its transient nature not less than its momentary existence; because it lets nothing impose upon it, and is in its essence critical and revolutionary."[19]

That critical and revolutionary character is manifest in Marx's analysis of capitalism in *Capital* precisely because of its scientific and dialectical precision.

It is evident, on the other hand, that the theory of revolution cannot be reduced to a study of the socio-economic forms or objective conditions that might broadly explain the necessity for revolutionary change. It must also draw constantly on an analysis of the practical human activity conditioned by that necessity and of revolutionary praxis in particular. In this sense practice provides an inexhaustible source of reference for theory; that is why Marx, absorbed though he was in a scientific task that was to continue until his death, returned to the analysis of practical experience whenever that experience seemed to overflow the boundaries of a theoretical framework erected on the basis of previous revolutionary activity. The revolutions of 1848-51 had called forth new contributions to the Marxist theory of the State, but they had, at the same time, posed a series of questions to which no answer could be found in the historical experience to which reference could be made at that time. It was therefore necessary to wait for history to yield the materials, as Lenin observed, with which to resolve the concrete problem of what was to *replace* the military-bureaucratic machinery of the bourgeois State.[20] As Marx had expected, history did respond. The Paris Commune of 1871 was a first attempt at proletarian revolution, a first attempt to destroy and replace the bourgeois State machinery. Marx analysed this concrete experience in *The civil war in France,* a significant and far-reaching contribution to theory. Lenin stressed the importance of practical experience for the elaboration of theory as a characteristic feature of a method designed to free us from Utopianism: "(Marx) examined the actual experience of a mass proletarian movement and tried to draw practical lessons from it. He 'learned' from the Commune, just as all the great revolutionary thinkers learned unhesitatingly from the great movements of the oppressed classes..."[21]

Lenin's method itself presupposed the role of practice as the basis of theory in his own contribution to revolutionary theory, a contribution that draws upon the revolutionary experiences of the Russian people in 1905 and in February and October 1917. The revolutionary practice of those great movements led him to confirm Marx's basic theses, although Lenin had to deal with concrete historical experiences that went beyond those on which Marx had based his analysis. It is important to remember that, on the international level, the capitalist world had entered a new, imperialist phase. If he was to pose the question of proletarian revolution in an objective and scientific way, Lenin had to analyse this fundamental change. His analysis of the economics and politics of imperialism led him to conclude that the world capitalist system was ripe for revolutionary transformation. Yet that transformation was clearly not going to conform to the perspectives developed by Marx and Engels in their time; the simultaneous victory of the revolution in a majority of capitalist countries, for example, seemed less real a possibility for Lenin, who discussed the possibility of revolution in one country and indeed saw that possibility realised in concrete historical conditions that Marx had not anticipated; those of a backward capitalist country in which the fundamental contradictions between the forces of production and relations of production had not yet reached their sharpest point. On the basis of revolutionary experience, and a concrete analysis of concrete situations (the basic elements of revolutionary theory in Marx), Lenin enriched that theory through the introduction of a number of new concepts of fundamental importance; the idea of the hegemony of the proletariat, and for the existence of a number of paths to revolution—chief among them being the violent path; the conception of the Party as a conscious, organised and advanced detachment of the proletariat; the fundamental notions of "the revolutionary situation", "the revolutionary crisis" and "the unity of the subjective and the objective factors (or conditions) necessary for the success of the revolution"; the thesis of the alliance of the proletariat and the peasantry within the socialist revolution etc. Lenin had held more rigorously to the spirit than to the letter of Marx's ideas. He had applied his own methods of analysis of the concrete conditions that give rise to and make possible a revolutionary praxis, and had then applied his analytical method to that praxis itself. Like Marx he did not see the development of theory simply as a logical process, but as a response to, and a function of practice. Revolutionary theory does not progress in terms of theory itself, but in accordance with praxis; its rigorously objective and scientific character links it necessarily to a practice designed to resolve the contradictions experienced in the real world.

In present circumstances, the method developed and applied by Marx and Lenin is the only one that can ensure the unity of theory and practice with regard to the theoretical and practical questions that have caused such deep divergences within the world communist movement. These questions have covered an extremely wide range; the problems of war and peace, peaceful coexistence, the fundamental contradictions of our age, the decision as to which are the most important battle fronts, and which the principal battleground in the world struggle against imperialism, the role that the socialist countries should play in that struggle, the relative significance in the advance towards socialism of the proletariat in the advanced capitalist countries and the peoples of the so-called Third World, the priority of the peaceful or the violent road to socialism etc. No research into the writings of Marx, however thorough, can provide direct answers to any of these questions. The significance of those writings lies in the fact that they represent a response to concrete situations of greater or lesser historical importance, and that they were confirmed in practice. When actual experience goes beyond the historical experience that Marx had at his disposal, then his theses must be amplified and brought up to date if they are to continue to be of value. The method of analysis, on the other hand, is as valid today as ever; a concrete analysis of concrete situations, coupled with an analysis and evaluation of the corresponding political activity. This is our only guarantee of the unity of theory and practice, a principle whose value all Marxists acknowledge, though not all apply it consistently. Any analysis of the contemporary situation, for example, must, as Lenin insisted, take into account the changes that have occurred in the capitalist system in recent years with the development of State monopoly capitalism and the resulting modifications in capitalist relations of production. These changes do not, of course, signify that capitalism has in any way changed its basic character. The theory must also consider the enormous expansion in the forces of production, due to unprecedented scientific and technological advances, as well as the contradictions between the growth of these forces and the maintenance of existing relations of production. The influence and repercussions of the October Revolution, that so radically changed the course of human history, must also cause Marxist theory to be modified accordingly; nor can that theory neglect the historical contribution of the Chinese Revolution, the far-reaching impact of the decolonisation of two continents—Africa and Asia—and the implications of the Cuban Revolution, which opened the way to the foundation of the first socialist state in Latin America. These profound world-historical changes have repercussions for Marxism, implying an increasingly complex set of theoretical demands; a higher scientific and ideological level, for example, which can only be achieved by close reference to social practice, and in particular to the revolutionary movement of the working class and the struggle of oppressed peoples for their national emancipation. Marx, Engels and Lenin demonstrated in an irrefutable way that theoretical activity can only be fruitful if it does not lose its nexus with that reality that is the object both of interpretation and of transformation. It must retain throughout its links with the practical activity that is its source.

Practice as the end of theory

The development of theory cannot be tied exclusively to the demands of current practice. If it were, it could neither anticipate nor influence (and that influence is often decisive) developments in practice. It follows that the relation between theory and practice must be considered at a new level; as a relation between an already elaborated theory and a practice that has still to be developed. This problem merits a slightly more detailed discussion.

Revolutionary theory must be responsive not only to an ongoing practical activity that gives sustained impetus to the development of theory, but also to a still non-existent practice, or one that is present only in embryonic form. It is possible for man to recognise the need for new levels of practical activity in his struggle to transform the world, even if he lacks the appropriate theoretical framework. In this instance, the direction of theory is determined by an anticipated practice from which it is not yet possible to glean any concrete lessons. Thus theory is determined by something that as yet exists only in an ideal form. What repercussions does this have for theory itself? It confirms that theory is limited by what we have called the end, the ideal anticipation of an activity that cannot yet be seen in action although there exists a desire that it should. In this case, practice is the end that determines theory. Like every other end, this practice—or rather the project or ideal anticipation of it—will only be effective to the extent that it is informed by theory. For practice, seen as the end of theory, demands a consciousness of the relationship that must exist between the two, or a consciousness of the practical necessities which theory may help to resolve. The transformation of theory into a theoretical instrument of praxis requires a heightened consciousness of the links that mutually connect theory and practice, without which the practical significance of theory could not be understood. It is in this light that new branches of science are being developed today, that look ahead to a practice that does not currently inform any level of action (cosmic practice), and whose beginnings are even now scarcely discernible.

The demands made by practical activity broaden the scope of both the problems and the solutions that are sought for them; in this sense, practice is the origin of theory. Yet it is also an end, the anticipation of an ideal practice. This demonstrates that the relation between theory and practice cannot be discussed in simplistic, mechanical terms, as if every theory were based in a direct and immediate way on practice. There clearly are specific theories that bear no direct relation to practical activity; but what we are concerned with here is the relationship that is established between theory and practice in the course of a socio-historical process that has both theoretical and practical implications. In fact the history of theory (of human knowledge in its totality) and of praxis (of man's practical activities) are abstractions from a single historical process; the history of man. It would be simply mechanistic to divide that history into two abstract parts, and then try to establish some direct or immediate relation between a practical and a theoretical segment. The relationship is neither direct nor immediate, but operates by way of a complex process that sometimes moves from practice towards theory, and sometimes from theory to practice. The practical activities that are the current source of theory call up, in their turn, a practice that does not yet exist. In this way theory (the project for a practice yet to come) determines actual, effective practice. Theory that is not as yet related to practice, because it is in some sense in advance of it, can establish the link at a later stage. The theories or mathematical concepts that found no practical application when they were first developed, but which have now proved their usefulness in specific practical situations, demonstrate the point. To speak of practice as the basis and the end of theory does not require us to assert that the relationship is direct or immediate, for it is possible for a theory to emerge—and the history of science offers frequent examples of occasions on which it does—that satisfies directly or immediately certain theoretical exigencies, that is, that resolves difficulties or contradictions encountered in another theory. Moreover, theory emerges in the last instance as an element of the socio-historical process, not as a result of some parallel but rigidly separate process of development, but in response to practical needs: thus its source is in practice.

The dependence of theory on practice, and the role of the latter as the final object of theory demonstrate the primacy of practice, seen as total human praxis. Far from implying that practice provides a counterpart to theory, however, this conclusion confirms the intimate connection between the two.

Praxis and the comprehension of praxis

To deny the relative autonomy of theory is to falsely interpret the unity of theory and practice, and to maintain that practice automatically evolves into theory, and that the rationality or truth of practice becomes automatically clear. The unity of theory and practice can only be correctly discussed if practice is presented as an objective activity, directed at the transformation of the natural and social world, and not as any kind of subjective activity, even if that subjective activity is called objective practice, as the pragmatists do. The mystical and fantastic experiences of alchemy, accumulated through fifteen centuries, had not been capable of revealing any new truths nor of provoking any new theory.

By practice, then, we understand a practical social activity transforming reality in obedience to practical needs and implying a certain degree of knowledge of the reality it transforms and the needs it satisfies. Yet practice cannot explain itself; it is not directly theoretical. As Marx points out in his Eighth Thesis on Feuerbach, beyond practice lies a further stage—the comprehension of that practice, without which its rationality remains hidden. That comprehension requires the development of an adequate theoretical framework. Experimental scientific practice, for example, can only be meaningful for the scientist whose knowledge of the corresponding conceptual language enables him to interpret it. Science provides the key to an understanding and knowledge of its own experimental practice. It falls to the physicist or the chemist to interpret and evaluate the laboratory experience. Economic practice—production—is an everyday fact; but its truth, its rationality, can only become apparent to those who are able to interpret the corresponding economic categories. Commodities do not immediately present themselves as the embodiment of a social relation, a product of social labour, but, as Marx shows in *Capital*,[22] as "fetishes." The struggles of the proletariat do not in themselves lead to an understanding of the socio-historical necessity of the proletarian revolution and the world-historical mission of the working class. Only the transformation of socialism from Utopia into science, together with the development of an adequate theoretical framework, have allowed the proletariat, and in particular its most conscious vanguard, to reach an understanding of its own revolutionary praxis.

It may be said that practice will clarify itself, rendering theory superfluous, when relations between men lose their mystified character, cease to have the character of relations between things and become clear and transparent; then practice might seem to have rendered its theory unnecessary. That is the situation that should occur with the disappearance of the capitalist mode of production and the creation of a new society, above all when it has reached its highest stage of development—communism. When they are freed of such mystification, social relations lose their opacity. Marx has sometimes been interpreted in this way,[23] so that the realisation of philosophy would signify either an end to its usefulness or its conversion into a positive science which would, in its turn, become little more than theoretical technique. Science would be a mere reflection of practice, and practice would become the foundation of a science which could offer, on the other hand, no reciprocal source of reference for practice. Human praxis, and the comprehension of it, would coincide and it would then, perhaps, become meaningless to speak of philosophy or of spiritual production under communism, since the distinctions between spiritual and material production would have disappeared.[24] The kind of communist society that Marx had envisaged would be characterised, in this view, by such a primacy of the practical that the theoretical element would be reduced to practice and finally disappear. In a word, praxis would necessarily be of itself theoretical.

This conception of the unity of theory and practice was maintained by some Soviet economists during the early years of socialist construction in the USSR. They held that social relations in socialism would lose the mystified character they had had under capitalism (where things are personified and people reified), and from this they concluded that a science or economic theory of socialism had become unnecessary, since socialist social relations were clear and transparent. In our day, there is no shortage of Marxist writers who draw inspiration from analogous arguments—the transparency of social relations, the conscious and creative nature of praxis—in order to continue to speak not of the unity, but of the *identity,* of theory and practice, in the sense that "all practical activity involved in the process of communist construction is, at the same time theoretical."[25]

However clear and transparent social relations may be, and however high the level of consciousness and creativity of human practical activity, far from excluding the need for theory and its relative autonomy, that activity itself necessarily presupposes that autonomy. Theory and practice are linked, and their boundaries in this connection are relative; but they can never break down completely. It is impossible to move from a recognition of the determining role of practice as a basis, an end and a criterion of true knowledge, to the conclusion that theory and practice are one and the same thing, and that theoretical activity transforms itself automatically into practice. Practice, as we have said, does not speak for itself; it is necessary that there should be a theoretical link, and that link is the comprehension of praxis.

Praxis as a criterion of truth

We must guard against the possibility that this interpretation might lead us into another, equally false, thesis that has been characteristic of the Idealist theory of knowledge, namely the negation of practice as a criterion of truth. In our view, such a negation is incompatible with the Marxist conception of praxis and with Marxist theory in general. Practice cannot speak for itself, and its position as basis for theory or as a criterion for testing the validity of theory is not given in a direct or immediate way. We are bound to reject this empiricist conception of practice, for practice can only be used as a criterion of truth if there is a theoretical link with practical activity itself. Clearly, every science has at its disposal concepts and methods that allow it to establish the appropriate practice as a criterion of truth. Practice alone cannot determine whether something is true or false, that is without a mediating theory. This does not mean that it is not, in the final analysis, the criterion of truth, nor that we should seek confirmation of this criterion in logical or esoteric procedures which are the exclusive province of theoretical activity.[26] It is the practice of the working class movement and the socialist revolutions of our century that have confirmed, for example, the Marxist theory of the world-historical role of the proletariat. Nonetheless, it has been incumbent upon theory to establish, through analysis and interpretation, to what degree practice did confirm theory.[27] It is perfectly correct to renounce the empiricist thesis that practice is a criterion of truth; there is no justification, however, for going on to renounce practice altogether as a criterion of validity in order to seek that criterion in theoretical activity alone, whether it is called theoretical or scientific praxis or not. To do so is to abandon a thesis fundamental to Marxism, and to substitute for it an old Idealist thesis from which Marx had already broken in his *Theses on Feuerbach*.

The relative autonomy of theory

Although practice retains its primacy with respect to theory, this does not entail the dissolution of theory into practice, nor of practice into theory, for their relation is one of unity, but not of identity. Theory can enjoy a relative autonomy, but the determinant role belongs to practice, which is the foundation, the criterion of truth and the object of theory. Yet that autonomy is an essential element of theory's role in practice itself, allowing theory to move in advance of practice, rather than restricting it to a rearguard, confirming role. Knowledge of an object or phenomenon can provide a basis for an ideal representation of its present and future development; knowledge of the laws governing an object can enable us to foresee certain tendencies in its development and thus anticipate future phases in its progress. The relative autonomy of theory enables it to produce an ideal model of the object and hence to propitiate a non-existent practice by moving in advance of actual progress at the level of the ideal. Were it not able to do so, theory would be no more than a simple and direct expression of existing practice, and it would be difficult to see what practical function it could fulfil as a theoretical instrument. For example, non-Euclidian geometries, like that of Lobachevski,[28] or Einstein's theoretical formulation of the relation of mass and energy, retain a certain autonomy with respect to practice, since it was only later, and precisely because they had advanced from a basis in practice, that their theories could become directly relevant to practice. So the instrumental capacity of theory derives from its capacity to elaborate an ideal model of a future process, and only thus can it achieve a role in productive or social praxis. That role, however, requires that theory allow itself to be permeated by practice, for, as we have underlined more than once, theory itself cannot transform anything real; that is, it is not praxis.

The unity of theory and practice implies at once a relative opposition and a relative autonomy, located in practice itself. A theory that does not demand realisation, that cannot be given shape, sustains a merely theoretical existence divorced from practice. The Utopian socialist doctrine, for example, failed to be realised because its autonomy actually reflected its distance from practice; here, then, the autonomy which had been presented as the condition of possibility of its practical influence, now merely testifies to the sterility and impotence of theory. So from the point of view of praxis, the autonomy of theory can be positive or negative. But if theory, independently of its practical consequences, can enjoy a relative autonomy with respect to practice, practice requires a minimum of theoretical ingredients, a) knowledge of the reality that will be the object of his transformation; b) knowledge of the instruments and their use, of the techniques demanded by each practice, with which that transformation is to be carried out; c) knowledge of accumulated practice, in the form of a synthesis or generalisation of previous practice in a given sphere; for man can only transform the world, by starting from a given theoretical level, and inserting his own actual praxis into the corresponding practico-theoretical history; and d) a teleological activity, anticipating objective results in the form of ideals or ends which, in order to fulfil their practical function, must respond to real conditions and needs, take root in the consciousness of men and be able to count on adequate means for their fulfilment.[29]

So the dependence of theory upon practice has its counterpart in the fact that practical transformation of the world is tributary, in its turn, to certain preexisting theoretical elements. Thus the unity of theory and practice implies, in this way, their mutual dependence.

Practice as subjective and objective activity

Theory and practice, therefore, are two modes of human behaviour in the real world, which develop historically in a firm unity. It remains to examine the particular facets of that unity in the particular behaviour of given individuals, groups or social classes. We have already seen that praxis is a theoretico-practical activity, and that the separation of the theoretical from the practical, material side would be no more than an abstraction. To reduce it artifically, therefore, to theory alone, or even to speak of theoretical praxis, is equivalent to restricting praxis to its material aspect alone. Neither objective, theoretical activity, nor individual material activity, even though both can culminate in the production of objects (like the nest built by a bird), can become praxis as long as the subjective, theoretical aspect represented by the consciousness of action, is absent.

Practical human activity as such transcends the limitations of subjectivity when the practical subject transforms some material thing, external to him, thus integrating the subjective into the objective process. But this can only occur when the material or object of that activity exists independently of the subject's consciousness; the practical subject requires a sphere of activity that is something more than a simple projection of his own subjective world. In this way, the result of his activity comes to have an objective character that we may call human, but which retains its independence from the life, ends or projects with which it was genetically associated. The activity of the practical subject unfolds, then, along a double axis: on the one hand it is subjective, insofar as it represents the activity of his consciousness; it is also an objective process, in a more restricted sense, to the extent that the acts or operations which he executes upon a given material can be objectively perceived by other subjects. To this extent we can say that man's activity is objective because a) it is executed upon a reality independent of consciousness; b) it is carried out through a process, and with the aid of objective means and instruments, and c) it gives rise to an objective product or result.

Practical activity, therefore, is subjective and objective at the same time, dependent and independent of his consciousness, ideal and material. On the one hand, the subject preserves his individuality, but without confining himself within it; he is practical insofar as he objectifies himself, and to the extent that his products testify to that process of objectification.

The relation between the end, or product of consciousness, and the product in which it is given material form, as the actual result of activity, should not be seen in the Platonic sense of a relation between an original (the subjective) and a copy (the objective). In this light, what is realised would be no more than a simple duplication of a model existing ideally and subjectively prior to its realisation. The objective, or product, is the actual result of a process which has the ideal result, or end, as its starting-point. This end indeed presides over the whole process, and governs its various phases; yet there is always a certain disequilibrium between the ideal model and its realisation, which is deeper the greater the resistance offered by the material to the imposition of a form envisaged at the ideal level. As Marx says, the end governs "the modalities of action"; if the end is to be realised, however, the non-ideal must in its turn come into play and the ideal consequently enter a sphere in which its very dominion is constantly at risk. It is important, however, that the end continue to preside over the practical process; were it not so, consciousness would simply dissolve into practice. The role of consciousness is not simply to elaborate one end or immutable ideal model; the dynamic and unpredictable quality of the objective process must have its reflection in a dynamic consciousness. The game can never be won before it starts, other than in the case of inferior forms of praxis which we shall discuss later. The actual result is the culmination of a practical, objective process which always goes beyond the result ideally conceived. Consequently, consciousness remains active throughout the process, not only through its attempts to impose an original end, but also in transforming that end in the course of its realisation.

Practical activity entails not only the supremacy of the material over the ideal aspect, but also the modification of the ideal in the light of the exigencies of reality itself (raw material, objective acts, instruments or means, and products). Practice demands a constant movement from one level to another, a movement which can only be a result of the continuous intervention of consciousness in the practical process. So while it is true that practice, or individual praxis, is inseparable from the ends set out by consciousness, these ends are not finished predeterminations, but elements of a process in which the end or ideal result itself undergoes changes in the course of practice. Theoretical and practical activity adapt themselves to one another, moving in different ways (from hypothesis to hypothesis, or from one test to another), they converge in the objective product, or actual result. The modifications imposed on the original end in the pursuit of a more defined transition from subjective to objective, from the ideal to the real, provide additional proof of the unity of theory and practice in practical activity. For it is through an activity at once subjective and objective that the real, objective transformation of matter is achieved and the end realised or objectified. The most complete expression of the unity of theory and practice is this: that the realisation of an end is guided by a consciousness which can only fulfil that function to the extent that it is itself guided by the mode in which its ends are realised.

Notes

1 Marx and Engels' comments on Feuerbach in this respect can be applied to all speculative philosophy, that is, to all philosophy that limits itself to merely interpreting the world; "Feuerbach wants... like the theorists, merely to produce a correct consciousness about an *existing* fact, whereas for the real communist it is a question of overthrowing the existing state of things." (Marx/Engels: *The German Ideology: ed. cit.:* p. 54).

2 Gramsci attempts to establish what kind of link existed between "common sense" and religion on the one hand, and religion and philosophy on the other, and endeavoured to extend his analysis to the relations between Marxism, as a philosophy of praxis, and "common sense" (Cf: *Historical materialism and the philosophy of Benedetto Croce: ed. cit.*) Gramsci defines philosophy as "an intellectual order" which requires the overcoming of both religion and "common sense". Indeed he regarded the philosophy of praxis initially as a critique of "common sense", and therefore of religion: "... it tends not to maintain simple people in their primitive common sense philosophy, but on the contrary, to lead them towards a higher conception of life." (*Ibid.* p. 17). This is a necessary process because "active man, as part of the masses, works practically but has no clear theoretical consciousness of the significance of his labour." (*Ibid.* p. 17.). The importance which Gramsci attributes to his critique of common sense from the point of view of praxis is particularly manifest in his study of Bukharin's *Historical materialism,* where Gramsci reproaches him with not having carried out such a critique of common sense, or the "philosophy of the non-philosophers", and with having reduced his critique to the level of the systematic philosophers. (*Ibid.* p. 121.). On the

196   The Philosophy of Praxis

other hand, Gramsci did not hold to a unique and suprahistorical view of common sense, since he regarded it as a historical product; hence his references to the need to create a new common sense, and his assertion that "in Marx allusions are often found to common sense and the solidity of its beliefs . . ." which Gramsci interprets as "the implicit affirmation of the need for new beliefs, for a new common sense and hence for a new culture and a new philosophy rooted in popular consciousness with the same solid and imperative character as traditional beliefs." (*Ibid.* p. 123).

3   Cf. the pragmatist conception of truth expounded by William James in his works: *Philosophical conceptions and practical results* (1898); *Pragmatism: a new name for some old ways of thinking* (1909) and *The meaning of truth* (1909).

4   The following works provide more detailed analyses of the contradiction between Marxism and pragmatism from the Marxist point of view: Josef Linhart: *Americky pragmatismus* (Prague, 1949); Adam Schaff: *Z zagadnien marksistowskiej teorii prawdy* (Warsaw, 1951); M.N. Rutkevich: *Praktika-osnova poznanija i kriterii istiny* (Practice on the basis of knowledge and its criterion of truth—Moscow 1952) and Guy Besse: *Practique social et théorie:* (Paris, 1963).

5   F. Engels: *Dialectics of nature:* (Progress Publishers, London/Moscow, 1941), p. 172.

6   Cf: on the origins of theoretical knowledge in relation to practice, and on the formation of logical categories, A. Spirkin: *Proijozhdienie soznanija* (Moscow, 1960).

7   For an exposition of the historical relations between science and practice, particularly material production, see J.D. Bernal's excellent study *Science in history:* ed. cit.

8   F. Engels: *Anti-Dühring:* (Lawrence and Wishart, London, 1969) pp. 51-2.

9   It should be noted that in opposing the Idealist conception of geometry, Engels omitted one element which, as Manuel Sacristan correctly points out, "is essential from the Marxist point of view—the importance of practice in every aspect of human life, and therefore in the structure and function of scientific activity itself. That is why he conceived the construction of science in a static sense, as copies of nature, rather than as human responses to the problems posed by nature." (Manuel Sacristan: "La tarea de Engels en el *Anti-Dühring*" in the Spanish edition of *Anti-Dühring:* Mexico, 1964, pp. xx-xxi).

10   Cf. I. Toth: "Geometrie euclidienne et développement de la pensée" in *Etudes d'histoire et de philosophies des sciences* (Editions de l'Academie de la Republique Populaire Roumaine, Bucharest, n.d.), who, like Engels, stresses that geometry, and science in general, is not merely a reproduction of nature, but is constituted by building new concepts in various ways, including the concrete negation of existing concepts.

11   "The description of the properties of atoms requires not only the data

provided by adding machines, but crucially demands new physical concepts and mathematical abstractions" (V.A. Fok: "Polémica con Niels Bohr" in *Revista de filosofía,* Havana, No. 2, 1965, p. 101). Bohr, in his turn, agrees with Fok that "in order to explain the new laws revealed by research in the atomic processes characterised by their emission of large amounts of energy" it is "necessary to introduce new abstractions into our mathematical apparatus" (Niels Bohr: "La física cuántica y la filosofía" in *Ibid.* p. 110).

12 On the immense possibilities offered by contemporary science and technology for the satisfaction of basic human needs, see the interesting contribution by the Soviet sociologist M. Semenov to the International Colloquium at Toyaumont (May 1961), published as *Quel avenir attend l'homme?* (PUF, Paris, 1961), pp. 249-262.
13 Marx's *Grundrisse* (translated by Martin Nicolaus, Harmondsworth, Penguin, 1973) p. 706; [Hereafter referred to as *Grundrisse*].
14 *Ibid.* p. 706.
15 Lenin: *State and revolution* in *Works:* vol. 25, p. 406.
16 *Ibid.* p. 409.
17 *Ibid.* p. 409.
18 Karel Kosik lays great stress on this connection in *Capital* between commodity "as the historical form of the social labour of men" and "the practical-spiritual activity of human groups in production i.e. classes." Knowledge of the system, of its laws of movement and of its destruction if the "*sine qua non* if the odyssey of historical praxis is to culminate in revolutionary praxis." (K. Kosik: *Dialektika konkretinho: ed. cit.:* pp. 126-8).
19 *Capital I:* p. 20.
20 Lenin: *State and revolution* in *Works:* vol. 25, p. 409.
21 *Ibid.* p. 425.
22 *Capital I:* especially chapter 1, section 4: "The fetishism of commodities and the secret thereof."
23 For example Kosta Axelos in his *Marx, penseur de la technique* (Paris, 1961). Despite the clear position expressed by Marx from *Theses on Feuerbach* onwards, confusion will arise if Marx's early work is considered without reference to its ideologico-historical context, and if we ignore his radical departure from simple speculative philosophy on the one hand, and on the other his search for a scientific theory consciously integrated into the process of transformation of the real world.
24 K. Axelos: *op. cit.:* pp. 254-8.
25 Cf: A.S. Kovalchuk: "The correlation of theory and practice in the process of communist construction" in *Voprosy filosofii,* Moscow, 1966, no. 4 p. 13. The author rightly criticised that conception.
26 This is Althusser's view: for example, "science has no need of verification from *external* practices in order to categorise as 'truths', that is as the knowledge that it produces" (*Reading Capital:* ed. cit.: p. 67); "It alone

provides the validating criteria for its own knowledge." (*Ibid.* p. 67).

27 Althusser, on the other hand, maintains that "the criterion of the 'truth' of the knowledge produced by Marx's theoretical practice is given in that practice itself, that is, through its demonstrative value, which provides the proof of the *scientific nature* of the *forms* ensured by the production of that knowledge." (*Ibid.* p. 67).

28 The fact that it is possible to build a non-Euclidian geometry on the basis of the negation of an existing theory, Euclidian geometry, does suggest a certain autonomy of theory with respect to the development of practice. Nevertheless, this new geometry born of the denial of the old geometry purely on the theoretical level, later had practical application in physics and in mechanics. In this way, theory rediscovers its nexus with practice.

29 On the relation between ends and means, see A. Sánchez Vázquez: "Contribution to the dialectic and finality and causality." *loc. cit.*

VI. Creative and reiterative praxis

Levels of praxis

As Marx said, "social life is essentially practical."[1] This sociopractical totality can be broken down into various sectors according to the object or material on which man executes his practical, transforming activity. As human, material praxis leads to the creation of a new, humanised reality, it is possible to speak of a praxis that occurs on a number of levels in accordance with the degree to which the consciousness of the active subject penetrates the practical process, as well as of the extent to which the creation or humanisation of the material which is the object of his activity is realised in the actual product. These two aspects can be expressed in terms of oppositions; between creative and reiterative, imitative praxis on the one hand, and between reflective and spontaneous praxis on the other. These distinctions of degree, however, in no way eliminate the links between various forms of praxis occurring at different levels. Reiterative praxis, for example, connects with spontaneous praxis, and creative with reflective praxis; these links, however, are not immutable, occurring as they do in the context of a total praxis determined by particular forms of social relations. The spontaneous is never devoid of creative elements, nor reflection divorced from reiterative praxis. On the other hand, the concept of degree is itself relative; the level, or degree, of a particular praxis is determined by reference to a) the degree of consciousness revealed by the subject in the practical process, and b) the degree of creation manifested in the product of his activity. Neither criterion takes exclusive account of the subject on the one hand or the object on the other. Since subject and object are themselves closely interlinked within the practical process, the criteria too are closely connected; the degree of consciousness revealed by the subject in the practical process, for example, cannot fail to be reflected in the degree of creativity manifest in the object—and vice versa. These mutual influences are neither static nor absolute, since they are modified by the social context in which praxis unfolds.

Praxis can have either a reiterative character, in that it conforms to a previously elaborated law so that it is reproduced in various products with analogous characteristics, or an innovating, creative character to the extent that it is not totally obedient to existing laws, and in fact culminates in a new and unique product.

Creative praxis

The term 'creation' has a variety of meanings in both ordinary and philosophical language, which concur in regarding creation as the production of something new, whether in the Greek sense of limited creative action, in the Christian sense of divine creation *ex nihilo* or in accordance with the Renaissance concept of a human creation whose point of departure is the world of real objects. In another context, it has been used to denote evolution in a global sense, in order to emphasise the new and unpredictable character of that process; Bergson, for example, referred to "creative evolution" and C. Lloyd Morgan to "emergent evolution". Traditionally it has had mythic, religious or magical undertones, which still present an obstacle to its conversion into a more precise, scientific term. So it is important to clarify at this stage that we understand 'creation' to mean the activity of man as a social being which enables him to produce a new object out of pre-existing elements or realities, and whose properties are the result of man's capacity to bring forth actual from potential existence. Specifically, creation is a concept that cannot be used without reference to man, or with reference to natural processes or the universe alone. Wherever man is present as an active subject—in art, science, labour, technology, social relations etc.—the term has legitimate use, for creation would then refer to the production of new concepts, works of art, objects, political institutions, social relations etc. New forms may be potentially present in existing elements; their actual emergence depends not on some inexorable logical determination, but on man's active intervention. Though new forms must emerge from existing ones, existence is not a sufficient condition for the appearance of something new. In this sense, creation is a specifically human act, yielding objects which could not exist without the mediation of consciousness and of human practice.

From the standpoint of total human praxis, translated into the production or self-creation of man himself, creative praxis is the determining factor insofar as it allows man to deal with new situations and the new needs to which they give rise. Man must constantly invent or discover new solutions; and once they have been put into action, he cannot simply go on repeating or imitating what had previously been the case, in the first place because he is constantly creating new needs which invalidate previous solutions, and in the second, because their inadequacy was revealed by the new exigencies of life itself. The solutions that are developed, however, enjoy a certain period of applicability, during which there exists a possibility and a need to generalise and extend them, that is to repeat them as long as they remain valid. Repetition, in other words, is justified so long as life itself does not require creation; man does not live in a constant state of creativity, but creates out of necessity, in order to adapt himself to new situations and to satisfy new needs. He will repeat what is given until he is called upon to create something new. Nonetheless, creation is the first and most vital human necessity, because only by creating or transforming the world can man (as Hegel and Marx pointed out from different philosophical viewpoints) make a human world, and thus make himself. Man's fundamental practical activity, then, has a creative character; yet it coexists with repetitious, relative, transitory activity which is always open to the possibility of displacement. Praxis, therefore, is essentially creative; yet between one creative period and another, during periods of truce in his active debate with the world, man may repeat an already established praxis. Considered both in its totality and in its specific political, artistic or productive forms, therefore, praxis is characterised by this alternating rhythm of creativity and imitation, innovation and reiteration. How, then, can we determine on what level to locate particular forms of praxis?

We must first consider the relation, characteristic of the practical process, between the activity of consciousness and its realisation. In a truly creative process, there is an indissoluble unity between the subjective and the objective, the internal and external aspects of the process. Artistic creation, the inauguration of a new society, or the production of a useful new object are examples of the conscious activity of the subject upon a given material worked or structured according to the end or project elaborated in the consciousness. A real, objective act is always preceded by a psychic, subjective act; and in its turn, the material act provides the foundation for a new psychic act, by bringing forth new problems that need to be solved, and the basis for new material activity, whose framework has been built in the course of the initial activity. Creative practical activity cannot be conceived as a continuous series of acts in consciousness corresponding to and reflected in another, equally continuous, process of material acts which occur in the practical process in the order in which they occurred in consciousness. The subjective is not merely the starting-point for the objective; the objective reality is not simply the completed product of subjective activity already disposed to being objectively realised, or reproduced. Consciousness devises an end or project which is open and dynamic, and will remain so throughout the practical process. The function of consciousness is not simply to conceive the project, and then return to itself; it must constantly transform the end at the level of ideals, not in response to intrinsic, ideal exigencies, but in terms of the external demands that arise as a result of the use of objective means and instruments, and of the objective activity itself. It is not a matter of two planes which unite on a purely external nexus, but of two intimately interlinked aspects of a single process. To form or transform matter does not simply involve stamping upon it a form already envisaged in a finished way at the level of the ideal, so that its objectification or materialisation entails little more than the simple reproduction or duplication of that form at another level. The production of the ideal product is inseparable from the production of the real, material object; they are reverse and obverse of a single fabric, twin aspects of a single process.

The form that the subject seeks to impose on matter is generated in consciousness; but the form ultimately given to the material is neither the same nor a duplication of that which had already existed in an ideal form. Certainly the final result had been prefigured at the level of the ideal; but it is the real and not the ideal result, or the generating project, that is definitive. The original model can only be realised through a process whose result may not reproduce that model in its totality. Why is it that this ideal prefiguration must suffer modifications throughout the practical process? Principally because matter does not passively allow itself to be transformed; it offers resistance, refusing to allow its form to be replaced by another, giving rise in artistic praxis in particular, to that creative torment which most artists experience. While it is true that the practical subject approaches his material with some knowledge of its properties and possibilities, and of the means most appropriate to inducing its submission, it is also the case that the particular character of the end or project in question evokes in its turn specific modes of resistance on the part of matter; for this reason it is never possible to fully know what the final outcome of the process will be until it is complete. An unexpected adversary, for example, could undermine all our preconceived plans and strategies; in the same way, the unforeseeable resistances of matter can force us to constantly modify our projects and our ends. Thus consciousness is obliged to be constantly active, to move from interior to exterior, from ideal to actual; for in the course of the practical process the distance between the ideal model, or end, and the product (the final or actual result) tends to grow, introducing, as far as the ideal model is concerned, an element of indeterminateness or uncertainty into the process.

All truly creative practical processes involve the loss of the original project which set them in motion; yet this does not mean that the end, or project, ceases to be a determining factor, indeed as Marx says, that end or purpose "gives the law to (the worker's) *modus operandi.*"[2] The end which in the beginning had presided over the practical process is itself modified during, and as a result of that process, and becomes in the end a law governing the *totality* of practical acts. It is only revealed as a law, however, when the process is complete; it could not have been established prior to the initiation of practical activity properly speaking, nor identified with the law that governed the first steps in the practical process. The whole creative process, then, is subject to a law that can only be discovered *a posteriori,* and it is this that gives to the practical process governed by it, and to the final outcome, the unique, unforeseeable and unrepeatable character characteristic of all creation. The distinctive features of all creative praxis can now be summarized: a) the indissoluble unity, in the practical process, of internal and external, subjective and objective elements; b) the indeterminate or unforeseeable nature of both the process and its result; and c) the unique unrepeatable quality of the product.

Revolution as creative praxis

These features may be found in all the various forms of praxis which have a creative character. The October Revolution of 1917 provides an example of creative social praxis, of the material activity of men engaged in the radical transformation of society and the inauguration of a new social regime. The Russian revolutionaries, under the leadership of the Bolshevik Party, started from an initial project of social transformation and creation elaborated by Lenin in the course of a number of Party congresses, and deriving in its turn from more general basic projects formulated by Marx and Engels. The initial project for the transformation of the State, for example, was set out by Lenin in a work written on the eve of the revolutionary upheaval, in the summer of 1917. The transition from the ideal model of the revolutionary transformation of the State machine to its effective realisation, however, was so direct and immediate that the author himself, as he acknowledged on the final page of his manuscript, decided to leave his writing and join the actual struggle, since "it is more pleasant and useful to go through 'the experience of revolution' than to write about it."[3]

The elements of the process, then, were the internal, subjective gestation of the revolution (the ends and theories which guided the Bolsheviks when they set it in motion) and its actual realisation; but this original project had to be adapted to human, social material that offers resistance, and to means and instruments whose possibilities were only fully revealed in the course of the practical process. For this reason the project had to undergo modifications, taking into account the very resistance of the social material, the presence or absence of certain objective conditions and the development of the subjective factors. It had to move constantly between the ideal and reality, and as a result there was established a growing breach between the original project and the practical revolutionary activity whose object was to transform social reality in accordance with that project. Not everything could be planned beforehand; unforeseeable circumstances arose which had to be dealt with (like hunger, blockade, military intervention, peasant discontent, the failure of the German Revolution, the peculiarities of socialist construction in one country etc.) and which in their turn entailed modifications to the original project. Revolution, therefore, could not be a simple reproduction of something ideal, nor be subject to a law *a priori*. The distance between the result and the course of practical, revolutionary activity itself, necessarily entailed an element of indeterminateness and unpredictability. The course of the revolution and its product, the building of socialism, were not subject to any immutable law governing all its modes of action; it was impossible to know in advance what socialism in the USSR would be like as a finished product resulting from the actual revolution and the concrete experience of building socialism; it could not, therefore, be considered as the materialisation of a complete product or of an ideal product. The modification motivated by the unforeseeable and indeterminate aspects of the revolutionary process emerge more clearly if we compare its developments and its results with the original project formulated by Lenin and the Bolsheviks, and especially if we set it against the models of the transition from capitalism to socialism previously elaborated by Marx and Engels.

This must necessarily lead us to consider the third distinctive feature of creative praxis; its unique and unrepeatable character. The Russian Revolution was governed by laws that only became apparent *a posteriori,* in the sense that it was elaborated in the course of its realisation; the process was not governed by a law conceived without reference to the practical process itself. The revolution yields its own law; in this sense it is a unitary practical process in which the ideal and the real combine in a dynamic and unpredictable way, and constantly overflow the limits of the original project. Further, it is a unique and unrepeatable process, whose governing law cannot be directly applied to other revolutionary processes without ignoring its particular objective and subjective conditions. This is not to exclude the possibility that revolutionary processes share certain common features; but far from excluding the unique and inimitable character of each revolution, those common features necessarily presupposed it. The experience of subsequent revolutions in China, Vietnam, Algeria and Cuba reveals the dialectical unity of their common, essential features on the one hand, and their specific and unrepeatable qualities on the other. The specific character of each revolution stems from the need to radically transform capitalist social relations in a given country and in the particular historical conditions, at both the objective and the subjective level, of that country. That is why the first socialist Revolution, that of October 1917 in Russia, has distinctive features of its own; and that is why subsequent revolutions have followed different paths as far as the mode of taking power, the role of the Party and the administration of the State (which it sometimes shares with other parties), the forms adopted by the organs of popular power, the particular mode of organisation in industry and agriculture etc., are concerned. The distinctive character of each revolutionary process has been further confirmed in recent years, as Lenin foresaw, by the fact that peoples liberated from colonialism seek modes of advancing towards socialism that do not involve passing through a capitalist phase. On the other hand, however exceptional the particular form of each revolution, and however individual the paths chosen to achieve its realisation, there remain those fundamental, shared features with respect to the objectives, essence, conditions of emergence and development of the revolutionary process, which arise not from a general and abstract proposition, but from the specific historical circumstances in which the working class movement and its vanguard develop in a particular country. What is unrepeatable and singular about each revolution is the particular way in which the essential features of all revolutionary movements have emerged and unfolded in a given case. Nevertheless that development is not predetermined by virtue of some universally applicable general law, nor solely by the existence of objective factors in a society, however peculiar the forms they adopt there; the process can only be realised as the result of the intervention of subjective factors—the popular forces and their vanguard. That is the source of that unforseeable quality, although this should not be taken to exclude completely the possibility of foreseeing or anticipating the mode of development of revolutionary praxis at the ideal level.

Artistic creation

The distinctive characteristics of creative praxis emerge particularly clearly in a domain where man's creative capacity is expressed most directly: art. The fact that we speak of "artistic creation" is evidence of the degree to which the products of art embody those essential features. Clearly, for example, art has a unitary and indissoluble character which makes it impossible to separate its internal and external features, subjective and objective, content and the form that it is given, in anything other than a totally abstract way. The artist's labour is formative in a double sense: it gives form to a particular content, yet the formative process can only be carried through by transforming matter itself. The form given to matter in the work of art does not exist ideally prior to the construction of the real artistic object; it cannot, therefore, be regarded as the mere reproduction of a product of consciousness. The material worked by the artist yields gradually to the nascent form, which takes direct account of the nature of the material itself; yet this form is the product of a content, as well as of a particular material. Artistic creation is a practical process; it has a beginning and end. In the beginning it is no more than an initial form or project, and a material ready to be worked. The result of the process is that a) the original form is materialised, losing its original ideal quality; b) the content now has form; and c) the material, its resistance overcome, has yielded to a form. All three, however, are indissolubly linked in the now finished product, which is the work of art.

The final form of the artistic product cannot be identified with its original form, nor its content with the psychic fact from which the creative process began, nor can the worked material be considered in the same way as the raw, primary material prior to its submission to the artist. The work of art is the product of an objective, practical act, which is also located in the subjective field; it is an object whose reality is independent of the experiences and ideas of the subject during its gestation, and its objective existence is the result of a process of materialisation or objectification of a series of subjective, psychic facts. The artistic product is much more than a transposition of the subjective into a medium. The object is not merely an expression of the subject; it is a new reality that transcends him. The error of psychological or sociological aesthetics, which see the work of art simply as an expression of the ideas, feelings and personal or social experiences which the artist wishes to communicate, consists in their failure to understand that the products of consciousness must be formed, or materialised, and that in the process they cease to be what they had been before the process had begun. The artistic product does not simply reproduce an experience existing prior to the practical process, when it was still without (artistic) form, but it shapes that experience itself. Thus Benedetto Croce, for example, was wrong to describe this formative process as simply internal, and subjective, the result of an intuition through which a content, or psychic fact, is given internal form; in the end, this perspective led Croce to disregard the external or objective materialisation altogether, because it did not fall strictly into the framework of aesthetic facts. Artistic creation cannot tolerate this separation between interior (the aesthetic sphere, properly speaking) and exterior (the extraaesthetic sphere) since here, as in every other practical, creative process, there can be no distinction between internal gestation and external execution, for the simple reason that the execution itself represents the unity of interior and exterior, subjective and objective.

Artistic creation is also an uncertain process; the artist begins with the aspiration to realise an initial, ideal project through his practical activity; but this internal model is determined and specified in the course of realisation itself. The result is thus indeterminate, and its uncertain character will only finally be overcome when the process is completed. And by then the product will bear little resemblance to the initial project. So there is something of an adventure about the artist's activity, since it seeks to realise a possibility which will only prove to have been realisable once it has found its final form. The work of art cannot exist as a potentiality, but only to the extent that it achieves material form; thence the element of risk, which so torments the artist, in every artistic venture. For example, the aesthetic possibility realised by Picasso in "Guernica" is accessible to us only to the extent that it is the realised product of practical activity. In the same way, Picasso realised possibilities that would have been unthinkable at other times, or from other perspectives—a further proof that one can never set limits to artistic creation, nor reduce it to its already realised historical forms, let alone to one such form alone. For the implication would be that it was possible to fix once and for all the aesthetic possibilities of form, style, language or content for the art of the future. Picasso's constant renewal of his own art, his search for new possibilities, is one outstanding example of the unique and unforeseeable quality of all true artistic creation. In the field of art, then, there can be no *a prioris;* if the work of art were obedient to preexisting laws or norms external to the creative process itself, then art would lose its characteristic uncertainty and the artist could proceed with absolute confidence. The laws that govern art, however, emerge from the creative process itself; a unique law presides over each work, which is itself a unique and inimitable product.

The examples of both revolutionary social praxis and artistic praxis reveal that true creation demands a heightening of the activity of consciousness, and its materialisation an intimate relationship between interior and exterior, subjective and objective. Similarly, creative activity cannot arise when the subjective is divorced from the objective, such that the latter becomes a mere duplication of the former, but only when consciousness starts from a law or original form which is transformed at the same time as matter itself.

Reiterative or imitative praxis

The inferior forms of praxis, characterised by the absence or weakness of the three distinctive features of creative praxis, are simply reiterative or imitative. In this form, the unity of the practical process is undermined because the project or end exists in a finished form prior to its realisation. The subjective is presented as a kind of Platonic ideal model which is copied, or duplicated, in the real world. As in Platonic metaphysics, the model is the determining factor; the real product can be only said to exist to the extent that it approximates to the ideal, and concomitantly that the failure to adjust itself to the ideal would imply a loss of reality. In creative praxis, the product requires not only a modification of the material, but also of the ideal (or end); the ideal of reiterative praxis, on the other hand, remains immutable throughout, exists already in a completed form which is not affected by the vicissitudes of the practical process. In creative praxis, not only does the material adapt itself to the end or project whose realisation is the object of that praxis, but the ideal itself must adjust to the demands of the material and to the unforeseen changes that occur during the practical process.

In imitative praxis, on the other hand, the range of unforeseeable possibilities is narrowed down as far as possible; the ideal remains immutable, and before activity occurs both its purpose and its methods are known. In other words, the law that is to govern the practical process exists in a finished form prior to the process and to the product that is its outcome. In creative praxis, the mode of behaviour is invented; in reiterative praxis, it exists already in finished form, and there remains little room for the improbable or unforeseeable eventuality, given that planning and realisation are one and the same. There is a total correspondence between the real and the ideal result, which determines both the methods and the location of praxis; there is neither adventure nor uncertainty in this form of activity. And in this sense, to act means simply to repeat or imitate other acts such that all activity is governed by a single, known, law, and thus remains within the boundaries of known and tried practice. Since the law is known *a priori,* the practical process can be repeated in the same way any number of times and any number of analogous products produced. The basis of imitative or reiterative praxis, then, is the existence of an already realised creative praxis, from which it derives its governing law. It is a second-hand praxis, which produces no new reality, provokes no qualitative changes in the present reality nor transforms anything in a creative sense; it does extend the world of created things, however, multiplying purely quantitatively the products of a previous, qualitative change. But it neither creates, nor brings into being any new reality; that is its limitation, and the source of its inferiority with respect to creative praxis. Yet it does have a positive aspect, insofar as it extends what has already been created.

If man simply repeated the same practical activities, and if the world represented for him no more than a mere reiteration of tried and persistent qualities, then man would not maintain himself at the human level, for what defines him and distinguishes him from the animals is precisely his radical historicity, or the creation, formation and production of himself through a theoretico-practical activity which is never exhausted. Thus however positive his reiterative praxis in given circumstances, there comes a time when he must give way, in the same field of activity, to creative praxis; for the determinant of man is the fundamentally historical character of his being and the creative character of his praxis on a world-historical scale.

To the degree that imitative practical activity has its roots in a previous creative praxis, it does offer positive aspects; but these are counterposed to a negative consequence, which is that it bars the way to true creativity, particularly in the fields of revolutionary social praxis and artistic creation, which can brook no imitative features, and reject even the positive features of reiterative praxis. The October Revolution, for example, fulfilled the three conditions of creative praxis. An imitative revolution (saving the expression) would have limited itself to developing further a preexisting law, whatever the obstacles to its realisation or the particular conditions in which the process unfolded. The experience of the great social revolutions, however, shows the extent to which each revolution must bring forth its own laws, if it is to be able to respond to particular subjective and objective conditions, rather than seek its legality elsewhere, outside itself, indiscriminately transplanting as a finished product the laws that had governed other revolutions at other times. We could say of revolutionary praxis what Marx said of history: that it tends to repeat itself, the first time as tragedy, the second time as farce. Certainly any revolution whose perspectives were limited to reproducing a previous revolution would come very close to farce or caricature, and would be anything but a true revolution. This does not exclude the possibility that similar historical conditions or a common stage of development in given societies could explain the existence of essential features common to two or more revolutions, or even the assimilation by one such movement of certain fundamental elements of previous revolutionary praxis. There is, for example, a clear relationship between the French bourgeois revolution of 1789 and the Independence struggles which were to shake Latin America from the beginning of the nineteenth century onwards. Similarly, one could point to a single nexus common to the first socialist revolution and similar revolutions that have occurred since then. These examples serve to prove the point that revolutionary social praxis is not a proper object of imitation, but only of a *creative* assimilation which has nothing to do with simple reiteration of what is the creative social act *par excellence*.

Bureaucratised praxis

The total divorce between interior and exterior, between form and content, is the characteristic feature of mechanical or reiterative praxis in social life. And it is this external or formalised practice that characterises bureaucracy, or the mechanical application to new processes of forms derived from a previous process. Bureaucratic practice is governed by a law that has been converted into an *a priori* which takes no account of its actual content; therefore such activity can be repeated indefinitely, provided that it fills requirements which were laid down prior to the particular content and without reference to the practical process itself. In bureaucratic, or more precisely, bureaucratised practice, practical acts are merely the facade that hides a form which already exists as a finished, ideal product. It is not, of course, a specific form of praxis with its own object, since by bureaucratic practice we do not understand the combined activities of a body of functionaries whose actions in practice transform nothing other than a state-social praxis, or a political, cultural or educative praxis executed in a bureaucratic way. They are all degraded, inauthentic forms of praxis, diametrically opposed to creative praxis and incompatible with it.

Praxis becomes bureaucratic wherever formalisms or formulas predominate, or whenever the formal element becomes its sole content; the content is sacrificed to the form, the real to the ideal and the concrete particular to the abstract individual.[4] These are the characteristic features of a degraded, bureaucratic state practice. Indeed Marx, in criticising the Hegelian concept of bureaucracy, suggested his own definition of bureaucratic practice, "(which gives) the formal as content and the content as formal."[5] Bureaucracy renders everything formal and unreal such that "real being is treated in terms of its unreal, bureaucratic being."[6] Lenin, too, was very conscious of the nexus between bureaucratism and deformations of the activity of the State; he returned time and again to the necessity of the struggle against bureaucratism, a struggle which he regarded as "a vital and necessary condition of successful socialist construction."[7] After his debates with Trotsky on the role of the trade unions, Lenin proposed that the unions should be given a certain degree of autonomy so that they could control the tendency of the bureaucracy to evade democratic control from below. He recognised that bureaucratic deformations could find favourable soil in the objective conditions of the transition to socialism, and consequently gave priority to the need to counterbalance those tendencies through the democratisation of social life. The key plank of his policy in this respect was the incorporation of the masses into the administration of the State; to this end he advocated a series of measures during the first years of the Soviet regime with the aim of integrating the masses and ensuring control from below of the State apparatus. Like Marx he took account of the tendency on the part of the bureaucracy to regard the State, as long as it existed, "as its private property," so that even under socialism there existed a permanent danger of bureaucratic deformations. Despite his efforts, those deformations reasserted themselves during the Stalin period, and it was not until after the 20th Congress that Lenin's warnings were again heeded, and positive steps taken to try and eliminate bureaucratic survivals in the State, economic and Party apparatus.

It is important to distinguish, in this respect, between the bureaucratic deformations of a given practice, which can degrade or bureaucratise even the government and administration of a socialist state, and the bureaucracy which is an essential feature of an oppressive and exploitative State machine which oversees a society divided into antagonistic classes. It was this latter situation that Marx had in mind when he analysed the Hegelian concept of bureaucracy and to which Lenin referred in pointing to the close and essential relationship between bureaucracy and exploitation.[8] Bureaucracy is a permanent characteristic of systems of government in which the State is divorced from the people, where bureaucratic methods of control exclude any possibility of popular control of or participation in the administration of society; bureaucratism, then, is fundamentally incompatible with true democracy. In the past it reached its apogee in the most anti-democratic, absolutist regimes; in our own day, it is a central feature of imperialism, which tends to fuse the State apparatus with the power of the monopolies. The contemporary example of the United States is eloquent testimony to the characteristic rise of bureaucracy in imperialism, as State power merges with that of the big private corporations, and the process of bureaucratisation comes to control not only State institutions properly speaking but the whole of social life, penetrating all levels of culture and even the form of human relations themselves. In the conditions of State monopoly capitalism, bureaucratism is no longer an isolated deformation, but an essential feature of a system which requires by its very nature the bureaucratisation of the economy, of politics, of culture and of social life in general. In fact the process is so clear that many commentators have devoted studies to the phenomenon, testifying to the depth and extent of bureaucratic penetration, although they rarely manage to discern its class basis.[9]

The danger of bureaucratism is not confined, of course, to the institutions of the State; it threatens all those economic, political, social, trade union and party organs that employ a body of functionaries to carry out their plans, so that even political and trade union activity can sometimes take on the character of a bureaucratised praxis.

This degraded form of praxis, then, is the polar opposite of creative praxis. It is limited to developing a law established and known in advance, which takes no account of the concrete peculiarities of its application in given conditions; it shapes a form without reference to its content. It represents a mechanical praxis whose extreme formalisation provides a guarantee of infinite repetition, insofar as it negates the role of content and imposes a form external to it. The practical process under these conditions becomes abstract and formal, beyond all determinations and successfully eliminating all the unforeseeable and adventurous qualities characteristic of every truly creative praxis.

Reiterative praxis in human labour

The negative consequences for man, the practical subject, of reiterative praxis are revealed with particular force in production, or human labour, and above all in its most highly mechanised forms—assembly-line, mass production or piecework—which are the very opposite of that creative labour which is distinguished by its determinate and concrete character, particularly as regards the needs which it is designed to satisfy and its concrete products or results. For creative labour presupposes the unified activity of a consciousness which projects and shapes a product at the ideal level, and a hand that gives material form to that project. The product of this unitary activity represents the culmination of a conscious and active process on the part of the producer; thus the object or product expresses the man who produced it. Creative labour is manifested in the form of manual activity in which the consciousness and the body combine under the guidance of consciousness. Manual labour recognises no distinction between intellectual or physical work, since all manual labour is at the same time labour of the consciousness. In this light, creative labour possesses all the features of creative praxis; it has the unitary character of a practical process whose product is not a mere duplication of an ideal object, nor the reproduction of one object in an infinite series.

Historically, it was the work of the craftsman that most clearly presented a creative character, the craftsman's labour brought the practical subject into direct and immediate contact with his material so that the relationship between the consciousness and the hand was always either direct or expressed through tools that were a direct extension of the hand. It is a form of labour possessing a universal character, in the sense that its various operations are realised by the same individual as parts of a totality which is not broken down into a number of partial operations carried out by different individuals. The creative character of the artisan's labour consists in the fact that it cannot be reduced to the repetition of one or various operations, and insofar as it brings directly into play the activity of consciousness. Labour, however, is a social activity whose principal function is to produce use values for society; in this respect, the activity of the artisan is characterised by its low level of productivity. Social developments demanded increased productivity, however, and a multiplication of products. In the long term the interests of society, which for some time now have coincided with those of capitalism, have encouraged not the production of unique articles such as those produced by the craftsman, but mass, serialised production made possible by the introduction of machines and the mechanisation of industry.

Mechanised production brought an enormous increase in the productivity of labour; in this sense, it was a positive force in social development, since society as a whole benefitted from the possibility of extending the ambit of human needs and increasing the production of objects designed to satisfy those new needs. Both Hegel[10] and Marx recognised, however, that this entailed in its turn a number of negative consequences for man, and particularly for the labourer, consequences which involved the loss of the universal character of labour, the rupture of the unity of the practical labour process etc., which were the necessary outcome of the growing division and specialisation of labour, and its fragmentation into a series of practical operations. In the particular conditions of capitalist material production, governed in Marx's view by the law of the production of surplus value, the worker came to be regarded solely as the medium and instrument of production, so that in contrast to the total development of the individual which was made possible by the universal character of workshop labour, the worker became exclusively subject to the demands of production. The division and specialisation of labour which was a necessary consequence of technological development brought in its train a division in man himself, who put his whole being at the service of a single activity which corresponded to one of the operations of the machine. The universality of labour from the worker's point of view disappears, to be replaced by the narrow and unilateral specialisation of the labourer who thus ceases to be anything other than an appendage of the machine, ascribed to a single operation, so that his labour is reduced to a monotonous, repetitive activity which rarely, if ever, requires his conscious intervention.

The features characteristic of creative praxis thus disappear from his labour, whose piecemeal, unilateral and monotonous nature has been fixed in advance without reference to him. Not only does the finished form, or end of his activity exist from the outset in the form of an ideal object that must be realised, but each step in the process of realisation is mapped out beforehand, allowing of no deviations. Not only must the end conform to a preexisting plan, but the activity must conform in the same way, since by avoiding deviations the possibility of unforeseeable circumstances arising is reduced to a minimum. The result is that not only does the worker's consciousness not intervene in that prior, ideal activity, but he is not even aware of the place occupied by his partial activity within the total process of which it is but one fragment. In order to avoid any unknown or unforeseen distortions of the global result, the very rhythm, duration and movement of the worker is determined to the highest possible degree and the operations that his hands must realise simplified wherever possible, since the more delicate the operation the greater the risk of deviation from the fixed norm. Although the conscious intervention of the worker at that point could correct any errors, deviations must be excluded in principle since any deviation could affect the production of profit which is the foremost task of production.

The negative consequences of the division of labour in the conditions of capitalist production, and particularly those that lead to the division of man himself, to the perpetuation within each man of the division between the physical and the spiritual which occurs when man becomes an appendage to the machine, should not lead us into nostalgia for the era of the craftsman, when that mutilation and fragmentation did not occur. The movement from workshop to mechanised production to automation in our time, is an irreversible process which brings not only technical progress, but also human, social progress; its very basis is the social division of labour which made possible increased production and the growth of productive forces, both of which are essential preconditions of progress at every level. The division of labour is an objective necessity inherent in all modes of production; it cannot disappear even in communist society. What can change and disappear are the historical forms of that division corresponding to their respective modes of production, and imposing upon men a given form of activity. Under capitalism, for example, the social division of labour brings with it a narrowly specialised activity, which is a minimum part of a more general activity to which man is always subject so that he can never experience the universal and harmonic development of his personality. This permanent ascription of man to a single activity engenders what Marx calls the "stultified professional". This form of the social division of labour forces a man to remain tied for life to a fragmentary activity, a narrow, limited and impoverished specialisation which must be destroyed, even though the social division of labour itself could not disappear except by relinquishing technological and social progress, and returning to outdated modes of production. That narrow specialisation, which in turn entails a mutilation of man himself, can be overcome when there have been established not only new social conditions (as Marx and Engels emphasised) but also technological conditions. We are witnessing today a technological and scientific revolution which has made it possible to speak of the dialectical negation of atomised labour, so that labour can reconquer its universality but at a level much higher than that of the craftsman of earlier times. Until those technological and social conditions do exist, however, the division of labour in the conditions of mechanised production leads to an extremely simple, unskilled, mechanical form of labour of the most impersonal and unconscious kind; for until there exist actual alternatives which offer a choice to the worker, consciousness has no role to fulfil and simply constitutes a hindrance to the successful execution of simple repetitive labour, whose most radical form is the assembly line. In the highly industrialised capitalist countries, this mode of production has a specific form developed under the influence of Taylorism, time and motion, or "the science of the organisation of production." Taylor's methods were designed to achieve maximum profits by depersonalising as far as possible the task of each worker. The success of the method depends upon the absolute passivity and ignorance of the worker, the radical destruction of the unity of the consciousness that projects ideally and the hand that realises; it was based, in other words, on the extreme atomisation of labour. Productivity and profit, increased as a result, but at the expense of the worker's creative capacity to adapt himself consciously to the performance of a number of different tasks. His hands are deprived of all spiritual content, so that he becomes nothing more than an appendage of the machine. With time, Taylor's methods have yielded their place to other, more refined methods of exploiting labour, though this has not in any sense meant the abandonment of assembly line production. In all the industrialised countries, including those of the socialist bloc, mass production has been the necessary result of technological progress; and this will continue to be the situation until the development of technology introduces the mode of production appropriate to the next phase—the phase of automation.

This absolutely reiterative praxis imposed by technological progress in a social context governed by the law of maximum productivity of labour, obtained through mass production, brings with it a mutilation of the worker much more serious than physical mutilation. For although the hand continues to operate in a physical sense, and continues to execute the mechanical tasks ascribed to it in mass production, it can be said that the human hand has ceased to exist, insofar as its significance derives not only from the fact that it is part of the body, but from the fact that it is moved and guided by consciousness. By separating the hand from the consciousness, mass production labour automates and enslaves the human hand, and radically changes its destiny, its capacity to link man and things, consciousness and the material world.

Supremacy and the decline of the hand

The privileged role of the hand, as opposed to other parts of the body, had already been acknowledged by the Ancients, who had perceived the relation between intelligence and the hand. Anaxagoras the elder, for example, noted that relation; Aristotle had gone further and attributed to the hand a decisive importance, since in his judgment man was the most intelligent of beings precisely because he had hands. The superiority of the hand derived from its capacity to utilise a large number of tools and instruments; it is "the instrument of instruments."[11] In modern times, that superiority has been definitely recognised as a result of the attempts to discover the specific difference between men and the animals. The evolutionists, and Darwin and Haeckel in particular, linked man's preponderance in the world to his use of the hand, a hand that has liberated itself in the course of natural evolution.[12] From the conception of its natural liberation Engels derived the notion of the liberation of the hand through labour, and of the hand as a product of labour.[13] And it was Engels, drawing inspiration from Hegel and from Marx, who formulated the central idea of the role of labour in the formation of man: "man alone has succeeded in impressing his stamp upon nature... And he has accomplished this primarily and essentially by means of *the hand*. Even the steam engine, so far his most powerful tool for the transformation of nature, depends, because it is a tool, in the last resort on the hand."[14] With his hands, man has been able to transform nature, so that the hand is both the organ and the product of labour. The Mexican philosopher José Gaos stressed, in his turn, that the hand fulfils its highest function in the use and fabrication of tools, precisely because it is linked to intelligence, so that "it is related not only to *material culture,* but to the whole of *human culture,* even to those aspects of it furthest from matter."[15] For the Vietnamese Marxist Tran-Duc-Thao, it is the use of tools that characterises and distinguishes human behaviour from animal behaviour, however advanced this animal behaviour may be: "The Anthropoid *uses* instruments, but only man understands the use of tools."[16] So it is the hand, with its capacity to employ tools, that allows man to achieve, through a series of stages, "human life in a properly human sense."

Why does the hand enjoy supremacy in comparison with other parts of the body? Clearly its origin is in the link between the hand and the intelligence, its spiritual value properly speaking. The intellectual nature of the hand is a consequence of the particular way in which it relates to things, which is radically different from other, analogous, animal organs. The hand can realise an infinity of movements and adapt itself to the most diverse uses; its plasticity allows it to impress its form on an object and in turn to let itself be formed, in a sense, by the object that is sheltered there.[17] As we have stressed, man is a practical being, who forms and transforms his world; the hand is the instrument of the transformation, and all tools are in the end simply extensions of that original instrument.

By using his hand, man had learned to overcome the resistance of matter and begun to dominate material things. With his hands, man came to put his mark on nature; the hand is his first tool, and its use marks the beginning of a properly human relation between man and the world of things. For not only do the hands shape things by overcoming their material resistance, but they also touch and explore; it is this contact with things that endows them with human significance. In the same way, the work of the hands establishes a special relationship between men themselves; the hands caress, and bring men together in a handshake, and they can also give sensitive expression to human relations, either between individuals or between human groups. And this capacity of the hands to express the most diverse emotions has its root in its close links with consciousness.

The transformation of material things often requires the most delicate and precise movements. The activity of the surgeon, the artisan, the painter or the sculptor bear witness to the unique and irreplaceable quality of this "tool of tools", the hand. Thus a worker like Georges Navel conceives life itself as a function of the hand.[18] "Man" he says, "lives through his hands. Life is what we touch." It follows that the hands that are devoted only to mechanical or empty labours are lifeless hands, which do not involve the intelligence of the worker. Through his hands, man is in contact with things, and gives them form; his relation with matter cannot be simply external. With his hands, man makes things his own, humanising both them and himself, by letting himself be touched, by adapting himself to their form, opening himself to things and consummating thus a human relation in the deepest sense.

The truly human hand is not simply and exclusively a part of the body, but a part formed and deformed in order to form the better; a hand that does not move blindly, in a natural or mechanical way, since its very movements are dictated by intelligence; a hand able to overcome the resistance of material things precisely because of its plasticity, its capacity to respond to the most varied, complex and subtle demands. And because it is plastic, flexible, the hand does not easily accept the petrification, repetition or simplification of its movements, nor let itself be reduced to its lowest level in the monotonous and simple labour of the production line, for this can only be achieved by robbing the hand of its spiritual sap, severing or separating it from consciousness and setting it in an external relation to consciousness, so that it ceases to be a human hand and becomes indeterminate and abstract; in the end each hand becomes identical to every other, and shares with others a common universe of perfectly measured and defined actions, whose form, rhythm and duration are all pre-established.[19] Thus my hand ceases to belong to me and every link that it has with my consciousness is severed; these are the characteristics of absolutely repetitive praxis like the labour of mass production which, under the influence of Taylorism, totally separates intelligence from the hand. These forms of labour must abolish every possibility of conscious, reflective intervention and make of the hand a pure extension of the machine; to this end, every element of creativity is eliminated, and the unity of the practical process destroyed. Consciousness not only becomes superfluous, but even an obstacle, as is demonstrated by the fact that less intelligent workers more easily adapt themselves to the requirements of this partial, monotonous and mechanical form of labour, and as is evidenced by the fact that it is the industrialists themselves who have insisted upon this separation of intelligence and the hand.

Nevertheless, there has in recent years been a turn away from the most brutal methods of exploitation (as advocated by Taylor) and towards a "human relations" approach. There are many reasons for this, chief among them is a growing resistance on the part of a working class whose demands have extended from simple wage claims to demands for better working conditions. The industrialists themselves, for their part, have been quick to recognise that Taylorism limits productivity in the final analysis, since its radical separation of decision from execution has induced among workers a complete disinterest. The resulting falls in production had serious effects on profits; so these methods were abandoned and replaced by attempts to integrate the worker "at a human level" and bring about changes in his attitude to work. The resulting mechanisms and methods have had a single aim, to bring the worker to regard his own destiny as linked inextricably with the fate of the enterprise, that is its profitability. The ends in view, however, are identical to those of Taylor; the means may change, but here as before the worker's labour is an instrument designed to produce an external end—the production of surplus value. So the "human attitude" of the industrial relations school ensures that alienated labour will persist. For the movement from repetitive to a truly creative praxis cannot occur as a result of "human relations" elaborated on the basis of the principle of profit maximisation, but only through a transformation of the material and social conditions of labour itself.

What is involved is not a return to the kind of unity between the consciousness and the hand that had characterised the era of the craftsman; social and technological developments have made such a return impossible except in an anachronistic sense. On the contrary, the recognition of the humanity of the worker, and of man as the ultimate end of production, will permit us to give much greater weight to the role of consciousness in production, and in turn to acknowledge the significance of the worker in the management, control and regulation of the practical process, which is increasingly carried out by machines. Thus automation emancipates man from his direct involvement in the production process, so that his hand can cease to be indeterminate and abstract and hence separated from his consciousness. Liberated from the assembly line, the hand, which for centuries was responsible for the development of material human culture, will raise the "culture of the hand" to which Gaos refers to higher levels and not be exhausted in its direct, material contact with things in labour. This does not mean that the hand will lose its purpose, since however automated production itself may become, there will always be a role for the intelligent hand of man to play. Even automated production requires a human hand to set it in motion, to repair the broken machine and so on; but it will no longer be the mechanical, dehumanised hand of the age of the assembly line, but the human hand obedient to consciousness.

We have spoken of the negative consequences of reiterative praxis in the sphere of human labour; it remains for us to ask the question posed by the French sociologist G. Friedmann, as to whether these consequences remain in the relations of production in a socialist society. For although as a matter of principle the socialist countries reject the application of the brutal methods of exploitation followed in capitalist society in accordance with the principles of Taylorism, it is equally clear that for the moment the socialist countries are not yet in the position to renounce completely the organisation of production in the form of the assembly line. Nevertheless, most of the negative features of this method of production have been successfully eliminated in socialist countries, by reducing the rhythm of work in such a way that the speed of the line is adapted to the normal possibilities of a man whose mental and physical health must be conserved, and not sacrificed on the altar of production. Yet even under socialism it has not been possible to abolish all the negative consequences of the production line—the separation of thought and action, of consciousness and the hand, typical of that form of labour which forces the worker into uniform, monotonous labour which can offer him no satisfaction. The situation can only be overcome to a relative degree, by becoming conscious of it, and by seeking means to fill the 'vacuum' in consciousness created in this process; and the worker takes a further step when he recognises that his labour has a social end which is not necessarily external to him. It is only this kind of moral, ideological stimulus that can enable men to confront and overcome the problem. Socialism does reduce and attenuate, if not abolish, the negative consequences of this kind of work.[22] In the end, however, it is only technological progress itself that can provide a final answer; automation alone can abolish monotonous, uniform labour, suppress unsatisfactory, partial labour and raise again the question of the role of consciousness, as a result of the need for highly skilled labour, which the production line had tended to limit and reduce. Automation itself has a series of social consequences which can be negative; but because they have a social character not necessarily linked to automated techniques, these consequences tend to lose their negative character under socialism.

Imitative praxis in art

The negative effects of imitative praxis can be discerned in spheres of praxis other than that of human labour. Even art, which is by its very nature creative praxis, does not escape the dangers of an imitative praxis expressed in this case in the form of academicism, or of artistic creation obeying principles or laws of a normative kind.

Artistic academicism or routinism dissociates internal and external, the law and the practical process, just as they are separated in other domains of praxis; the result is that the artist is pressured into making his creation conform to an already established canon, or law of subjectivity, extrapolated from an artistic experience whose day is past. On the other hand, that canon can be imposed beforehand, from a standpoint external to artistic creation, by considerations of an extraaesthetic order, whether moral, political, or religious (artistic normativism). In the first case, creation is governed by a law established in advance, leaving no room for the unforeseen, the surprising, the unique or the unrepeatable qualities of creative work. And since the activity of the artist holds to an already creative law, rather than to a law that has arisen in the course of creation itself, the actual result can be nothing other than the mere duplication of an ideal end or result. In a word, there is no creation, properly speaking. All great art can in principle give rise to forms of academicism which degrade artistic praxis by simulating and holding back the creative forces that have found expression in great works of art. In this way, a superior manifestation is a premise for an inferior one. It is true to say, then, that this inferior, degraded artistic activity, culminating in the academicism of the nineteenth century, arose on foundations laid by the great classic works. Academic deformations can be the direct result of true, creative praxis, wherever the principle given living, external shape in previous creation becomes a norm or a rule external to the subsequent artistic process. In this sense, the authentic art of our time, which is characterised by the will to break with or negate previous canons, and an antiacademic perspective, can in turn give way to a new academicism based on this very rejection; this we could call an anti-academic academicism.

Whereas in the previous case the clearest manifestation of reiterative praxis is the attempt to subordinate the practical process to an artistic principle shaped or developed in a previous praxis, artistic normativism is characterised by this attempt to mould the work to an external principle, so that it becomes an illustration of extraaesthetic criteria (politics, morality, religion etc.). Thus the relations between the principle governing the work and the form of the work itself are external; the work neither changes nor develops in the course of creation, it never comes down, in other words, from its conceptual pedestal. It retains the same being at the beginning and at the end of the process; the material has not assumed a shape of its own, nor has there occurred any fusion of form and content. The principle remains throughout external to the creative process, its substantive character and conceptual structure unaffected. Once the law governing a process of this kind assumes an *a priori* character, it can no longer be regarded as a unique law, since it can inform as many processes as required and always yields the same results.

It should be stressed, however, that what determines the transformation of artistic activity through imitative or reiterative praxis is not the political or religious principle itself, but the mode in which the principle governs the practical process. It can only become a unique principle, linked to a unique mode of realisation, when the principle stands in a dynamic unity with the process of realisation itself in a unity of subjective and objective. Only in this way can tendentious works, informed by a given ideological tendency of a political, moral, social or religions kind, become true works of art rather than mere illustrations of certain principles.

We have suggested that there are three fundamental types of praxis—social-revolutionary, productive and artistic—operating on two distinct levels: creative praxis and reiterative, imitative praxis. It is in both cases a human activity that transforms a given material, but both the practical process and its product can have either character. The criterion for distinguishing between the different forms of praxis is the existence, or absence in an extreme case, of the three distinctive features of creative praxis: the unity of internal and external, of subjective and objective, in the practical process; the unforeseeable quality of the process and its results; and the unity and uniqueness of the product. There are no absolute barriers, however, between the levels of praxis, for in total human praxis innovation and tradition, creation and repetition alternate and at times intertwine and mutually condition one another. The determining praxis, nevertheless, is creative praxis.

Notes

1. *Theses on Feuerbach:* p. 653.
2. Marx: *Capital I:* p. 131.
3. Lenin: Postscript to *State and Revolution* in *Works:* Vol. 25, p. 492.
4. In our study of the hero in Kafka's *The trial,* we have pointed to the characteristic of that bureaucratic practice in which the concrete individual existence becomes abstract as a result of an empty or formal universality with which he identifies. (Cf. "A Kafka hero: Joseph K" in A. Sánchez Vázquez: *Art and Society,* pp. 136-154.)
5. Marx: *Critique of Hegel's philosophy of the State.* This work was written in the summer of 1843, but remained unpublished until 1927. In it Marx criticised the Hegelian conception of bureaucracy as "formalism of the State" (as Hegel called it): "As this 'formalism' of the State becomes a real power and provides its own *material* content, it becomes evident that the 'bureaucracy' is a tissue of practical illusions, or the 'illusions of the State'. The bureaucratic spirit is a totally jesuitical, theological spirit... The true finality of the State appears to the bureaucracy then to be a finality opposed to the State." (*Ibid.*)
6. Marx: *Critique of Hegel's philosophy of the State: ed. cit.:*
7. Lenin: *Works:* 5th Russian edition: volume 38, p. 93.
8. Lenin: "The economic content of populism and a critique of Herr Struve's book" in *Works:* vol. 1. See also "Tasks of the social democrats" in *Works:* vol. 11, pp. 365-375.
9. See for example, the work of C. Wright Mills, M. Lerner, Vance Packard, David Riesman, Erich Fromm, William H. Whyte, E.L. Bernays etc.
10. Cf. above, Chapter 1.
11. *Aristotle on the Soul:* (Ed. W.D. Ross: O.U.P. 1961): Book III Chapter 8 and *Book of Animals:* (Heffer's, Cambridge, 1967), IV, 10, 687-719.
12. Jean Brun, in his work *Le main et l'esprit* (P.U.F., Paris, 1963) carries out a historical study of the conception of the hand from Aristotle to the modern evolutionists.
13. "Before the first flint could be fashioned with a knife by human hands, a period of time must probably have elapsed in comparison with which the historical period known to us appears insignificant, but the decisive step was taken; the hand became free... Thus the hand is not only the organ of labour, *it is also the product of labour.*" Engels: *The dialectics of Nature:* Progress Publishers, Moscow, 1941: p. 281.
14. *Ibid.,* p. 18.
15. José Gaos: *Dos exclusivas del hombre: la mano y el tiempo:* Mexico 1945: p. 28.
16. Tran-Duc-Thao: *Fenomenologia y materialismo dialectico:* (Lautaro, Buenos Aires, 1959): p. 243. He adds "The perception of the instrument as an instrument, in its intrinsic efficacy, is constituted with the *use of tools,* which marks the appearance of Man" (*Ibid,* p. 242). As distinct from the Anthropoid, who only uses instruments occasionally, there emerges with man "a new structure in which the mode of utilisation is definitively

absorbed and repressed, and lived out in constantly renovated parts which makes the object appear to the subject who produces it and preserves it as an *object bearing powers of its own*." (*Ibid.* p. 244). So when the hand is considered as an instrument, it can be said, according to Tran-Duc-Thao, that man not only utilises the hand, but he can also repress its use and live it as "an intentional movement in which the subject is conscious of the utilisation at the ideal level" of a hand that he prepares and keeps in abeyance.

17 Cf: Jean Brun: *op. cit.:* Chapter IX.
18 Cf: Georges Navel: *Travaux:* Paris, 1946.
19 As Friedmann says, "The rationaliser breaks down a given operation into a certain number of parts and ascertains, from several workers, the minimal times for each part. Finally, he assembles the most rapid movements in a stereotyped series which will henceforth be imposed as the standard and only method, on all the workers." G. Friedmann: *Industrial society:* Free Press of Glencoe, 1955: p. 53.
20 For Taylor "the full possibilities of functional foremanship, however, will not have been realised until almost all of the machines in the shop are run by men who are of smaller calibre and attainments." Taylor: *Shop Management:* quoted in Friedmann: *op. cit.:* p. 63.
21 Cf. G. Friedmann: *7 études sur l'homme et la technique:* Ed. Gonthier, Paris, 1966: p. 175.
22 On the personality of the worker in the conditions of mechanised production in the Soviet Union, and on their attitude to their work, see the collection entitled *O chertaj lichnosti novogo rabochego* (Aspects of the personality of the new worker): Moscow, 1963. As far as the negative consequences of assembly line work, see the essay by N.G. Valentinova: "Roll lichnosti v predolinii monotonnostiraschlennogo truda" (The role of personality in overcoming the monotony of piecework) in the same collection.

VII. Spontaneous and reflective praxis

Consciousness in the practical process

We saw in the previous chapter that creative praxis demands a high level of activity on the part of consciousness, not only in setting out at the beginning of every such process the original end or project to which the subject will give material form in the course of his activity, but also throughout the process. A rich and creative practice required a proportionately greater level of activity on the part of consciousness, since the problematic, unpredictable character of the process and its uncertain result oblige that consciousness to intervene constantly. It would be incorrect, however, for us to devote our attention exclusively to the role of consciousness in *creative* praxis, for consciousness is also an element of lower levels of praxis, although its intervention is less significant. At the bottom end of the scale, what remains is a totally reiterative praxis in which there is a radical divorce between consciousness and the hand, between planning and execution, not so much because there is a tendency to exclude the hand from production as a result of automation, but because the hand becomes mechanical, abstract and indeterminate; in other words, the hand ceases to be a human instrument. Yet even this attempt to submerge the hand in total unconsciousness cannot completely eliminate the conscious aspect of an activity which purports to be blind; in the end the subject must make a conscious decision to accept an attitude to things which would entail abrogating the function of his own consciousness. Indeed even in order to ensure the mechanical character of the operation and the exclusion of the intervention of a consciousness which, from the point of view of production, has become largely superfluous, requires some minimal activity of the consciousness. A case in point is the efforts of the Surrealists to exclude all conscious intervention from the practical, creative process; André Breton, for example, defined surrealism as the reduction of creative activity to "a pure psychic automatism through which the real functions of thought may be expressed verbally, in writing or in any other form."[1] The problem is that consciousness does not give up its place that easily; to advocate the exclusion or elimination of consciousness is itself a completely conscious position. The Surrealist, for example, regarded "automatic writing"[2] as the most radical form of artistic unconsciousness; yet even this could only be achieved by encouraging the active intervention of consciousness, rather than by attempting to paralyse it. Consciousness asserts its existence both through its decision to automate the psyche, since it alone can determine the rate of progress towards that automatism, and also throughout the process and in its result. The very radicalism of the Surrealist project, in this sense, demonstrates that it is impossible to exclude consciousness from the practical, artistic process.

Practical consciousness and the consciousness of praxis

The role of consciousness in practical activity reveals the existence of two types of praxis, which we have called creative and repetitive praxis. The consciousness active at the outset and in the course of practical activity, in intimate unity with the shaping and realisation of its ends, we shall call *practical consciousness,* insofar as it intervenes in the practical process, inserting itself at the point where the ideal end becomes the actual result. Practical consciousness could equally well signify that consciousness which devises an end, or an ideal model to be realised which is itself modified in the process of realisation, in response to the unforeseen exigencies of practice itself. This practical consciousness is heightened through creative praxis, and weakened if not eliminated when the material activity of the subject assumes a mechanical, abstract or indeterminate character, when formal ends are materialised (as in bureaucratic practice) or when ends and projects are shaped outside the process and without reference to consciousness itself. Practical consciousness exists only where its ideal products are given material form; it does not cover that consciousness which develops exclusively on the theoretical level marginal to practice, or when it fails to respond in an immediate way to the demands of a practical process.

Consciousness, moreover, is not only projected and shaped; it knows itself to be projected and shaped, knows that it is its own activity that governs the modalities of the practical process and knows, furthermore, that that activity is necessary and integral to the process.

Without separating the two, it is important to distinguish between practical consciousness as a *practical state,* and the consciousness of practice. Both refer to the relation between consciousness and the practical process, but while the first is consciousness to the extent that it impregnates that process, governing it and giving it material form throughout, the second refers to that consciousness that knows itself, that is conscious of that impregnation, so that it governs the practical process as an end. Practical consciousness entails in every case some consciousness of praxis; but the two are on different levels. In a practical process, it can happen that the first occurs at a very much lower level than the second, for example, in the case of the intelligent or class-conscious worker who becomes aware of the monotonous, partial or mechanical nature of his work. His consciousness of praxis is not in a direct relation to his practical consciousness, which is virtually nullified by the fact that he does no more than apply an end or law which is imposed on him from without. In an inverse way, something similar can be said of artistic praxis, in the case of a painter or sculptor who, despite a high level of consciousness of his activity, does not manage to realise his sketch or plan; here practical consciousness is at a lower level than the consciousness of praxis. These two levels should neither be confused nor separated, since on the one hand practical consciousness, as an ideal activity which is materialised, makes it possible for the consciousness of what is being mounded to be heightened and made more transparent, and for the consciousness of practice in turn to contribute to enriching real, material activity and thus to heighten the (practical) consciousness which finds form in that activity. Thus the consciousness of praxis is practical self-consciousness.

The new levels of praxis

According to the degree to which this practical self-consciousness is manifest we may distinguish at this point two new levels of practical, human activity which we shall call *spontaneous praxis* and *reflective praxis.* Practical consciousness never disappears, even in spontaneous praxis; for this reason we have avoided reference to spontaneous and conscious praxis, given that consciousness is always present in spontaneous activity. What determines whether praxis is spontaneous or reflective is the level of consciousness of practical activity, which in the one case is weak or virtually absent, and heightened in the other. It is not, therefore, a matter of two new modulations of the forms of praxis we have already discussed (creative and repetitive); reflective praxis does not correspond directly to creative praxis, nor spontaneous to non-creative, mechanical or repetitive praxis. There is some correspondence, but it has special characteristics according to the form of praxis involved. As far as artistic praxis is concerned, for example, the notions of rationalist aesthetics (like the Classical aesthetics of the 18th century) which established a direct relation between consciousness and creation, and the theses of irrationalist aesthetics, with their source in Plato's *Ion*, and their development in contemporary surrealist aesthetics which regards artistic creation as the product of unconscious activity, are equally false, because they are both unilateral explanations. What could be lacking from this activity is not so much practical consciousness as a consciousness of praxis; and it is that absence that determines the spontaneity of artistic creation. Artistic praxis shows that spontaneity is not necessarily opposed to creative activity; they are simply two different levels. The opposite of creation is reiterative, mechanical praxis; in this sense, repetitive praxis, like the assembly line, is at once the negation of spontaneity and of creation. For this reason spontaneous praxis must not be confused with the supposedly unconscious praxis, or any other kind of praxis that excludes consciousness, nor set in an external relation to the practical process. Creative praxis can be to a greater or lesser degree reflective and spontaneous. Reiterative praxis, on the other hand, is characterised by a weak intervention on the part of consciousness, yet that does not justify calling it spontaneous. For in this respect, repetitive praxis is opposed both to practical creation and to spontaneous praxis.

Two new problems arise from the recognition of the existence of these two levels of praxis: a) what type of relation obtains between them? and b) how is the transition from one to the other effected? The answer will not come from an analysis of the existing relations between these two levels of consciousness or of the mode of transition from practical consciousness to the consciousness of praxis. A study of praxis involves an approach to practical questions like the relations between praxis and consciousness; the products of practical activity cannot be indifferent to that relation, since a spontaneous relation with consciousness does not lead to the same results as a reflective relation.

The spontaneous and the reflective in revolutionary praxis

The practical character of these problems gives them a vital importance for revolutionary praxis, and it is for this reason that Marxism, in accordance with the Eighth Thesis on Feuerbach, has acknowledged their special importance. If revolutionary activity is to become reflective, and thus truly revolutionary, its consciousness of praxis must be heightened; that is the import of Lenin's formulation—"without revolutionary theory there can be no revolutionary movement." It is no coincidence that divergences about the ways of transforming society should have taken the form of debates about the relations between spontaneous and conscious (reflective) activity in the revolutionary movement, and particularly about the role of consciousness, and its highest expression, revolutionary theory, in the practical transformation of society. A correct conception of the relations between spontaneity and reflection, and their corresponding practical levels, must deal with two extreme positions whose practical consequences are equally pernicious: the overestimation of the spontaneous element, on the one hand, or of the reflective element on the other. In the first case, the result is a depreciation of the role of theory in revolutionary practice; in the second, a failure to recognise the spontaneous elements that emerge at the beginning of and during the practical, revolutionary process.

Marx's task with regard to the revolutionary transformation of society, had as its basis a clear perception of the relations between spontaneity and reflection. The proletariat can only overthrow the socio-economic order that estranges it through a highly conscious, reflective praxis. Thus the workers' movement must be endowed with a consciousness of its historical mission, of its ends, of the social structure of capitalism and the laws that govern that structure, as well as of the objective conditions and possibilities of its emancipation at a given stage in its socio-historical development. The proletariat can only liberate itself once it has become conscious of its exploitation, and of the necessity of developing a revolutionary praxis that will abolish it; and this, in turn requires a praxis developed in the context of given objective conditions as well as a high level of consciousness of those conditions, both in terms of the obstacles they present and in the light of the ends and possibilities that can be realised under those conditions. In this sense, revolutionary praxis has an objective aspect, insofar as its necessity, its limitations and its possibilities, are objectively determined by social and historical factors, and a subjective aspect, to the extent that the proletariat is conscious of that historical necessity, of its limits and possibilities, and in consequence prepares its plans for the transformation of society.

The possibility of an effective transformation of society is linked to the objective aspect; but it can only be realised where the subjective consciousness of praxis and its objective possibility exist at the same time. In this respect Marx said that ". . . mankind always sets itself only such tasks as it can solve."[3] This does not mean that we can only pose those problems or goals which are capable of solution in advance, but that the question has its origins in the exigencies of socio-historical development itself which already demand and suggest the possibility of a solution.

Humanity can only advance when the proletariat negates itself as a class, and overcomes the reified or commodity status of the proletarian. Consciousness of the worker's reified condition and of his reduction to a mere means of production necessarily precedes the negation by the proletariat of its own negation, as well as of the conditions and possibilities of action designed to carry through that negation. Action in itself is not sufficient; the workers can destroy the machines in a gesture of protest, but this will not produce substantial changes—as the working class learned in an early stage of its movement. Their actions must be integrated into a perception of their historical mission, which provides them with a consciousness of their own class being, and of what they actually represent as a socio-historical force. Furthermore, they must act in accordance with that being; it is not enough to pursue an end, whatever it is, for they must act in pursuit of an end that is consonant with their historical mission. "The question is not what this or that proletarian, or even the whole of the proletariat *considers* as its aim. The question is what *the proletariat is* and what, consequent on that *being*, it will be compelled to do."[4]

The historical mission of the proletariat in our time

Marx's conception of the historical mission of the proletariat has nothing to do with the kind of proletarian messianism attributed to him by some Catholic theologians in their excursions into Marxism, or by those "marxologists" who have insisted on interpreting Marxism in an ethical sense, ignoring the scientific character which distinguishes it radically from any ethical or Utopian version of socialism. When Marx and Engels spoke of the historical mission of the proletariat, they clearly understood its mission to be the radical transformation of capitalist society through class struggle, and through revolutionary struggle in particular. That mission was not providentially attributed to the working class, but arose as a possible and necessary consequence of socio-historical development itself which had sharpened the contradictions between the social character of production and the private appropriation of the means of production. As the mission of the proletariat is objectively determined, and as the realisation of that mission involves both theoretical and practical activity, it requires too a consciousness of the objective situation and its possibilities as well as forms of organised struggle. In this sense the mission of the class is determined both objectively and subjectively, responding to a historical necessity rather than to an ineluctable destiny fixed by some unknown party. The proletariat is the class most directly linked to production, particularly to its most advanced forms, and thus its mission is clear. Given the key role of production in socio-historical development, the function of the working class in that production explains the superiority of its socio-historical tasks, as compared with the tasks of other oppressed classes, whether today or in the past. On a world-historical scale, the proletariat is the revolutionary class par excellence; and this role is not affected by advances or setbacks in the fulfilment of its mission in a given country or at a given moment. Furthermore, its mission is no less crucial in the present conditions of State monopoly capitalism, although some reformist theoreticians have falsely asserted that it has become less significant. In fact, there are some Marxist theorists, too, who have come to the same conclusion, and have sought proof of their position in a false interpretation of the undeniable fact that there exists at the present time a powerful and developing revolutionary movement in some colonial or dependent countries which still do not possess an industrial proletariat. The point is that however willing State capitalism may be at a favourable conjuncture, or under the pressure of working-class struggles, to absorb some important social and economic demands, no legal or peaceful reform within the system can overthrow the fundamental contradiction that characterises the activity of workers, and which is the source of their alienation—namely, the contradiction between labour governed by the laws of the production of surplus value, and truly social labour. From the worker's point of view, that contradiction presents itself as between the creative, social essence of his activity and the external purpose to which he remains subject. There are some who consider their mission to be complete, seeking the proof in a comparison between the struggles of the proletariat in the advanced industrialised countries and the struggles of the oppressed people of the oppressed or dependent nations. The truth, however, is that far from having been exhausted, the potential of the proletariat, its disposition to struggle, has persisted in new forms. Furthermore the world-historical mission of the proletariat does not mean that other classes (the peasantry, petty bourgeoisie, intellectuals, and in certain cases the national bourgeoisie) cannot fulfil a revolutionary role where, for objective reasons, there does not as yet exist a proletariat constituted as a class. On the other hand, the activity of these classes does not negate the mission of the proletariat; if anything, it serves to underline it insofar as the triumph of socialism and the fulfilment of this vanguard role by the proletariat since the first socialist revolution came to power, has created favourable conditions for the revolutionary struggle against imperialism of the oppressed classes in the colonial nations. If those oppressed classes are to maintain the revolutionary character of the struggle which they have initiated, and which often retains a strong spontaneist orientation, their initially national, democratic revolution must develop without interruption into a socialist revolution. These classes can only be revolutionary, moreover, to the extent that they fuse their mission with that of the proletariat, even in those situations where the working class exists but has not, for historical reasons, fulfilled its role, or where that class does not yet exist at all. The mission of the proletariat is an imperious necessity; indeed so vital is it that the revolution in those countries where it is not led by the proletariat itself can only advance to the extent that the vanguard whose origins are in other classes takes up as its own mission the world-historical mission of the proletariat and its vanguard. In these conditions, the presence in the struggle from its outset of spontaneous elements, far from weakening the need for a reflective, conscious praxis, makes it all the more necessary and urgent precisely in order to achieve the fusion of its interests with those of the proletariat. If the process is not carried through in this way, the revolutionary movement can be halted, and liberation, thus detained, will give way to other forms of domination.

The revolutionary experience of recent years testifies to this danger, especially in those countries where those classes, instead of merging their interests with those of the working class, have surrendered the leadership of the national liberation movement. Where the working class has been unable to assume the practical, political and ideological leadership of that movement, the tasks of the revolution cannot be fulfilled unless other revolutionary forces take up the task before the national bourgeoisie, which tends to vacillate and inclines towards compromise, leads the revolutionary movement to its annihilation. In the present situation, the realisation of the mission of the working class is more urgent than ever, not only in the countries of the developed, capitalist world, but also in the dependent, colonial nations where economic and political independence can only be ensured by revolutionary means. In the end, no other class can arrogate to itself the mission of the proletariat; the growth of the socialist world, for example, is simply an expression of the leadership of the working class on a world scale.

Let us now return to the problem of the relations between spontaneity and reflection in the praxis of the proletariat.

Flashes of consciousness and class consciousness

In characterising the revolutionary praxis of the proletariat as spontaneous or reflective, the consciousness of praxis plays a decisive role, since it is closely linked to the consciousness on the part of the proletariat of the historical process, of its class interests and of its mission. For Marxism that is what is meant by *class-consciousness,* whose highest expression, socialist consciousness, requires concrete knowledge of the structure of capitalist society, of the class character of the State, of the relations between different classes in that society, of the level and meaning of social and historical movements and the role of the working class within them, and of the historical mission of the class. Class-consciousness, therefore, presupposes a capacity to situate the specific manifestations of oppression and exploitation within a total vision, and thence a possibility of guiding apparently weak actions in a general way towards a more distant objective which gives these actions their significance. This is the only certain way of escaping the tendency towards spontaneity and of integrating all the actions of the class into a reflective, purposive praxis.

The proletarian may live enclosed within his immediate interests and his individual consciousness weave a web of illusions around him that could even turn against his class being. In that case he cannot rise to a total vision of the process; his acts will not correspond to his interests, because he ignores his own powers, possibilities and limitations. His praxis, then, is spontaneous because it is marginal to consciousness, which in the proletariat is class consciousness. Yet spontaneity and reflection are not separated by an absolute wall; they are correlative insofar as both acquire meaning as a result of their relation. Spontaneity is not absolute, for it always contains elements of consciousness. As Lenin explained, "the 'spontaneous element', in essence, represents nothing more nor less than consciousness (or reflection in our own precise terminology) in an *embryonic form.*"[5] The systematic strikes of the Russian workers in the 1890s, for example, were no longer simple manifestations of desperation or revenge as the machine-wrecking of previous decades had been, for Lenin saw in them "flashes of consciousness,"[6] embryonic forms of conscious activity, not in the sense that spontaneous activity already contains the seeds of reflective praxis, so that it would be simply the internal, immanent development of a content already present in the spontaneous activity in an embryonic form. "Flashes of consciousness" in themselves do not lead either to class consciousness or to conscious revolutionary praxis. There is no automatic transition from spontaneous to reflective praxis.

From spontaneous to reflective praxis

The proletariat cannot by itself overcome the spontaneous level of praxis; it cannot by its own efforts raise itself to that of reflective revolutionary praxis. Marx himself pointed out that neither oppression nor misery are sufficient to convince the proletariat of its revolutionary, historic mission. There have always been, and still are members of society living under conditions as extreme, or more so, as those of the proletariat. The superiority of the proletariat over other classes or oppressed social groups resides precisely in its capacity to raise itself to a level of consciousness—class consciousness—which allows it to assume its socio-historical mission, and thus to orientate its own activity in the framework of given objective conditions, in such a way that it can pass from spontaneous praxis to reflective revolutionary activity, or the conscious transformation of society.

We have already stressed that the proletariat cannot raise itself spontaneously to the level of reflective, revolutionary praxis, nor act in a spontaneous way in accordance with its class being, since such action would require the intervention of a class consciousness which does not arise of itself from his class being nor from his spontaneous praxis. If class consciousness is not internally present in the proletariat, if it is not given but acquired, and if it does not automatically result from its class being, then class consciousness must be inculcated into the proletariat. Lenin was clear on the point: "*There could not have been* Social-Democratic consciousness among the workers. It would have to be brought to them from without. The history of all countries shows that the working-class, exclusively by its own effort, is able to develop only trade-union consciousness."[7]
By trade-union consciousness we should understand consciousness of the situation and of possible perspectives as a function of immediate material interests, but devoid of understanding of the true historical

mission of the proletariat and its general class interests. So trade-union consciousness can shed no light on revolutionary praxis, informing only the economic struggles aimed at winning immediate material gains. These economic struggles, it is true, reveal a higher level of consciousness than is manifested in those spontaneous acts of desperation and revenge which express the earlier forms of working-class discontent; yet trade union consciousness still remains inferior to class consciousness.

The Leninist conception of socialist consciousness

If the proletariat cannot raise itself through its own powers to a consciousness of its being and its praxis, in response to the spontaneous development of capitalist production and the concomitant class struggle, then class consciousness can only come to it from without, as Lenin always maintained. Lenin underlined the point by quoting Karl Kautsky's comment that "socialist consciousness appears to be a necessary and direct result of the class struggle." Lenin adds that although socialist consciousness emerges from the class struggle, it is not a direct consequence of it, for as Kautsky had observed, "There would be no need (to introduce this consciousness from outside) if it derived automatically from the class struggle."[8] Lenin's conclusion is unequivocal: "There can be no talk of an independent ideology formulated by the working masses themselves in the process of their movement."[9]

There arises at this point a crucial question; if the working class cannot raise itself alone to a reflective praxis, who will introduce the consciousness indispensable to the transition from spontaneous praxis to reflective, revolutionary consciousness? Since there can be no practical activity conforming to class being, that is no revolutionary praxis, without that consciousness, the question is a vital one. Further, it needs to be posed on two distinct historical planes: a) when neither class consciousness nor its most complete theoretical expression—Marxism—exist, a revolutionary theory of the proletarian movement must be elaborated; b) when theory does exist, albeit never in a complete form, and there already exist within the working class sectors who have assimilated its basic principles and have thus acquired class consciousness, the task is one of inculcating an increasingly profound and broadly applicable socialist consciousness. It is a task imposed by the need to develop a revolutionary praxis. On the other hand, if the spontaneous development of the workers' movement leads neither to class consciousness nor to revolutionary praxis, any reinforcement of spontaneity will simply weaken further the possibility of revolutionary praxis. But this does not occur in an ideological vacuum, since the space that rightly belongs to an absent proletarian consciousness is occupied by bourgeois ideology. "The *spontaneous* development of the workers movement leads precisely towards its subordination to bourgeois ideology . . ."[10] The spontaneous praxis of the proletariat ends by entering into contradiction with its own class being by subordinating itself to bourgeois consciousness. The working class tends spontaneously towards socialism, as Lenin recognised; but it cannot strive at it spontaneously.

> "It is often said that the working class *spontaneously* gravitates towards socialism. This is perfectly true in the sense that socialist theory reveals the causes of the misery of the working class more profoundly and more correctly than any other theory, and for that reason the workers are able to assimilate it so easily, *provided*, however, that this theory does not yield itself to spontaneity, *provided* it subordinate spontaneity to itself. The working class *spontaneously* gravitates towards socialism; nevertheless, most widespread (and continuously and decisively revived) bourgeois ideology spontaneously imposes itself upon the working class to a still greater degree."[11]

Thus the task of inculcating class consciousness as a necessary precondition for the working class movement to move towards reflective revolutionary praxis cannot be conceived as a spontaneous task that can safely be left to the free will of individuals or social groups; it is a task that must be consciously organised. The next question to answer, therefore, is how and by whom class, or socialist consciousness can be introduced into the proletariat so that it can develop a conscious praxis.

Marxism as a philosophy of the proletariat

The proletariat exists historically as a *class in itself* before becoming conscious of its interests and its historical mission, or to use the Hegelian terms that Marx sometimes employs, as a class *for itself*. The proletariat exists *in itself* as a social reality before becoming conscious of it, that is, before it comes to exist *for itself*. It exists objectively even when consciousness grasps its own reality in a limited or deformed way, as when workers see themselves through the ideological veil of trade unionism or reformism. This does not mean that consciousness is indifferent to its actual existence, in the sense that it is not integral to that existence nor that it does not provoke certain changes in that existence. Even though its consciousness cannot alter its objective situation as an exploited class, whose members, because they have no control over means of production, are forced to sell their labour as a commodity, class consciousness introduces a qualitative change into the very existence of the working classes; this qualitative change consists in its transformation into a revolutionary class. It is not, of course, merely a matter of heightened consciousness, for the elevation of the consciousness of the proletariat to the level of revolutionary class consciousness passes through that stage which Lukács, in his *History and class consciousness* calls, in very Hegelian terms, "self-consciousness as commodity." The transformation of the working class into a revolutionary class is decisive, for it is in that process that it rises to the condition of the conscious subject of history and becomes capable of fulfilling its historical mission. In opposing all Messianic or mythological approaches to the proletariat as an oppressed and exploited class, Marx said that *the proletariat is a revolutionary class or it is nothing*. Although it exists objectively as an exploited class subject to the iron law of the production of surplus value, independently of the consciousness it may have of its own existence as a class, it is also true that the proletariat *as a revolutionary class* cannot exist without some degree of consciousness of its class being, or socialist consciousness. On the other hand, that consciousness is not simply an expression, or reflection of its existence. It is a *theoretical* consciousness, with all that this implies from the cognitive point of view. Marxism is the theory which at a given moment provides the proletariat with a consciousness of its particular class interests, of its place in the socio-historical process and of its mission in the context of the objective possibilities present in that process. That is why Marxism can legitimately present itself as the philosophy of the proletariat, whose analysis of the socio-economic structures of capitalism reveals the true situation of the class and in turn expounds the historical necessity and the objective possibility of a revolutionary praxis whose end is the creation of a new society. Marx does not see that new society as an abstract or Utopian ideal to be realised by the proletariat, but as an end or ideal that already exists as a possibility and a historical necessity in the process of social development. It is an end that is sketched out at the beginning of the process, but whose definite features will only be revealed in the practical process of realisation. Marx always regarded the building of ideal, finished models as Utopian, for it assumed that practice would restrict its function to giving material form to a duplicate of the original: "Communism is for us not a *state of affairs* which is to be established, an *ideal* to which reality will have to adjust itself." [12] This does not mean that every end or ideal should be discarded and thrown on to the pile of Utopian of ideological projects; the significance of the end stems from the fact that it is not conceived as a mere ideal result or product of man's will and understanding, but as a real possibility deriving from the development of history. In this case, realisation demands consciousness of the object and of activity as a further development from previous human praxis.

Marxism provides the proletariat with the consciousness of its revolutionary praxis, and with knowledge of the necessity, extent and limitations of that activity. Obviously the proletariat could not arrive at that theory simply as a result of its struggles; so it has reached the class from without, the theoretical instrument of its revolutionary activity placed at its disposal by thinkers of a different and even opposite social extraction. Marx and Engels, for example, had a bourgeois social background and were formed in bourgeois institutions. Yet despite their social origin, and indeed by taking as their starting point the theoretical framework learned in those institutions, they elaborated a new economic-philosophical conception that responded to interests and ends opposed to those of the social class from which they came. Marxism, then, arises as an interpretation of a given socio-historical situation characterised by the existence of sharp contradictions between productive forces and the relations of production, and provides the theoretical instrument whereby the proletariat, definitively constituted now into a class, can bring about its radical transformation. As the philosophy of the proletariat, Marxism offered not only the theoretical solution to theoretical problems, but a theoretical instrument for the practical resolution of real problems. The actual solution requires the unity of philosophy and the revolution, of theory and practice, and this can only pass into reality when the proletariat has made it its own and passed to action. In this way, Marxism offers the proletariat, from without, the possibility and the indispensable precondition of the transition to action, of a raised consciousness of its world-historical mission and of the need to negate itself as a class, thereby abolishing all classes, in order to achieve its emancipation.

Marxism has both an internal and an external relation to the class whose philosophy it aspires to be: internal because it responds to its interests and its mission; external because the proletariat as such does not intervene in its elaboration, and because neither its development as a class nor its struggles have brought forth that philosophy. This does not imply a radical negation of Marx and Engels' thesis that social existence determined consciousness, which could be seen to yield the conclusion that the social existence of the proletariat must itself engender proletarian consciousness, that is consciousness of their situation, class interests and historical mission, all of which Marxism provided. It remains to consider to what extent Marx and Engels' notion compaginates with Lenin's assertion that the proletariat, by itself, can never go beyond bourgeois ideology.

Marxism as science and ideology

The conception of ideology elaborated by Marx and Engels for the first time in *The German Ideology* stressed the links between predominant ideas and class interests in a given society. "The ruling ideas are nothing more than the ideal expression of the dominant material relationships, the dominant material relationships grasped as ideas; hence of the relationships which make the one class the ruling class; therefore, the ideas of its dominance."[13]

The consciousness that aspires to interpret reality is an interested consciousness, whose products carry the stamp of a class interest which had contributed to the narrowness or extension of their field of application, or to an emphasis on certain problems to the exclusion of others. In this sense, Marxism can relate to a certain social structure of which the proletariat forms a part, since not only is it a product of a given historical situation and could have not existed prior to the reality it seeks to explain, nor until it had reached full maturity, but it also responds in an objective sense to certain class interests. The Marxist theory of alienation, its conception of labour, its vision of history etc. respond to the class interests of the proletariat and are the theoretical expression of its social being and its movement, as Engels says in *Anti-Dühring* ("modern socialism is the expression of the modern workers' movement"), and as is emphasised in *The German Ideology* whose authors regard the ruling ideas as "the ideal expression" of dominant material relations. Ideas express a reality—material relations, historical situation, workers' movement—not only in the sense that they presuppose the existence of that reality, but also to the extent that they respond to the needs and interests of men living those relations, situations or movements. Ideas are expressive because they arise in relation to concrete circumstances without which they would not have been produced, and because they reflect a reality through the prism of certain needs and interests which have a fundamentally class character. The fact that ideas are expressive in this sense, however, tells us nothing about the type of link that joins them to a previous ideological period or with the material of preexisting ideas, nor about their cognitive value either as regards their truth or their falsity. Ideas can be expressive and responsive to a social, class situation, for example, or to certain interests and needs precisely by being false, deformed or illusory. In this case the fact that they do express certain interests limits or even invalidates their cognitive value, so that the ideas, while they are expressive, are not true. Such a system of ideas could not by definition be articulated or constituted as a science. Furthermore, their invalidity has an objective, rather than a subjective base; for example, there are objective reasons why bourgeois consciousness cannot achieve a fusion of ideology and science: "The barrier which converts the class consciousness of the bourgeoisie into 'false' consciousness, is objective; it is the class situation itself. It is the objective result of the economic set-up, and is neither arbitrary, subjective nor psychological."[14] Socialism, on the other hand, as it was developed by Marx and Engels is the *expression* of the interests of a social class and a response to certain historical conditions, yet it is also a science that "demands that it be pursued as a science."[15] In other words, it has not only an ideological (expressive) character, but also a scientific one (which yields true knowledge), and it is impossible to consider one aspect without taking account of the other. Were we to stress its ideological character at the expense of its scientific content, we would reduce it to mere ideology, discarding socialism as a science and with it the very foundation of the praxis of the proletariat in a scientific knowledge of reality. That is the effect, for example, of Sartre's position when he underlines the ideological aspect of Marxism as the only theory that, in our day, responds to the needs and actions of a rising class, the proletariat. "In certain well defined circumstances *one* philosophy is constituted which gives expression to the general movement of society . . . it is above all the mode whereby the rising class takes cognisance of itself."[16] Later, he characterises Marxism as "the philosophy of our time" which "Cannot be surpassed because the circumstances that gave rise to it have still not themselves been surpassed."[17] Neither Sartre nor Gramsci for that matter can be reproached in any way with not having seen Marxism in relation to actual history, since Gramsci too conceived every philosophy, and especially Marxism, as "the expression of a society."[18] We have seen that both Marx and Engels stressed this relation in applying to their own philosophy the cardinal thesis of historical materialism with regard to the needs and interests of a social class and to the concrete circumstances which both give rise to it and justify its supremacy in historical terms. But Marxism is a scientific theory, and in this sense Althusser was right to stress that the "relationship of direct expression" does not by itself distinguish Marxism from other philosophies with respect to its character of scientific knowledge.[19] Certainly the historicist interpretation of Marxism, particularly in the absolute form which it adopts in Sartre, evaporates its scientific content. Marxism cannot be reduced to an expression of actual history and practice. As a theory, it is a product of a thought that constructs concepts and categories in order to reproduce reality in an ideal way as part of the process of development from concrete to abstract. The concept of "expression" of society or of actual history fails to establish the conceptual, cognitive or scientific character of Marxism. In a word, Marxism is not merely ideology; its ideological aspect is inseparable from its scientific character. If it is not correct to reduce it to the mere expression of a historical situation, of a society or of class interests, it is not admissible either to reduce it to the level of a scientific theory devoid of expressiveness in the sense that Marx and Engels themselves used the term. The fact that a philosophy responds to social interests does not in principle entail the setting aside of its cognitive function, as Marxism itself demonstrates. Not only are the two functions perfectly compatible, but it is clear that in certain cases, particularly in the case of historical materialism, it is able to fulfil its cognitive function precisely because of class interest, and its perspective on knowledge. There is no justification, therefore, for establishing a radical opposition between Marxism as a science and Marxism as ideology, whether or not we take into account the basis of that supposed contradiction in the concept of expression on the one hand, or the concept of truth on the other. The unilateral character of both positions leads to a misrepresentation of the true character of Marxism, which Lenin underlined, as the scientific ideology of the proletariat. There can be no justification for stressing its ideological character at the expense of its scientific content, or for relegating this latter aspect to a secondary role, as Sartre does; nor is it legitimate to emphasise its scientific aspect, as Althusser does, to the exclusion of its ideological element. Marxism is at once science and ideology, knowledge and expression; it is a theory that responds to given circumstances and social interests yet does not for that reason cease to be a true, scientifically-based ideology. The expression "scientific socialism" was coined in order to emphasise the differences between Marxism and Utopian socialism. Scientific socialism rejects all Utopias, but not all ideologies, given that it responds to the needs and interests of the struggle of the proletariat. On the other hand it can only fulfil its ideological role on the basis of scientific understanding, that is, of a knowledge of reality. In this sense, Marxism has a class character; it is the ideology of the proletariat, and as such it must have a scientific character. As a theory it is the product of the theoretical activity of bourgeois intellectuals like Marx and Engels, closely linked, of course, to social practice. The class character of Marxism, however, should not be confused with the social, class origins of its founders, for it was neither proletarians nor intellectuals of the working class who elaborated the constituent concepts of the scientific theory of the proletariat. How, then, can we explain this contradiction between ideas and their class origins, between consciousness and existence, even though it is true that this contradiction occurs in concrete cases, not at the level of the consciousness and existence of a social class, but of certain of its members only? We are left with the need to explain why it is that those who do contribute to that development come from a different, and even opposed, social background.

The intellectual and the proletariat

In the conditions of a society divided into antagonistic classes, the cultural patrimony that includes the philosophical heritage, is not equally at the disposal of the dominant and the oppressed classes: as Marx and Engels put it, "the class which is the ruling *material* force of society, is at the same time its ruling *intellectual* force."[20] In this situation the elaboration of a new philosophy, or indeed of any philosophy that does not respond to the interests of the ruling class, must take permanent note of this close relation between material and spiritual domination. The oppressed class, the proletariat, is separated from the superior cultural formation, its access to the highest cultural benefits, among them the benefits of philosophy, is restricted. Where there are exceptions, these serve simply to prove the rule. For in a class society, only the intellectuals formed in the institutions of the ruling class enjoy the right to take advantage of the existing cultural legacy, so that only they are in a position to reelaborate it in one sense or another. A philosophy like Marxism could not have emerged from an act of spontaneous generation marginal to the philosophical or theoretical legacy existing at a given moment. Marx, for example, while submitting Hegel to a profound critique, particularly in the *1844 Manuscripts,* stressed time and again his debt to Hegelian thought; similarly, in the *Theses on Feuerbach* he recorded the important contribution made by German Idealism as a whole through its development of the active side of knowledge. Engels in turn affirmed that "the German working class movement is the inheritor of German classical philosophy,"[21] and developed this further in his prologue to *The peasant wars of Germany,* where he said that "the German workers have two important advantages over those of the rest of Europe. First, they belong to the most theoretical people of Europe; and they have retained that sense of theory which the so-called 'educated' classes of Germany have almost completely lost. Without German philosophy, which preceded it, particularly that of Hegel—German scientific socialism—the only scientific socialism that has ever existed—would never have come into being."[22] Lenin, who regarded German Classical philosophy as one of the three fundamental sources of Marxism, refers to Engels' words in support of his contention that the German working class rather than any other, was the inheritor of that philosophy precisely because of its special relation to theory, or its "theoretical sense", as Lenin called it. If, as Engels said, scientific socialism could not have existed but for the German philosophy that preceded it, then there can be no justification for separating Marx from his immediate philosophical roots; it is equally illegitimate to insist on reducing his philosophy to an intrinsic development of previous philosophical premisses, and particularly those of Hegel.

Leaving aside the question of the relations between Marxism and its immediate philosophical past, what is certain is that Marxism not only responds to given historical circumstances and class interests, but that it also forms part, as theory, of a historical process which has its own logic and therefore some autonomy. However a philosophy breaks with its philosophical past—as Marxism, the philosophy of praxis, broke radically with its past—all philosophy responds to previous philosophical movements, which had opened and closed various avenues of development, and provides the material basis for new philosophical constructions. As far as Marx's philosophy was concerned, it was Hegelian philosophical thought that provided its preexisting ideological material, as well as the reelaboration and critique of that thought by the Young Hegelians, and by Feuerbach in particular, and theoretical contributions taken from other fields, like English political economy and the socialist and communist doctrines of his time. In this way, Marx's philosophy was a response to historical exigencies and social interests, not in the context of a theoretical situation emptied of ideas, but by reforming existing ideological materials.[23] In the specific conditions of the society of their time, the members of the oppressed classes could not gain access to the institutions or modes of thought which could have made Marxism available to them, opening the way to understanding and assimilating the rich contents of the *Phenomenology of the Spirit* and the *Logic,* for example; but new philosophies were simply not accessible to the proletariat, so that only bourgeois intellectuals were at that time in a position to understand, assimilate and reelaborate critically the Hegelian philosophical inheritance. Thus Marxism, the philosophy of the proletariat, arose on a foundation of existing ideological materials, but was created by intellectuals who had not yet become estranged from the social class which that philosophy was designed to serve. The question, then, is what leads the intellectual to break with the class from which he comes and within which he has been formed. How are we to explain the fact that, after breaking with his own class, he can go on to contribute to the class consciousness of the proletariat? The pressures of reality itself can provide part of the answer, insofar as the sharpening of social contradictions is such that society can no longer be understood in terms of earlier categories. The new facts do not fit into the old conceptual schemes and their significance is lost; their meaning can only be discovered by evolving a vision of the social and historical reality as a whole. It is in the search for this totality, this understanding of the movement as a whole, that the schemes that were linked to the point of view of a class now outmoded, come to grief.

In the *Communist Manifesto,* Marx and Engels discussed the concrete historical conditions in which the bourgeois intellectual moves towards socialism; and they are the same conditions under which it had been possible for him to move, in a complex and contradictory process, from Hegelian idealism and a merely speculative philosophy to a philosophy of action.

> "In the times when the class struggle nears the decisive hour, the process of dissolution going on within the ruling class, in fact within the whole range of old society, assumes such a violent glaring character, that a small section of the ruling class cuts itself adrift, and joins the revolutionary class, the class that holds the future in its hands. Just as, therefore, at an earlier period, a section of the nobility went over to the bourgeoisie, so now a portion of the bourgeoisie goes over to the proletariat, and in particular, a portion of the bourgeois ideologists, who have raised themselves to the level of comprehending theoretically the historical movement as a whole."[24]

But what does it mean to pass from one class to another? In certain cases, the worker can become bourgeois, not only in the sense of acquiring the mental attitudes of a bourgeois, which for reasons we have outlined is not uncommon, but in the sense of *being* bourgeois. This means, in fact, that the worker ceases to be a worker because he has changed his class being. The same can be said of the bourgeois who becomes proletarian; he too ceases to be what he was, because he has changed his class being. On the other hand, the intellectual of bourgeois social origin who unites with the proletariat, thus breaking with his own background, continues to be an intellectual. Indeed it is often the case that the very act of breaking his links with the ruling class serves to affirm, or develop under more favourable conditions, his condition as an intellectual. Clearly, this requires further explanation.

The intellectual tied to the ruling class by social origin or education, can become divorced from that class, though this does not entail the loss of his intellectual being. If his previous links do continue to have an influence on the content of his activity, this can be attributed to the specific condition of intellectuals in modern society. Intellectuals do not, in the Marxist sense of the term, constitute a social class in themselves, since they do not occupy a specific position in the system of relations of production; that is to say, they are not necessarily linked to the social class that occupies the dominant position in the system of productive relations. On the other hand, intellectual production is subject to the law of capitalist material production, and their work does have the quality of a thing or commodity; to that extent their interests as a class are those of the working class, since it suffers in like manner the consequences of the subjection of labour (in this case labour that is by its nature free and creative) to the law of capitalist material production, or to narrow exigencies which constrain the field of activity available to them. Thus, when the intellectual of bourgeois origin, with a bourgeois ideological formation, adheres to the objectives of the ruling class, his links to that class *as an intellectual* do not have a forced, principled, class character, given that his activity as an intellectual is not necessarily ascribed to the ends of a given social class. He can sever his connections with that class and change his class and yet still continue to be an intellectual; the worker and the bourgeois, on the other hand, do not have such a choice. The specific situation of the intellectual who is tied to certain class interests by virtue of his social origins and formation, yet not necessarily linked to them, explains why in the past many intellectuals of aristocratic origin were able to abjure their class origins and the education they had received and pass over to the bourgeois revolutionary camp, without losing their role as intellectuals. The break between the founders of Marxism and the bourgeoisie can also be explained in this way, for they were not *necessarily* linked to the bourgeoisie on a class nexus. This does not mean that the intellectuals are marginal to classes or above them, enjoying an imaginary liberty to absolve themselves of any class interest, and thus to develop their activity in a manner free from all ideological contamination. The Marxist theory of ideology, and contemporary writings in the sociology of knowledge which ultimately derive from it, have shown that no such pure, uncontaminated intellectual activity can exist so long as man is both the subject and the object of knowledge. On the contrary; in a society divided into classes, where the class that dominates material activity also dominates the means of spiritual production, the intellectual is generally ascribed to the class interests represented by the material and spiritual power, not only because the education he receives generally responds to those interests, but also because it is education that disposes of the material and spiritual means to acquire and develop that formation. The intellectual is what he is, nevertheless, because he exercises thought, and because he has the power to explain and criticise things, although he only exercises those powers in relation to actual praxis. This explains why, in certain circumstances, when his links with the ruling class become an obstacle to the exercise of his critical, rational power, the intellectual should feel impelled to break with the ruling class precisely in order to safeguard his own position as an intellectual. In objective terms, however, his efforts to maintain his position put him on the side of the revolutionary social class which also opposes the ruling class, although for other reasons. If, as Lenin and Gramsci say, "the truth is always revolutionary," the intellectual who seeks the truth at any cost can thus find himself on the side of the revolution—which is precisely what happened with Marx and Engels. This explains, too, why the intellectuals can often fulfil a vanguard role in the creation of a revolutionary consciousness.

Marx, for example, was a bourgeois intellectual with a bourgeois education; yet he came to formulate a theory which not only transcended the particular interests of the class from which he came, but became the highest expression of the interests of the class most directly opposed to his own, that is the proletariat. This philosophy of the proletariat was necessarily the culmination of a complex process, and the product of a critical confrontation between his thought and the philosophy of his time, English political economy and contemporary Utopian socialist and communist doctrines, and at the same time the product of the constant tension between his thoughts and reality itself. From his position as a bourgeois intellectual immersed in the dominant philosophical, economic and social ideas, Marx used them as preexisting ideological materials which provided a starting point for his own philosophy, unconscious at that point of the fact that, with his first steps, he had embarked on the creation of a theory that was to provide the proletariat with the consciousness of its own revolutionary praxis. In this way he passed from complete confidence in the ideas of previous philosophy, to confidence in the conscious activity of men, in their practical, transforming activity. In this way, Marx moved on to create the theoretical instrument of the revolutionary transformation of the world, and put it in the hands of the social class which was able to use it.

The Party as a "Collective intellectual"

Having created the philosophy through which the proletariat could raise itself from spontaneous to reflective, revolutionary praxis, Marx went on to demonstrate in the *Communist Manifesto* that the proletariat was not in a position to turn it spontaneously into a guide for action. It would still be necessary to carry out organisational and educational work in order to imbue the working class with heightened class consciousness and raise its praxis to a reflective, highly conscious level. Marx dedicated his life to this task, combining in a tight unity theoretical work and activity devoted to the education and organisation of the proletariat as a revolutionary class. Marx's own example, as an organiser and a leader of the working class proved in practice his conviction that it would never be possible to achieve socialism through a spontaneous, automatic process originating in the maturing of objective social conditions, but that he regarded it as essential to force the hand of history a little by preparing the social forces that would transform society. Marx's behaviour in practice showed too his belief that the proletariat must move from spontaneous to reflective praxis, and that it was necessary to introduce socialist consciousness since neither exploitation nor misery nor the class struggle can lead by themselves to an understanding of the historical movement as a whole, and thus of the mission, ends and possibilities of the action of the proletariat.

The task of inculcating this socialist class consciousness, an indispensable precondition for conscious, revolutionary praxis, cannot rely exclusively on intellectuals who have broken with the bourgeois class, nor can the task fall in a major way to them since it surpasses by far what they can contribute directly. Education is necessary, but so too is the organisation and leadership of a reflective, revolutionary praxis which lies well beyond the possibilities of a handful of ex-bourgeois intellectuals. The principal task, therefore, must fall to that sector of the proletariat which is most conscious and resolute in its conviction of the need to link revolutionary theory and practice; that sector of the proletariat which possesses a theoretical understanding of the conditions, limits and goals of revolutionary struggle, and the practical activities that compose that struggle. This conscious and organised sector, whose task it is to inculcate into the rest of the working class a consciousness of its own mission, to lead and organise its struggle and carry it beyond immediate interests towards the general interest of its emancipation, is the Party of the proletariat. Two circumstances impose the necessity for its existence: a) the liberation of the proletariat is not a spontaneous automatic process; however ripe the objective conditions for its emancipation, these alone do not lead to the revolutionary transformation of society—there must also be conscious, revolutionary activity; b) the proletariat cannot by itself achieve this reflective praxis as a result of the development of objective conditions and the class struggle, but only as a result of a process of education, extension and enrichment of socialist class consciousness.

If the simple development of objective conditions could guarantee the transition to socialism, or if the proletariat could raise itself by its own powers to a reflective, revolutionary praxis, this more conscious, organised and decisive detachment of the class would be redundant. The Party, however, does not exist as a separate sector or detachment, but represents the class consciousness of the proletariat at its highest level, and hence the most developed consciousness of its own mission, of its limits and its goals as a revolutionary class. To that extent it fulfils a theoretical role. This function is not limited to elaborating general philosophical, economic or aesthetic theories, but involves educating the workers at the ideological level and studying concrete situations with a view to preparing concrete guidance for action for the whole period of struggle; a political line. Through the Party, theory passes to the working class, and theory and practice are fused; yet neither this movement nor this fusion should be considered as a completed state, but as a process without an end. The task must be realised continuously, since its debilitation or abandonment can only lead to the submission of the working class to bourgeois ideology and the renunciation or distortion of its revolutionary praxis, leaving the field to reformism or adventurism.

If action is to avoid the infusion of adventurist or Utopian features, it must be based on knowledge of the concrete situation and on an objective appreciation of the level of consciousness of the working class. The political line that emerges as a result of this analysis opens a perspective for struggle which has its roots in actual, concrete developments. If the policy of the party is mistaken, however, it indicates not only ignorance of the objective conditions (which can lead to subjectivism) but also a false evaluation of the level of consciousness and organisation of the masses to whom that policy must apply. In that case, their distance from the party is an unmistakable sign that subjectively, that is from the point of view of their consciousness and organisation, the conditions are not yet mature enough for them to carry the programme into practice. The party's insistence on carrying forward its political line in that situation would simply serve to reinforce the subjectivist tendency arising from ignorance of the objective conditions. If it persists in this path, the party will find itself isolated, and become a separate detachment which fails to fulfil its essential function in promoting the unity of theory and practice. Given that objective conditions exist, the subjective conditions become decisive, and if these do not exist then the task is to create them. The first exist independently of the activity of the party; the second must in large part be the result of its work.

There are no guarantees against error. The party can wrongly evaluate the level of maturity of objective conditions or the potential of the revolutionary forces. Yet although there exist no absolute guarantees, given that the reactions of the adversary can never be completely foreseen, nor the composition and preparedness of the revolutionary forces, there does exist a relative guarantee to the extent that the political line is based on sound knowledge of the objective and subjective conditions under which the political line confronts reality. Hence the need to keep in close contact with the masses, who are not masses in the sense of a docile, inert material susceptible to education and guidance; as Marx said in his Eighth Thesis on Feuerbach, "the educator (in this case the Party) must in turn be educated." Lenin, too, was at pains to stress the need to take into account their level of consciousness and their combativity, and even to learn from them. Far from implying the primacy of spontaneous over conscious activity, this simply serves to prove (albeit in a negative way) the importance of the reflective praxis among the masses which the party has the task of leading and organising. It can only fulfil this mission to the extent that its own theoretical function is conceived as a collective task, rather than as the exclusive province of specialized intellectuals. For this reason, Gramsci referred to the party as a "collective intellectual", a type of intellectual that unites the theoretical and the practical aspects in a given theoretical product, the political line, which is formulated and applied in the course of the practical process.

As a result of its theoretical understanding of the movement as a whole and of its significance and role at a given stage; through its task of educating and leading the working class, the party continues to represent throughout the process the power of consciousness, and hence is the indispensable vehicle of reflective praxis. That too is the basis of our rejection of two extreme positions which tend to derogate the role of the reflective element: on the one hand, the position that restricts proletarian praxis to spontaneous activity, and on the other the position that completely rejects these spontaneous actions and accepts only a total revolutionary praxis, seeing this revolutionary principle as incarnate from the outset in the elemental spontaneity of the proletarians. To reduce the role of consciousness in revolutionary praxis is to reduce or even deny that praxis itself, since it has meaning above all as reflective, revolutionary praxis.

* * *

In general terms, then, and by way of summary, we can point to two levels of the practical process which are distinguished by their respective degree of consciousness: the level of reflective praxis, which requires heightened consciousness of praxis, and that of spontaneous praxis which implies a low or negligible degree of consciousness. Nevertheless, the relations between spontaneity and reflection cannot be absolutely maintained, since they do not always occur on the same level. It would be simplistic, for example, to see spontaneity as a radical negation of consciousness. On the contrary, the almost total elimination of spontaneity in the practical, productive process leads, as we have seen, to a repetitive, mechanised praxis, whose negative consequences Marx dwelt on at length in *Capital*. The destruction of spontaneity has similar consequences in bureaucratised practice. Both examples show that the relation of spontaneity and consciousness cannot be derived from any simplistic correlation, for example, from the suggestion that spontaneity disappears as consciousness manifests itself to its fullest extent. For reiterative productive praxis and bureaucratised praxis entail the annihilation of both elements.

On the other hand, we cannot achieve a truly creative praxis by raising the spontaneous element in it to the level of the absolute, as the anarchists do with respect to revolution, and the surrealists in the field of art. So all praxis presupposes a relation between spontaneity and reflection, and establishes two levels of that relation according to the relative predominance of one or the other element. Although we cannot ignore the role of spontaneity, above all in artistic activity, it is clear that creative praxis can only occur at the level of reflection.

Notes

1. That was the definition of Surrealism given in 1925 by André Breton in the *Revue surréaliste*.
2. It was hoped that "automatic writing" or "automatic graphics" would succeed in completely excluding logical thought and allow the subconscious world to reveal itself. To this end the hand must move freely, beyond conscious control, and itself sketch something on paper or canvas.
3. Marx: *Preface to a contribution to the critique of political economy* in Marx/Engels: *S.W.:* vol. 1 p 363.
4. Marx/Engels: *The holy family:* London/Moscow, 1957; p 53.
5. Lenin: *What is to be done?* in *Works:* vol. 5 p 374.
6. *Works:* vol. 5 p 375.
7. *Ibid.:* p 375.
8. Karl Kautsky quoted in *Works:* vol. 5 pp 383-4.
9. *Works:* vol. 5 p 384.
10. *Ibid.:* p 384.
11. *Ibid.:* p 386
12. *The German Ideology:* p 47.
13. *Ibid.:* p 60.
14. G. Lukács: *History and class consciousness:* Merlin Press, London, 1971: p 54.
15. Engels: Preface to *The peasant wars in Germany* in Marx/Engels: *S.W.:*

258   *The Philosophy of Praxis*

vol. 1 p 653.
16   J.P. Sartre: *Critique de la raison dialectique:* Gallimard, Paris, 1960. p 15.
17   *Ibid.:* p 29.
18   Gramsci: *Historical materialism. . .: ed. cit.*
19   L. Althusser: *Reading Capital: ed. cit.:* pp 129-131.
20   *The German Ideology:* p 60.
21   Engels says, in the final paragraph of his pamphlet *Ludwig Feuerbach and the end of Classical German philosophy:* "The new tendency which recognised that the key to the understanding of the whole history of society lies in the history of the development of labour, from the outset addressed itself by preference to the working class and here found the response which it neither sought nor expected from officially recognised science. The German working class movement is the inheritor of German Classical philosophy," in Marx/Engels: *S.W.:* vol. 2 p 402.
22   Marx/Engels: *S.W.:* vol. 1 p 652.
23   Cf: Engels' letters to K. Schmidt (27th Oct. 1890) and F. Mehring (14th July 1893) in Marx/Engels: *S.W.:* vol. 2 pp 486-8 and 496-501.
24   Marx/Engels: *The Communist Manifesto* in Marx/Engels: *S.W.:* vol. 1 p 43.

VIII. Praxis, Reason and History

Intentional praxis

The previous chapter concluded with the assertion that there can be no blind praxis, no praxis without a conscious subject or author with respect to whom that praxis can be seen as an end or result of activity. The alternative would be an opaque praxis, or an activity whose results did not fit in with an ideal model elaborated by a subject, or a number of subjects, and in which those subjects had not acted collectively in pursuit of a shared project or end in whose realisation they had collaborated after combining their individual ends and products. It is hardly necessary to reiterate at this point that when we speak of individual praxis or of the collective praxis of a group of individuals, we always have in mind an individuality impregnated with the quality, or social essence that defines the individual understood as a complex of social relations.[1] In this individual or collective praxis, activity obeys an existing purpose; its product, therefore, is an objectification of practical subjects, whether individual or collective; to this extent there must always be some adjustment of the ends or means, to the result of their action. The process of realising an intention, in the course of which the subjective assumes objective form, the intention is realised and the objective becomes the subject, occurs in the sphere of practice and thus requires the intervention of consciousness; what is realised, therefore, corresponds to a greater or lesser degree, according to the vicissitudes of the practical process, to a certain primitive intention. This takes us into the realm of intentional praxis, or the reflective praxis that is counterposed to the unintentional forms of practical activity which are not guided by any previously formulated end, project or intention. It embraces, for example, the activities of the worker who produces a given object, particularly in the craft industries; of the artist who, in transforming a given material creates a work of art; of a proletarian who unites consciously with other workers in a strike in order to achieve a certain end—a change in the worker-management relationship; or the revolutionaries who consciously organise their actions in order to provoke a radical change in social relations, destroying existing powers and creating a new social structure. There are in all these cases ends and intentions whose realisation is sought after, and there is therefore an activity of consciousness which unfolds both in the production of the project which is the starting point for activity, in the practical process whereby it is realised, and finally in the result of the process, to the extent that the subject is objectified or materialised in that result.

Intention and result

Since it is practical activity, the activity of the subject is determined by its product, or by what remains in an objective or material form as the result of his activity. Practical activity is relevant to our analysis, in other words, only to the extent that the subjective is objectified as a result of action. If there is some disparity between the starting point (the original intention) and the culminating point (the product)—and this seems to be inevitable, particularly as regards creative praxis—then it is neither the original project nor its level of realisation that is of primary importance, but the result. This should not lead us to discount the subjective element, of course, since it is impossible to consider the product as an object in itself without seeing in it the objectified activity of the subject. Unlike the conductivist or objectivist conception of praxis, the subjective is here presented in its proper light, in indissoluble unity with the object, that is as an intention made objective or realised. The sphere of praxis does not embrace intentions that have not assumed objective form, however good those intentions may be; what concerns us here is the product realised by the worker, rather than the ideal object which existed only in his consciousness; the realised work of art, rather than the sketch that served as a point of departure for creative activity; the revolution carried through and fulfilled rather than the revolutionary images which could not be given shape or form, either because their Utopian character condemned them to remain a dream, or because the vicissitudes of the practical, revolutionary process forced them to be modified or abandoned altogether.

The subjective is of interest, then, through its effects and through the products in which it is given objective form. The problem is, how can we define practice in terms of subjective elements if the characteristic feature of the practical process is, as we have seen, the constant modification of an intention or original project? For this would seem to demand that we dissociate elements that are intimately fused in the practical process, and to require a return through its various modifications or objectifications, to a pure, original intention before it assumed objective form; for it is only by situating the analysis at a point prior to the practical process that we could assess a purely subjective activity, a pure intention, without reference to its realisation. But what point would there be in defining these unrealised intentions? What could the knowledge we might derive from it contribute to the evaluation of a process that is of interest precisely because it is practical?

All intentional praxis, then, presents two kinds of problems: 1) To what extent is the intention of the subject present in the object and how does that intention acquire an objective form or shape? How, in other words, does the subjective become objective, and what modifications does the intention, end or original project undergo in the course of the practical process? As we have already pointed out,[2] praxis requires a conscious activity not only at the outset but throughout the practical process, given that the material to be transformed constantly offers up new resistances which make the result once again relatively uncertain and unpredictable. 2) What significance has the intention in the practical subject in the evaluation of that result? This is obviously of key importance in our mode of judging practical activity, be it artistic, productive or political.

We can begin by giving a single, common answer to these two related questions. If intentional praxis is the realisation of an intention modified in its turn by transformations occurring in the course of the practical process, then the product of the activity of the subject is simply an intention realised. In this sense it is impossible to separate the intention from the product in which both subjective and objective have been given form. If there is a lack of adjustment between the two, what is in the end decisive is the intention in its material form, or the product as it appears actually and objectively before us. For it is through the material product that we evaluate the activity of the practical subject and seek the validating criterion of praxis.

Intentional praxis in art

Artistic praxis provides an illustrative example of this proposition. As practical activity, art is the production of a new reality, the culmination of a process which began in consciousness, in the form of an intention, sketch or project, and was modified throughout the process until it acquired an objective reality; the product transcends the subjective acts that occurred during the practical process, yet preserves them at the same time in an objective form. Yet the fact that the original intention is modified, necessarily establishes a disparity between the intention and its product; it is this distinction that prevents us from reducing the being of a work of art to a creative intention. The artistic product is not, or at least is not entirely what the artist intended it to be. It is evidence of a subjective reality, or the result of an intentional praxis, to the extent that it is the product of a doing and not the mere expression of a life. The product of praxis, and thus praxis itself, has value to the extent that it is an object, and not simply as a result of its author's intentions. Its value is internal, rather than the fruit of something which the artist proposed to inject into the material from without. If he did not succeed in investing it with that intention, it is valueless; and if the intention is present within his product, it is worthwhile only to the extent that it has been given objective or material form. This serves to underline the distinction between intention and result, and thence the necessity to evaluate a work of art not in terms of its author's intentions but in terms of the practical, objective result of his creative activity. This distinction does not imply that there is no relation between the original intention, abandoned or modified in the course of the practical process, and its result; for although the result may be very far from, and even contradict the artist's proposition, it does not negate the original intention, but is the realised intention. It is the demands of this practical process of realisation that lead to the disparity between intention and result, since the original intention is modified in practice. We do not judge what the painter wanted to render on canvas, but only what he actually put there. Artistic praxis, even if it is intentional, should be judged or evaluated in its product rather than with reference to any intention that may be attributable to the artist. Intentional artistic praxis, then, cannot be used as a justification for intentionalist criticism,[3] which evaluates the work on the basis of the real or imagined intentions of the author, and forgets that the product of subjective activity is an object with its own existence and its own value.

Artistic praxis, in sum, is a practical activity whose intentional character is made manifest through a subject-object relation. The subjective is revealed in praxis to the extent that it is the objectification of the subject in the product of his activity that determines the way in which his praxis should be judged and evaluated.

Intentional praxis in social life

Let us now turn our attention to another type of intentional praxis: social praxis leading to the production of a new reality, be it political, economic or social. As we have seen, its highest and most creative form is revolutionary praxis, which can be characterised as intentional praxis to the extent that it has as its starting point a fundamental intention, project or objective conceived pragmatically, which is then modified as a result of the vicissitudes of the practical process until it achieves its final form, its result or product. In judging a revolution, we must be careful neither to ignore nor underestimate the result of the practical, revolutionary process, nor to overestimate the project, plan or programme that was its point of departure. For the project may not correspond to the objective realisation, since the exigencies of the process itself, the unforeseen factors arising in the course of activity, may impose modifications, even though they do not mean the abandonment of its essential content. The revolution, like the work of art, is a product, a new reality transcending the projects or intentions of the revolutionaries, the party or the vanguard that led and organised it. It is an objective reality that should be judged in the same way as the practical activity of the party—not by its declarations, programmes or projects, but by its practical acts and their result. In politics as in art, what matters is not the intention but the act, or to be more precise not the pure intention, but the intention objectified through action. Intentions are put to the test in the field of practical action. In the same way it is in practice, and only there, that the revolutionary character of a party or social class may be actually put to the test. Historically, for objective reasons to which we have referred, the working class is the revolutionary class *par excellence;* that is the source of its world-historical mission as it was formulated by Marx and Engels. On the other hand, as both they and Lenin explained, it is possible for this class to become bourgeois in certain historical situations and in certain countries; and here too it is practical activity, rather than the projects or aims of its organisations, that will tell whether it is acting in accordance with its class being, that is as a revolutionary class. In a more developed way, Marx, Engels and Lenin stressed the need for a working class party which would be the conscious and advanced detachment of the class, and would lead and organise its revolutionary struggle. Without this vanguard, represented in our day by the Marxist-Leninist parties, the working class cannot emancipate itself. Whether a party actually fulfils its function can only be judged on the basis of its concrete activity, its education, leadership and organisation of the masses, and not by its intentions or programmes, nor the declarations to which it subscribes. The necessity for a revolutionary vanguard, a conscious and organised detachment of the class, is a historical necessity so overwhelming that it has sometimes emerged in opposition to a vanguard which, though it was so in name, had failed to fulfil its vanguard role in practice. Far from undermining the theses of Marx, Engels and Lenin on the need for a revolutionary party of the proletariat, this serves to confirm their contention, for it is practice, as a realised intention rather than programmes and declarations of principle, pure intentions, divorced from their realisation, that enables us to judge practical activity, or the intentional praxis of a class or a party.

In 1921, for example, when Russian agriculture was experiencing a very difficult phase and the peasants were beginning to openly demonstrate their opposition to the economic policy of "war communism", there emerged a radical contradiction between the plans and intentions of the Bolshevik party and their practical realisation, or result. In the event, Lenin did not judge that policy simply on the basis of its intention, but in terms of its practical outcome. The Soviet regime's economic policy during those years had been dictated by the exigencies of the civil war, with the aim of mobilising all its agricultural resources. This led to a worsening of the situation of the peasantry and to a series of risings in the countryside, which undermined the basis of Soviet power. Lenin did not hesitate in that case to recognise that

Party policy had gone too far, that is to say that its intentions had led in practice not to a strengthening but to a weakening of the relations between the city and the countryside, between the workers and the peasantry; and in order to resolve that situation, Lenin proposed the New Economic Policy (NEP). In the event Lenin judged political practice not by its intentions, plans or projects but by its results, that is its objective character in practice.[4]

Two conclusions emerge from this: a) that there exists an individual or collective intentional praxis, to the degree that we can relate it to the intention or project of one or several individuals (group, class, party etc.); b) that a praxis of this kind, even if it is intentional and conscious, is explained and has value not by reference to its intentions, that is its merely subjective side, but in terms of its results, or its practical objectification.

Unintentional praxis

It remains to put intentional praxis in its relation to history. If man is essentially defined as a practical being, that is as a being who transforms a given reality and replaces it with a new one at the same time as he transforms and produces a new human reality, then the history of man is the history of his praxis. Man is historical precisely because he is a practical being. In historical terms, this human praxis is always the practical activity of conscious human beings, practical subjects who aspire to realise their intentions and who pursue their own ends. Nonetheless, if we pass from individuals to social groups, be they large or small (social classes, nations, social structures or even society as a whole), who act in a collective way, the question that arises is whether it is possible to establish a relation between intention and result, subjective and objective, which is characteristic of praxis, independently of the degree of parity between one moment and the other. Is it possible to attribute this practical activity to a given agent who has ideally anticipated the product of his activity and who has in consequence directed and organised the practical process in the light of an intention, project or end which has guided his actions?

History shows that man in the past transformed nature through his productive praxis and concomitantly transformed his own social relations. History, in fact, has been a total practical process carried out by men. Yet if the practical, transforming character of his activity is a fact proven throughout history, it is equally clear that men have not carried out that practical activity according to any preexisting end or common original intention which was intentionally modified in the course of collective practical action. Practical human activity has overthrown social systems and created new ones; the productive praxis of men has created the conditions for the successive disappearance of various socio-economic formations (slavery, feudalism, capitalism), and their social praxis (protests, rebellions or revolutions) has contributed to the abolition of capitalist social relations and to the overthrow of the old colonial systems. Men have abolished slavery, developed productive forces, created national markets, made war etc., yet in none of these cases can it be said that the result of their activity was the practical objectification of a common project or intention. The individual praxis of concrete individuals as conscious beings is integrated into a common praxis that culminates in a product or a result. Each can be related to an original intention, but not so the collective praxis which subsumes these individual activities. When a sixteenth century peasant fled from his dwelling-place to seek work in an incipient industry, his decision opened the possibility of a new individual praxis, as a worker in industry, and thus contributed to the gestation of a capitalist mode of production. When he abandoned the lands he had cultivated and went in search of free work, as a wage-labourer, however, it was not his intention to contribute to the development of a new mode of production. Nor did the industrialists themselves have such an end in view. Both pursued their own ends, and in doing so contributed to the gestation of the capitalist mode of production. Social praxis, collective praxis, when it combines a number of individual acts, resulted in the emergence of a new socio-economic formation which could not be referred back to the intention or project of any individual or collective practical subject. In this sense, it was an unintentional praxis.

If we consider the socio-economic formation as a social structure in which different elements or phenomena are integrated into a totality on the basis of a given mode of production, it becomes clear that changes in the socio-economic formation (that is, changes or the displacement of one complex structure of this kind by another) imply a radical, qualitative change in human history. This change or displacement does not emerge historically as a realisation or shaping of a subject's intention or project, but spontaneously, that is without reference to men's consciousness of the possibility that their activity could have these results. On the other hand, Marx and Engels emphasise in *The German Ideology* and thereafter that the displacement of one social formation by another, even if it is blind or spontaneous e.g. unintentional, is nevertheless neither arbitrary nor chaotic. It occurs in the first place on the basis of conditions that have been gestating in the previous social formation, whose members unknowingly contribute to its overthrow by pursuing their own ends, like the lumpen slave who flees his master's lands in search of liberty and better conditions, and goes to work in an atelier or a factory in the town. Marxism has shown that what determines the transition from one social formation to another are the contradictions that arise within the mode of production, between productive forces and the relations of production. This contradiction is the result of a cumulative series of changes in the framework of the system such that the relations of production, and particularly the form of ownership of the means of production, no longer correspond to the increase in productive forces. As it becomes sharper, this contradiction begins to demand resolution, and thus provides the historical necessity for the transition to a new social formation in which the relations of production do correspond to the progressive growth of productive forces. And this necessarily entails the abolition of the old relations of production and their substitution by new relations, which in turn brings with it the necessity for correspondingly radical changes in the political superstructure; political power, in other words, must pass into the hands of a new class.

Thus human history appears as a process at once continuous and discontinuous; the conditions created by the praxis of previous generations provide the basis for a new productive and social praxis, and historical continuity is thus assured. On the other hand the break with a previous social formation introduces an element of discontinuity into the historical process, as a new socio-economic structure arises in place of the old.

Men, the subjects of history

All the elements of history are the product of the practical activity of men. It is they who have developed productive forces, creating thus a contradiction which demands resolution; it is they too who have created the social relations of production and who destroy them with real concrete actions when these relations hold back the development of productive forces and of social progress in general. Men do not only develop productive forces, but also themselves form part of those forces; in the same way, men find themselves at the centre of the relations of production which are in the end simply the relations which they contract in the process of production. Similarly, the transformation of nature through labour, an index of which is the level of development of the productive forces, and the transformation of the relations which men contract in production, are both the work of actual men. Productive praxis is as human as social praxis, not only in the sense that man is its object, but also in the sense that he is always the subject of praxis; nothing can happen in history without his intervention. Both the development of productive forces and the overthrow or replacement of given social, economic or political relations are the product of human practical activity.

In his letter to P.V. Annekov, Marx delimits precisely the human character of all social relations and transformations: "what is a society, whatever its form may be? The product of man's reciprocal action."[5] Men are the subjects of all activity, economic and social as well as ideal: "men who produce their social relations in accordance with their material productivity, also produce *ideas, categories,* that is to say, the abstract ideal expression of the same social relations."[6] Men alone can destroy what they themselves have created, and this in order to open the way to a new creation; they make their own history, although they are constrained, as Marx pointed out, by existing conditions. From his early work onwards, Marx established an indissoluble unity of man and history; man cannot exist on the margins of history, that is of the history of his own praxis, nor can history exist as a separate power or as a superhuman subject. "History does nothing" "it possesses no immense wealth" "It wages *no* battles", Marx said, setting between inverted commas the speculative, metaphysical affirmations of the Young Hegelians; "it is *man,* real, living man that does all that, that possesses and fights: 'history', is not a person apart, using men as the means for *its own* particular aims; history is *nothing but* the activity of man pursuing his aims."[7] Thus history only exists insofar as it is made by men who themselves justify their existence by producing a new reality through their productive praxis and producing themselves in a process without end; men transform things and transform themselves—their own true history is the history of their transformations. Man is the subject of history, as he affirms *in* and *through* the historical process; history by the same token is solely the history of man's activity. The indissoluble unity of history and its human subject is a guard against the abstraction of either of the terms, since they are in fact one and the same reality. Unless we are to fall into a new abstraction, however, while affirming that there can be no history without men because they are its only subjects, we must make this concept of "man" and "human relations" more concrete.[8] What are these men who make their own history? What kind of relations do they contract in order to develop that collective praxis whose history constitutes the very content of human history as we understand it?

In the first place, men are not individuals abstracted from social relations, as Marx had already stressed in 1845. Individuals do not have an essence which is the same within or outside those relations; they are not social atoms who permit the social whole to be composed or destroyed. We have to do more than reject this traditional atomistic, robinsonian conception, however, in order to find the key to the explanation of society and of history. Sartre, for example, believes the actions of individuals to be endowed with a structure through which we can perceive the movement of history itself and thence the common praxis that transcends individual praxis. For Sartre, this individual praxis has a determinate character: "the only concrete basis for the historical dialectic is the structure of the individual act."[9] The individual is the basis because he is concrete; the movement of history is intelligible to the extent that his praxis is intelligible. "Starting from the individual worker, we have discovered that individual praxis reveals the full intelligibility of the dialectical movement," Sartre asserts.[10] In this context the rationality of the common praxis must also be sought in individual praxis: "the dialectical rationality of common praxis does not transcend the rationality of individual praxis. On the contrary, it is nearer to the ground than the latter."[11]

In Sartre's view, men are not atomised or isolated individuals; on the other hand, the movement of history can only be explained in his theory by starting from the actions and reciprocal relations of individuals, since their praxis is the very foundation of the historical dialectic. Sartre purports to remain within the bounds of historical materialism; but in that case, it is hard to see how we can compaginate Sartre's ideas with the cardinal thesis of historical materialism, namely that objective situations, modes of production, have a determinate role, and that economic and social relations cannot thus be reduced to mere relations between individual and individual. Further, if insufficient weight is accorded to objective factors, and to the role of social motor forces which surpass the limits of individual praxis and escape the consciousness and plans of individuals, how can we then discover the basis of the revolutionary, political actions of men, unless we adopt a Utopian or adventurist position? Common collective praxis cannot be understood simply on the basis of a conception of history as the totalisation of individual projects, for however many mediations may be discovered between the individual and that totalisation, individual praxis is still not its principal foundation. When Marx and Engels assert that men make their own history, those men cannot be individuals in an atomistic, private sense.

Individuality and sociality

The social is not the product of individuals; on the contrary, individuals are a social product. From a socio-historical point of view, individuality is not the point of departure; it is something man has conquered and enriched in a socio-historical process. Individuality, and the forms in which individuals relate to one another are socially and historically conditioned. The way in which they produce or insert themselves into the productive process, their links with the organs of power, their way of loving and facing death, their tastes and preferences are socially conditioned. A whole series of social relations merge in the individual, as Marx underlined in speaking of his social character or quality. This social quality does not completely determine individual behaviour, but it does determine some of its fundamental forms and limitations. Far from eliminating individuality, the individual acquires in this way a physiognomy of his own. The social relations that merge in the individual and the conditions that create the fundamental forms of his behaviour are not something supraindividual, for if we cannot abstract man from society, neither can society and social relations be abstracted from individuals. In the letter to Annekov to which we have already referred, Marx went on to say that "the history of men is never anything but the history of their individual development, whether they are conscious of it or not. Their material relations form the 'basis' of all their relations. These material relations are only the necessary forms in which their material and individual activity is realised."[12] The concept of man loses all its speculative undertones, all its empty generality if it is clearly understood as that double and intimate relation between the social and the individual. Society does not exist apart from concrete individuals, nor do they exist outside society and its social relations. Those who act materially, in practice, are concrete individuals, and social relations are the necessary forms through which their activity develops. And precisely because it does develop in these forms, individual praxis is integrated into a common praxis whose results transcend the ends and results of individual action. Beginning from given social relations rather than from the abstract individual or man in general, then, we can understand men, that is concrete individuals who are members of a given social formation, as the subjects of historical praxis. In this sense it is men, not atomised individuals who are merely supports of social relations or simple effects of a social structure,[13] who make their own history. Because the individual is a social being, the relations between men cannot be reduced to intersubjective human relations. The relations of production are certainly objective, social relations between men, independently of how they live or know them. But men do not contract these relations as mere supports or effects, but as concrete individuals endowed with consciousness and will, although a particular type of social relation, like capitalist relations of production, tends to make mere supports or effects of them and to convert human relations into simple relations between things.

Unintentional products of an intentional praxis

As concrete individuals, whose practical activity necessarily adopts the form of a social relation, men act socially, but at the same time act as individuals who produce and work consciously and in accordance with ends, independently of their degree of consciousness of the relations of production in which they are involved, of their membership of a given social class, of the type of social relation which they contract with other men and of the results to which their individual praxis leads when it is integrated and conjugated in a common praxis. In this way the intentional praxis of the individual is fused with that of others in an unintentional praxis which neither one nor the other has pursued, and which yields results neither sought after nor desired. It happens thus that individuals as social beings, endowed with will and consciousness, produce results of which they are not conscious, results which respond neither to the objectives which guided their individual actions nor to any shared proposition or project. Nonetheless, these results are the fruit of their activity. Man's praxis, therefore, has a double aspect: it is intentional insofar as his activity as a conscious being takes a social form and is integrated into a collective praxis (production as a social activity) leading to global results which escape his consciousness and his will (the production and conservation of given social relations). Decisive historical events occur in this way: the collapse of feudalism, the birth of capitalism, the formation of modern centralised states, the transformation of capitalism into monopoly capitalism etc. have not occurred as the result of anyone's conscious intent, yet they are results of human activity. To take another example, the labour of the worker is not intended to unfold his essential powers in an object, nor to develop productive forces: he works in order to subsist. Yet the results of his activity are integrated into a global result that escapes his consciousness. The worker in capitalism, then, is a concrete individual whose praxis consists in selling his labour-power as a commodity and putting it into action, throughout the working day; he is exploited and lives out his relation to his own labour in a negative way, blind to its true character and confused in his response to it, at least at first, although he may later become conscious that he is tied to a social relation of exploitation.

In this sense, then, we can speak of an unintentional praxis that necessarily presupposes the conjunction of a multitude of particular intentional praxis culminating in a result or product which cannot be referred back to a particular consciousness or will. Subjects who act consciously, therefore, can carry through an unintentional praxis.

We can now reduce the question to these terms: how can a multiplicity of unintentional practical activities lead to a result that does not respond to a prior end or intention, or to a result neither foreseen nor sought after and yet which, far from being casual or arbitrary, does have a clear raison d'être? We have to face the fact that subjects endowed with consciousness and will can, without consciously planning it, and acting in accordance with their own ends, produce something which is beyond the ambit of their will and consciousness—although this does not mean that it lacks meaning for them, nor that it fails to respond to certain laws.

Historical rationality and teleology

The situation would present few problems if we were to begin by recognising the unintentional character of man's praxis, its marginality to human intentions or projects, and go on to establish its relation with a superhuman power. In this case, the intentions of the superhuman subject would provide the rationale for unintentional human praxis; that is the teleological explanation of historical becoming, which reduces this latter to the realisation of the designs of a power transcendental to man, which is the true subject of history; it has its most complete expression in Hegel's philosophy of history. For Hegel, history is not properly speaking human history but the history of God's becoming, a process whose orientation is in accord with an objective, namely "that the spirit achieve knowledge of what it truly is and make that knowledge objective, realise it in an actual world and produce itself objectively."[14] History is the process of the (objective) spirit's realisation in time; thus the true subject of history is *spirit*. The purposive character of the universal historical process ensures both its rationality and its unity. Every society represents some degree of realisation of the spirit, and is therefore rational; further, every society is rational insofar as it forms part of a unique process. History, then, as a rational, unitary and completed process of the realisation of spirit is a true theodicy. Yet the spirit needs men in order to be realised; their actions serve the realisation of the universal objectives of the spirit. They move through a series of particular ends, trying to satisfy their interests and passions, and in doing so they fulfil the objectives of the spirit. That is what is meant by the "astuteness" or "trickery" of reason, which governs universal history: "reason makes the passion

relations of production in which they are involved, of their membership of a given social class, of the type of social relation which they contract with other men and of the results to which their individual praxis leads when it is integrated and conjugated in a common praxis. In this way the intentional praxis of the individual is fused with that of others in an unintentional praxis which neither one nor the other has pursued, and which yields results neither sought after nor desired. It happens thus that individuals as social beings, endowed with will and consciousness, produce results of which they are not conscious, results which respond neither to the objectives which guided their individual actions nor to any shared proposition or project. Nonetheless, these results are the fruit of their activity. Man's praxis, therefore, has a double aspect: it is intentional insofar as his activity as a conscious being takes a social form and is integrated into a collective praxis (production as a social activity) leading to global results which escape his consciousness and his will (the production and conservation of given social relations). Decisive historical events occur in this way; the collapse of feudalism, the birth of capitalism, the formation of modern centralised states, the transformation of capitalism into monopoly capitalism etc. have not occurred as the result of anyone's conscious intent, yet they are results of human activity. To take another example, the labour of the worker is not intended to unfold his essential powers in an object, nor to develop productive forces: he works in order to subsist. Yet the results of his activity are integrated into a global result that escapes his consciousness. The worker in capitalism, then, is a concrete individual whose praxis consists in selling his labour-power as a commodity and putting it into action, throughout the working day; he is exploited and lives out his relation to his own labour in a negative way, blind to its true character and confused in his response to it, at least at first, although he may later become conscious that he is tied to a social relation of exploitation.

In this sense, then, we can speak of an unintentional praxis that necessarily presupposes the conjunction of a multitude of particular intentional praxis culminating in a result or product which cannot be referred back to a particular consciousness or will. Subjects who act consciously, therefore, can carry through an unintentional praxis.

We can now reduce the question to these terms: how can a multi-

work for it."[15] "Men satisfy their interests; but in doing so they produce something else, something that is present in what they do, yet was not present in their consciousness, nor in their intention."[16] In brief, Hegel admits that historical praxis may be unintentional from the point of view of men, but argues that it remains intentional to the extent that it fulfils the ends of the spirit. Not only does the rationality lie outside its particular ends, but it is necessarily excluded from them; in the realm of the spirit which uses men in order to realise its own ends. Rationality, for Hegel, is inseparable from this universal purpose.

The rationality of actual history

From his earliest writings, Marx fought against this transcendental or teleological conception of history, basing himself on four principal objections: a) that according to this conception the subject lies outside the real history of man and reduces historical becoming to a history of the spirit; b) that it reduces the true subjects of history—men—to the condition of means or instruments acting on behalf of a superhuman subject; c) that it considers history as a teleological process, that is a process directed towards the realisation of an end; and d) that it bases the rationality of history on its purpose.

Marx counterposed to the teleological conception of history, the actual history of men made by themselves in a rational process, although this process has the teleological character of the development of humanity towards an end. As distinct from Hegel, for whom the rationality of one phase of historical becoming, as well as the rationality of the process as a whole, necessarily entailed that it had a purposive character, Marx never accepted the notion that the objective rationality of a system, or of one phase of the historical process of becoming, or indeed of history in its totality (a totality which was never closed) necessarily led to the conclusion that the actual movement was subject to a purposive process to which it could not but submit itself. Marxism, in other words, rejects all prophetic or teleological conceptions of history. For the rationality of historical movement rests not in the purpose of action, even where man, rather than a power like God, Spirit etc., is regarded as the true subject of the historical process of becoming. In this respect, Marx represented a radical break with every transcendental conception of history; and precisely because he acknowledged the existence of unintentional praxis, while insisting that it is still rational, Marx was obliged to pose another problem which had never arisen within the context of teleological conceptions: how can history be said to be rational, when men have not consciously structured it in accordance with their own ends? Where does this rationality come from?

The problem would not arise, of course, were it simply a question of seeking the rationality of history in certain phases or parts of the historical process, rather than in terms of the totality. It was in the Enlightenment that this 'partial' perspective was most clearly sustained, and achieved its highest expression, in the work of Voltaire. The Enlightenment philosophers regarded man as being rational by his very nature, although he has not always lived in accordance with his rational being. For the most part, in fact, he had always behaved irrationally in the past; to this extent it could be said that history itself was irrational. This irrationality, characteristic of the history of man until the Enlightenment, was now called upon to give way to the realm of reason. Society organised according to the principles of reason would leave superstition, error and the mists behind, and develop thenceforth in a rational way, in accordance with the permanent, universal essence of man.[17] In this conception, history becomes rational when man becomes conscious of his rational essence. Reason in history appears together with the history of reason; as long as reason is not acknowledged as the substance of humanity, however, all is chaos, confusion and obscurity and there can be no rationality in history. Hegel's great contribution with respect to Enlightenment thought, was to have introduced reason into everything and in particular into the process of historical becoming. For him, history is reason, not only in one privileged segment or area but in its totality as well as in each of its areas. Despite the Idealist, teleological form in which historical rationality appears in Hegel, his conception of history as a unitary, rational process, at once intentional and unintentional, was in the end to prove more fruitful than that of the Enlightenment. The Hegelian conception of history can only be surpassed when we acknowledge the need to explain rationally the whole historical process, up to the present, as well as each one of its essential phases. As man acts in accordance with ends on the one hand, and on the other produces results which do not correspond to his intentions, a rational history must integrate into its own rationality both the intentional praxis of individuals and the unintentional praxis on which multiple individual praxis is founded. Such an explanation should delimit the precise location of this historical, objective rationality; whether in the intentional praxis of individuals or whether, in contradicting Sartre, we do not regard the teleological behaviour of individuals as the key to the intelligibility of the historical process, but find it in an objective rationality which escapes the will and intentions of individuals. In that case it would be necessary to determine the precise relation between the various forms of praxis, above all when collective praxis responds, like individual praxis, to a prior intention or project, so that the product of that praxis is a result in which the practical activity of a subject (in this case, a collective subject) will be given objective form.

If historical changes obey a historical necessity rather than an end sketched out beforehand, or are in accordance with human essence (once human reason has discovered that essence, as the Enlightenment philosophers, as well as Feuerbach and even the young Marx, might have added), then the rationality must already exist within the social structure itself, for only in that way could changes in that structure, and therefore the continuity and discontinuity which constitutes the tissue of history, be rational. If the transition from capitalism to socialism, for example, responds to an objective rationality and not simply to the desires, ends and intentions of men, it is because capitalism has its own rationality which itself imposes the necessity of passing to a new social formation, endowed with a rationality of its own as objective, that is as independent of the will and consciousness of men, as the rationality of capitalism itself.

If the whole of history is rational, rather than one phase of it, there can be no socio-economic formation that does not possess its own laws which in turn provide its own rationality. The narrow and privileged conception of rationality characteristic of the Enlightenment—that rationality emerges in a given phase of historical becoming and is inherent only in a given society—has not disappeared completely even today; there are even echoes of it in purportedly Marxist writings. If Marxism and historical materialism in particular proposes to explain man's actual history, the general laws that govern its socio-economic formations, their change and succession, it must do so in objective and scientific terms; this requires that it accept the objective rationality both of the historical process as a whole and of each of its social structures, as well as of their change and displacement. Historical rationality cannot be regarded as having begun at a given point in time, or in a given socio-economic formation, whether it is capitalism, socialism, or whatever; objective rationality is not exclusive to the capitalist system, for example, unless it is suggested too that socialism is based on little more than subjective rationality e.g. the subjection of society to laws consciously established by men.

The universal rationality of history

The objective rationality of social development or of a given social formation does not immediately emerge; there must first be a whole process of abstraction, production of concepts etc. before it can be grasped as such, and that is the task of science and particularly of historical materialism. What can be scientifically explained or reduced to laws obeys an objective rationality. If historical materialism has been constituted as a science of the general laws of different socio-economic formations and their change and succession, it is precisely because, contrary to what the Enlightenment philosophers believed, the rationality of the socio-historical process is not limited to a single phase of the process; for this would entail dismissing everything that had happened previously because it belonged to an earlier, irrational phase.

What, then, is the significance of restricting historical materialism to its explanation of the social structure of capitalism, as Lukács did in his *History and class consciousness,* so that in his view, the very function of historical materialism would change after the triumph of the proletariat?[18] Since it is implicitly related to the problem of rationality in history, we can discuss this problem briefly at this point.

Historical materialism, according to Lukács, is "the self-knowledge of capitalist society,"[19] its field of validity and its sphere of application is, above all, bourgeois society. "Historical materialism is, in the first place, a theory of bourgeois society and its economic structure,"[20] a theory which, in capitalist society, as Lukács observed, is not only an instrument of knowledge but also a means of struggle.[21] By limiting its validity to capitalist society, however, or at least by pointing up the limitations of its applicability to pre-capitalist epochs, Lukács brings into question its character as a universal theory applicable not only to capitalism but also to the societies that preceded it: "historical materialism cannot be applied in quite the same manner to pre-capitalist social formations as to capitalism."[22] The unexceptionable suggestion that historical materialism should take account of the distinction between one social formation and another, and particularly of what separates capitalism from previous societies, is not sufficient reason to restrict its universal validity. What is debatable here is not the contention but the arguments which Lukács adduces to underline the necessity of seeing historical materialism as primarily the theory of bourgeois society, emerging within it and in relation to the situation of the proletariat not only as an instrument of knowledge but also of its action. Lukács provides ideological rather than objective reasons why materialism should in the first place afford us knowledge of capitalist society to the exclusion of earlier societies. "The purest, indeed one might say the only pure form of the control of society by its natural laws is found in capitalist production."[23] Capitalism is the culmination of the process of the socialisation of nature; reality can only become transparent when "the reification of all man's relations... (a product of capitalism) ensures that all 'natural limits' recede,"[24] which makes it difficult to distinguish in the past between economic forces and other forces, like religion, which express the social being of man.

If we limit the problems posed by Lukács to the terms of the present discussion, we can say that historical materialism is a science, the expression of an objective rationality, and as such can only be applied in societies in which that rationality is fully realised, that is, where society is totally subject to objective social laws. Thus Lukács would not regard it as being applicable, at least not on the same scale, to societies whose economic life rests on immanent, autonomous laws and in which human relations have still not reached the point where men become mere ciphers, as they do under capitalism. The feudal economic system, unlike capitalism, does not present the features of a system whose relations are "independent of all man's human characteristics." For Lukács, then, there are differences between structures which are to be explained first and foremost in terms of a difference in their rational structure. Historical materialism, then, cannot explain or define precapitalist societies because they are irrational from the point of view of the peculiar rationality of capitalism—that is, the subjection of society to natural social laws which operate as blind forces. For Lukács, economic determinism corresponded to the period governed by an objective rationality; the presence of a non-economic determinism (whether religious, political etc.) introduced a coefficient of irrationality typical of precapitalist societies, and thus negated the determinant role of economic factors. Lukács was able to arrive at this position because he failed to distinguish between the determining role of economic factors *in the last instance,* and the principal role of non-economic forces like religion or politics, in given historical situations. If, however, we begin by establishing a Marxist distinction between the determinate, and the principal role of the economic factor, it then becomes apparent that it is that very economic factor that determines whether religion or politics shall occupy a principal role in a given situation. At this point, the problem of the determining role of economic factors will have to rest; we can conclude by summarising Lukács' position in this way: Lukács acknowledges the existence of an objective, historical rationality at the economic level in capitalism. In precapitalist societies, however, the economic factor does not occupy this determining role; therefore such societies do not operate according to rational principles, and historical materialism cannot be applicable to them.

In the end, this is the key question: How can men unconsciously make a rational history while acting in a conscious way? If historical praxis cannot be explained by reference to the reflective, intentional praxis of individuals, it then becomes necessary to ask how a collective, historical praxis can be at once unintentional and rational?

The universal and structural rationality of history

Our analysis of the conception of historical rationality and historical praxis in the context of those conceptions in the work of Sartre and Lukács leads us now to try and establish the distinctive features of historical rationality in accordance with the basic theses of historical materialism.

The rationality of the historical process, or the history of human praxis, is universal. There are neither societies nor changes or displacements of one society by another which have no raison d'etre, or do not respond to a given legality. So this rationality embraces all societies, from the so-called primitive societies to those of the present day. There is no society that enjoys some special privilege because of its rationality; from the point of view of their structure and of the necessity of their change and displacement, all societies are equally rational. Yet commentators have spoken, and continue to speak of the irrationality of a previous, or alien society: the ancient Greeks, for example, judged other peoples in this way and qualified them as 'barbarous'; the enlightened philosophers of the 18th century made similar judgments about the Middle Ages. Indeed capitalism itself has sometimes been judged to be irrational or to have a limited rationality; the Young Hegelians justified their critique of German society in their time, for example, in terms of the need to destroy its irrational aspects by calling human reason into play. In all these cases the concept of irrationality as applied to a society at a given stage of development, or when it is undergoing change or being replaced by another, is profoundly unscientific; its only justification, in this respect, appears to be an ideological one, either in justifying the continued existence of a given social order, or in providing an ideological basis for the struggle to transform or accelerate the transformation of a given social structure.

The rationality of a society cannot be gleaned from the mass of facts and phenomena that appear on the surface, casual facts unrelated among themselves, but only when the fundamental elements or relations constituting a totality, or a whole of structured elements and relations, that is a system or a structure, are discovered and exposed to view. Behind the accumulated casual facts and individual activities lie other elements and relations, like "productive forces", "relations of production", "mode of production", "social classes", "the State", "religion", "art" etc. Such a system or complex structure is what is meant by a socio-economic formation (capitalism or socialism for example), whether on a universal level (a world capitalist or socialist system) or on the level of one country. There exist within this complex structure, simple structures, like relations of production in a given society, or dependent structures (although their dependence presupposes a certain degree of autonomy rather than excluding it) like the art or the political superstructure of a given socio-economic formation. As a complex structure, the socio-economic formation is characterized by a manifest rationality, which cannot be discerned in any internally related organic whole, embracing simpler relations and structural dependencies.

The rationality of complex structures, then, is not reproduced in any single element or structure in abstraction or separation from the whole; in this sense, neither the economic, the political nor the religious factor are uniquely or exclusively determinate. This is not to deny the possibility that the determinant role in that totality (although not in one abstracted structure or relation) may belong to the economic factor; if the economic element, or indeed any other factor were abstracted from the totality its reality would become extremely precarious. And the economic is determinate in the last instance, but the expression "last instance" itself indicates the existence of other realities or structures which cannot be reduced to the economic factor, although they are in the end conditioned by it—hence the relative autonomy of their development. The central role of economic factors corresponds to the place occupied by production in human society and its history, to the degree that it is not only the production of a world of objects and useful goods; its social character also involves the production of social relations, which is a necessary consequence of all types of production. In the final analysis, man's economic, material relations with nature and the consequent economic relations between men condition all others; but that conditioning is not one-dimensional, a matter of cause and effect, but one that develops *in* and *through* a totality. So the economic does not determine every aspect of the structure as a whole, and neither the totality nor its individual elements can be reduced to the economic aspect. If, on the other hand, non-economic factors must ultimately be explained by the economic, (although this should not be understood in a simple cause and effect sense) the economic cannot be explained by reference to itself alone, despite its determinate role. It too is one element of a totality, whose explanation must in turn be sought in non-economic factors; political and ideological levels, for example, influence and are necessary factors in its appearance and development. The relations between economic and non-economic factors, then, are therefore neither fully dependent nor completely independent of one another. The economic is both determining and determined; but its determinate role remains even in those socio-economic formations where it does not fulfil the fundamental role. In the end it is economic factors that determine when non-economic elements shall predominate. Marx himself made this clear distinction, in replying to one of his detractors: it is the economic structure itself, he said, that can explain why structures which are not economic properly speaking can come to dominate a society.[25]

The determinate role of the base and the principal role of one or another non-economic structure can only be determined by reference to the dependent relations of the parts with the whole, and to the interrelationship of partial structures. The actions and relations of men constitute a system; in this sense, historical praxis has a structural rationality, in that it is that praxis that reveals the law or laws that govern the totality of the structure. These are the fundamental laws of a given mode of production; and it is they that govern its structural functioning.

The rationality of changing social structures

Each structure is underpinned by a structural rationality; yet the rationality is also universal, and explains the appearance and disappearance of structures in time and the transition from one to the other. Each system has its own functional law, determining the interrelation of its various elements and the relation of those elements to the whole; but the historical process is also subject to laws that can explain radical, qualitative changes and the transition from one society to another. It is not a question of the emergence or transformation of one element in a structure, nor of a new relation between two or more elements generated within the structure; what is at issue here is the appearance and disappearance of whole structures, the transition from one socio-economic formation to another, or the process of development itself. Marx and Engels characterised it as a natural-historical process subject to objective laws which escape the will and consciousness of men.[26] But in that case, how does the transition from a structure A to another structure B actually occur?

The appearance of new structure, or socio-economic formation B necessarily presupposes a previous structure A, which like all complex structures had combined a number of related elements and was, therefore, a totality of relations and dependencies. The internal structure of these integral elements is not static, but dynamic, subject to constant internal change consequent upon the appearance of new elements and relations, the transformation of one element into another etc. These internal changes can effect an element or a given relation without affecting the structure as a whole. This does not mean that every element of the structure is affected by the changes, for there can be changes which do not penetrate the fundamental laws of the structure. The structure can absorb a series of changes without undergoing a qualitative transformation. Thus the appearance of a new structure implies a whole series of changes: the appearance of new elements, or new relations, the transformation of an element or relation involving modifications of other elements of the structure etc.[27] For the modification of one element may not provoke structural change at one stage of its evolution, and yet bring about changes whose effects are felt throughout the structure at another. The productive forces, for example, are a dynamic, constantly developing element of the structure closely related to another of its fundamental elements the relations of production which is characterised by its stability within the structure; while the first continually develop and grow, the second remain unchanged. For a period of time the productive forces do correspond to the relations of production in a given structure; in this situation, the relations of production contribute directly to the growth of productive forces rather than holding back their development, and the increase in productive forces—men or means of production—neither provokes nor requires a change in the relations of production—the form of appropriation of the means of production or its products. When, on the other hand, the relations of production present an obstacle to the development of productive forces, the previous correspondence gives way to a conflict, a contradiction, whose solution can only lie in the establishment of new relations of production. And this entails a radical, qualitative change in the whole structure and the appearance of a new socio-economic formation.[28]

Structural change, therefore, is determined by the structure itself, and the conditions for its change are internally generated. To the extent that the new structure gestates at the heart of the previous one, there is a relation of continuity between one and the other. Insofar as a new structure assumes the breakdown of previous structural elements and their relations, however, the relation is one of discontinuity. Thus a historical process, or a change of structures, [29] is at once continuous and discontinuous. New structures arise on the basis of previous ones; men make their own history, but their point of departure is the conditions created by previous generations; nevertheless, new structures must overflow the boundaries of previous ones. Some elements of the old structure are integrated into the new totality, entering into new relations there and fulfilling new functions; but new elements and relations emerge, and underline the aspect of discontinuity in the process of transition.

As is revealed by the fact that structural change cannot occur except under certain conditions and unless certain changes take place at the heart of a given structure which make the transition to new stages possible, the historical process, defined as the change and displacement of socio-economic formations, is subject to laws. There is thus a historical rationality in all social structures, and in the process whereby they are changed and replaced.

Marx's analysis of the economic base of society and its related and dependent political and religious structures, made it possible to consider the rationality of social life as a totality, and the rationality of the historical process as a transition from one structure to another. It also provided the basis for understanding how changes in one structure (the relations of production) can provoke changes in other, related structures. Finally the structural conception of the historical process elaborated in his *Preface to a contribution to a critique of political economy* of 1859, perceived the new structure as a consequence of the liberation of certain component elements of a previous structure and the exposure of contradictions in the economic structure. These were the necessary conditions of the transition to a new social structure or social formation. Marx, in fact, was the first to apply the concepts of structure and the historical process, in the sense in which we have defined it, to the study of history and society. Furthermore, he applied the same criteria in his concrete research. The Soviet philosopher Grushin, for example, who attempted to employ the structural principle in his economic, historical and social research by close reference to Marx's own work, asserts that: "the historical works of the Classic Marxists show that, by means analogous to those of contemporary science, history's task is to study the objective *systems of relations* and the reproduction of historical processes in the mind as organic systems."[30]

The structural analysis of a system cannot be substituted by a genetic analysis, although they are in no sense opposed; in fact despite their essential differences, they are in many ways mutually dependent. On the one hand, no structure can be analysed without reference to previous structures which it has liberated, in Marx's terms; on the other, we cannot study the genesis or evolution of a system unless we possess the means to understand what it is that is engendered and evolves in its place. As Grushin says, "the investigation of the historical processes of development of a complex whole presupposes a study of its *structure* and of its *genesis*."[31] Historical analysis of a system requires a theoretical, structural analysis with a historical basis which should not, however, be allowed to subsume its other elements. The Marxist, structural point of view, then, permits neither an (absolute) historicism, nor an atheoretical theorism which gives absolute primacy to the theoretical, structural analysis.

Unintentional historical products

The fundamental historical rationality is that of socio-economic formations, their appearance and disappearance, and the transition from one to the other. Social structures, however, are human products, and it is human activity that makes their change and transformation possible; men are the subjects of the historical praxis that erects or overthrows social structures, so that the laws which govern their function and change are simply laws of historical and social, human praxis. Men are the creators of their own history, not as shipwrecked mariners but as concrete individuals acting in conjunction with others in the framework of a structure that fixes their relations of interdependence with other members of society as well as the general forms of their activity. Individuals act not only socially, but consciously, as individuals who have set themselves certain objectives. Men have acted consciously since they came to exist as social beings, yet they have for centuries been unconscious of the laws and results of their activity. "In the history of society," as Engels says, "the actors are all endowed with consciousness, are men acting with deliberation or passion, working towards definite goals; nothing happens without a conscious purpose, without an intended aim." A little later, he adds; "The ends of the actions are intended, and the results which actually follow from these actions are not intended; or when they do seem to correspond to the end intended, they ultimately have consequences quite other than those intended."[32]

What men do, then, does not correspond to their intentions. It is not a matter of the disparity between ends and results imposed in all intentional praxis by the exigencies of the practical process, but that when the individual acts as a social being and integrates his praxis into a common praxis, this later becomes blind to its own results and its products cannot be referred back to any intention. In the framework of a given social structure, like feudalism for example, it is human acts that produce the changes in its elements and relations that overflow the qualitative limits of that structure. This entails the appearance of a new structure, capitalism, with new structural elements in new relations. Nobody, either individually or collectively, had proposed to create a new social structure in conformity with an individual or common project, and the same can be said of the elements and relations internal to that structure. Nobody had intended to develop the productive forces with an eye to the contradictions that this development would provoke with respect to the dominant relations of production and the form of ownership in particular. Although, as Marx says, the development of productive forces is "the result of the practical energy of men," its fundamental consequences escape their consciousness; their growth does not respond purely and simply to the sum of individual wills, since that very practical energy "is itself circumscribed by the conditions in which men find themselves, by the productive forces already acquired, by the social form which exists before they do, which they do not create, which is the product of the preceding generation."[33]

The duality of individual praxis

The fact that the results of common praxis cannot be referred to a consciousness or a will, nor to a sum of them, confirms that historical rationality cannot be discovered at the level of individuals, of their ends, their interest or their individual praxis. The rationality of historical praxis, of a collective praxis whose results do not respond to intentions or ends, must be sought at the level of social structures and fundamental changes in them. For this reason it is a universal structural and objective rationality. The laws that govern the functioning of structures and the changes in them operate on the margins of consciousness and of the will of concrete individuals, nevertheless govern their activity, or, more precisely, exist and are fulfilled through their activity. The objectivity of the laws that give the historical process a natural quality does not consist in a supposed metaphysical existence which has no reference to men (since historical laws are simply laws of human praxis) but in the fact that they exist and develop on the margins of his will and consciousness. The fundamental laws of capitalist socio-economic formations, for example the law of the production of surplus value, dominate from a point external to the will and consciousness of both capitalists and workers, and even independently of the knowledge they have of them. Since both capitalist and worker act in their capacity as elements of a particular structure of the relations of production within a complex totality (the capitalist socio-economic formation), their individual behaviour necessarily assumes the social form imposed on it by the structure, and the results of those acts correspond to the laws that preside over its functioning. The worker neither proposes nor wishes to produce value in excess of the value of his labour-power; the capitalist, for his part, can believe that when he pays a given wage he is paying at its true price, not the worker's labour-power but his labour itself. Each acts according to the fundamental economic law of the production of surplus value which objectively governs through his acts, but independently of his intentions, will or consciousness. The behaviour of the individual in this case responds to the exigencies of a social structure, and in that sense it is socially determined. The individual produces something that was not in his consciousness and which surpasses his intentions—something for which he is not individually responsible. The individual behaviour of both worker and capitalist, insofar as their individual activity responds to an objective law, necessarily adopts a social form which Marx analyses in

Capital, and which represents its subjection to the governing law of the structure on which the individual depends. Thus we can speak of "the rationality of the worker's behaviour" to the extent that it is in accordance with the fundamental law of the structure. Yet the individual as a social being does not employ all his possibilities of behaviour in the social form of his activity which accords with the laws of the system and which, under capitalism, takes the form of unintentional praxis. This point should be borne in mind whenever we speak of the "rational" behaviour of the worker in capitalist society.

Though he continues to be an agent of capitalist production, and his activity necessarily adopts a social form whose results escape his will and consciousness, the worker is a concrete individual who acts as a conscious being and pursues his own ends. Thus his individual, practical activity has a double character: intentional, insofar as he acts in the belief that he is realising his own ends, and unintentional to the extent that in acting, as he must, in a social form, the results of his acts do not respond to previously devised ends of his own. There is revealed in his practical activity at the same time an internal contradiction; because it is at once intentional and unintentional, and is itself the expression of a contradiction between the individual and the social, the social, unintentional form of his praxis is opposed to the individual form it assumes in intentional praxis. The existence of this duality at the heart of one and the same practical activity—the work of the labourer—prevents us, bearing Marx's warning in mind, from making the individual responsible for an activity necessarily imposed upon him by the corresponding structure. Yet the activity of the individual cannot be reduced to its social form, for it is also the activity of a subject endowed with will and consciousness so that his praxis necessarily has an intentional character; it is not merely the personification of a social relation, supporting or reflecting a structure. If men were no more than the bearers of given social relations or the effects of a structure; if all the possibilities of their individual behaviour were exhausted in the forms necessarily imposed upon them by that structure, the historical process, particularly, for the present and the future, would be a process operating through the activity of men but without their conscious participation in the abolition of an outmoded social structure or in the creation of a new one—socialism. While the individual is the personification of functions and social relations, there is at the core of his individual activity a duality which in the end explains why the worker is not only the bearer of relations of production but also their gravedigger.

The need to take this intentional aspect of human activity into account does not affect the fact that individual praxis cannot be explained starting from the intentions of individuals, but only by taking as the point of departure the social structure within which they carry out their activities. It is this that explains not only the social form of his praxis but also its individual form properly speaking, that is the intentional form that it presents in a given structure. It is the social structure itself, then, that is the source of the contradictions between the intentions of individuals and the results of their acts, between the intentional and the unintentional aspects of praxis or between their social form and their actual individual content. Subjective factors alone cannot explain the failure to realise individual intentions; the social structure itself determines why the intentional praxis of different individuals yield in their combination a result neither desired nor projected by any consciousness.

From intentional praxis to common, intentional praxis

How, then, is it possible to pass from these individual praxis which seek certain results in accordance with given ends to a common praxis integrating the various activities of individuals, in order to produce a result neither foreseen nor desired, yet whose raison d'être stems from its correspondence with the fundamental laws of the system?

It is clearly not enough to point to the existence of a contradiction between individual ends and results and indicate that its cause lies in the general laws of the structure or the forces associated with those laws. Engels pointed up the contradiction, in this way: "that which is willed happens but rarely... the ends of the actions are intended, but the results which actually follow from these actions are not intended."[34] Engels also points to the need to go beyond these motives and seek the historical explanation, both in the general laws that govern history and in the motor forces that impulse them. The problem persists, however, for while it is true that we cannot start from individual ends in order to explain a result unconnected to any previously conceived end, nor derive the sum of individual praxis from any common praxis or its results, the fact is that unintentional common praxis and its products remain inseparable from the praxis of the concrete individuals who act within the framework of a system, since this unintentional product necessarily entails their intervention as conscious beings. Unintentional praxis is always the result of a multitude of intentional praxis, of the acts of individuals who, in pursuing their own ends, give rise to a result that had not previously passed through their consciousness in an ideal form, as intention or project. The problem can now be stated: how and in what conditions does the structure determine the passage from conjugated individual praxis to the unintentional praxis that corresponds to the rationality of the system? How and in what different conditions does another structure permit the transition from a multitude of individual praxis to a common, intentional praxis?

Engels explains the transition in the following terms:

"History is made in such a way that the final result always arises from conflicts between many individual wills, of which each again has been made what it is by a host of particular conditions of life. Thus there are innumerable intersecting forces, an infinite series of parallelograms of forces which give rise to one resultant—the historical event. This may again itself be viewed as the product of a power which works as a whole, *unconsciously* and without volition. For what each individual wills is obstructed by everyone else, and what *emerges* is something that no one willed. Thus past history proceeds in the manner of a natural process and is essentially subject to the same laws of motion. But from the fact that individual wills—of which each desires what he is impelled to by his physical constitution and external, in the last resort economic, circumstances (either his own personal circumstances or those of society in general)—do not attain what they want, but are merged into a collective mean, a common resultant, it must not be concluded that their value is equal to zero. On the contrary, each contributes to the resultant and is to this degree involved in it."[35]

From this passage we can deduce that 1) individuals are impelled to act by their aspiration to realise their own ends; 2) the ends they aspire to realise are interconnected and opposed among themselves; 3) the results obtained do not correspond to desired ends; and 4) the ends fuse into a mean, a common result to which every individual has contributed.

Engels emphasises the role of concrete individuals in historical praxis by taking to task these false interpretations of Marx's doctrine which made of the economic factor the *sole* determinant and consequently converted the economy into the subject of history. Yet in deriving the common unintentional result from a totality of individual praxis, albeit through a series of mediations, interconnections and conflicts, he neither explains why these individual praxis come into conflict, nor why they are translated into a mean, a common resultant, which does have meaning. The result of individual praxis, the unintentional result of intentional praxis, is not a statistical mean. Individual wills are not fused into a total resultant mean, but into an outcome required by the social form that individual activities necessarily adopt in the context of a given social structure. Consequently it is the structure that determines the contradiction between ends and results, and the conflict between different individuals; it is the structure, too, that imposes the unintentional character of the common result by making an intentional praxis impossible, not at the level of individuals but of society as a whole. Although history cannot exist without reference to concrete individuals, it is equally true that its unintentional products cannot be explained simply by reference to concrete individuals whose individual praxis are interconnected or opposed, in the first instance, only to become fused for unknown reasons into a common result in the end. Only by taking as a basis the laws that govern the functioning of the social structure can we explain why historical praxis has had in the past an unintentional character, and why in the present it could have an intentional quality, given that one and the other are the praxis of individuals endowed with consciousness and volition.

Within a given social structure, the social relations of production, and particularly the form of ownership of the means of production, determine to a large degree the intentional character of common praxis; as we have repeatedly underlined, individual praxis, whatever the structure in which it develops, always has a conscious, intentional character. It is the social structure as a whole, and particularly the form of the ownership of the means of production, that determines on the one hand the intentional or unintentional, spontaneous or reflective character of historical praxis, and on the other, the functioning of the law of a given social formation.

Interests and social structure

In the conditions of the private ownership of the means of production characteristic of the social formations of the past and of capitalism in our own day, the interests of individuals and of society as a whole do not coincide; when their social position with respect to the means of production, that is as capitalists or workers, are diametrically opposed, their interests are also opposed and antagonistic. If we wish to explain the activity of individuals, social groups or society as a whole, we cannot begin from their ideal motives, as the Idealist conceptions of history are wont to do, but from their interests, that is from the attitude of individuals, classes or society towards their conditions of existence which is in turn closely linked to their position relative to the means of production. Interests, then, have their source in objective conditions.

The activity of men—individuals, social groups or society as a whole— is an interested activity; to understand it, we must start from the human interests expressed in certain ends, from the objective conditions and especially from the form of ownership of the means of production, according to which the character of individual and social interests itself changes. Similar changes occur in the relations between the personal interests of individuals and those of the class to which those individuals belong, or between their interests and those of society as a whole. The character of those interests determines in its turn whether their praxis can be transformed, in the case of individuals and social classes, into an intentional praxis. Personal interests reflect the attitude of individuals to their own concrete conditions of existence; but because they occupy the same position with regard to the means of production and are thus members of the same social class, individuals also have common, class interests which are more than the sum of their personal interests, since they express the attitude of a social group towards its existence as such, and above and beyond the strictly personal interests of individuals. In social structures governed by the private ownership of the means of production, the interests of opposing classes enter into bitter conflict; in the same way, the interests that impel the ruling class to defend a social structure riven by a contradiction that can only be resolved by the disappearance of that system, enter into conflict with the interests of the whole of society.

Interests have an objective content to the degree that they are determined by the conditions of existence of men and thus give impetus to their activity, although they may have no clear consciousness of the link. In the conditions of a society characterised by private ownership of the means of production it is the character of these means that determines their consciousness of their interests. Personal interests are obviously more immediately recognisable, so that men tend to act primarily in terms of them; consciousness of class interests, or class consciousness, on the other hand, requires that immediate personal interests be transcended, so that a common, intentional praxis becomes feasible. And that class consciousness does not emerge spontaneously, but from the elaboration of ideological material. While class interests are formed spontaneously, in concert with the process whereby the class itself is constituted, the consciousness of those interests arises only in the process of the struggle between opposing classes, as a result of the elaboration of the corresponding ideology and with the creation of class parties to inculcate that ideology. Bourgeois class consciousness, for example, arose in the 18th century; proletarian class consciousness from the middle of the 19th.

In all progressive classes, class consciousness entails a consciousness of the interests of society as a whole. Because their class interests do not coincide with the rest of society even during the epoch in which they are the ascendant class, the bourgeoisie has only a limited consciousness of the interests of society in general, corresponding to its limited class interests. Only the class consciousness of the proletariat can grasp the interests of society as a whole, once its class interests coincide with those general interests.

Since interests depend on the social structure, or more precisely on the character of the relations of production and the predominant form of ownership, interests are formed objectively, have an objective character and their satisfaction demands a similarly objective praxis. The consciousness of interests in no way affects either their objective content or their formation, but does affect their realisation; hence the kind of collective praxis required to satisfy them, for only the consciousness of class interests can give that praxis an intentional character. Every praxis responds to certain interests, whether or not they are consciously held. Until individuals achieve a consciousness of their class interests, therefore, their collective praxis cannot have an intentional character, for it is only that consciousness that can enable them to set common objectives and develop a common, collective praxis. As long as individuals lack the consciousness of their class interests, only their individual praxis can have an intentional quality, in that it responds to personal interest.

Limits of an intentional, collective praxis

Interests and the consciousness of them cannot give rise to practical activities that contradict the fundamental functional laws of the structure. An intentional praxis that contradicted the objective conditions would necessarily bring about a conflict between objectives and results and these results would therefore assume an unintentional character. The structure thus makes its determining role effective when the ends of individuals or social groups are in contradiction with its fundamental, governing laws.

On the other hand, in the conditions of a social structure characterised by its internal antagonisms, the limited interests of the ruling class prevent it from acting on the basis of its understanding of the legality of the structure; in this sense, that legality escapes conscious control, and is spontaneous. In a structure dominated by private property, the structure itself engenders a conflict of interests which obviate the possibility of a denominator common to all those interests; in these circumstances the common, social activity of the ruling class cannot yield an intentional product—like a planned economy, for example. Private ownership of the means of production and the law of the production of surplus value admit only limited economic planning and regulation. By their very nature, the fundamental economic laws of capitalism govern blindly, spontaneously, and however developed the conscious class activity of the bourgeoisie, it cannot prevent these laws from acting in a blind, external manner. In the conditions of monopoly capitalism, the conscious activity of the bourgeoisie can achieve certain results which correspond to their intentions, but in the end its activity must yield results which it had neither envisaged nor desired: the sharpening of the fundamental contradictions in the structure of monopoly capitalism.

The limits of an intentional, collective praxis under the regime of private property are imposed by the structure itself, and by the laws that govern it. The action of these laws sharpens the contradiction between class interests, and makes any intentional praxis at the level of society as a whole impossible. If the actions of individuals, groups or social classes are to be founded on a common, intentional praxis whose results correspond to a common objective or project, there must be a radical change in the structure and thus new governing laws. Only in this way can historical development assume the character of a rational, intentional process, so that history ceases to be merely an objectively rational history, and becomes a history produced rationally. Thus historical praxis becomes a common intentional praxis on a social scale. And this is possible only under socialism.

Under socialism individual praxis are fused in order to yield a desired, anticipated product. The paths that lead through individual praxis to this global result are only freely laid to the extent that they are adjusted to a common end or project, and this can only occur on the basis of a fusion of personal and social interests such that the social structure ceases to witness conflict between opposing interests, that is by the overthrow of the system of private property and the abolition of the source of the division between contending classes. The disappearance of these contradictions (though other contradictions may persist) creates conditions in which social and personal interests may be merged and a conscious, common praxis developed. Where praxis with an intentional character had previously been restricted to the level of individuals, and to a greater or lesser degree, to the vanguard detachments of a social class, it may now become the distinctive feature of praxis at the level of society as a whole.

This collective, intentional praxis is not possible as long as the structure prevents the coincidence of class interests and the appearance of common objectives; it is impossible, too, as long as the consciousness of the ruling class expresses interests that contradict those of a society as a whole, and thus cannot raise itself beyond ideology to a theoretical consciousness of the existing social structure and of the whole historical process. The possibility of developing an intentional, historical praxis, based on knowledge of the functional laws of capitalist society and the historical process as a whole, only arose historically with the constitution of a social class like the proletariat, whose class interests gave impetus to the acquisition of that knowledge.

Subjectivism and voluntarism in intentional, historical praxis

By virtue of this common, intentional praxis whose products can be referred to the intentions or products of the conscious, advanced detachment of a class, radical changes in a social structure, and the transition from one socio-economic formation (capitalism) to another (socialism) can be for the first time the result of a conscious, historical process. The October Revolution was the first movement to put the revolutionary praxis of a social class and of the whole of society (the construction of socialism) in relation to consciousness, and thus to have the character of an intentional, historical praxis. The role of consciousness and of subjective activity as the intentional praxis of man acquires an entirely new dimension; but this elevation of the subjective factor, to the extent that historical praxis ceases to be unintentional and becomes the conscious, practical activity of a social class or of society as a whole, must not be interpreted in a subjectivist or voluntaristic sense. How, then, are the subjectivism and voluntarism manifested?

Whatever degree of consciousness men have of their interests and their actions, and despite the unintentional character of the products of their common activity, the results of their activity do have meaning because in the last instance they respond to the functional laws of a given social structure. As we have said, what is unintentional is not necessarily irrational. Feudalism, for example, was not unreason in history. When the slaves acted in accordance with the fundamental laws of feudalism they were acting rationally, although of course they could not act in any other way. Those who insist that the history of pre-Columbian peoples in the past, or of the colonial peoples in our own day are characterised by their irrationality, can only do so for ideological reasons. The universal rationality that embraces the whole of history, however, is an objective fact; although it does not exist outside men but rather as the rationality of their praxis, it does exist objectively, outside and independent of their consciousness and volition. Each structure or social formation has its own rationality, its own fundamental laws that determine the character of collective, intentional or unintentional praxis. In this sense, socialism as a social structure has its own functional laws, its own objective rationality which like every other structure opens certain possibilities and closes others as far as the rational, practical behaviour of its members is concerned.

The transition from unintentional social praxis, which has predominated until now, to a collective, intentional praxis of the kind that can develop most fully under socialism, does not in any sense imply the end or culmination of objective rationality, so that praxis can develop in accordance with laws (or more precisely the rules or norms) fixed by consciousness, even where it is a question of a common project or intention. For if that were the case, the rationality would cease to be objective or independent of the consciousness and volition of men to become their subjective product; that would be the conclusion of a subjectivist conception of intentional, historical praxis, which starts from the correct premise that there can be neither social development nor intentional or unintentional historical praxis without men endowed with consciousness and will (which holds good for all social structures, including socialism), and derives the false conclusion that the laws that govern a social structure cease to be objective when they are known, and thus become dependent on the will and consciousness of men. The result is a confusion of the rationality of a structure with the knowledge of it, and the incorrect conclusion that when a conscious, common, practical activity develops, the rationality of a structure like socialism loses its objective character. It is true that, since it is primarily a matter of structuring human relations, there can be no social structure without reference to man; we cannot deduce from that, however, that the practical acts and objectives of men, although they are consciously integrated into a common praxis, are not conditioned in their appearance, development, character and possibilities by the rationality inherent in that structure. It is only a socialist formation that can create the conditions in which, unlike the structures of the past, the integration of individual praxis or of the non-antagonistic classes that still exist into a common, intentional praxis is possible. Thus the difference between historical praxis in socialist conditions and that in presocialist societies does not consist in the subjectivity of the first and the objectivity of the second, but rests on the fact that in the first case rationality governs consciously and in the second, spontaneously. In both cases it is men who make their own history: in the past they did it unknowingly, unaware of the laws of social formations and of their change and displacement and thus unable to consciously utilise these laws in their favour by accelerating historical development; in the present, men make their history knowingly, conscious of the fundamental laws that govern the structure and, on the basis of their knowledge, directing and accelerating social development. The rationality can govern spontaneously in one structure, and consciously in another. The lack of knowledge of the structural rationality under capitalism, and the knowledge of it under socialism, create opposite possibilities as far as a common, collective praxis is concerned. In the last instance, however, it is the type of rationality of the system that creates the conditions for such a praxis, since the socialisation of the means of production, and the corresponding disappearance of class antagonism, facilitates not only knowledge of that rationality unlimited by class interests, but also the possibility for that knowledge, on the basis of a unity of interests and objectives, to be used on behalf of the whole of society. The unity of ends and knowledge permits the development of intentional, common, practical activity in accordance with the fundamental laws of the system. It is precisely the unity of ends and interests, and the conscious utilisation of laws that ensure that the results obtained correspond to a greater or lesser degree to the objectives proposed. If, for reasons or circumstances that sometimes occur in the course of socialist construction, the laws of the system are ignored or violated, their rationality will not disappear, since it is objectively inherent in the system itself, but it will then, as in the past, govern with unexpected results and thus produce a conflict between the objectives and the results of practical activity. This transitory and prejudicial reappearance of unintentionality in common praxis, however, cannot undermine the objective rationality of the structure.

The subjective factor and objective rationality
In the specific conditions of a social structure not based on the

private ownership of the means of production, the existence of an objective structural rationality not dependent on the consciousness or volition of men adds weight to the role of the subjective factor. This elevation of the role of men's consciousness and volition does have limits imposed on it by objective rationality itself, since this is not reducible to a product of consciousness. The laws that govern the functioning of the socialist economic formation are not laws in a juridical sense, that is norms or rules created by men in order that the behaviour of the members of a given society conform to them. In this sense, the laws of socialism are no different from those of capitalism. Marx *discovered* the laws that govern the movement of the capitalist structure; he neither produced nor invented them. The law of the production of surplus value does not govern as a norm to which both capitalist and worker should submit themselves. The law governs objectively, independently of the knowledge that one or another may possess of it and also of their will or reluctance to be subjected to that law; the capitalist, or the owner of the means of production cannot fail to use those means and the labour power which he purchases in order to accumulate surplus value; the worker in turn cannot avoid selling his labour-power as a commodity and putting it into action in order to produce surplus value. Here the law acts objectively; it is not a creation of Marx nor the fruit of a decision on the part of the capitalists. The knowledge of it cannot lead to its abolition; it can only disappear together with the system whose functioning it governs.

The socialisation of the means of production under socialism governs as a law of the system and not as a juridical or moral norm. Although the degree of knowledge of the rationality does not meet the structural limitations which manifest themselves as limitations of class interests, that rationality is not completely transparent, nor do all the members of a society reach towards it in the same way. Thence the fact that intentional, common praxis, whose framework and basis is the social structure itself, does not always entail an adaptation of objectives to results despite its conscious character and its objective basis. On the other hand, knowledge of the objective rationality of a structure and the analysis of the concrete situation in that light, is not enough to ensure the success of a reflective praxis based on that knowledge. This engenders certain ends which it is hoped to realise in combination, but between these and the results there is inserted a whole practical process which, above all when it has creative character, entails a certain margin of unpredictability and uncertainty.

So collective, intentional praxis based on knowledge of the laws that govern the functioning of a socialist structure, far from excluding the existence of an objective rationality necessarily presupposes it. Further, the objective character of this structural rationality, far from excluding the subjective factor, the conscious activity of men, supposes it necessarily, since only this activity can ensure that social development is duly directed and accelerated so that men can be saved the untold sacrifices required by the historical process whenever it has a blind, spontaneous character.

Rationality and purpose in historical praxis

In sum, common praxis, conscious and organised human activity, in the same way as the unintentional and spontaneous praxis of the past, rests on the structural rationality of social relations and on structural changes in socio-economic formations, which are subject to objective laws. In both cases, history progresses rationally, not as the march of men towards an end or ideal that was written beforehand by some unknown hand; but this does not imply that purpose is absent from human praxis. That purpose is always at the level of individual practical activities which, because of their social character, are fused in the past into a common praxis whose products or results do not correspond to the ends and intentions of practical subjects. It is present in collective praxis, too, insofar as men organise and combine their practical activity in terms of a common project or end. There is in historical development, then, precisely because it is a history of the praxis of men endowed with consciousness and volition, a subjective purpose which gives praxis its intentional character, whether the intentionality is manifest at the level of the individual praxis which is translated into a common, unintentional praxis, or only in the common praxis of given groups, classes or society as a whole. This subjective purpose, however, necessarily presupposes an objective rationality which fixes its limits and possibilities.

The objectivist conception of human praxis which does not take into account the role of the subjective factor will evidently underline the features common to historical development and natural processes—that is, their subjection to objective laws—but will in turn be unaware of what is specific to human praxis: its character of activity adjusted to ends, even when human acts culminate in an unintentional product, since there intervene in all praxis subjects endowed with consciousness and volition.

A teleological conception of historical praxis lays stress on its purposive character in the name of the specific character of its subject, and makes of history a successive process of the realisation of ends that progress towards an ultimate objective: it too, lacks any scientific basis.

There remains only the history made by men in particular conditions which they also create; men make history and history makes men. There is no history outside the objective, historical rationality which makes a certain purpose, or a certain intentional praxis possible, nor outside a certain purpose in human acts on the individual and the collective level. But when praxis is conceived on a world-historical scale as intentional or unintentional human, practical activity, human history appears as a natural-historical process subject to laws, and therefore rational.[36]

Notes

1. *Theses on Feuerbach:* p 654.
2. Cf: Chapter Six above.
3. The intentionalist critique first tries to determine what the artist intended to realise and then to establish to what extent he achieved the realisation of that intention. This mode of judging the work of art rests on what Wimsatt and Beardsley have called "the intentional fallacy". (See: Wimsatt and Beardsley: *The Verbal Icon:* University of Kentucky Press, 1954 and also Beardsley's: *Aesthetics:* Harcourt, Brace, New York, 1958: pp 26-9 and 458-60).
4. Cf: Lenin's speeches and articles on the historical turn away from "war communism" towards the NEP in *Works:* vol. 32.
5. Marx to P.V. Annekov: 28th December 1846: in Marx/Engels: *S.W.:* vol. 2 p 442.
6. *Ibid.* p 448.
7. Marx/Engels: *The holy family: ed. cit.* p 125.
8. Cf: E. Balibar: "The basic concepts of historical materialism" in *Reading Capital: ed. cit.:* pp 251-2 and 270-71.
9. J-P. Sartre: *Critique de la raison dialectique:* Gallimard, Paris, p 279.
10. *Ibid.* p 198.
11. *Ibid.* p 532.

12 Marx to Annekov: Marx/Engels: *S. W.:* vol. 2, pp 442-3.
13 "Men do not appear in the theory except in the form of supports for the connexions implied by the structure, and the forms of their individuality as determinate effects of the structure." (Balibar: in *Reading Capital: ed. cit.:* p. 252).
14 Hegel: *Lectures on the philosophy of history:* p 77.
15 *Ibid.* pp 62-3.
16 *Ibid.*
17 "Voltaire thinks of reason as universal and constant. All human progress is indebted to it, insofar as diversions, evils and imperfections derived from its absence. Thence the fact that the efforts of the enlightened tend to make manifest the irrationality of the present and to sketch out a future in conformity with that universal and eternal reason. But this supposed universality and eternity of reason is no more than the reason that expresses on an absolute plane the particular, class interests of the bourgeoisie; its own reason presents it as universal, and in this way the order created according to it and in contraposition to the real, concrete order acquires the universal value which gives it the right to see itself as in conformity with man's rational nature." (A. Sánchez Vázquez: "La filosofía de Rousseau y su influencia en Mexico" in *Presencia de Rousseau:* UNAM, Mexico, 1962: p. 41.)
18 In referring to this central thesis of Lukács' work expounded in his *History and class consciousness,* first published in 1923, we should point out that later the author refuted its basic philosophical content, arguing that he had only understood Marx properly, and in particular the relations between Marx and Hegel, much later. (Cf: "Mein Weg zu Marx" in *Festschrift Lukács:* Berlin 1955).
19 G. Lukács: *History and class consciousness:* Merlin Press, London, 1971: p 229.
20 *Ibid.* p 229.
21 *Ibid.* p 224.
22 *Ibid.* p 238.
23 *Ibid.* p 233.
24 *Ibid.* pp 236-7.
25 He was refuting comments made by a German newspaper published in the U.S. on publication of his *Contribution to a critique of political economy* in 1859. Marx wrote "This paper has said that my thesis that the dominant mode of production and its relations of production at a given time—in a word 'the economic structure of society'—is the real basis on which the juridical and political superstructure is raised and to which given forms of social consciousness correspond, and the idea that the regime of production in material life conditions the whole process of social, political and spiritual life, was undoubtedly correct with respect to the modern world in which material interests predominate, but could not be applied to the

Middle Ages which were governed by Catholicism, nor to Athens and Rome, where politics reigned. Far from it: what explains why in one case politics and in another Catholicism were fundamental is precisely the way in which each earned their living."

26 Marx: *Preface to Contribution to a critique of political economy* in Marx/Engels: *S.W.:* vol. 1 pp 362-4.
27 Cf: B.A. Grushin: *Ocherki logiki istoricheskogo issledovaniya* (Essays in the logic of history investigation): Moscow, 1961: pp 37-53.
28 Marx: *Preface to a contribution...* in *S.W.:* vol. 1 pp 362-4.
29 On the conception of the historical process from a structuralist point of view, see M.A. Barg: "Strukturny analiz u istoricheskom issledovani" in *Voprosy filosofii:* no. 10, 1964, pp 83-92.
30 Grushin: *op. cit.,* p. 17.
31 *Ibid.* p 94.
32 Engels: *Ludwig Feuerbach and the end of Classical German philosophy* in Marx/Engels: *S.W.:* vol. 2, p 391.
33 Marx to Annekov: *loc. cit.:* p 442.
34 Engels: *Ludwig Feuerbach and the end of Classical German philosophy; loc. cit.:* p 391.
35 Engels to J. Bloch (21st/22nd September, 1890) in *S.W.:* vol. 2, p 489.
36 With respect to some of the questions discussed in this chapter and particularly the problem of the structural rationality of history, see A. Sánchez Vázquez: "Estructuralismo e historia in *Estructuralismo y marxismo:* Grijalbo, Mexico, 1970: pp 41-80.

IX. Praxis and Violence

Violence as a human attribute

All praxis is a process of forming, or rather transforming matter. Having dismembered and violated a material, the subject impresses a new form on it; in doing so, he must be cognisant of the legality of the object, for the subject can transform only to the extent that the object surrenders its own substantive character and accepts another. It is torn from the ambit of its own governing laws to become subject to a new law, established by the subject in the course of his activity. In this sense, the object suffers the invasion of an external law, and the degree of acceptance of that alien legality determines the degree of its transformation. That law, however, cannot be completely alien; were it so, it would encounter an absolute and insurmountable resistance in the object. Its properties, or its level of development must make it susceptible to transformation, or the activity of the subject would be null and the object totally invulnerable to change. The initial, ideal project in the consciousness of the subject leaves the object intact; its realisation is dependent, then, upon the internal character of the object. The object must be subjected to force, or violated, in order that the transformation can occur; only thus can its implicit potential for transformation be realised. On the other hand, that potential exists for the subject only, and can only be realised through his real, objective activity.

The transformation of the object demands on the one hand recognition of and submission to its legality, and on the other its disturbance or destruction. When it is executed on a real, physical object, the process may be qualified as violent, and the actions realised in order to disturb or destroy it, as violent acts. In this respect, it can be said that violence accompanies praxis. Violence is manifested wherever the natural or human material of the object of his activity offers resistance to man; thus it is characteristic of those activities whose aim it is to detain, change or overthrow a particular natural or social legality. In this sense, violence is exclusive to man, since he is the only being who needs to violate or do constant violence to an external legality (that of nature) in order to maintain his own human legality.

In a stable and self-identified world violence would be unknown, given that violence always conduces to undermining stability, immobility or identity. If man lived in complete harmony with nature, or passively subordinated to it, he would not have recourse to violence precisely because violence is the expression of a radical disequilibrium. In this sense, only man can be violent; the relations between man and nature, for example, as a constant violation of the established natural order, are always governed by violence. The transformation of nature itself, which impresses a human form upon it by disturbing its legality, is itself a violation; the humanisation of nature is simply a process whereby a law external to nature, a human law, violates natural legality. Society is the constant violation of nature.

Violence is a human attribute, insofar as man destroys the established order in violent ways; yet violence is not simply the effect of the presence of force. For there are natural forces too, yet violence is not force in itself, or in the act, but the *use* of force. Forces can act without being used; man alone uses force, and can use himself as a force—in this sense force in itself is not violence, until it is *used* by men, and violence has an exclusively human character.

Violence in productive and artistic praxis

We can now consider the relations between praxis and violence. The question cannot, however, be posed in an abstract or general way, but only in relation to specific forms of praxis and in accordance with the terms that unite and are opposed in the practical relation.

In productive praxis, for example, the human is opposed to the non-human (nature). The properties of the object of action are disturbed, destroying the mode of articulation of its parts. Matter offers resistance to these inroads, and obliges the subject to realise a series of violent acts in order to dominate it. The resistance is blind, opaque, the dumb resistance of a natural order that refuses to be broken. Praxis, then, is opposed by an established order that reacts, to use Spinoza's words, as if it were fighting to preserve itself in its own being. Productive praxis knows resistance, limits, forces that must be overcome; but it knows no anti-praxis, no system of acts tending to nullify praxis itself and ensuring the survival of a given reality.[1] It cannot be said, however, that the violence of the subject is met by counter-violence on the part of the object, or of matter; matter resists, but does not oppose the praxis of the subject in the form of anti-praxis.

A similar relation operates in the case of artistic praxis. Matter resists artistic praxis even more than productive praxis, because the form that the subject seeks to impose violates its legality to an even greater degree. For it is the way men impress themselves on matter in the fullest sense; hence the violence done to the object is greater, and greater too the resistance of matter. Yet however determined that resistance, it always has a blind and opaque character, and for that reason does not fall within the exclusively human framework of an anti-praxis. Similarly, the marble moulded or violated by the sculptor cannot be said to offer counter-violence to his activity. Thus in both productive, material praxis and artistic praxis, violence is the exclusive province of the subject, and fulfils a double function: on the one hand, it is the negation of a given legality (the destruction of a form, an order or a reality); on the other it is the negation of this negation, a dialectical negation of the matter that refuses to be overcome and resists a new form and a new legality. Violence is not, as simple negation, creative in itself; it is not sufficient to destroy a given legality, in order that a new reality may emerge. Violence, too, must be submitted to the ideal end or form which it is hoped to shape or mould in practice. Thus when we speak of a violent praxis, we mean that violence is at the service of praxis itself. Neither in productive nor artistic praxis can the violence exercised upon matter or materials have any status other than that of a means at the service of an end. Through violence, the transition is made possible from the merely natural to the human, materialised or objectified in the product of labour or the work of art. Praxis here cannot be reduced to violence; but violence as a means is indispensable to praxis.

Violence in social praxis

What is the role of violence in social praxis, when man is both subject and object? For social praxis is both the action of some human beings on others, and the production of a human world as a result of the subversion of an established social reality. Social praxis thus takes the form of a practical, revolutionary activity which brings about the destruction of a given social order and the creation and installation of a new social structure. In this way, a wide field is opened to violence, for the material of human action resists the transformation and human actions assume violent form, since violence alone allows obstacles to be removed in order that creation may take place. Praxis and violence are so intimately linked that it is sometimes easy to overlook the purely instrumental character of the latter. Indeed violence has been so clearly linked to all historical production or creation, that many commentators have seen violence as the very motor force of historical development—for example, those who, like Dühring or Gumplowicz have tried to find a theoretical justification for racism or fascism. We must, therefore, attempt to delimit the actual relations between praxis and violence and to determine whether and to what extent it is an indispensable part of social praxis, and of creative praxis in particular.

To repeat what we have already said about the praxis whose object is not man but non-human matter, it cannot be reduced to violence, but violence is its indispensable instrument. We have seen, too, that violence is integral to those forms of praxis because of the resistance offered by the material, a resistance of a non-human order which reacts blindly to human attempts to disturb or destroy matter. Action encounters a limit, not another action or contrary intent designed to annul it; praxis, in other words, is not met by anti-praxis, but by a physical, corporeal limit set by the resistance of a physical structure. Violence here involves the use of physical force to destroy or break down a physical resistance. The production of a useful object presupposes a series of physical acts which man executes directly with his hands, or indirectly with the tools or instruments that prolong his hands, in order to alter the physical state of matter. Without this violence applied by the worker or the artist, there could be no productive or creative praxis properly speaking. However rich and profound the spiritual meaning of the artistic object and however far the work of art is irreducible to its simple physical constituents, artistic creation is a process of objectifying a human spiritual content in a given material, and as such could not be achieved unless the artist won the submission of the material through violence.

In both forms of praxis, violence represents the destruction of a physical order, or a given material structure; it therefore has a physical character, in the restricted sense of the use of physical force in order to achieve the destruction or alteration of a given natural or social order. In these two specific forms of praxis, the transformation of matter necessarily entails violence, or the alteration or physical destruction of the properties or legalities of a physical object.

Social praxis involves action exercised on concrete men and human relations which constitute its object and material. These men are beings endowed with a body, men of "flesh and blood" as Unamuno would say. The acts aimed at them, however, involve their social rather than their physical, corporeal being, that is their condition as subjects of given economic, social and political relations embodied and crystallised in certain institutions and relations that cannot exist externally to concrete individuals. Social praxis tends towards the destruction or alteration of a given social structure and its social relations and institutions. It can only occur when men act as social beings, and exercise their activity on other men, who are such not only insofar as they relate to other men, as members of a community, but also to the extent that they are individuals endowed with a will and consciousness. Social praxis directed towards the transformation of a given social reality must also overcome the resistance of the social and human material that it wishes to transform; here praxis encounters the limit imposed by human individuals and groups. As we have said, violent action characteristically overcomes these limits by the use of force, force which has a material, physical character, since spiritual force cannot overcome a physical resistance. Thus, although concrete individuals are endowed with a body and consciousness, violence is exercised on them at the physical, corporeal level; the body is the first object of direct violence, even where that violence is directed against man as a conscious, social being. Violence seeks, in this case, to obtain the submission of consciousness and to enforce recognition. The alteration or destruction of the body as such is of no interest, except insofar as it is the body of a conscious being whose consciousness itself is affected by violent action directed against his physical being. Thus the violence executed on the body does not stop there, but has repercussions in consciousness; its true object is not man as a natural, physical being, as a mere body, but man as a conscious, human being. Although violence may be exercised on the body in the first instance, the violence that accompanies social praxis or anti-praxis entails the recognition that the body is not merely a body, but the body of a human being.

Violence and counter-violence

As in all forms of praxis, the violence of social praxis is determined by the need to overcome the resistance of matter (in this case, social matter). But in this case the resistance that it encounters is not of the same kind as the resistance offered by the natural or physical material of productive or artistic praxis. Man's being is not totally subsumed in the physical or natural being of the object of his activity in other forms of praxis; he is a being endowed with consciousness and volition, and not only does he blindly resist any attempt to alter or destroy a human order, but he also reacts consciously against a given social praxis precisely because he is a social being who sees his interests as linked to the maintenance of the order whose destruction is threatened. The violence that accompanies praxis is met by the counter-violence of those who resist it. While in the forms of praxis that do not have man as their object, there is violence and consciousness on one side, and blind resistance, pure opacity, on the other, in social praxis its object not only presents a limit that resists violation or suppression, but which has some degree of consciousness of the fact that it is offering up resistance. Man does not resist in a blind way, passively subject to a legality that fixes or determines his resistance, but can vary it according to his degree of consciousness until he transforms it into an open opposition, an anti-praxis developed in response to the violence of counter-violence. Thus violence is both in the subject and in the object, and accompanies both praxis and anti-praxis, both the activity which tends to subvert the established order and that which fights to preserve it.

Ever since violence has become a feature of society and been employed in the service of given social relations, it has always given rise to an opposing activity; violence has bred violence, understood as the application of different forms of coercion, including armed actions, with the object of conquering or maintaining an economic or political dominion or of achieving privileges of one kind or another. In class society, violence dominates both the internal relations of different social classes and the relation between countries; its extreme form is internal (civil) war on the one hand, and external war (sometimes wars of aggression, sometimes defensive wars of independence or liberation) on the other.

The appearance and development of violence in social relations is linked to objective factors—the rule of private property and the division of society into classes—which have made it impossible until now to solve the fundamental contradictions by peaceful means. The class struggle has developed historically with a varying coefficient of violence, but historical experience shows that when the existence of a ruling social class is endangered, that class has no hesitation in employing the most extreme forms of violence, including massive terror; for no social class is prepared to voluntarily abandon the stage of history.

Potential violence and violence in the act

Violence does not only exist in the act, or as a response to actual violence. It can be organised or structured as a potential violence ready to be enacted; this organised violence, or potential violence disposed to be realised as soon as the class interests which it serves demand it, is represented in the State. In class society, violence is the final rationality of the State: violence in the act when its character as an organism of domination of one class over another demands it, or potential violence when the State feels able to ensure that domination, or the establishment of class interests by other, non-coercive, means. In every class State, however, violence is the ultimate rationale, present throughout as potential violence, and prepared to become the act at any time. In societies based on the exploitation of man by man, like contemporary capitalism, violence is not only present in the direct, organised forms that offer real or potential violence, but also in an indirect and apparently spontaneous way, a violence linked to the alienated and exploitative character of human relations; that is, the violence of misery, hunger, prostitution or disease which is not the response to another, potential or active violence, but violence itself as a way of life imposed by a social regime of which it is an essential aspect. This quiet violence causes many more victims than the noisy violence of the coercive organs of the State.

Revolution and violence

If it is to avoid Utopianism, a true social praxis must begin by recognising that violence governs contemporary society. Force has always existed and has always been used. At the same time, the same people who have made use of violence have refused to recognise openly the role that violence fulfils; because he did acknowledge that function, Machiavelli still evokes shocked and horrified reactions. Other than in arbitrary or despotic regimes, there is always a tendency to deny it or hide it, although it is sometimes recognised as a necessary evil in the defence of certain principles deemed to be pure, for in that case its application leaves the purity of those principles intact, since it is assumed that violence is in an external relation to those principles. In other cases, violence is no longer considered as a necessary evil that leaves the purity of the ends intact, but as inherent in the ends themselves in the form of a normal and natural exploitation of man by man, or the legitimate development of a superior civilisation which requires the colonisation of other peoples. Violence, then, is represented as a fact as natural as the ends from which it is inseparable, since their fulfilment could not fail to be violent, unless the ends themselves were denied.

In both cases, violence is inseparable from politics. Yet while in the one case great abstract universal principles are put on the first plane, and violence is practised as an evil which is not necessarily related to its content but to its application, in the other case it appears as inherent in the very principles themselves and thus in their application. While in the one case the principles do not assume the presence of violence, and indeed attempt to ignore or hide it or dismiss it as external to them, in the other it is assumed as a universal, metaphysical principle consubstantial with man and history.

In a world governed by open, unstinted violence, what role does it fulfil in that practical, human activity whose object is to transform the social reality itself? The historical experience of the past shows that, in class societies, the great social changes that entail a true, revolutionary transformation of society have never been able to dispense with violence. The examples of the English Revolution in the 17th century, the French and North American in the 18th, the Mexican, Russian and Chinese in the 20th, to which should be added the Latin American Wars of Independence in the last century and the liberation movements of Asia and Africa in our own day, would all seem to confirm Marx's contention that "force is the midwife of every old society pregnant with a new one,"[2] but taking this phrase in its true sense: the midwife does not herself give birth, but helps those who do give birth. Violence was not invented in some previous revolution; the revolutionaries of all ages have had recourse to it because only with its aid could new social relations be created. Violence emerged, in the first place, as a means to the destruction or overthrow of a social order incarnate in concrete men of flesh and blood who in their turn exercised a certain type of violence. The recourse to violence on the part of the revolutionaries was an indication in each historical situation that they had reached the conclusion that non-violence could not eliminate established violence, and that therefore in order to transform given social relations and create new ones, it was necessary to destroy by violence the social reality that was itself rooted in a real and possible violence.

The historical necessity of violence

Marx and Engels always recognised the historical necessity of violent methods of struggle in the revolutionary transformation of society, and therefore argued against underestimating the role of violence in that transformation. Opposing them on this vital question, Karl Kautsky and the leaders of social-democracy underlined above all the possibilities of carrying out the social revolution by exclusively peaceful means within the parliamentary context of bourgeois democracy. It was precisely this negation or underestimation of the role of violence, progressively emphasised by the reformist leaders of German social democracy from the seventies of the last century onwards, which led Lenin to firmly recall the role that Marx and Engels had attributed to violence in the transition from capitalism to socialism. In *State and revolution,* written on the eve of the October Revolution, Lenin said: ". . . the theory of Marx and Engels of the inevitability of a violent revolution refers to a bourgeois state. The latter *cannot* be superseded by the proletarian state (the dictatorship of the proletariat) through the process of 'withering away', but, as a general rule, only through a violent revolution. . . The necessity of systematically imbuing the masses with *this* and precisely this view of violent revolution lies at the root of the *entire* theory of Marx and Engels."[3]

Marx and Engels affirmed the importance of violence in opposition to the tendency of bourgeois historiography to negate or mask its role in the historical process and in the revolutionary transformation of society; Lenin, for his part, made a similar affirmation precisely in order to challenge the reformist and opportunist conceptions of Marxism which raised non-violent methods of struggle to the absolute plane. Neither Marx, Engels nor Lenin ever attempted to offer apologies for violence, less still did they consider it as the exclusive method of struggle or as an end in itself. For them, violence was a necessity imposed by the irreconcilable contradictions of class society and utilised, with diametrically opposed objectives, both by the ruling and the oppressed classes. Historical experience showed them that no ruling class was willing to voluntarily concede its vital economic and political positions, and for this reason they refused to be tied down by pacifist or humanitarian considerations; it showed them too that, faced with that resistance, the oppressed and exploited classes found all peaceful roads closed to them so that only the violent way was left. They did not extrapolate any apologia for violence from this objective, historical lesson; on the contrary, their objective, scientific analysis of historical developments, and of capitalist society in particular, led them to understand the necessity and the possibility of the abolition of violence, although the violent revolution had to play an important part in realising that possibility. On the other hand, Marx, Engels and Lenin resisted the tendency to exaggerate the role of violence; Marx had in his time already challenged the adventurist slogans of the Blanquists and the anarchists, who inflated the role of violent methods in order to substitute it for the real, objective conditions for revolutionary praxis; at the same time he condemned the crude and primitive conception of socialism or communism which reduced those two superior forms of social organisation to a form of organisation rooted in violence.[4]

Faced with the typical underestimation of the role of violence on the part of the opportunists and the reformists, and with its characteristic exaggeration in the subjective, voluntaristic perspectives of the Idealists, Marxists cannot fail to stress the fundamental role of violence, although they must analyse it historically, as it arises in different epochs, in various revolutions and above all in distinct concrete situations. Revolution and violence appear to be interlinked; yet their mutual relation exhausts all the possibilities of neither one nor the other. The revolution represents a radical, qualitative change in social relations and particularly in the relations of production, overthrowing an outmoded social structure and building a new one in its place. Thus it entails a change in the political, economic and ideological leadership of society such that power passes from an already reactionary social class to another, revolutionary class. The problem of the conquest and maintenance of power is thus a vital one for every revolution, but we should not confuse the character and content of the revolution with the means whereby the transfer of power from one class to another is realised, nor believe that the conquest and maintenance of that power represents the totality of its content. The concept of revolution cannot be reduced to the concept of violence, that is to the application of revolutionary violence. The essence of the revolution derives from the contradiction that it seeks to resolve, the social tasks to be fulfilled and the need to overturn the class in possession of the means of production, which is also the class that exercises power. Only in this sense can we speak of bourgeois, bourgeois-democratic, national liberation and socialist revolutions.

If revolution and violence are not historically identified, then violence in itself cannot have a revolutionary character, but can only be endowed with that content by the revolution that it serves.

Violence and revolution meet in history, but their respective contents are neither merged nor exhausted in that encounter. If violence is a fundamental condition of historical development it is not, on the other hand, an immutable, invariable or a priori condition of every socio-historical process. Should the recognition of the determinant role of violence in social revolutionary praxis, therefore, lead to the radical exclusion of the role which can or could be played by non-violence in relation to historical praxis, that is in the infinite process of man's formation or self-production? There can be no answer to this question that is complete, however, until we have dealt with the question of non-violence.

Non-violence

Non-violence is not passivity, but activity. We can legitimately speak of non-violent action to the extent that it seeks in a particular way to produce a certain effect in men. We have said that what characterises violence is not force itself but the human use of force to break or alter a given, physical, corporeal resistance. Violence imposes itself necessarily whenever there is a need to change a physical object, or in the case of men, to act on their material, corporeal relations or institutions, although in the end this action points to conscious and social aspects of that activity. Non-violent action, then, would leave its object intact as far as its physical quality is concerned; and that would make it inoperable where there is a need to alter a structure in a physical sense. In artistic praxis, for example, non-violent activity would be inapplicable, given that such activity entails the real, physical transformation of a given material; thence the doubtful validity of Croce or Collingwood's conception of art which, translated into our own words, present themselves as philosophies of artistic non-violence. The work of art only emerges as such as a result of the artist's violent action upon the material that he transforms. It is not that man cannot enter into a non-violent relation with objects—indeed it is the characteristic feature of acts like perception, contemplation, thought or the evaluation of an object, acts in which its physical properties or its own legality are not affected by the action of the subject. The object remains intact, since no violence is done to it. A change of level is necessary if the properties of the physical object are to be altered, a move from this non-violent, spiritual action to a violent corporeal or material act.

Like violence, non-violence would approach man as a social and conscious being: but while in a limited sense violence seeks to reach consciousness through the body, non-violence would try to generate a transformation in consciousness without touching the body, that is without acting directly upon it. Educative action provides an example of non-violent action tending to transform the individual as a conscious, social being without submitting his physical being to violence. On the other hand, it would be legitimate to speak of ideological or moral violence, since at this level action is designed to transform or orientate the consciousness through a weakening of human defences. On a social level, however, non-violence generally accompanies the attempt to transform social relations peacefully, in a purely spiritual sense, by persuasion, education at all levels, edification by example etc., and it is here that non-violence reveals its inefficacy at a historical level, since it seeks to affirm its particular mode of activity in a world that, for its part, affirms itself by violent means. Non-violence has to operate, in other words, in a climate of social violence, since the spontaneous violence of daily life has as its background the ultimate rationale of established, organised violence against which non-violent activity can avail nothing. Furthermore, the *non* in non-violence, while it implies restrictions on violence inasmuch as it renounces the use of force, can only restrict it unilaterally. When it sets itself to restrict actual violence, it also limits the level of potential violence that can be opposed to established violence; and since external violence then finds no limits on its expansion, non-violence can be said to contribute to that extension of organised violence. When violence is renounced as a matter of principle in a world where violence predominates, there exists the objective danger that non-violence will become the accomplice of organised violence, precisely by removing the obstacle to its growth, that is, the potential violence of its victims. And it is not a matter of personal choice: man does not enjoy an objective choice between violence and non-violence, since to date man has lived in a world which, on the world-historical scale, has never offered any such alternative.

The consciousness of non-violence

If non-violence has never affirmed itself in actuality, however, the history of thought offers numerous expressions of the consciousness of non-violence. In its religious form, it appeared in ancient slave-owning society, in the guise of Christianity; in its philosophical form it arose during the decline of the Graeco-Roman world in the guise of Stoicism, and in modern times in the form of German Idealism; in its socio-political form, the consciousness of non-violence has found expression in certain Utopian socialist or communist doctrines of the last century and in the reformist political theories that rejected or underestimated the role of revolutionary violence in the struggle for the socialist transformation of society.

The consciousness of non-violence nearly always expressed an actual impotence; the impossibility of transforming the world in ways required by non-violence. Man can be offered a non-violent progress towards heavenly liberation, like the Christian doctrine of salvation, towards the liberation from external goods in self-sufficiency, or towards a spiritual liberation through the autonomy and sovereignty of the subject, as the German Idealists promised. Reformism in its turn offered hope of liberation within the system itself through a gradual accumulation of reforms that would not require recourse to violent methods, and made no attempt to accelerate history itself. In all these cases, a virtue is made of necessity, and violence is presented not as an index of power, but of weakness. True power, they contend, resides in the spirit, or according to reformist economism, in the spontaneous progress of things.

Against this consciousness of non-violence, historical experience has shown that the liberation of man necessarily passes through violence; social praxis, in its decisive moments, has never been able to dispense with it. On the other hand, in underlining its role in history and its presence in the radical transformations of society, we must also challenge the tendency to raise violence to the level of the absolute.

The apologia for violence

The apology for or absolutisation of violence with respect to all human, social praxis, real or possible, takes the following forms: a) the assertion that history is violence, and that violence is ultimately the subsoil, the root or the motor force of history. (History as the history of human violence.) b) the notion that social praxis, which is dominated by violence, could never take the form of a non-violent social praxis. (Violence as an indispensable element of all praxis, present or future.) c) the assertion that one violence will historically succeed another. (The impossibility of a new society without a State or similar mechanism of coercion.)

These three affirmations rest on a metaphysical conception of violence in isolation from the socio-historical context in which violence serves a given social praxis. They forget that violence is only the result of the rejection of a given social order which it is hoped to transform and replace with another (praxis), and arises because this attempt at transformation meets with the conscious and organised resistance of those who insist on maintaining and defending what exists (anti-praxis). There is violence, then, because there are antagonistic irreconcileable contradictions between men and between social classes. In this sense Marx and Engels in the *Communist Manifesto* spoke of history as the history of class struggle.[5] Inasmuch as social classes confront irreconcileable ends and interests, this antagonistic contradiction must be resolved in a violent way. Violence is the means to the conquest and maintenance of power, but no social class prefers violence when it can achieve its objectives by non-violent means, just as no social class will hesitate to resort to it in the last resort when its vital interests are threatened. This explains why, ever since society has been divided into antagonistic classes, violence has been present in all its decisive historical crises. Whether or not history is full of violence, however, we must not concentrate on it exclusively without also considering the human interests and ends of social classes whose entry into the conflict gives impetus to violence.

The objective elements of violence

The persistence of violence throughout history, and the extension of certain of its forms even beyond the socialisation of the means of production, might seem to justify the historical explanation. Man cannot cease to speak the language of violence; that was the position of those religious conceptions which regarded violence as the expression of a human nature corrupted by sin or by the living presence of evil. In our times, a supposedly objective explanation has sometimes been suggested which starts from a biological or naturalistic conception of man in order to see violence as an instinctive feature of men which will therefore never disappear from social life. Sartre, for his part, expounds a conception of violence in the context of his existential anthropology, according to which violence is a structure that accompanies human action as long as man dwells in the realm of necessity, or more precisely in the realm of "scarcity."[6] Violence is thus linked to "man's fundamental determination" or "the fundamental relation of our history." Scarcity, according to Sartre, makes history possible and is both its motor force and its ontological basis.[7] It not only engenders human labour but also the struggle between men, understood not properly speaking as a class struggle, but in the Sartreian sense of a struggle between "each" and "the other". Violence establishes a reciprocal relation between men, but it is a relation of an inhuman, alienated kind, which is the inevitable consequence of scarcity.[8] It might be thought that the actual fact of scarcity ("there is not enough for everyone")[9] leads directly to violence. Given the privileged place that Sartre accords to consciousness, however, what matters is not scarcity as an objective fact but scarcity lived and internalised to use Sartre's own terminology; hence his assertion that "violence is the constant inhumanity of human conduct as scarcity lived out, that is as the scarcity that makes each man see in every other man an other and a principle of evil."[10] The Sartreian idea of violence, then, rests on the concept of scarcity, which for him is the very basis of the division and opposition between men. There exist violent relations because scarcity makes us see the other as a danger. In the social field, the attitude I maintain towards the other is determined by my consciousness of his dangerous character in the light of scarcity. Men confront one another, but not in the Marxist sense of finding themselves in objectively opposed situations with respect to the ownership of the means of production.

For a Marxist and it is Sartre's pretention in his *Critique of dialectical reason* to complete and enrich Marxism, taking the thesis of historical materialism as his starting point—what holds back the men who objectively form a class, or leads them to violence, is not their consciousness of a situation of scarcity but their objective situation, not with respect to products but fundamentally with regard to the means of production. It is the appropriation or dispossession of these means of production, and not of goods or products in general, that divides and opposes them among themselves. These means of production in capitalist society are not "scarce" for the proletarians; they do not exist for them at all. They lack these means and this lack determines their attitude and their violent activity, in given circumstances, towards capital (in the form of strikes, demonstrations, protests of various kinds and even armed insurrections). The consciousness of this situation gives the actions of the proletariat a more conscious and organised character, but in the last instance its violence is economically and socially, that is objectively determined. On the other hand, the link between violence and scarcity can explain neither the sharpening of class conflicts, nor the extension and deepening of that conflict in capitalist society, precisely at that point where the increase in productive forces considerably augments the amount of wealth available.

Historically, the division of society into antagonistic classes and the appearance of organised violence, whether potential or in the act, are linked to the production of goods in excess of direct or immediate consumption. Scarcity, on the other hand, as a lived fact does not necessarily engender a violent attitude; furthermore, it is not always experienced as scarcity. It is historical and social conditions that allow the consciousness of scarcity to develop. The alienated member of capitalist society, for instance, who suffers a daily process of impoverishment of his spiritual life under the pressure of capitalist mass media cannot be conscious of the scarcity of things which subjectively he does not need, until the corresponding need is inculcated or awoken in him. The transitory scarcity that can occur in a socialist society (when there are insufficient copies of a book by Balzac to go round for example) is a lived scarcity that is at the same time an index of spiritual wealth, and as such does not necessarily engender a violent reaction. So that while it is true that the passage to a higher stage of communism requires that scarcity be overcome as far as a series of fundamental goods or products are concerned, overcoming a concrete contradiction between production and consumption which cannot be finally or definitively overcome simply because the wealth of human needs is never satisfied, the transitory and relative scarcity that occurs at an early stage of socialist construction need not engender divisions between men, nor violence. This implies that there is a qualitative difference between a society based on the private appropriation of the means of production and a society in which the socialisation of those means eliminates the real, objective basis of the division into antagonistic classes and of the violence caused by it. If violence survives even after the socialisation of the means of production (as violence directed against enemies of the class or in some cases, as during the years of the Stalin cult, against the members of socialist society themselves) its cause must be sought at levels very distant from that of scarcity.

If an explanation of violence based on scarcity seems unconvincing, it cannot gain plausibility simply because it is linked to the consciousness of scarcity or, as Sartre puts it, to the understanding of the motives and intentions of men in the context of scarcity. When I become conscious of him, the Other is for me something strange, alien, with whom I can only contract a violent relation. It is not scarcity properly speaking that engenders violence, but the consciousness of violence which makes the Other present to me. Violence, therefore, takes on a subjective undertone so that its social, class roots disappear. Violence exists objectively, however, insofar as men struggle among themselves in terms of their class interests, even when they are not conscious of the objective situation which moves them to violence as a result of this clash of interests.

Once the objective socio-economic, class roots of violence are ignored, it again becomes possible to concentrate on violence itself rather than on the system that necessarily engenders it: consciousness of violence itself, therefore, does not penetrate to its social roots. This consciousness is revealed above all in relation to the most direct and immediate forms of violence (colonial oppression, political violence, terror, armed intervention or war), that is, with respect to the forms of violence that can be lived and understood in a direct and immediate form. What is lost from view here is the fact that the violence that appears on the surface and is experienced directly, is the expression of a deeper violence; the exploitation of man by man and the economic violence served by that exploitation. In the case of colonial oppression—pure violence "in its natural state" as Fanon called it[12] — the source of oppressive, human relations is the economic exploitation of the colonial peoples. And one cannot build a wall between the exploited of the metropolis and the colonies, because that would simply replace one abstraction with another. British imperialism, like all imperialisms or colonialisms, offers proof of Fanon's words: "For centuries the capitalists have behaved in the under-developed world like nothing more than war criminals. Deportations, massacres, forced labour and slavery have been the main methods used by capitalism to increase its wealth, its gold or diamond reserves, and to establish its power."[13] But British imperialism could only exercise this violence *as capitalism,* having constituted itself as such on the basis of a terribly inhuman economic violence which Marx objectively and vividly described in his analysis of the primitive accumulation of capital.[14] If today, imperialism does not apply the same yardstick to the workers of the metropolis and the population of a colonial or dependent country; if there is an attempt to integrate the first into a "system of human relations" from which direct and immediate violence is excluded, insofar as beyond its frontiers only the law of the jungle and unstinted violence (armed intervention, war, terror etc.) are applied, the reasons must be sought in objective factors which determine the type of relation that can exist in each case and which determine, in accordance with those factors and with the level of revolutionary consciousness, the type of response that might come from the relevant social classes. This response can oscillate between relatively peaceful struggle, when there is no revolutionary situation, and armed struggle when the legal and peaceful means of transforming a given society have been closed. The fact that he ignores the objective factors in violence leads to a total concentration on situations of extreme oppression in which violence appears in a direct and immediate form, relegating to a secondary level those situations in which violence appears in more subtle and indirect forms. The basis of both extreme, direct violence in a colonial or dependent country, and a quiet, hidden violence exercised on the working class of a developed capitalist country, is the same. Imperialist and colonial violence is merely the extension, in a more extreme, direct and immediate form, of that violence which is exercised by imperialism in its own country in a potential form. The tendency to dissociate colonial violence from its objective, class roots, culminates in an underestimation of the working class as a revolutionary class and even in the gratuitous counterposition of the objectives of the so-called Third World on the one hand and the socialist countries on the other,[15] when it is undeniable that the construction and fortification of socialism, together with the struggle of the working class in capitalist countries and in the colonial and dependent nations are inseparable currents of the world revolutionary movement.

Thus if we concentrate our attention on the extreme forms of violence, like political violence, it could lead us to forget that in the colonial countries it can open the way, as Fanon points out, to other, less direct and immediate forms of violence after national liberation. Hence the need to uncover the economic, class roots of violence, for only thus can we find the ultimate basis of the various forms that it can adopt in a society divided into classes. From the Marxist point of view, this link between violence and economic and social factors is an essential one, for that recognition is also the key to the creation of a society in which the violent relations between men are abolished.

Men and the instruments of violence

Engels, in his *Anti-Dühring,* challenged the tendency to make of violence the decisive factor or motor force in historical development, stressing its subordination to the economic factor. In contrast to Dühring who regarded "force as historically the fundamental thing" Engels affirmed that "force is only the means and that the aim is economic advantage."[16] In another passage from the same work, he affirms "that force is conditioned by the economic situation, which furnished the means for the equipment and maintenance of the instruments of force."[17] In fact, the level of violence that can be exercised in a given society, above all in the case of military violence that Engels had in mind in these passages, is determined by the level of development of the productive forces and of technology.

Obviously the condition for violence cannot be reduced to this: there are other, more important conditioning factors, particularly in the case of social violence. The level of economic or technological development determines the nature of the instruments of violence at a given moment (from the stone thrown from a sling to the atomic bomb dropped on Hiroshima). The development of productive forces, of science and of industry are here the instrumental condition of one kind of violence, since it fixes the means of destruction and annihilation that can be used at any one moment. What determines their use, however, and the force embodied in them, is the type of relations of production, of social organisation and the State, and the correlation of classes in conflict. Violence is not a metaphysical or suprahistorical entity; it is socially and historically conditioned and it is in the end concrete men who determine its use and its extent, for as Hegel said, "weapons are nothing but the essence of the combatants themselves."[18]

Non-violent social praxis

In class society, violence governs as the *ultima ratio* of the ruling class; but we cannot deduce from that that violence can rule in an absolute way. In the first place every State, even if it is essentially an instrument of domination over other classes, aspires to obtain the active consensus of the governed; as Gramsci notes, "the State is the whole complex of practical and theoretical activities with which the ruling class not only justifies and maintains its rule but manages to win the active consent of the governed. . ."[19] It leaves some room for non-violence. Even in the most violent regimes, some social groups or sectors escape the effects of violence, namely the sectors that institute it and which could not, therefore, apply it to themselves.

Although history, as man's self-production, has progressed by violent means in its role as "the midwife of history", in our time a non-violent social praxis cannot be dismissed—although it would be exceptional. If in the end the violence of one class is a response to the violence of another, we cannot exclude a situation in which the ruling class might find itself forced, taking account of the correlation of the existing forces, to restrain itself from the use of violence because of its relative weakness in that correlation. During the eighteen seventies, for example, Marx and Engels dwelt at length on the

question of the peaceful conquest of power. Their conclusion was that in states with a highly developed military and civil bureaucracy, like France or Germany, the socialist party could conceivably come to power by the electoral road, but would soon be called upon to defend its victory in a civil war. Where that apparatus was weak, however, as in England and the United States, Marx recognised that there existed other possibilities and argued thus in his commentary on a projected law designed to proscribe the Social Democratic Party, which came before the Reichstag in 1878: "If, for example, the working class in England or the U.S.A. were to achieve a majority in Parliament or Congress, it could legally put an end to the laws and institutions that presented obstacles to its development. . .
Nevertheless the 'peaceful' movement could become 'violent' as a result of the rebellion of those whose interests were tied to the old order. . . (but they would then) be like rebels against the 'legal power'." Lenin, too, in his famous *April Theses*, written several months before the October Revolution, foresaw the possibility of a peaceful transfer of power to the proletariat. He based his conclusion on the provisional government's apparent reluctance to use violence against the working class. The counterrevolutionary coup of July 1917, however, turned the movement in a violent direction, and Lenin was quick to acknowledge the error of his earlier assessment. As he said, "all nations will arrive at socialism. . . but all will do so in not exactly the same way; each will contribute something of its own."[20]

Today, this possibility remains as exceptional now as it was in Marx and Lenin's time,[21] and it should not lead us to underestimate the role of violence nor to put on the same plane violent and non-violent methods, to counterpose the latter abstractly to the first nor to place our hopes of transformation exclusively on the peaceful road to socialism. For this would lead us back to reformism. The peaceful transition to socialism, then, is a possibility but an exceptional one; historical experience should be consulted in this respect and we should beware of adhering too rigidly to what remains a possibility until it is actually realised. When radical, qualitative changes are on the agenda, violence remains the general rule, though this should not lead us to dismiss those exceptions that do arise.[22] Creative praxis, and the revolution which is, as we have seen, a form of it, never permits a rigid determination of what is possible.

The violence that negates itself

History has shown that until now, violence has been the last rather than the first resort of the ruling classes. We have pointed out that not even the most violent State is a sphere of pure violence, nor of constant violence in the act. Nevertheless the predominance of violence over non-violence is patent both in praxis and in social anti-praxis. Faced with the use of force in the past, we cannot adopt an abstract, moralising position marginal to history and its concrete, class content. Social praxis has necessarily had recourse to violence, but this should not lead us to forget what it means when it is applied not to a physical object, but to man as a conscious, social being and his physical, corporeal body. If the progress of man's self-production is progress towards his humanisation, towards his elevation as a social, conscious, free and creative being, then violence, even where historically it appears to be positive, proves to be in some sense antihuman, opposed to that free and creative nature which man aspires to achieve. Truly human relations, as they are beginning to be forged in socialist societies, in which man is actually treated as an end and not as a means, as subject not object, as man and not thing, cannot admit violence. The violence that has historically accompanied class societies will be abolished together with the classes themselves, and with the State as an instrument of domination and coercion. The exclusion of violent means of resolving social conflicts and contradictions will be one of the clearest indices of a superior form of society in which the personality of each man can develop freely within a free and conscious union of individuals, and in which the coercive and administrative organs of the State are replaced by the organs of social self-management. The revolutionary violence of today contributes to a future state of affairs in which violence will be excluded from human relations. In this sense it is the potential negation of itself, and as such, is the only legitimate form of violence; for it is a violence which, though historically determined, contributes directly to its own future disappearance.

Towards the exclusion of violence

The philosophers of non-violence have been incapable of seeing this historical function of revolutionary violence. Hegel, for example, did situate violence on the historical level, but simply in order to underline its negativity. In the pages devoted to the Terror in *Phenomenology of Mind*, for example, he examined this form of extreme violence in relation to the historical experience of the French revolution. The revolution is an attempt to realise reason on earth, he says, and to put absolute freedom into effect, but this attempt to realise absolute liberty culminated in terror, in the negation of what it wished to be: "All that remains to that liberty is to *work negatively:* it is only the fury of things that must disappear."[23] From absolute liberty and the terror that negates it, man must rise to a new realm of "spirit certain of itself"; from revolution one must pass to "the moral conception of the world." Thus Hegel rejected revolutionary violence. Terror, however, as its extreme form, is only the negative element; creation, praxis, exists in another realm, the sphere of spirit. Thus one may pass to a new ground from which violence has been successfully uprooted; the soil of the spirit. Hegel saw, albeit in an Idealist form, that a truly human history must negate violence—though for him that history was a spiritual one. He did not recognise the positive aspect of violence itself, in making possible its own disappearance.

In Marx, revolutionary violence appears as an historical necessity which will necessarily disappear, as the socio-historical conditions that engender it themselves disappear. Its content is neither unique, universal nor abstract; it is violence and counter-violence, it serves some interests and not others; it is an element of praxis and of anti-praxis. Thus it is neither simple positivity nor pure negativity; it is ambivalent. In the conditions of class society, it is positive insofar as it serves a revolutionary social praxis. In a truly human world, where men unite freely and consciously, violence must be eliminated.[24] In a world like this, in which the liberty of each presupposes the liberty of all, violence and external coercion will give way to an elevated moral and social consciousness which will make it unnecessary. Social praxis will no longer necessarily be obliged to have recourse to violence.

Thus if it is true that violence, as "the midwife of history", has accompanied human social praxis in its decisive changes of direction, all violence of a positive kind works definitively against itself, that is against the violence of tomorrow. Thus in making possible a true, non-violent, human praxis, revolutionary violence and especially that of the proletariat is not only directed against a particular class violence, from which there emerges, in a transitory way, a new violence—the dictatorship of the proletariat—but is directed against violence in general, and makes possible the effective transition to a non-violent State. Only then will social praxis, having ceased to be violent, achieve the truly human dimension.

Notes

1. In his *Critique de la raison dialectique* (N.R.F., Paris, 1960) Sartre also uses this term, but with a very different meaning from that which we have given it. Sartre conceives *anti-praxis* as a process stemming from a multitude of individual praxis as a result neither sought after nor foreseen in those praxis; it is a blind, authorless praxis, opposed to a free praxis. (Cf: J.P. Sartre: *op.cit.*: pp 202 and 235-6). For us *anti-praxis* is the practical activity that tends to destroy a creative praxis or to maintain the dominance of a praxis whose products have lost their vitality.
2. Marx: *Capital I:* p 751.
3. Lenin: *State and revolution:* in *Works:* Vol. 25, p. 400.
4. Lenin, in his discussion of the insurrection, made a clear distinction between Marxism and Blanquism. Cf: *Works:* vol. 26, pp 22-23.
5. Marx/Engels: *S.W.:* vol. 1, p 34.
6. Sartre: *Critique. . .: ed.cit.:* p 209.
7. *Ibid.* p 201-3.
8. *Ibid.* p 209.
9. *Ibid.* p 204.
10. *Ibid.* p 221.
11. *Ibid.* pp 103-111.
12. Frantz Fanon: *The wretched of the earth:* (Penguin, Harmondsworth, 1967) p 48.
13. *Ibid.* p 80.
14. *Capital I:* pp 713-774.
15. Fanon paints a masterly picture of what violence means in the colonial world as an oppressive, political violence, at the same time as he reveals its illuminating and liberating power. Like Sartre, however, he fails to uncover the economic, class roots of violence. For that reason he failed to point out the true reasons why colonial violence is succeeded by the new form of political violence that corresponds to neo-colonialism. This also explains the Utopian nature of the means he suggests for countries

to free themselves from the colonial yoke, and accelerate their economic development. It should be said, however, that Fanon did see the necessity for a permanent revolution and to sustain the need to impulse national liberation until it acquires a social content, a process that can only be realised by leaving the bourgeoisie behind.

16 Engels: *Anti-Dühring:* Lawrence and Wishart, London, 1969. p 192.
17 *Ibid.* p 200.
18 Quoted in Lukács: *History and class consciousness: ed.cit.:* p 247.
19 A. Gramsci: *The modern prince:* Lawrence and Wishart, London, 1967, p 182.
20 Lenin: *Works:* vol. 23, p 69.
21 Lenin refers to Kautsky's insistence on quoting Marx "who in the 70s allowed for the possibility of a peaceful transition to socialism in England and America", and goes on to point out that "Firstly Marx regarded it as an exception even then. Secondly in those days monopoly capitalism i.e. imperialism did not exist. Thirdly, in England and America, there was no militarist clique then—*as there is now*—serving as the chief apparatus of the bourgeois state machine." (Lenin: *The proletarian revolution and the renegade Kautsky:* in *Works,* Vol. 28, p. 108). Of course, that conclusion would have to be open to question once again in our day, given changed conditions and forces.
22 The Hungarian Revolution of 1919 can be considered an exception to the rule which led to the assumption of power by the working class. It is also worth recalling that the intervention of the imperialist powers soon put an end to this socialist revolution that had been initiated and developed in a relatively peaceful way, without an insurrection or a civil war.
23 Hegel: *Phenomenology of Mind: ed. cit.:* p 446.
24 "Our ideal", Lenin said, "does not allow violence against people . . . (historical) development leads to the abolition of the (violent) dominion of one part of society over the other . . ." (Lenin: "On the caricature of Marxism" in *Works:* vol. 23, p 69).

Conclusion

This study set out to clarify some fundamental problems related to the philosophical category of praxis which, although it is central, as we have tried to show, has merited little attention from philosophers until very recently. Other epochs had deemed it worthy of more attention, but it only overcame its limited conception as moral activity opposed to theory when Marx gave it a new content: that of practical, material activity that tranforms the world. On the other hand, the category could only occupy its principal place within Marxism when two cardinal premisses—the one philosophical, the other socio-historical—had been clearly established. As long as philosophy conceived man almost exclusively as a theoretical, rational or spiritual being, it was not possible that his practical activity could pass to the first level as the principal object of investigation; on the other hand, while the revolutionary transformation of society did not present itself as a radical possibility, because the objective social conditions for that transformation had not yet matured, the consciousness of praxis and of productive, material and revolutionary praxis could not be raised.

Hegelian philosophy, by carrying the principle of the autonomy and activity of the subject to its ultimate Idealist conclusions, opened the way for a transition to the conception of human activity as actual, practical revolutionary activity. Feuerbach did not grasp the significance of that active dimension of consciousness which German Idealism had underlined. Clearly, he did anthropologise the subject, and put real man in place of God or the Idea; but in reducing true human behaviour to its theoretical aspect, he ignored the practical side of man's relations with the world. Marx was able to carry forward the principle of the activity of the subject, once anthropologised, by conceiving actual man not as a theoretical being but as a practical (or more precisely theoretico-practical) being who develops his transforming, material activity as a socio-historical being. Consequently the true characterisation of Marxism must start from the recognition of the central place occupied by the category of praxis within it. Every attempt to reduce the importance and limit the content of praxis entails a risk of falling into a scientific, objectivist conception or an interpretation that returns to philosophical positions which Marx himself had aspired to overcome, and did overcome, precisely by making praxis the key to his philosophy.

In the present study, we have taken Marx's conception as our starting point, and considered praxis as material, human activity that transforms both the world and man himself. This real, objective activity is at once ideal, subjective and conscious. To this end, we have insisted on the unity of theory and practive, a unity that also entails a certain distinction and a relative autonomy of one and the other term. Praxis has a precise ambit here, for it is neither so broad that it can embrace even theoretical activity itself, nor so narrow that it can be reduced to simple material activity. Praxis presents itself in various forms, but all concur in their transformation of a given raw material and the creation of a world of human or humanised objects. All these are specific forms of a total praxis whose result or product is in the end social man himself. Independently of the degree to which each individual, social group or society participates in this social praxis, it is the activity through which man produces or creates himself. Even though the object of human action is not actually man, as in productive or artistic praxis, all the specific forms of praxis are integral to a universal, practical process of the production of man. Conceived in this way, this total praxis has through all its advances and retreats, its hesitations and insecurity, a creative character. As a result man has advanced historically with regard to nature, and there has emerged a specifically human world in both a material and a spiritual sense. Although the total praxis is creative, or humanising, it can oscillate between one form or level and another, or between a properly creative praxis and a reiterative, mechanical praxis. We have also analysed the role of consciousness in praxis conceived both as cognitive activity and as an activity producing ends that govern the modalities of action. To this end we have discussed practical consciousness (conscious activity moulded in the practical process) and the consciousness of praxis (the consciousness that becomes praxis itself). In this light we have examined two new levels of practical activity, which we have called spontaneous and reflective, whose relations are of crucial importance in and for the revolutionary praxis of the proletariat.

For similar reasons, we have attempted to clarify the relation between praxis, reason and history. The need to do so arose from the fact that, where practical human activity is distinguished by its conscious, intentional character, historical praxis, or collective praxis which fuses a multitude of individual praxis, has almost always had an unintentional character. Men, the true subjects of history, have made history without knowing it and only in our time have they made any attempt to carry it out in an intentional way, on the basis of knowledge of the laws that govern social structures and of those that preside over the transition from one social structure (capitalism) to another (socialism). It is here that Marxism shows its practical value, precisely because of its scientific character. Thus the conscious, collective activity of men, far from abolishing rational objectivity, requires a scientific knowledge of that rationality such that human acts do not stray into Utopianism or adventure. Historical creation, as a conjunction of subjective and objective factors, entails both the elevation of the subjective factor and knowledge of the objective rationality.

Finally, having underlined the creative, affirmative character of praxis, we have emphasised that it can also bring with it some element of violence since it represents the disturbance or destruction of a given order. With particular reference to practical, social activity, we have studied the role of violence in the special conditions of class society; setting aside all illusions and taking our cue from historical experience, we have underlined its repeated presence in the great social transformations. Nevertheless, violence conceived not in the abstract, but socially and historically, yields the conclusion that it is not a constitutional element of every social praxis. Having considered the very limited possibilities of non-violent praxis in class society, we have tried to extend the perspective into a society without antagonistic classes. The transition to non-violence can only occur on the basis of the disappearance of the forces of violence themselves; this transition, however, itself presupposes violence, since it can only emerge as a consequence of a whole violent praxis on a historical scale.

Through our study, we have tried to raise the philosophical consciousness of man's practical, material activity. That consciousness must open a path for itself through the deeply rooted conception of man as a being whose only reality lies in the world of culture, and which today is threatened by the impetuous development of productive, material praxis itself. We have pressed for man's practical, material activity to be acknowledged in its true worth and value, and stressed that the world of material praxis cannot be artificially separated from the world of human culture, for it is only that praxis that can enable man to become a cultural being.

The true consciousness of praxis should contribute to the overcoming of the characteristic spiritualism that, for twenty five centuries, has persuaded men to regard their own material, productive praxis in a negative light. The human factor is not present only in theory, but in man as a theoretico-practical being who affirms himself in and through praxis.

Our study set out to show practical activity as an essential dimension of man as an historical and social being. Far from covering every aspect of the theme, it has simply opened a new area of discussion to a concept that has undergone changes in recent years in the light of the development of praxis itself, and of advances and changes in material production, as automation creates the technical and material conditions for ending, in large part, man's direct participation in the productive process itself. On a social level, the primary role of productive praxis will never disappear. Whatever the degree of participation of individuals, or whole social sectors, in the process of production, however much man breaks his direct contact with material things in that process and however long the chain of mechanisms that act as intermediaries between man and nature, human beings can only affirm themselves as such by dominating and transforming nature. This dominion, on the other hand, can only become possible with a fully automated industrial system. But in that case, what direction will the lives of individuals or social groups take in a future in which men are excluded from material praxis? Any attempt to answer this question must take account of the dominant type of social relations, for on them will depend whether automated industry creates new calamities and alienations for man, or makes it possible for man to develop his essential powers in practice in new directions, having liberated them from material, productive activity.

The liberation of man, his true human liberty to develop his practical, creative potential, is linked to the possibility of raising and developing the organisation of material production along rational lines, so that the labour-time imposed by necessity is progressively reduced. Marx, for example, clearly underlined the relation between human freedom and the liberation of material, productive activity:

"The realm of freedom actually begins only where labour which is determined by necessity and mundane considerations ceases; thus in the very nature of things it lies beyond the sphere of actual material production... Freedom in this field can only consist in socialised man, the associated producers, rationally regulating their interchange with Nature, bringing it under their common control instead of being ruled by it as by the blind forces of Nature; and achieving this with the last expenditure of energy and under conditions most favourable to their human nature. But it nonetheless still remains a realm of necessity. Beyond it begins that development of human energy which is an end in itself, the true realm of freedom, which, however, can blossom forth only with this realm of necessity as its basis. The shortening of the working-day is its basic prerequisite."[1]

This liberation of material production cannot be ensured, as is sustained by some of the idolators of technological progress or the panegyrists of "industrial society", without taking into account the dominant role that will be played in that process of liberation by the dominant relations of production. The transformation of Nature by man cannot be isolated from man's transformation of himself; productive, material praxis, whose development is an essential component of Marx's realm of freedom, cannot be separated from the social relations that govern its future fate. It is only socialist relations of production that can ensure that the liberation of material production does not become a source of a new enslavement and a new alienation. They alone can ensure that the time freed from production will become a genuinely free time, so that the exclusion of the individual from direct participation in productive, material praxis serves to ensure the development of his capacities in other fields—artistic, scientific, social etc. When this is achieved, then free time, and not working time will, as Marx says, be the true measure of wealth.[2]

These perspectives, however, which in our day seem still more extensive, demand the prior installation of the social relations that can convert these possibilities into a reality.

However much his activity may develop and change, then, man is a practical being; the conception of his role and of praxis itself, however, must maintain a dialectical relation with a changing reality in which both productive, material and social praxis undergo significant change too. And this is only possible on the basis of an enriched and more rigorous concept of praxis, to the development of which this study has been a contribution.

Notes

1 Marx: *Capital III:* (1972): p. 820.
2 "But to the degree that large industry develops, the creation of real wealth comes to depend less on labour time and on the amount of labour employed than on the power of the agencies set in motion during labour time... In this transformation, it is neither the direct human labour (the worker) himself performs, nor the time during which he works, but rather the appropriation of his own general productive power, his understanding of nature and his mastery over it by virtue of his presence as a social body— it is, in a word, the development of the social individual..."

"As soon as labour in the direct form has ceased to be the great well-spring of wealth, labour time ceases and must cease to be its measure, and hence exchange value must cease to be the measure of use value... The free development of individualities, and hence not the reduction of necessary labour time so as to posit surplus labour, but rather the general reduction of the necessary labour of society to a minimum, which then corresponds to the artistic, scientific etc. development of individuals..."

"Capital itself is the moving contradiction, in that it presses to reduce labour time to a minimum, while it posits labour time, on the other side, as sole measure and source of wealth. Hence it diminishes labour time in the necessary form so as to increase it in the superfluous form; hence posits the superfluous in growing measure as a condition-question of life or death— for the necessary. ... Forces of production and social relations—two different sides of the development of the social individual—appear to capital as mere means, and are merely means for it to produce on its limited foundation. In fact, however, they are the material conditions to blow this foundation sky high..." (Marx: *Grundrisse: ed. cit.:* pp. 704-6).

APPENDICES

Appendix One

"The Concept of Human Essence in Marx"

I

In the *1844 Manuscripts* Marx speaks time and again of man's essence—of "the human essence."[1] When he uses expressions like "human reality", "true human reality",[2] they have a similar conceptual content. Clearly, Marx found that content in labour which for him is man's essence, his essential reality.[3] In his analysis of the socio-historical reality, however, Marx—unlike Hegel—discovered its negation. The labour that he found in the real, concrete existence of men was alienated labour. Just as labour is the essence of man, this essence is only given in a negative or alienated form in the actual, concrete relations that exist between men and their products, their own activity and other men (the non-workers) in production.[4]

To summarise Marx's analysis, then: a) man has an essence; b) his essence is labour; c) in his actual existence his essence occurs only in an alienated form; d) man's essence is therefore separated from his existence.

It might be thought that this relation of man's essence in the real world characterises a given historical stage only. Marx certainly saw it as characteristic of a given type of society—bourgeois society; it is the worker whose essence is negated, and the labour analysed by Marx is labour in the peculiar conditions of capitalist production. But the problem is treated historically throughout the *1844 Manuscripts*, for Marx poses both the question of the origin of that negation of man's essence and the problem of its reappropriation. If the actual, concrete form of that negation—alienated labour—is linked in its origins to private property, it is rather as an effect than as a cause of that negation.[5] Its origins go back further in time, to man's original material weakness in the face of nature itself. It follows, therefore, that man has never lived in accordance with his essence. Thus we must add a fifth proposition to the previous four: e) the essence of man has never had a concrete, historical expression.

Human essence is conceived as non-alienated labour, that is, as creative labour. This implies that man should be able to recognise himself in his products, in his own activity, in the relations he contracts with others. That human essence has never been realised in the course of man's existence; throughout history man's essence has been divorced from his existence. This will continue to be the case until, under communism, that separation is overcome; then, existence will no longer be the negation of man's essence, but its realisation.[6]

This conception of the relationship between human essence (labour as creative, conscious and free activity through which man affirms himself) and social and historical existence (alienated labour as an activity through which the worker does not recognise, but negates himself) implies two fundamental determinants of man: his practical nature and his social nature, even though his practical, social activity appears as the negation of his own essence. Albeit in alienated form, man is praxis and history; these define the frontiers of his self-negation and the limits of his victory. In the production of a humanised world—even with alienated labour—and in the production of new relations, there appears the possibility of realising man's essence in his existence. Thus, in the first place as a possibility engendered by history itself and later as its historical realisation, it is possible to realise the essence which throughout history has occurred only in the form of negation. Communism, in resolving the contradiction between essence and existence, does no more than realise a possibility necessarily engendered in the historical process. In other words, (alienated) human existence develops socially and historically in a way that leads necessarily towards the identification of existence with essence.[7]

This conception of human essence cannot be considered as a variant of the traditional speculative and metaphysical view, that is, as an essence alien and indifferent to historical and social existence. It emerges clearly from the *1844 Manuscripts* that human essence is driven to realise itself, to fuse with existence; furthermore, history and the social existence of men lead necessarily to that realisation. The historical process is simply the history of this essence, first of its negation and later of its fulfilment. Its negation and its realisation are therefore historical. Since history is part of man's essence, that essence ceases to be an inaccessible norm counterposed to actual existence. In this sense, the concept of human essence in the *Manuscripts* cannot be reduced to a metaphysical concept of abstract and universal human essence incapable of social or historical realisation. Nor can it be reduced to the equally abstract and universal idea of a human essence that is merely the conjunction of the particular features of all individuals. For Marx, individuals will continue to live out the negation of their essence until the fusion of essence and existence is achieved.[8]

The conception of human essence that emerges from the *1844 Manuscripts* is perceived in relation to history and to praxis; in this sense, it goes well beyond earlier speculative, metaphysical conceptions. Nonetheless, it is not completely free from the speculative quality that characterised all discussions of this kind from the 18th century up to Feuerbach. The speculative element of Marx's conception arises from the divorce between essence and existence, even though that divorce must be overcome. If men have lived, and continue to live, in a real world in which their activity (labour) negates their existence; if, in other words, there is a mode of being which does not find expression in man's existence, then what is the source of this concept of human essence? It cannot arise from the actual relations between men, nor from the actual behaviour of individuals. It has been derived from the negation, at the ideal level, of actual human existence. By negating alienated labour, in which man neither recognises nor affirms himself, it is possible to arrive at the conclusion that man is defined by his labour, but by creative labour through which he recognises and affirms himself. Having interpreted actual existence as the negation of something which is not given in the real world, the concept of human essence becomes an element of a critique of bourgeois society. At the same time, history is conceived as a process through which that essence is first negated and later creatively realised.

What then is the import of Marx's slightly speculative conception? That there is an essence which is not given in reality, but which is a potentiality within historical reality itself. In real terms, the loss or conquest of that essence is located within the history of alienated labour. Actual, concrete man is *without* an essence—he does not exist *essentially* as a human being. Yet through his labour he produces a humanised world and produces himself; he marches through a history that contradicts his essence, towards his true human reality. In this sense, Marx's conception of history as the process of overcoming the contradiction between essence and existence, and of communism as the resolution of that contradiction, does still have a certain speculative colouring. But beneath this speculative element of the concept of human essence as presented in the *Manuscripts,* there lies the great hypothesis to which Marx later sought to give a scientific basis: man makes history through and *in* his praxis, and *with* it creates and produces himself.

II

From the *German Ideology* onwards, Marx and Engels abandoned the conception of history as a process of the humanisation and dehumanisation of men, of the negation and affirmation of his essence. The historical process is no longer presented as the development of a human essence first negated, then given as a possibility and finally realised. The starting-point for the analysis is no longer human essence but verifiable, empirical facts: production and the relations that men contract within production. Man's real nature is now sought in the contradictory movement of reality, that is, in the actual existence of men. What is at issue is no longer the essence of man but the nature of real individuals in actual life and history. Marx himself sets a clear distance between himself and both the traditional speculative, metaphysical view of man's essence and his own interpretations, to the extent that elements of the former conception were still to be found in the *1844 Manuscripts.*

> "The individuals, who are no longer subject to the division of labour, have been conceived by the philosophers as an ideal, under the name 'Man'. They have conceived the whole process which we have outlined as the evolutionary process of 'Man', so that at every historical stage 'Man' was substituted for the individuals and shown as the motive force of history. The whole process was thus conceived as a process of the self-estrangement of 'Man'..."[9]

If we take as our starting-point real individuals, their practical acts and the material conditions of their existence, rather than the essence of man; if men are not set apart from what they seem to be, that is from their real life and history, then we can no longer speak of a human essence divorced from existence. There does not exist on the one hand an essence and on the other an existence so distant from it that, until the moment of their fusion men have actually lived on the margins of their own essence. Man defines himself essentially through production; when he begins to produce, which he can only do socially, man enters the human sphere. In the *German Ideology,* Marx establishes clearly the essential relation between man and production.

> "Men themselves begin to distinguish themselves as soon as they begin to *produce* their means of subsistence... By producing their means of subsistence, men are indirectly producing their actual material life."[10]

Man has existed since production began. Ever since man has transformed nature and produced himself, there has been history—not a history in contradiction to his essence, but a history in which man lives, to use the language of the *Manuscripts,* according to his essence (man as a productive, social being), which is existence itself. "What they are, therefore, coincides both with *what* they produce and with *how* they produce."[11]

The *German Ideology* set Marx on the firm ground of real history; neither human essence indifferent to social life and history (the traditional speculative, metaphysical conception) nor human essence as a potentiality to be socially and historically realised (the conception of the *1844 Manuscripts*) but an essence that is revealed only in the social and historical existence of individuals "as they really are, that is, as they develop their activity within material limits and conditions which exist independently of their will."[12]

Speculation, when it is located in the real world, becomes real and positive knowledge. Essence separated from concrete history is no more than an empty abstraction. Its place is now occupied by a study of what men are in real life—productive, practical beings.

III

The human essence that knowledge reveals in concrete relations is not an attribute or set of attributes that all individuals possess and from which, by abstraction, the essence of man and the human essence of each individual can be derived. The idea of a human essence not divorced from its existence, that is, an essence abstracted from real men, might be understood in this way. But in that case, the human reality would be no more than the reality of individuals, and essence simply an abstraction from some characteristic of all individuals. This conception of human essence ignores the fact that the individual is himself a social product determined by social relations, and in the first place by the relations of production, which determine his individuality in given conditions. Marx challenges this conception of human essence as a universal attribute occurring in real individuals: "The human essence is no abstraction inherent in each single individual. In its reality it is the ensemble of the social relations."[14]

In the first place, Marx's interpretation reasserts that the human essence is not to be found in the individual but in the social relations of which that individual is himself a product. It is mere abstraction to speak of individuals existing outside those relations, just as it is to conceive human essence as an individual attribute. There is no human essence which is an attribute common to all individuals, for the simple reason that the isolated individual does not exist in reality. The universal human essence and the human nature of individuals can only be discovered in the ensemble of social relations that produce the nature both of social man and of the individual. The concept of human essence cannot be built, therefore, on the basis of characteristics common to all individuals, but only on the basis of the relations between man and nature (production, human labour) and between men (social relations).

The human essence of individuals, abstract men, will always be an abstract essence; its reality is to be found only in the social relations that make of individuals real, living men. Yet when we say that man is an ensemble of social relations, we have gone no further than to establish the location of human essence, but not its nature. Having rejected the notion that human essence is to be discovered in the ambit of individual activity, it remains to define what it is that is essentially human. It cannot occur independently of the actual relations between men; it is not to be found in the individual separately or collectively. Human essence is given socially, in the practice that is the basis of all human activity. Man is, in essence, a productive being. Production, and in the first place material production, is what determines the very existence of human society, of each individual and of history itself.[15]

IV

Man has an essence to the extent that he is a social being who produces. The process whereby the objective reality is transformed, and in which man produces himself, is in turn a process that develops through time. Since he is a social and practical being, man is never fixed within any particular social form of his practical activity. Thus human essence resides in man's social, practical-productive and historical nature. Man produces socially and in this process produces himself; this self-production, as a process in time, makes of him a historical being.

These three essential dimensions of man are inseparable; each necessarily implies the other. Man's *social* being entails the other two essential features, since he does not exist only within a relation or a network of social relations. Those relations are at the same time a human product; he himself produces his own social relations. On the other hand, these relations change historically in accordance with each given social structure. In an analogous way, the productive, transforming nature of men is only revealed socially and in different historical forms. Man is historical because he produces socially, and thus produces both himself and his social relations. Human history is thus the history of man's praxis.

The unity of these three essential features excludes any concept based on one of them alone. We cannot reduce that essence to labour in general, without taking into account the social relations that man produces. Nor can we assert man's social nature, as Aristotle did, without reference to the fact that man, as a practical being, also produces social relations and the forms of individuality determined by them.[16] Finally, we cannot speak of man's historicity in an absolute sense, excluding all the essential dimensions except its very historical character (e.g. the historicist thesis that "man has no nature, only a history"), for only a being that produces, and further that produces himself, can be said to have a history, which is in its turn the product—the labour—of a practical, transforming being (i.e. "men make their own history"). It is the unity of praxis with the social and historical being of man that determines his essence, and prevents the latter from being dissolved into history; on the other hand, these elements cannot be considered in a nominalist sense as something immutable or indifferent to history. Human essence is historical in a double sense: a) because it only occurs historically, and b) because it too is a product of history.

The social, practical and historical human essence is therefore never fully expressed in any of the concrete forms of man's social and individual existence. Insofar as praxis, and human labour in particular, is a determining element of history, this essential productive, practical and creative dimension is never totally submerged nor negated for sociohistorical man. Thus after the *1844 Manuscripts,* Marx never returned to the contradiction between alienated labour and human essence. The alienated labour that is discussed in the *1844 Manuscripts* implies a negative attitude on the part of the worker towards the products of his labour, his own activity and towards others, as well as a devaluation of himself as a human being to such an extent that the world of products that he created turns against him.[17] Nevertheless alienated man is a social being who develops his practical, creative potential by producing a world of products that bears his mark, even though its human aspects are not revealed in the process; in the same way, men produce their own history through their practical, social activity, although for centuries they have not recognised that history as a product of their labour. Lastly, men contract given social relations, although in a capitalist society these do not present themselves to him as social or human relations, but as relations between things.

From *The German Ideology* onwards, then, Marx no longer presents a human essence that has occurred socially and historically only as negation. The essence of man occurs historically in the form of real men, not men conceived individually, in isolation from one another, but in their social relations. Thus Marx moved beyond his own earlier conception of an essence divorced from existence, to affirm its social quality; in other words, he rejected any attempt to discover that essence empirically in an attribute common to all individuals. This essential human mode is not an idea, an archetype, an ideal human norm, nor does it occur once and for all in empirically identifiable individuals. This human essence—praxis—occurs only socially and historically and not as a common attribute of individuals. A given individual in a given society or historical epoch may be neither producer nor transformer; he may devote himself to activities that are neither transformative nor creative. If we considered practical activity as an attribute inherent in every isolated individual, we should not have solved the problem of the individual whose activities contradict his human essence. Yet the contradiction ceases to exist when that essence is conceived in a social sense, for individual activity can then only be considered as a social product; the predominance of this or that activity in the conduct of an individual, or even the predominance of a certain activity in a given society—politics, religion etc.—is determined in the last instance by the practical productive activity of men and the social relations they contract through that activity. The practical activity of social man, whatever the social structure in question or its stage of development, determines and makes possible in the last instance the behaviour of individuals. The apparent contradiction between individual and human essence can only occur in terms of that conception which Marx finally rejected in his Sixth Thesis on Feuerbach: namely, individuals perceived in isolation, some of whose common characteristics are then assembled into common, universal essence.[18] If essence is conceived as social essence, man's essential behaviour explains not only the determining role of production in a given society, but also the location, scope and validity of all human activity as well as individual behaviour, since in the last instance that activity and that behaviour can only be understood in terms of man's essential dimension as a practical being who produces and reproduces himself socially and historically.

In the transition from the *1844 Manuscripts* to *The German Ideology* and the *Theses on Feuerbach,* Marx established a concept of the essence of man as praxis, that is, as a productive, transforming creative being. This essence is in turn revealed in the actual life of men, in actual social and historical existence.

V

What changes, then, occur in Marx's concept of human essence in his later work, particularly in such representative mature works as *Capital?*

In *Capital* Marx sets out the theory of a given social structure—the capitalist mode of production—that is, the theory of the social relations that men contract in a given socio-economic formation—capitalism. The ultimate objective of the work is to "lay bare the economic laws of motion of modern society."[19] Men now appear as products or functions of concrete, objective social relations within a social structure that determines their individual behaviour. What interests Marx above all is the essence of that structure, its fundamental governing laws, the essential contradictions in its development that in turn explain the historical necessity of its disappearance. It is a question of laying bare the social, human character of the relations that men contract within a structured whole which determines the fact that those relations, which are social and human, present themselves as relations between things. It is men and the relations between them that are at issue; but the men in this case are capitalists and workers, insofar as they represent the social forms that the behaviour of concrete individuals adopts when it is inserted into capitalist relations of production.

Marx saw the essence of one and the other as agents of production, as the personification of given social relations.[20] This clearly excludes the kind of conception of man's essence touched on in the *1844 Manuscripts*. *The German Ideology* and the *Theses on Feuerbach* mark Marx's definitive rejection of the idea that essence is not actually given in existence but engendered in that existence as a possibility which must necessarily be realised. Now, the concept of the essence of man as a productive, socio-historical being, whose theoretical basis Marx had laid down in his earlier work, is always more or less explicitly assumed in *Capital*. In *Capital* Marx no longer uses the expression "human essence" (so charged with speculative and metaphysical resonances) but prefers to speak of "human nature in general"; yet the conceptual content is the same in both cases—that through which man produces himself and maintains himself as such, that is praxis.

In refuting the English Utilitarian Bentham, who had raised a particular mode of being of men (that of the English shopkeeper or philistine) to the category of human nature in general, Marx pointed to the changing character of that nature, stressing the necessity of recognising how this human nature in general is given particular historical form:

"... to know what is useful for a dog, one must study dog-nature. This nature itself is not to be deduced from the principle of utility. Applying this to man, he that would criticise all human acts, movements, relations etc. by the principle of utility must first deal with human nature in general, and then with human nature as modified in each historical epoch."[21]

Here Marx is merely underlining what he had already elaborated in his earlier work: that man has a universal nature (or essence) which differs from that of animals because it is historical.

In *Capital,* too, Marx expands the meaning of labour as an essential and universal dimension of man. We already know, from the *1844 Manuscripts* and *The German Ideology,* that man is defined and defines himself by his productive activity and that he is the product of his own activity (a man who produces and thus produces himself). In *Capital* Marx devoted several pages to labour in general, independently of the concrete forms it adopts in certain given social relations like those contracted, for example, between the worker and the capitalist; thus he analysed labour as the determinant of human nature in general. Marx's definition of it, and his analysis of the labour-process are applicable to every social formation and are true for the men who work in any given society.

"Labour is, in the first place, a process in which both men and Nature participate, and in which man of his own accord starts, regulates, and controls the material reactions between himself and Nature. He opposes himself to Nature as one of her own forces . . . By this acting on the external world and changing it, he at the same time changes his own nature."[22]

Man is thus defined—essentially—by his labour, by his productive praxis, that is by a practical activity through which not only does he produce a world of objects that satisfy his needs but also transforms and therefore produces himself.

Marx also presented the elements that make labour as activity not only essential and universal to man, but also a specifically human activity. "We presuppose labour in a form that stamps it as exclusively human . . ."[23] Unlike the animals, man projects or produces ideally before producing materially.

"At the end of every labour-process, we get a result that already existed in the imagination of the labourer at its commencement."[24]

Thus man is defined by labour, but he only works *in a human sense* when he transforms matter in order to realise his ends through it, "an end that, as he knows, governs the modalities of his activity as a law."

The labour-process, as universal human activity, is also broken down into the simple elements that invariably intervene in it: "1. the personal activity of man i.e. work itself, 2. the subject of that work, and 3. its instruments."[25] Lastly, Marx stressed its essential and general human quality in these terms:

> "The labour-process, resolved as above into its simple elementary factors, is human action with a view to the production of use-values, appropriation of natural substances to human requirements; it is the necessary condition for effecting exchange of matter between man and Nature; it is the everlasting Nature-imposed condition of human existence and therefore is independent of every social phase of that existence, or rather, is common to every such phase."[26]

VI

What, then, are the implications of these pages in *Capital* in which labour in general is analysed with tacit reference to human essence or, explicitly, to universal human nature? Clearly Marx was not looking for the theoretical basis of the capitalist social formation in human essence; nor did he try to explain that formation by reference to Man or to human nature in general. That explanation had to be found in the social formation itself, where the fundamental law that governs capitalist social structures must be sought behind the appearances that hide true social relations; and that was the sole objective of the work. Although man, human nature and labour in general are mentioned, the main issue is the worker and the capitalist, labour in the special conditions of the capitalist mode of production (wage-labour, abstract and concrete labour etc.), and the relations of production that men contract in the context of a given social structure. Marx referred to human nature and to labour in general[27] for the methodological reasons expounded with reference to Bentham; but he then passed on immediately to the concepts and categories necessary to explain what constituted the true task of the section to which these pages belong—the exposition of the production of surplus value.

In affirming "that the general character of the labour-process is evidently not changed,"[28] and that "it is the everlasting Nature-imposed condition of human existence,"[29] Marx paused, albeit in a transitory way, on the apparently anthropological problem of human essence. As long as he was presenting the problem in this way, as he himself recognised, there was no need to present the worker in his relations with others.[30] But Marx devoted very little space to the subject; in the first place, because man's essence—as he recalls with reference to Bentham—is historical; in reality, neither human nature nor labour exist outside the concrete forms that they adopt in a given society. For this reason, if his brief analysis of labour in general precedes an analysis of its specific social form under capitalism—labour carried out by the worker for the capitalist—it is only for reasons of exposition that Marx refers, in parentheses, to one specific form. The reference to universal human nature and to labour in general in *Capital* is only a necessary presupposition or starting-point from which to embark on the explanation of a given social structure with its specific social relations and forms of labour.

From this two consequences flow: 1) the idea of a human essence and of labour in general as one of its determinants, as presented in *Capital,* in no way implies that Marx was falling back into a "philosophy of man" based on an anthropological conception of human labour and of the social relations of production. This would have entailed setting aside the fundamental objective of the work clearly expressed and scientifically developed by its author. 2) The fact that Marx, in accordance with that objective, studied human labour, social relations and the men that are determined by them within a given social structure without deducing all these categories and structures from human nature in general, presupposed rather than excluded the idea of human essence. That is why Marx felt it necessary to refer to a universal human nature —that of a working (practical) socio-historical being.

Notes

1. Cf: *1844 Manuscripts: ed.cit.:* pp 100,102,103,106,130,133,134,139 etc.
2. *Ibid.* p 139.
3. *Ibid.* p 140.
4. *Ibid.* p 69-71.
5. *Ibid.* p 68.
6. *Ibid.* p 99-100.
7. On the conception of history in the *1844 Manuscripts* cf: pp. 71,000, 146.

8   *Ibid.* pp 103,106,139,146 and 149.
9   Marx/Engels: *The German Ideology: ed.cit.:* p 83.
10 *Ibid.* p 31.
11 *Ibid.* p 32.
12 *Ibid.* p 35.
13 *Ibid.* p 36.
14 Marx: *Theses on Feuerbach: loc. cit.:* p 652.
15 *German Ideology:* pp 36-9.
16 On the relations between individuality and sociality. Cf: above pp. Ch. 4 "subjects of history section".
17 *1844 Manuscripts:* p 66.
18 This concept of human essence is therefore obliged: "1) to abstract from the historical process . . . and presuppose an abstract–*isolated*–human individual. 2) The human essence, therefore, can with him be comprehended only as 'genus', as an internal, dumb generality which merely *naturally* unites the many individuals." *Theses on Feuerbach: loc.cit.:* p 653.
19 Marx: *Capital I: ed. cit.:* Prologue to First German edition: p 10.
20 "Here individuals are dealt with only insofar as they are personifications of economic categories, embodiments of particular class-relations and class-interests. My standpoint, from which the evolution of the economic foundation of society is viewed as a process of natural history, can less than any other make the individual responsible for relations whose creature he socially remains, however much he may subjectively raise himself above them." *Capital I:* p 10.
21 *Ibid.* p 609.
22 *Ibid.* p 177.
23 *Ibid.* p 178.
24 *Ibid.* p 178.
25 *Ibid.* p 178.
26 *Ibid.* pp 183-4.
27 They are found throughout Section 1–"The labour-process or the production of use-values": in Chapter VII "The labour-process and the process of producing surplus value" in *Capital I:* pp. 177-185.
28 *Capital I:* p 184.
29 *Ibid.* p 184.
30 *Ibid.* p 184.

Appendix Two

"On Alienation in Marx"

What is the place, function and validity of the concept of alienation in Marx's thought, taking as our points of reference an early work (the *1844 Manuscripts*) and the most representative of his mature writings—*Capital?* We have to ask whether alienation is the central category of Marxism, or an ideological rather than a scientific concept, fulfilling a practical function but lacking a theoretical basis; or is alienation a concept that evolves and is enriched together with the evolution of Marx's thought, making possible the development of the basic concepts of historical materialism?

An answer to these questions clearly requires that we follow through Marx's work the theoretical changes that the concept undergoes in the course of Marx's development, albeit in a brief and summary way. At the same time such a study will enable me to clarify my own position as to which of these possible interpretations mentioned above seems to me the most valid.

I

It is clear that the concept of alienation originates in Hegel and in Feuerbach; in Hegel, its subject is the Spirit, in Feuerbach it is man. For both, however, alienation is a spiritual matter whose character is as abstract as its subject. Yet, as Marx pointed out in his own critique of the *Phenomenology of the Mind,* the concept does have in Hegel a real, anthropological character, albeit in a mystified form.

It is Feuerbach's concept of alienation—Hegel anthropomorphised—that provided Marx with his starting-point; for Feuerbach posed the problem of alienation on a human (anthropological) plane, and furthermore, provided Marx with the very structure of the process of alienation, which he was to develop in the *1844 Manuscripts.* That structure comprised the following elements: a) objectification of the subject in the product of his activity, b) objectification as alienation or estrangement, c) the inverse action of the object on the subject which expresses itself in the subject's impoverishment, submission or dispossession. This third element of the process, so characteristic of Feuerbach's view of religious relations, is not to be found in Hegel.

We can now present in schematic form the points of agreement and disagreement between the concepts of alienation elaborated by Feuerbach (in *The Essence of Christianity*) and Marx (in the *1844 Manuscripts*).

	Feuerbach	Marx
Subject who alienates himself	Man in general	The worker
Character of his activity	Theoretical	Practical
Product of his activity	An ideal object: God	A real object: the product of labour
Sphere of alienation	Human consciousness	Human labour
Content of alienation	Dehumanisation of man	Dehumanisation of the worker
Inverse action of the object on the subject	God dominates man	The product of labour turns against its producer
What is alienated and de-alienated	Human essence	Human essence

We shall not discuss this scheme in detail at this point; it will be sufficient to stress the points of contact between Feuerbach and the Marx of the *1844 Manuscripts*.

In both philosophies, the concept of an alienated human essence occupies a central place; both regard it as possible for man to live according to his essence only when his alienation has been overcome. Nevertheless, these aspects common to both Marx and Feuerbach should not obscure the very real difference between them. In Feuerbach, it is man in general who is alienated as a result of his human nature, the essence of man as a natural, sensual, mortal and circumscribed being. It is an anthropological necessity and as such alien or indifferent to concrete, social, historical men. In Marx, on the other hand, alienation is not an essential dimension of human nature even though, historically, it has been impossible to overcome it. Man (the worker) alienates his essence in a practical, material relation with nature (labour) that in turn determines relations between men (the worker and the non-worker). The concept of alienated labour takes us into the sphere of material production in a given historical form. Although Marx speaks of "alienated human essence"—and although, as we have suggested, the concept of essence still has a speculative character—alienation is presented as characteristic of man's productive activity in given historical conditions; it occurs in history and the conditions for its elimination are historically created. It is not inherent in human labour in general, but in a concrete, historical form of labour. On the other hand, the impossibility of reducing alienation to a simple relation between a subject, understood as an isolated individual, and an object, is proof of its concrete, social character. It entails an antagonistic social relation between the worker and the non-worker, for the dominion of products over the producers simply expresses the dominion of the non-worker (the capitalist) over the worker.

This shows that the Marxist concept of alienation, unlike that of Feuerbach, does not simply emerge from a universal and abstract human essence, although it is related to that essence as it is presented in the *1844 Manuscripts*—namely, a human possibility not *yet* realised but which historical development itself will necessarily lead towards such a realisation. On the other hand, since alienation occurs in the concrete form of human labour, and since its appearance and development as well as its elimination are historically conditioned, it cannot be reduced to a merely anthropological concept. It is precisely because it is rooted in the sphere of production, considered historically, that the concept of alienated labour can be fruitful for the later development of Marx's thought and, in particular, for the elaboration of some of the fundamental categories of historical materialism. But it is fruitful only to the extent that the young Marx overcomes his limitations and leaves behind what Feuerbachian elements still remain. This becomes clear, for example, when Marx abandons the conception of human essence which still permeated the *1844 Manuscripts,* ceases to conceive philosophy as the philosophy of alienation and alienation itself as a process (albeit a practical one) in which the worker experiences the negation of his human essence, through which he produces himself (the point at which alienated labour and human essence meet) and in which, finally, the conditions are created for him to overcome his alienation. Alienation, in other words, as the key to understanding what man is, has been and will be.[2]

II

The principal limitation of this key concept is its polivalence. It does explain, or rather provides a theoretical basis for the explanation of private property, the antagonistic relations between men (class society), the pauperisation of the worker etc. Alienation, then, explains a great deal without itself being sufficiently explained.

Alienated labour, whose clearest expression is to be found in capitalist society, is a concept that enables us to distinguish some of the essential features of the relation between the worker and his products, of his own situation as a man within that relation and, ultimately, of the relations that men contract with one another.

Marx perceives the alienation of the worker and his products as an economic reality, the analysis of which provides a key to the explanation of private property; it is these two linked elements that provide the basis for all the categories of political economy. Yet alienation itself, alienated labour, remains unexplained. Marx tells us, quite correctly, what estranged labour is and how it is manifested as a fundamental economic reality. It remains to consider, however, how much can be derived from a reality which is described rather than explained.

In the first place, Marx locates the phenomenon on both the objective and the subjective level. Although he never clearly establishes the demarcation of the two planes, he emphasises the subjective aspect of alienation, pointing to the worker's attitude a) to the products of his labour (he behaves towards them as he would towards estranged, alien objects); b) to his own productive activity (labour is something external to him; far from seeing it as a self-affirmation, he regards it with discomfort), and c) to other men (he behaves towards them as if they were alien beings).[3] Conceived from the subjective point of view, then, alienation is reduced to the problem of man's failure to recognise himself, the human factor, in his products, his activity or in other men. Thus the worker emerges as a real, empirical subject who creates yet fails to recognise himself, as a productive or creative being, in his products.

Marx rightly stresses this subjective aspect of alienation; but he does not reduce it to that aspect alone. Indeed the concept of alienated labour proved useful in his later work precisely because of its objective content, insofar as it indicated real facts which occur objectively, independently of the way in which they are subjectively experienced. These facts are:

a) The material and spiritual pauperisation of the worker in contrast to the material and spiritual wealth that he produces ("the worker becomes all the poorer the more wealth he produces... With the *increasing value* of the world of things proceeds in direct proportion the *devaluation* of the world of men").[4] The phenomenon of the pauperisation of the worker and of the contradiction between "increasing wealth on the one hand and misery on the other" is a major element in Marx's analysis of the structure of the capitalist mode of production *(Capital)*. Here it is considered as an objective manifestation of the economic reality of alienation;

b) alienated labour produces not only goods/commodities but also produces the worker as a commodity.[5] At this point Marx had still to clarify, as he did later, that the condition of the worker as commodity consists in the fact that he sells himself when he sells the only commodity he possesses, and which is inseparable from him—his labour power. But the objective situation of the worker who works for someone else, someone who buys him as a commodity, is thus clearly established;

c) the objectification of labour, and therefore of the worker in his product is objectively translated, independently of the attitude of the worker himself, not into a life-giving activity but into a pure means of subsistence;

d) the worker feels separated from his products and from the conditions of his labour because another person objectively appropriates those products and determines those conditions. Thus if his labour and the product of labour present themselves as something foreign to him, this estrangement has an objective foundation: the appropriation of his products and of his activity by another (the capitalist).

It is not the case, then, that in the *1844 Manuscripts* alienation is reduced to the behaviour of the actual, concrete worker towards his products, his labour and other men. On the contrary, it expresses the objective fact of the worker's moral and physical pauperisation, his transformation into a commodity, his exploitation insofar as he produces for someone else, and his separation from his labour and the conditions under which he realises that labour.

The concept of alienation, in sum, embraces a series of facts and phenomena of both an objective and a subjective nature, although Marx undoubtedly emphasises the latter; this does not imply, however, that he attributes to the subjective aspect a more decisive role, simply that he elaborates more fully the connection between alienated labour and the worker's failure to recognise human essence in his products, his labour and in other men. It must be stressed that Marx never abandoned the assumption that he was dealing with a concrete, empirical worker who is, at the same time, the active subject who fails to recognise himself in his own activity. To the extent that labour as defined in *Capital* is a practical process whereby matter is transformed in accordance with certain ends, alienation will always occur where the worker stands in an external relation, both subjectively and objectively, to his activity and the products of that activity. In *Capital,* however, alienation plays a very secondary role compared to its place in the *1844 Manuscripts,* for in his later work Marx addressed himself above all to those objective aspects which received scant treatment in his early writings. In summary, the concept of alienation as expounded in the *1844 Manuscripts* a) covers a series of subjective and objective facts whose complexity is not analysed with sufficient precision; b) provides a theoretical basis for the explanation of private property and all other economic categories; c) it is a basis, however, that has not itself been given a sufficient foundation. Whatever the limitations of the concept, its importance in the later elaboration of the fundamental categories of historical materialism—production, the relations of production, the division of society into classes according to the place they occupy in the productive process etc.—should not be forgotten. Nor must we lose sight of the fact that it was the conception of the worker alienated in labour that allowed Marx to move closer to the scientific concept of the proletariat and its world-historical role. The concept of alienated labour, therefore, cannot be reduced to a mere ideological concept, nor a radical separation made between the problem of alienation in the *1844 Manuscripts* and the question of historical materialism, unless we first reject the continuity, that is unless we establish a discontinuity in the process of formation of Marx's thought.

III

How, then, does the concept of alienation evolve from the *1844 Manuscripts* to a mature work like *Capital?* Let us first trace the general lines of the evolution, in the course of which alienation loses its centrality, its ability to provide a universal theoretical basis for those concepts that were later to emerge from historical materialism and which did not require explanation by reference to the category of alienation. As Marx's work evolved, alienation came to be a concrete, social phenomenon, like economic fetishism, which did not provide a basis of explanation but rather itself required a foundation.

As Marx began to establish the bases of his materialist conception of history in *The German Ideology,* he began to use the word 'alienation' in a more restricted way, and even with some scepticism. When discussing the German Idealist philosophers, for example, he pointed out that by conceiving history as the process of man's self-alienation "they transform the whole of history into the revolutionary process of consciousness."[6] Clearly, Marx is here referring to alienation in the Idealist sense. And although Marx gives it a similar conceptual content in *The German Ideology* when he refers to the fact that the products of men escape their control and dominate them, it nevertheless begins to lose its original, fundamental character and now appears conditioned in its turn by a real, historical fact—the division of labour.

> "The division of labour offers us the first example of how, as long as man remains in natural society, that is, as long as a cleavage exists between the particular and the common interest, as long, therefore, as activity is not voluntarily but naturally divided, man's own deed becomes an alien power opposed to him, which enslaves him instead of being controlled by him."[7]

This division of labour is "natural"; it is involuntary and furthermore, it is social. "Men", here, are individuals who contract a relation—which they neither accept nor reject voluntarily—that is: a social relation, independent of their personal volition.

In *The German Ideology,* alienation still refers to a particular subject-object relation in which the product appears alien to the subject; it is no longer spoken of as alien to his human essence, however, but as outside his control. It is not a matter of subjective attitudes, but of an objective fact—the subject cannot control the object.

> "The social power, i.e., the multiplied productive force, which arises through the co-operation of different individuals as it is determined by the division of labour, appears to these individuals since their co-operation is not voluntary but has come about naturally not as their own united power, but as an alien force existing outside them, of the origin and goal of which they are ignorant, which they thus cannot control..."[8]

Alienation appears wherever human products—not only the products of labour, but also the products of social activity, like the State—since they are human, social, acquire their own autonomy and power.

> "This fixation of social activity, this consolidation of what we ourselves produce into an objective power above us, growing out of our control, thwarting our expectations, bringing to naught our calculations, is one of the chief factors in historical development up till now."[9]

Clearly, then, Marx's presentation of alienation in *The German Ideology* cannot be reduced to the subjective attitude of the individual towards his products but must be seen as a social phenomenon emerging and developing historically on the basis of a given economic relation: the social division of labour. The use and abuse of the concept by the German Idealist philosophers explains the reserve with which Marx uses it:

> "This 'estrangement' (to use a term that will be comprehensible to the philosophers) . . . can of course only be abolished given two *practical* premisses: the sharpening of the contradictions of society and a huge development of productive forces."[10]

Thus the concept of alienation no longer occupies the central place it had held in the *1844 Manuscripts;* it is no longer the foundation of everything, but a concrete social phenomenon conditioned and based in its turn on another more radical social and historical phenomenon—the division of labour.

IV

The place occupied by alienation in a mature work like *Capital* and leaving aside for the present the fundamental link that is the *Grundrisse* is determined by the framework of that study—the capitalist mode of production—and its objective—to discover the fundamental laws that govern this complex structure. In *Capital,* therefore, whatever can be associated with the concept of alienation must occur in this context and in accordance with that fundamental law. The immediate implication is that a socio-economic structure cannot be explained by reference to alienation or any of its concrete forms; that had ceased to be possible as soon as alienation had relinquished its centrality in Marx's work. The corresponding concept would now have to be explained through the mechanism of capitalist production itself.

The problem of alienation was posed both in the *1844 Manuscripts* and *The German Ideology* in relation to the character of the products of human activity, insofar as such products, particularly the products of human labour, acquire a power of their own. In *Capital* Marx developed a theory of human labour in general and of its products in the concrete conditions of the capitalist mode of production. Human labour, whatever the social formation in question, is the transformation of a natural substance in accordance with particular objectives. As Marx clearly established, the labour-process requires the creation and use of instruments of labour, the material or object of labour that is to be transformed, and the objective or result that exists ideally.[11]

To affirm the existence of an end to be realised, and to which the worker submits his activity and his will therefore signifies an admission that labour is no more than the realisation, materialisation or objectification of a subject's ends. The objectivity of the product is the expression of his activity, his labour. And since this is the product of the activity of a human subject who is always a historical and social being, this conception of labour and its products cannot be reduced to an anthropological conception. In *Capital*, Marx analysed labour and its products in the concrete historical forms of the capitalist mode of production; the product is considered not only as a product of given, concrete labour, but also as general, abstract labour—or commodity.[12] Commodity is the form adopted by the concrete labour of a worker, to the degree that his concrete and determining function disappears to become a particle of general, abstract labour. The product of labour is not itself a commodity, but adopts this manifest social form in given social conditions of production. When the product of labour, the result of the determined concrete activity of a subject or group of subjects, adopts the commodity form, then the object has a double objectivity. One: whose result is the objectification of the concrete, determinate labour of the subject; the object possesses physical, sensual properties linked not to the material in itself but only to the extent that it has been sensually, physically transformed by the worker (Objectivity I). Another: arising out of this first objectivity, treats the product of human labour as an object-commodity which can no longer be considered as a product of the concrete determinate labour of the worker (Objectivity II). Objectivity I does not necessarily lead to Objectivity II, but the second is inconceivable without the first; in other words, every commodity is the product of human labour, but not every product of labour is necessarily a commodity. To repeat—commodity is the form adopted by the product of human labour set in relation to other products, that is when it is not used but exchanged. In *Capital* it is not the product of labour in general that concerns Marx, but the product of a given form of labour which, under the private ownership of the means of production, necessarily assumed the commodity form.

The product of concrete, determined labour, precisely because it has that character, can be traced back to a concrete worker. But to which worker can we refer that Objectivity II which arises on the labour? If it is not the product of concrete, determined labour, then we cannot relate it to a worker. If the commodity only emerges when concrete labour becomes a particle of general, abstract labour, then what is objectified in it is simply a social relation.

Since commodity is the objectification of a social relation or a product the substance of whose exchange-value is not the concrete labour of a worker but social, abstract labour, then there is clearly a disequilibrium between the nature and the appearance of the object. Insofar as commodity is the objectification of a social relation yet manifests itself as a thing, endowed with autonomy and a power of its own, it also presents itself, as Marx says, as enigmatic and mysterious and endowed with sensual and suprasensual being.[13] Its sensual, physical properties relate to the concrete labour of the worker; the sensual aspect externalises the human subject who has produced it. Yet these properties alone do not express the type of social relations that are objectified in the product when it adopts the commodity form. Further, the suprasensual properties impose themselves upon the sensual, and cannot be derived from the properties acquired by the object as a result of the concrete labour materialised in it. The product of labour in its commodity form objectified a social relation, a relation between men—yet it presents itself as a thing; the reified form hides and masks, rather than reveals the social relation that is its essence, its true social nature.

The product of labour thus becomes a fetish; its transformation into something enigmatic and mysterious when it adopts the commodity form is the phenomenon which Marx calls *commodity fetishism*. The commodity takes on this mysterious character "because in it the social character of men's labour appears to them as an objective character stamped upon the product of that labour; because the relation of the producers to the sum total of their own labour is presented to them as a social relation, existing not between themselves, but between the products of their labour."[14] A social relation, a relation between men, thus presents itself in reified form. "There is a definite social relation between men that assumes, in their eyes, the fantastic form of a relation between things."[15] But it is in no sense a subjective appearance; in the social conditions of the labour that produces commodities, the products of labour adopt the commodity form and thus must necessarily manifest themselves as fetishes.

Money and capital, too, are economic fetishes. Their fetishistic character emerges to the extent that the social relations they embody appear as things, and insofar as a social quality is presented as a quality inherent in a material thing. In this respect Marx's analysis of *fetish-capital* is of particular interest, although it merits less of his attention[16] than commodity fetishism. Marx says, "The relations of capital assume their most externalised and most fetish-like form in interest-bearing capital."[17] A social relation—capital—presents itself as a thing personified.

> "Capital appears as a mysterious and self-creating source of interest, the source of its own increase. The *Thing* (money, commodity, value) is now capital even as a mere thing, and capital appears as a mere thing. The result of the entire process of reproduction appears as a property inherent in the thing itself... In interest-bearing capital, therefore, this automatic fetish, self-expanding value, money generating money, are brought out in their pure state; in this form it no longer bears the birthmark of its origin. The social relation is consummated in the relation of a thing, of money, of itself."[18]

Nor is it in this case a subjective appearance; the mysterious innate capacity of a thing—capital—to increment itself by itself is simply the form in which a social relation necessarily presents itself in the conditions of capitalist production.

It is with particular relation to commodity fetishism that Marx develops his conception of economic fetishes. It therefore seems appropriate at this point to establish the true place of the concept of alienation in *Capital*. Bearing in mind its centrality in the *1844 Manuscripts*, to what extent does Marx sustain, modify or abandon this conception in *Capital?*

V

Marx speaks of the "mystical character" or "mysticism" of commodities, and makes an analogy between the world of commodities and the world of religion; that is evidence enough that he has not completely abandoned the concept of alienation. Yet neither this expression nor its corresponding expression "fetishism" should be taken to indicate that Marx had not progressed beyond the limits of the Feuerbachian structure of alienation, nor even that he had remained at the point he had reached in the *1844 Manuscripts*.

Before comparing the conceptions of economic fetishes *(Capital)* and alienated labour *(1844 MSS)*, however, it will be necessary to discover whether they can coexist within a common framework. In both cases men (the worker or social relations) are divorced from the human products in which they are objectified; in other words the objects (products of labour, commodities, money or capital) which exist to the degree that they are the fruit of human activity, present themselves to men as autonomous objects lying outside their control and endowed with an autonomous power. Nevertheless, we cannot speak of alienation in the two works in the same sense. Although economic fetishism brings us back to a conception of human labour, the distance that separates one concept (alienated labour) from the other (commodity–money–and capital–fetishism) is the distance that mediates between a conception of labour that lacks a scientific foundation, because the fundamental law of motion of the structure within which the concept operates has yet to be discovered, and a conception of human labour in which the latter takes the concrete form of labour-power, wage-labour, abstract and concrete labour etc. For these are all categories of an analysis of the structure of the capitalist mode of production which entails first the correspondence and later the contradiction between two structures: productive forces and relations of production. Of course it is men who through their praxis form and maintain that structure; it is they who develop the productive forces and they who contract given relations in production independently of their conscious will. But it is precisely this structuralist conception of the capitalist mode of production that determines the fundamental differences as far as the location, extent and content of the concrete form that alienation adopts in *Capital*–e.g. as economic fetishism–are concerned.

While in the *1844 Manuscripts* alienated labour refers to the negation of human essence, in *Capital* it is the reification of the relations between men that is central, as Marx analyses the fetishistic character of the objects (commodity, money, capital) in which these relations are given objective, material form. In the *1844 MSS* it is the worker who alienates his essence in the concrete relation with the products of his labour and in labour itself. The failure to recognise the self is thus an important element of this concept of alienation, although this in no way lessens the significance of the objective aspects of the alienated relation, which we have already discussed, nor its social character insofar as it determines in its turn a certain type of relation between men in the production process.

In the *1844 MSS* therefore, the personal subjective relation between the concrete, individual labourer and his products, has a central function, as does its effect upon the concrete worker as a man, that is in his human condition and human value. In *Capital* that relation is sometimes made explicit but is usually assumed; in fact Marx does occasionally discuss the way in which the real, individual worker is affected as a man—its effect upon his human dignity. He says, for example,

> "... within the capitalist system all methods for raising the social productiveness of labour are brought about at the cost of the individual labourer; all means for the development of production transform themselves into means of domination over and exploitation of, the producers; they mutilate the labourer into a fragment of a man, degrade him to the level of an appendage of a machine, destroy every remnant of charm in his work, and turn it into a hated toil; they estrange from him the intellectual potentialities of the labour-process in the same proportion as science is incorporated in it as an independent power; they distort the conditions under which he works, subject him during the labour-process to a despotism the more hateful for its meanness..."[19]

It cannot be said, therefore, that Marx loses interest in the labourer as a concrete individual, reducing him to the condition of a mere support or effect of social relations. On the contrary, he shows clearly that labour within the capitalist system mutilates, distorts and alienates the spiritual powers of the worker. The relation between the worker and his labour is considered in the passage quoted above as a relation whose distinctive characteristics are the same as those of alienated labour as expounded in the *1844 MSS*. It is precisely the idea of the labourer as a man that allows this relation to be interpreted as an alienated relation, both in its subjective aspect—as a relation lived by the individual worker—and in its objective aspect—insofar as objectively labour has for him all the negative consequences to which Marx refers in very precise terms in the passage we have quoted from *Capital*.

Although it no longer occupies the central place it has had in his early work, Marx never fails to consider the concrete relation between the worker, his labour and its products which had held his attention in the *1844 MSS*. Given the basic objective of *Capital*, however, it is not the concrete, personal relation of the individual worker with his labour and its products that interests him, but the social relations of production that that worker lives out. And that relation is of interest to the extent that it takes on objective, material form rather than as it is lived and felt by the worker. Finally, he is concerned not with the fact that the worker fails to recognise himself in the products of his labour—though Marx in no sense dismisses that relation—but with the objective fact that objects lack transparency because as commodities materialised by given relations of production, they present themselves as things whose social, human character is not manifest.

In the *1844 MSS*, the qualities of the product derive from the worker and from his concrete, determined activity, its objectivity from the real, concrete subject who takes objective form in it. Its objectivity is not in itself mysterious; but the material and spiritual pauperisation of the worker and the appropriation of the product of his labour by another (the non-worker) means that the subject does not act towards the object in the same way as he would towards a product of his own labour. In sum, the worker cannot recognise himself in that which negates (devalues) him and is alien to him (because it belongs to another). In *Capital* the limitations of this kind of explanation are overcome, and human labour comes to be considered not only as a determined activity through which the worker creates a product whose properties are appropriate to the use that is to be made of them (concrete labour), but also as general social labour, of which each determined act of labour is a part, for only thus can the products of labour be compared and exchanged. Without this second concept of labour (abstract labour), there would be no way of explaining Objectivity II, in which the products of labour adopt the commodity form. As a commodity, the product of labour acquires social properties which do not derive directly from the concrete activity of the worker. Furthermore, given that the product has properties which the worker has not put there, the problem of alienation can no longer be reduced to the subject-object relation, where the first is understood as the concrete worker and the second as the product of his concrete activity. It is now a question of the links between the social relations of production and the object in which they are given material form. The worker as concrete subject produces an object that adopts the commodity form only in certain social relations of production.

The fact that a human product assumes non-essential characteristics or powers emphasises the alienated character of both relations. If in the *1844 MSS,* the product of the worker's labour becomes an autonomous subject when in fact it is *his* product, that is the objectification of his labour, in *Capital* the product of human labour, both concrete and abstract, presents itself as an autonomous mysterious subject too, insofar as it is the objectification or materialisation of labour which is in turn a social relation. If in the *1844 MSS* the product negates the human essence of the product, in *Capital* the commodity-object hides the social essence to which it gives objective form. And if in the first case the product of labour renders the subject an object which it dominates, in the second the commodity reifies a social relation.

VI

In the transition from the concept of alienated labour to that of economic fetishism, then, the first clearly undergoes essential modifications. The alienation of the concrete worker gives way to the fetishisation of a social relation; the product that in the one case is the objectification of a determined, concrete activity, is in the other the objectification of a relation between men; the alien character of the product of labour now takes on the fetishistic character of an economic object; the human character externalised in an object yields to the social character of a product that presents itself, nonetheless, as a thing.

There is a contradiction in both conceptions between a) labour and human essence *(1844 MSS)* and b) a social relation and its manifest form *(Capital).* In both cases men (individual labourers or social relations) are separated from the products through which they assume objective form as these become autonomous and escape human control (either of the individual worker or of society), presenting themselves as autonomous powers. In both cases, we are presented with the fundamental structure of alienation; the contradiction between men and a human reality that presents itself to them as an alien and external reality. The transition from the concept of alienated labour to that of economic fetishism, then, does not entail Marx's abandonment of alienation; the latter is simply the concrete form assumed by alienation in production for the market in a developed capitalist society. The polivalent conception of the *1844 MSS*, which was still dependent upon a slightly speculative conception of human essence, evolves into a concept that explains the mode in which the social relations of production present themselves in a given socio-economic formation. Fetishism, integrated into the analysis of capitalist production and the social relations that men contract within that system, expresses both the reification of these relations and the fantastic character of the objects in which the process takes form. In this way the social products of human labour appear to function as fetishes.

But if economic fetishism expresses the most developed form of the alienation of social relations under capitalism, this does not mean that it exhausts the concept of alienation. *Capital* does not exhaust the analysis of the capitalist social formation, given that it is a complex structure involving the relations and mutual dependence of a series of structures, among them the political and ideological superstructure that Marx proposed to analyse at a later date. Nor does fetishism exhaust all the forms of alienation; there is political (*in* and *through* the State) and ideological alienation (*in* and *through* ideas) etc. All these are examples of human products that have become alien to men. In each case, what must be determined is the nature of the contradiction between the (human social) essence of a product and the form of its appearance. In ideological alienation, for example, it is a matter of investigating the mode of being of one set of human products—ideas—to discover how and in what sense they objectify social relations, and in turn how and why the objectification of these relations presents itself as a contradiction between its internal essence and its manifest form. It is a question of clarifying, for example, under what conditions and in what circumstances a theory functions ideologically. Only this kind of concrete analysis that moves from a basic structure of alienation to its specific forms. Marx pointed the way, in presenting the phenomenon of alienation under the concrete conditions of capitalist production as the fetishism of economic objects.

VII

For us the conclusion must be that alienation should be considered on the basis of concrete research rather than by turning Marxism into a philosophy of alienation. To reduce it to this, in the name of a conception of human essence which Marx himself abandoned after *The German Ideology,* would lead us to stray from the path that Marx followed in his evolution from the *1844 MSS* through the *Grundrisse* to *Capital.* We cannot, therefore, renounce a concept of alienation which can yield up all sorts of new possibilities through the concrete analysis of economic fetishes; nor, on the other hand, must we accept it, without modification, as it appears in Marx's early work—that would lead us into a similar process of development, only in an inverse sense.

As we have tried to show, Marx passed on from the concept of the alienation of human essence to that of the alienation of a concrete, human, social relation; he turned his attention, in other words, to the social mode of being of man that can be scientifically analysed in its socio-historical development. There is no radical discontinuity between the two conceptions. Without the concept of alienated labour, Marx would not have been able to arrive at the key concepts of "social production", "relations of production", "productive forces", "commodity", "capital" etc. which allowed him to discover the fetichistic character of the objectification of certain social relations.

Marx develops from a general theory of alienation which makes this concept the theoretical foundation of all his explanations of history and society, towards a conception of a concrete social and historical phenomenon which requires a sound basis of explanation. Similarly, he moves from a conception of alienation in which the subjective aspect fulfils a central role, to a conception in which alienation is above all an objective fact, independent of how men live and understand that relation. Finally, Marx raised himself from a philosophical conception of alienation, sometimes tainted with speculation, to a scientific theory integrated into the theory of the capitalist mode of production.

The concept of alienation, then, does not have a key, central character; but that is not to say that it is merely ideological. Its validity derives from its capacity to explain concrete situations. In this sense it has proved its value in relation to the mysterious, enigmatic character of the products of labour when they adopt the commodity form (economic fetishism). Therefore this concrete, specific form assumed by economic objects—real and unreal, sensual and suprasensual, object with an essence and an appearance—does not exclude the concept of alienation, but makes it all the richer. In sum, Marxism cannot be reduced to a philosophy of alienation; but that should not lead us to deny the scientific character of alienation. And this is ample justification, once freed of all speculative concent, for its right to exist.

Notes

1   Position a) is sustained above all outside the field of Marxism and is adopted, setting aside differences of degree and nuance, by E. Thier, J. Hyppolite, J. Calvez, H. Popitz, A. Mayer and M.G. Lange: position b) has been recently defended by Marxists like Godelier, Althusser, Ranciere, Balibar, Varret and, with other arguments, W. Jahn; finally position c) emerges clearly from the excellent work of A. Cornu, and others coincide—e.g. Oizerman, Pajitnow, Rossi, Garaudy, Bottigelli, Suret-Canale, Schaff, Kosik and other Marxists.
2   See, in the present work, our exposition of the concept of praxis in the *1844 MSS,* and on the significance of this early work in the evolution of Marx's thought: Cf. pp. (111-119) *supra.*
3   *Economic and philosophical manuscripts of 1844: ed. cit.:* pp. 67-74.
4   *Ibid.:* p. 66.
5   *Ibid.:* p. 66.
6   *The German Ideology: ed. cit.:* p. 86.
7   *Ibid.:* p. 44.
8   *Ibid.:* p. 46.
9   *Ibid.:* p. 45.
10 *Ibid.:* p. 46.
11 *Capital I: ed. cit.:* pp. 179-181.
12 *Ibid.:* Cf: all Chapter 1, Section 1: "Commodities": pp. 35-83.
13 *Ibid.:* p. 72
14 *Ibid.:* p. 72.
15. *Ibid.:* p. 72.
16 We refer to Chapter 24, entitled "Externalisation of the relation of capital in the form of interest-bearing capital": *Capital III: ed. cit.:* pp. 391-400.
17 *Ibid.:* p. 391.
18 *Ibid.:* p. 392.
19 *Capital I:* p. 645.

BIBLIOGRAPHY

I: Principal primary sources

a. Hegel
Early Theological Writings: Trans. T.M. Knox, Harper Torchbooks, New York, 1961.
Jenenser Realphilosophie: J. Hoffmeister, Leipzig, 1931-2. 2 vols.
Lectures on the Philosophy of History: Trans. J. Sibree, Bohn's Philosophical Library, London, 1852.
Lectures on the Philosophy of Religion: Trans. E.B. Speirs and J.B. Sanderson, London, 1895: reprinted by Routledge, 1962.
Lessons on the History of Philosophy: Ed. E.S. Haldane, Routledge, London, n.d. 3 vols.
Phenomenology of Mind: Trans. J.D. Baillie, Allen and Unwin, London, 1967 (2nd edition).
Philosophy of Right: Trans. T.M. Knox, Oxford University Press, 1942.
Science of Logic: Trans. A.V. Miller, Allen and Unwin, London, 1969.

b. Feuerbach
Kleine philosophische Schriften (1842-5): Leipzig, 1950. (Includes *Vorlaufige Thesen zur Reform der Philosophie).*
Manifestes philosophiques: textes choisies (1839-45): Ed. L. Althusser, P.U.F., Paris, 1960.
Principles of the Philosophy of the Future: Trans. M. Vogel, Bobbs Merrill, 1966.
The Essence of Christianity: Trans. Marian Evans; John Chapman, London, 1854. Also Harper and Row (trans. G. Eliot): New York, 1966.

c. Marx and Engels
MARX:
Capital: Vols. 1(1965), 2(1967), 3(1972): Lawrence and Wishart, London, in collaboration with Progress Publishers Moscow.
Critique of Hegel's Philosophy of Right: Ed. J. O'Malley: Cambridge University Press, 1970.
Critique of Hegel's Philosophy of the State: in *Young Marx on Philosophy and Society* (Ed. Easton and Gaddut): Doubleday, New York, 1967. pp. 151-202.
Critique of Political Economy: Lawrence and Wishart, London.
Grundrisse: Trans. Martin Nicolaus: Penguin Books, Harmondsworth, 1973.
Poverty of Philosophy: Lawrence and Wishart, London, 1956.
The Economic and Philosophical Manuscripts of 1844: Progress Publishers, Moscow, 1967. Trans. M. Milligan.
Theories of Surplus Value: Lawrence and Wishart, London, 1967-72. 3 vols.
MARX & ENGELS:
The German Ideology: Lawrence and Wishart, London, 1965. (Includes Marx:

Theses on Feuerbach.)
Selected Works in 2 volumes: Lawrence and Wishart, London, 1958.
ENGELS:
Anti-Dühring: Lawrence and Wishart, London, 1969.
Dialectics of Nature: Progress Publishers, Moscow, 1941.
Engels: A Selection edited by W.O. Henderson: Penguin, Harmondsworth, 1967.
LENIN:
Collected Works: Lawrence and Wishart, London, 1961-4.

II. Works by Marxists relating to the problem of praxis

L. Althusser: *For Marx:* Penguin Press, Harmondsworth, 1969.
L. Althusser, E. Balibar, R. Establet: *Reading Capital:* Trans. Ben Brewster: NLB, London, 1970.
J.D. Bernal: *Science in History:* in 4 volumes: Penguin, Harmondsworth, 1969.
Guy Besse: *Pratique social et theórie:* Paris, 1963.
M. Cornforth: *Theory of knowledge:* Lawrence and Wishart, London, 1956.
Jean T. Desanti: *Phenomenologie et praxis:* Eds. Sociales, Paris, 1963.
Yovo Eles and G. Davydova: "Materialisticheskaia dialektika-teorija revoluzionni praktiki" in *Voprosy filosofii:* Moscow, no. 9, 1965.
J.M. Fataliev: *Estestviennye nauki i materialno-proizvodstvennanya baza obshestva:* Moscow, 1962.
Y.G. Gaidukov: *Rol praktiki v prozesse poznanija:* Moscow, 1964.
R. Garaudy: *La theórie materialiste de la connaissance:* Paris, 1953.
    Humanisme marxiste: Paris, 1957.
    Perspectives de l'homme: Paris, 1961.
    Dieu est mort: Paris, 1962.
    Karl Marx: Paris, 1964.
M. Godelier: *Rationality and Irrationality in Economics:* Trans. Brian Pearce: NLB, London, 1972.
Eli de Gortari: *Introduccion a la lógica dialéctica:* UNAM, Mexico, 1965.
A. Gramsci: *Il materialismo storico e la filosofia de Benedetto Croce:* in *Opere:* 8th edition: Einaudi, Turin, 1966.
E.V. Ilenkov: *Dialektika abstraktnogo i konkretnogo v 'Kapitale':* Moscow, 1960.
G. Klaus and D. Wittich: "Zu eigenen Fragen des Verhaltnisses von Praxis und Erkenntnis" in *Deutsche Zeitschrift zur Philosophie,* Berlin, no. 11, 1961.
P.V. Kopnin: *Lógica dialéctica:* Grijalbo, Mexico, 1966.
K. Korsch: *Marxism and Philosophy:* NLB, London, 1970.
K. Kosik: *Dialektika konkretinho:* Prague, 1963.
G. Lukács: *History and Class Consciousness:* Merlin, London, 1971. Trans. R. Livingstone.
    Existentialisme ou marxisme: Paris, 1948.
    The Young Hegel: Merlin, London, 1975.
Mao Tse Tung: *On Practice:* 1937.

M.N. Rutkevich: et.al. *Praktika-kriterii istiny v nauke:* Moscow, 1960.
A. Sánchez Vázques: *Art and Society: Essays in Marxist Aesthetics,* Merlin Press, 1974.
Adam Schaff: *La teoría de la verdad en el materialismo y el idealismo:* Lautaro, Buenos Aires, 1964. (Original in Polish).
J. Stalin: *Problems of Leninism:* Moscow, 1960.
P. Togliatti: "Il leninismo nel pensiero e nell'azzione di A. Gramsci" in *Studi Gramsciani,* Rome, 1958.
Tran-Duc-Thao: *Phénoménologie et matérialisme dialectique,* Paris, 1951.

III. Works by non-Marxists relating to questions of praxis

H. Arvon: *Le marxisme:* Paris, 1960.
K. Axelos: *Marx, penseur de la technique:* Paris, 1961.
J.Y. Calvez: *La pensée de Karl Marx:* Paris, 1956.
G.M. Cottier: *L'athéisme du jeune Marx:* Paris, 1959.
    Du romantisme au marxisme: Paris, 1961.
E.L. Burke: *The notion of praxis in the early works of Karl Marx:* Doctoral thesis, University of Louvain, 1959.
F. Chatelet: *Logos et praxis:* Ed. Sedes, Paris, 1962.
G. Gentile: *La filosofia de la praxis:* in *Opere,* vol. 12, Florence, 1937.
J. Hommes: *Der technische Eros:* Freiburg (Breisgau), 1955.
B. Matteuci: *Antonio Gransci e la filosofia de la prassi:* Milan, 1951.
M. Merleau Ponty: *Humanism and Terror:* Beacon Press, New York, 1969.
    Les aventures de la dialectique: Gallimard, Paris, 1955.
P. Naville: *De l'alienation à la jouissance:* Paris, 1957.
R. Tucker: *Philosophy and Myth in Karl Marx:* Cambridge University Press, 1961.
E. Severino: *Studi di filosofia della prassi:* Universita Cattolica del Sacro Cuore, 1962.

IV. Other works cited (including articles)

H. Agosti: *Tántalo recobrado:* Lautaro, Buenos Aires, 1964.
H. Aphtheker (ed.): *Marxism and alienation:* Humanities Press, New York, 1965.
Aristotle: *Book of animals:* Ed. J.N. Mattock: Heffer, Cambridge, 1967.
    De Anima: Ed. W.D. Ross: Oxford University Press, 1961.
    Metaphysics: Trans. J. Warrington: Everyman/Dent, London, 1968.
    Politics: Trans. T.A. Sinclair: Penguin Classics, 1969.
H. Arvon: *Ludwig Feuerbach ou le transformation du sacré:* P.U.F., Paris, 1957.
Carlos Astrada: *El marxismo y las escatologías:* Buenos Aires, 1957.
    Humanismo y dialéctica de la libertad: Buenos Aires, 1960.
M. Ballestero: "Hegel, el joven Marx y el marxismo" in *Realidad,* Rome, no. 10, 1966, pp. 73-92.
M.A. Barg: "Strukturny analiz v istoricheskom issledovanni" in *Voprosy filosofii:* Moscow, no. 10, 1964. pp. 83-92.

F. Battaglia: *Filosofia del lavoro:* Ed. Patron, Bologna, 1951.
M.C. Beardsley: *Aesthetics:* Harcourt Brace, New York, 1958.
E. Bernstein: *Zur Geschichte und Theorie des Sozialismus:* Berlin, 1901.
Guy Besse: "Le marxisme est-il une religion?" in *La nouvelle critique:* Paris, no. 165, 1965.
P. Bigo: *Marxisme et humanisme:* P.U.F. Paris, 1953.
M. Blondel: *L'Action* Vol. 2 (L'action humaine et les conditions de son aboutissement): P.U.F. Paris, 1963.
Niels Bohr: "La física cuántica y la filosofía" in *Revista de Filosofía:* Havana, no. 2, 1965.
E. Bottigelli: "Les Annales Franco-Allemandes et l'opinion francaise" in *La pensee,* Paris, no. 110, 1963.
"Karl Marx et la gauche hegelienne" in *Annali 1963:* Feltrinelli, Milan, 1964. pp. 9-32.
"Introduction" to K. Marx: *1844 MSS:* Paris, 1962.
Jean Brun: *Le main et l'esprit:* P.U.F., Paris, 1963.
N. Bukharin: *Historical Materialism:* University of Michigan Press, 1970.
A. Camus: *The Rebel:* Penguin, Harmondsworth, 1969.
U. Cerroni: *Il pensiero giuridico sovietico:* Ed. Riuniti, Rome, 1969.
C. Cesa: "Figure e problemi della stopiografia filosofica della sinistra hegeliana" in *Annali, 1963:* Milan, 1964. pp. 62-104.
V.A. Chaguin: *Iz istorii borby protiv filosofskogo revixionism v germanskoi sotzial-demokratii:* Moscow-Leningrad, 1961.
D.I. Chesnekov: "Obschestvenny interes i mejanizm deistviya sotzialnyi zakonov" in *Voprosy filosofii:* Moscow, no. 9, 1966: pp. 3-14.
R.G. Collingwood: *Principles of Art:* Oxford University Press, 1963.
A. Cornu: *Karl Marx et Friedrich Engels:* (3 vols. 1958-65): Paris.
"Le materialisme historique dans 'L'Ideologie Allemande' " in *Annali 1963:* Milan, 1964. pp. 34-61.
B. Croce: *Estetica come scienza dell'esspressione e linguistica generale:* 11th edition, Laterza, Bari, 1965.
Y.N. Davydov: "Lefebvre v ego 'konceptizia otchuzhdenija' " in *Voprosy filosofii:* Moscow, no. 1, 1963.
R. Descartes: *Discourse on Method:* Trans. F.E. Sutcliffe, Penguin, 1970.
Documentos de las conferencias de los partidos comunistas y obreros celebrados en Moscu en 1957 y 1960: Mexico, 1963.
D. Dumitrescu: "Les mathematiques et le progrès technique" in *Etudes d'histoire et philosophie des sciences:* Bucharest, n.d.
Dynnik et.al.: *Historia de la filosofía:* in 7 volumes: Grijalbo, Mexico, 1960-66.
Ives Eyot: "La création 'travail créateur', 'conscience creatrice' " in *La nouvelle critique:* Paris, no. 178, 1966: pp. 119-126.
Frantz Fanon: *The Wretched of the Earth:* Penguin Books, 1968.
B. Farrington: *Greek Science:* Penguin, 1969.
P.N. Fedoseev: "Sotzializm i gumanizm" in *Kommunizm i filosofija:* Moscow, '62.

P.N. Fedoseev: "Gumanizm v sovremennom mire" (Humanism in the modern world) in *Memorias del XIII Congreso Internacional de Filosofía:* UNAM, Mexico, 1963. pp. 97-118.
"Materialistischeskoe ponimanie istorii i "teorija nasilija' " in *Kommunist,* Moscow, no. 7, 1964.
J. Ferrater Mora: *Diccionario de filosofía* (2 vols.): 5th edition Ed. Sudamericana, Buenos Aires, 1965.
Filofskaya Entziklopedija under the editorship of F.V. Konstantinov: vols. 1-5, Moscow, 1960-64.
Sidney Finkelstein: *Existentialism and Alienation in American Literature:* Central Books, London, 1965.
V. Flores Olea: *Política y dialéctica:* UNAM, Mexico, 1964.
V.A. Fox: "Polémica con Niels Bohr" in *Revista de filosofía:* Havana, no. 2, 1965.
G. Friedmann: *Industrial Society:* Free Press of Glencoe, 1955.
    Anatomy of Work: Free Press of Glencoe, 1962.
    Le travail en miettes: Gallimard, Paris, 1956.
    Sept études sur l'homme et la technique: Gonthier, Paris, 1966.
Erich Fromm: *Marx's Concept of Man:* Ungar, New York, 1961.
    (ed.) *Socialist Humanism:* Doubleday, New York, 1965.
Jose Gaos: *Dos exclusivas del hombre: la mano y el tiempo:* Mexico, 1945.
    De la filosofía: UNAM, Mexico, 1962.
R. Garaudy: *Qu'est ce que la morale marxiste?:* Eds. Sociales, Paris, 1963.
J.D. Garcia Bacca: *Humanismo teórico, práctico y positivo según Marx:* F.C.E., Mexico, 1965.
G. Gentile: *La filosofia di Marx...* in *Opere complete XII:* Florence, 1937.
G.E. Glezerman: *O zakonaj obschestvennogo razvitija:* Moscow, 1966.
L. Goldmann: "Socialisme et humanisme" in *Diogene,* no. 46: Paris, 1964. pp. 88-107 (see also Fromm: *Socialist Humanism* which includes this essay).
E. Gonzalez Pedrero: *Filosofía política y humanismo:* Mexico, 1957.
E. de Gortari: *Lógica general:* Grijalbo, Mexico, 1965.
A. Gorz: *La morale de l'histoire:* Ed. du Seuil, Paris, 1959.
    Strategy for Labour: Beacon Press, New York, 1967.
A. Gramsci: *Gli intelletuali e l'organizzazione della cultura* in *Opere:* 8th edition, Einaudi, Turin, 1966.
    The Modern Prince: Lawrence and Wishart, London, 1959.
Salvatore Graziano: "Alcune considerazioni intorno all'umanesimo di Gramsci"in *Studi Gramsciani:* Ed. Riuniti, Rome, 1958. pp. 149-164.
M. Grundwald, M. Hofer and H. Redecker: "Zum Verhältnis von Theorie und Praxis" in *Deutsche Zeitschrift für Philosophie:* Berlin, no. 8, 1962.
L. Gruppi: "I rapporti tra pensiero ed essere nella concezione di A. Gramsci" in *Studi Gramsciani: ed.cit.:* pp. 165-181.
B.A. Grushin: *Ocherki logiki istoricheskogo issledovaniaya:* Moscow, 1961.
C.I. Gulian: *Metoda si sistema la Hegel:* Bucharest, vol. i. 1957; vol. ii, 1963.

C.I. Gulian: "Les valeurs ethiques et la connaissance de l'homme" in *Memorias del XIII Congreso Internacional de Filosofia:* vol. vii: UNAM, Mexico, 1964. pp. 291-6.
"Connaissance et valorisation de l'homme" in *Recherches internationales:* Paris, no. 46, 1965.
G. Gurvitch: "La sociologie de Karl Marx" in *La vocation actuelle de la sociologie:* vol. 2: P.U.F., Paris, 1963.
A. Hauser: *Social History of Art:* 4 vols. Routledge, London, 1969.
M. Heidegger: *Being and Time:* Trans. J. Macquarrie and E. Robinson: Basil Blackwell, Oxford, 1967.
S. Hook: *From Hegel to Marx:* Ann Arbor Paperbacks, 1962.
J. Hyppolite: *Studies on Marx and Hegel:* Ed. J. O'Neill: Heinemann, London, 1969.
William James: *Philosophical Conceptions and Practical Results:* 1898.
Pragmatism: a New Name for some Old Ways of Thinking: 1909.
The Meaning of Truty: 1909.
Athanase Joja: "Valeur et pathos de la science" in *Etudes d'histoire et de philosophie des sciences: ed.cit.*
"Definición del hombre" in *Historia y sociedad:* Mexico, no. 6, 1966.
I. Kant: *Critique of Judgment:* Oxford University Press, 1969.
H. Klotz: "Einige Bemerkungen zum marxistischen Praxibegriff und zum Verhaltnis von theoretischer und praktischer Tatigkeit" in *D/Z.Ph.:* Berlin, no. 3, 1962.
L. Kolakowski: "K. Marks i klazyczna definicja prawdy" in *Studia Filozoficana:* Warsaw, 11th February, 1959.
Der Mensch ohne Alternative: Piper, Munich, 1960.
A. Kolman: "L'homme, maître de la nature" in *Memorias del XIII Congreso...*
V.D. Koniujov: "O soznatelmom jaraktere ekonomichsekogo razvitija pri sotzialisme" in *Voprosy filosofii:* no. 9, 1965.
F.V. Konstantinov: *Foundations of Marxist Philosophy:*
"Cheloviek i obschestvo" in *Memorias del XIII Congreso...* vol. 2, pp. 201-221.
V. Korac: "Vocation of Philosophical Anthropology" in *Ibid:* vol. 2. pp. 223-230.
K. Kosik: "Wer ist der Mensch" in *Ibid:* vol. 2. pp. 231-8.
"La dialectique de la morale et la morale de la dialectique" in *Recherches internationales:* no. 45, 1965: pp. 106-120.
A.S. Kovalchuk: "O sootnoshenii teorii i praktiki kommunistischsekogo stroitelstva" in *Voprosy filosofii:* Moscow, no. 4, 1966.
S. Kovaliov: "El humanismo comunista y la coerción revolucionaria" in *Revista Internacional:* Prague, no. 5, 1964.
H. Kreschnak: "Zur Dialektik von Praxis und Erkanntnis" in *D/Z.Ph.:* Berlin, no. 8, 1962.
N.I. Lapin: *Borba vokrug ideinogo nasledija molodogo Marksa:* Moscow, 1962.

M.G. Lange: *Marxismus, Leninismus, Stalinismus:* Stuttgart, 1955.
F. Larroyo: *Antropología concreta:* Mexico, 1963.
L. Lavelle: *De l.Acte:* Paris, 1946.
H. Lefebvre: *Critique de la vie quotidienne:* Grasset, Paris, 1947.
  Dialectical Materialism: Jonathan Cape, London, 1968.
  Les problèmes actuels du marxisme: P.U.F., Paris, 1958.
  Pour connaître la pensée de Marx: Bordas, Paris, 1948.
  Sociology of Marx: Allen Lane, Harmondsworth, 1968.
  (with N. Guterman) *Cahiers de Lenine sur la dialectique de Hegel:* Gallimard, Paris, 1938.
  (with N. Guterman) *La conscience mystifiée:* Paris, 1936.
M. Lerner: *America as a Civilisation:* Clarion, New York, 1957.
C. Levi-Strauss: *The Savage Mind:* Weidenfeld & Nicolson, London, 1966.
  Structural Anthropology: Allen Lane, 1968.
H. Lindner: "Fichtes Humanismus der Tat" in *D/Z.Ph.:* Berlin, no. 4, 1962.
W. Lonhard: *Les théories politiques* volume 2 of *L'ideólogie sovietique contemporaine:* Paris, 1965.
G. Lukács: "Mein Weg zu Marx" in *Festschrift Lukács:* Berlin, 1955.
  Ästhetik: vol. 1. Luchterhand.
N. Machiavelli: *The Prince:* Penguin, 1970.
V. de Magalhaes-Vilhena: "Progrès technique et blocage social dans le cité antique" in *La pensée:* no. 102, Paris, 1962.
S. Mallet: *La nouvelle classe ouvrière:* Ed. du Seuil, Paris, 1963.
K. Mannheim: *Ideology and Utopia:* Routledge, London, 1954.
Mao Tse Tung: *Selected Works.*
H. Marcuse: *Reason and Revolution:* London, 1954.
  Soviet Marxism: New York, 1958.
Imre Marton: "Sobre las tesis de Frantz Fanon." in *Historia y sociedad:* Mexico, no. 6, 1966.
Y.K. Melvin: "Man in the Space Age" in *Memorias del XIII Congreso...* Vol. 3.
C. Wright Mills: *Power Elite:* Oxford University Press, 1956.
  The Marxists: Penguin, 1969.
  White Collar: O.U.P., 1951.
M.B. Mitin: "Cheloviek-kak objekt filosofskij issledovanni" in *Memorias del XIII Congreso...:* vol. 1.
R. Mondolfo: *Marx y el marxismo:* F.C.E., Mexico, 1960.
  El humanismo de Marx: F.C.E., Mexico, 1964.
W. Muller and M. Thom: "Zu einigen Fragen des Verhaltnisses von Praxis und Erkenntnis" in *D/Z.Ph.:* Berlin, no. 4, 1962.
N.S. Narski: "Ob istoriko-filosofskom razvitii poniatija 'otchuzhdenie'" in *Filosofskie Nauki:* Leningrad, no. 4, 1963.
G. Navel: *Travaux:* Stock, Paris, 1945.
P. Naville: *Vers l'automatisme social:* Gallimard, Paris, 1963.

D. Nedelkovitch: "L'homme et l'humain" in *Memorias del XIII Congreso...:* vols. 2 & 3.
E. Nicol: *Historicismo y existencialismo:* F.C.E., Mexico, 1950.
    Los principios de la ciencia: F.C.E., Mexico, 1965.
T.I. Oizerman: *Formirovanie filosofii marksisma:* Moscow, 1962.
    Problema otchuzdenija i burzhuasznaja legenda o marksisme: Ed. Znanie, Moscow, 1965.
    "*Man and his Alienation*" in *Memorias...:* vol. 8.
M. Olmedo: *Sociedades precapitalistas:* vols. 1-4: Mexico, 1961-3.
J. Ortega y Gasset: *España invertebrada:* in *Obras completas:* Madrid, 1957, vol. 3.
    Revolt of the Masses: Allen and Unwin, 1951.
A. Ouibo: "L'elaboration des problemes du materialisme historique pour Marx et Engels dans 'L'idéologie allemande'" in *Recherches internationales:* Paris, no. 19, 1960.
V. Packard: *The Hidden Persuaders:* New York, 1957.
L.N. Pajitnov: *U istokov revoliutzionnogo perevorota v filosofii:* Moscow, 1960.
    "Les manuscrits economico-philosophiques de 1844" in *Recherches internationales:* Paris, no. 19, 1960.
F. Pappenheim: *The Alienation of Modern Man:* Monthly Review, New York, 1959.
M.I. Petrosian: "O marksistkom ponimanii suschnost chieloveka" in *Filosofskie nauki:* Leningrad, no. 4, 1963. pp. 19-27.
G. Petrovic: "El concepto del hombre en Marx" in *Cuadernos americanos:* Mexico, no. 4, 1962.
G.V. Plekhanov: *Selected Works.*
H. Popitz: *Der entfremdete Mensch* in *Philosophische Forschungen, Neue Folge* vol. 2, Basle, 1953.
Praktika-Kriteri istiny v nauke: Moscow, 1960.
D. Riesman: *Lonely Crowd:* Yale University Press, 1950.
    Individualism Reconsidered: New York, 1954.
I. Roguinski: "L'evolution de l'homme" in *Recherches internationales,* no. 46.
M. Rossi: *Marx e la dialettica hegeliana:* 2 vols. Ed. Riuniti, Rome, 1963.
B.L. Rubinstein: *El ser y la conciencia:* Grijalbo, Mexico, 1963.
M.N. Rutkevich: *Praktika-osnova poznaniya i kriterii istiny:* Moscow, 1952.
A. Sabetti: "Il rapporto uomo-natura nel pensiero de Gramsci e la fondazione della scienza" in *Studi Gramsciani:* Rome, 1958.
    Sulla fondazione del materialismo storico: Florence, 1962.
M. Sacristan: "La tarea de Engels en el Anti-Dühring. Introduction to Engels: *Anti-Dühring:* Grijalbo, Mexico, 1964.
A. Sánchez Vázquez: "Contribucion a una dialectica de la finalidad y la causalidad" in *Dianoia:* Unam, Mexico, 1961.
    "Ideas estéticas en los 'Manuscritos económico-filosóficos de Marx" in *Ibid.*

A. Sánchez Vázquez: "Mitología y verdad en la crítica de nuestra época" in *Memorias...:* vol. 4, Mexico, 1963.
Presencia de Rousseau: Mexico, 1962.
"Estructuralismo e historia" in *Marxismo y estructuralismo:* Grijalbo, Mexico, 1971.
J-P. Sartre: *Being and Nothingness:* Methuen, London, 1969.
Communists and Peace: Braziller, 1968.
Critique de la raison dialectique: Gallimard, Paris, 1960.
Sartre et.al.: *Marxisme et existentialisme:* Plon, Paris, 1962.
A. Schaff: "Le vrai visage du jeune Marx" in *Recherches internationales:* Paris no. 19, 1960.
Philosophy of Man: Dell, New York, 1968.
"Le conception marxiste de l'individu" in *Recherches internationales:* Paris, no. 46, 1965.
P.M. Schuhl: *Machinisme et philosophie:* Paris, 1947.
Etudes sur la fabulation platonicienne: Paris, 1947.
L. Sebag: *Marxisme et estructuralisme:* Payot, Paris, 1964.
J. Semprun: "Marxisme et humanisme" in *La nouvelle critique:* Paris, no. 164, 1965.
E. Shorojova: *El problema de la conciencia:* Grijalbo, Mexico, 1963.
M. Simon: "Marxisme et humanisme" in *La nouvelle critique:* Paris, no. 165. 1965.
G. Simondon: *Du mode d'existence des objets techniques:* Aubier, Paris, 1964.
G. Sorel: *Reflections on Violence:* Collier Macmillan, 1961, New York.
A. Spirkin: *Proisjozdenie soznania:* Moscow, 1960.
J.V. Stalin: *Problems of Leninism:* Moscow, 1960.
S.G. Strumilin: "Razdelenietruda y vsestoronnee razvitie lichnosti" in *Voprosy filosofii:* Moscow, no. 3, 1963.
B. Suchodolski: *Teoría marxista de la educación:* Grijalbo, Mexico, 1966.
J. Suret-Canale: "Marxisme et humanisme" in *La nouvelle critique:* Paris, no. 172, 1966.
M. Takiyettin: "Der Mensch als arbeitender wesen" in *Memorias...:* vol. 2.
E. Thier: "Anthropologie des jungen Marx nach den Pariser. okonomich-philosophischen Manuscripten" in Marx: *Nationalökonomie und Philosophie:* Koln u. Berlin, 1950.
Menschenbild des jungen Marx: Gottingen, 1957.
P. Togliatti: "Per una giusta compresione del pensiero di Antonio Labriola" in *Rinascita:* Rome, june 1954.
"De Hegel au marxisme" in *Recherches internationales:* Paris, 1960.
Tran-Duc-Thao: "Le 'noyau rationnel' dans la dialectique hégélienne" in *La pensée:* Paris, no. 119, pp. 3-23.
N.G. Valentinova: "Roll lichnosti v predolenii monotonnostiraschlennogo tuda" in *Ochertaj lichnosti novogo rabochego:* Moscow, 1963.
M. Verret: *Los marxistas y la religión:* Ed. Nuestro Tiempo, Buenos Aires, 1965.

M. Verret: "Marxisme et humanisme" in *La nouvelle critique:* Paris, no. 168, 1965.
J. Vialatoux: *Signification humaine du travail:* Eds. Ouvrieres, Paris, 1953.
G.N. Volkov: "Automatizatzia, novy istoricheskii etap v razvitii tejniki" in *Voprosy filosofii:* no. 6, 1964.
G. Della Volpe: *Rousseau e Marx:* Rome, 1957.
B.A. Voronovich: "Dialektika tseli truda y seedstv eio osuschestvlenija" in *Filosofskie nauki:* Leningrad, no. 2, 1963.
J. de Vries: *Teoría del conocimiento del materialismo dialéctico:* Bilbao, 1960.
J. Vuillemin: *L'être et le travail:* P.U.F., Paris, 1949.
G. Wetter: *Dialectical Materialism:* Routledge, London, 1958.
       Soviet Ideology Today: Heinemann, London, 1966.
Wm. F. Whyte: *Organisation Man:* Penguin,
W.K. Wimsatt: *The Verbal Icon:* University of Kentucky Press, 1954.
A. Zanardo: "Il 'manualo" di Bukharin visto dai comunisti tedeschi e da Gramsci" in *Studi Gramsciani:* Rome, 1958.

INDEX

(NB: MARX and ENGELS are not given specific entries in the Index, since they appear throughout the work.)

Absolute, The—42, 52, 64, 70.
Abstract and Concrete—163, 171.
Academicism—224
Activity:
  Cognitive/teleological—153-4
  experimental-scientific—159
  in general—149-50
  subjective and objective—153, 155, 195
  theoretical—161-3
Aesthetics:
  irrationalist—231
  rationalist—231
  psychological/sociological—208
Agent:—149
  of production—347
Alberti, Leon Batista—18, 20
Alienation:
  and division of labour—358-9
  ideological—368
  objective aspects—354-6
  and praxis—110
  religious—71-77
  subjective aspects—54, 357
  of workers—105
  in Feuerbach—352-4
  in Marx:
    in *1844 Manuscripts*—354-8
    in *German Ideology*—358-60
    in *Capital*—360-70
    evolution of concept in Marx—356-9
Althusser, Louis—30, 140, 245, 245
Analysis:
  genetic and structural—285-6
Anaxagoras—219
Annekov, P.V.—268, 271
Anthropology:
  Feuerbach's—82
  and religion—81-2
Antiphon—16
Archimedes—16
Aristotle—2, 11-14, 174, 219
Art:—158
  and craft—15-16, 19
  as imitative praxis—223-5

  as intentional praxis—262-3
  and violence—307
Artisan:
  in Greece—15, 18
Artist:
  and craftsman—19
Automatic writing—229
Automation—221, 222, 235

Bacon, Francis—17, 22
Bachelard, Gaston—140
Bauer, Bruno—94
Bernstein, Edouard—27
Blanqui, Louis—178
Blanquism:
  and Leninism—315
Bloch, J.—151
Breton, André—228-9
Bruno, Giordano—17, 19, 20
Bukharin, N.—30
Bureaucracy:
  as bureaucratised praxis—211-14
  Hegel's concept of—212-14
  and imperialism—213-14
  struggle against—213

Campanella, Thomas—20
Capital:
  as Fetish—361-3
Capitalism:
  and Science—17
Categories:
  logical: formation of—173
Cieszkowski—95
Class:
  for itself—241
  in itself—241
  working—263-4
  revolutionary—241, 263-4
Class Struggle—132
Collingwood, R.G.—316
Commodity—361-2
Common Sense—3, 169-70
Communism:—130, 242
  "War Communism"—264-5
Comprehension:

of praxis—188-90
Concept:
 geometrical—174-5
 and man (Hegel, Lenin)—58
Conditions:
 Subjective and objective—254
Consciousness:
 activity of (Kant)—40-41
 bourgeois—244
 class—237-8
 of God (Feuerbach)—76
 of non-violence—318
 of object—74
 practical—229-234
 in practical process—228-9
 of praxis—230, 233
 of self—74-5, 76, 77
 socialist—238-9, 253-4
 theoretical—241
 trade-union—238-9
Consciousness, Ordinary:
 and artistic activity—8
 political—7-8
 of praxis—2-10
 and theoretical activity—9-10
Consciousness, Philosophical:
 of praxis—10, 16, 20-21, 29, 235
Contemplation:—76
 and practice (in Renaissance)—16-18
 and work (in Renaissance)—20
Counter-Violence—310-311
Craft—215
Creation:
 artistic—206-9
 concept of—200
 revolutionary—204-6
Criticism:
 in art—261
 (intentional fallacy)
 radical—99-101
 as weapon—99
Croce, Benedetto—208, 316
Culture:
 of the hand—223
 Rousseau's critique of—23
Cybernetics—177-8

Daily Life—4-5, 8
Darwin, Charles—219
Davydova, G.A.—30
Depoliticisation—7-8
Descartes, René—22
Desire—48
 for recognition (Hegel)—53
Determinism:

Economic—296
Dialectical Materialism—30-31, 136-7
Diogenes—16
Division of Labour:
 and alienation—355-6
 social—15, 216-17
 and theoretical activity—173
Dualism (Kant)—41
Dühring, Karl—308, 324
Duncker, H.—30

Economic Factor:
 principal and determining role—278
 determining in the last instance—279-80
Economists, Classical—23-4, 104
Egoism—85
Einstein, Albert—191
Eles, Yovo—30
Empiricism:
 of praxis—140
Empiriocriticism—140
Encyclopedists—23
Ends—62-4, 152-3, 194, 203
 Adjustment to—150-1
 and knowledge—300
 and product—193-4
 of theory—186-8
Enlightenment:
 concept of social transformation—122-3
 idea of history—276
Epistemological Break—140-141
Essence, Human—83
 according to Feuerbach—72, 77-8, 87
 according to Hegel—53
 alienated—107, 353
 and history—344-6
 and human existence—338-41, 342-3
 speculative conception of—340, 342
Ethics:
 of action—45
Euclid—174-5
Existence, Human—338-41
Existence, Social:
 and consciousness—244
Experimentation—22
Expression:
 of actual history—246
 concept of—245-6

Factors, Subjective and Objective:

of praxis—28, 32-3, 286
and rationality—299-301
of revolutionary praxis—286
of violence—319-21
Fanon, Frantz—323, 324
Fetishism:
and alienation—363, 366-7
of commodity—361-3
Feuerbach, Ludwig—25, 31, 70-88, 96, 101, 105, 109, 122, 126, 138, 139, 140, 249, 277, 331, 352-4
Fichte, J.G.—2, 26, 41, 43, 44, 45, 50
Fogarasi, B.—30
Forces, Productive:—131, 132, 284, 287, 325
Formalism:
Kantian—41
of practice—211-13
of State (Hegel)—212
Fourier, Charles—165
Fourier, J.B.J.—176
Freedom:
human (Marx)—334-6
of will (Kant)—43
Friedmann, G.—223

Gaidukov, Y.G.—30
Gaos, José—219, 222
Geometry:
Euclidian—175
non-Euclidian—175
Germany:
as historical anachronism—44, 93
God—70, 71, 76, 83-4, 331, 352
Goethe, J.W.—122
Good, The:
in Hegel's *Logic*—61-3
Gramsci, Antonio—30, 32-3, 116, 245, 246, 252, 256, 325
Grushin, B.A.—285-6
Gumplowicz, L.—308

Haeckel, E.—219
Hand—218-19
Hegel, G.F.—2, 3, 25-6, 31, 40-65, 70-72, 88, 92-4, 107, 126, 126, 138, 140, 164, 201, 248, 273, 275, 276, 331, 353
Heine, H.—43
Herder, H.G.—122
Hesiod—16
Hess, Moses—95, 165
Historical Character:
of man—342-3

Historicism:
and Marxism—245-6
Historiography:
Bourgeois—313-315
History:—302
and alienation—356-7
and human essence—338, 339-40, 341
and violence—325-6
as science—284-6
continuity and discontinuity—267, 285
Hegelian concept of—273-4
materialist concept of—128-9, 131-4
men as subjects of—267-70
purpose of—301-2
universal structural rationality of—280-83
Homo Oeconomicos—24

I (Fichte)—41-2
Idea (Hegel):
absolute—58, 59, 62, 64
anthropological analysis of (Lenin) —60
of the Good—57, 61-2, 62, 63
of knowledge—58, 62
practical—57-64
theoretical—60-61, 62
Ideal:
abstract or Utopian—242
communism as—242
in practical process—209
Idealization:
of work (Hegel)—55-6
Ideas:—162
expressive capacity—244
Imperialism—185, 323
Individual, Social—335
Individualism—41
Individuals—269, 271, 346
social formation and determination of behaviour—288-90
social quality—270-1
and human essence—339-40, 343, 346
Industrial Revolution—179
Industry:
its anthropological basis—133
Instruments of labour:—156-7
and human labour—156-8
Intellectual:
and proletariat—247-53
and social classes—250-1

Intentionality—297
Intentions and results—260-1
Interests—292-5
Interior and exterior—200, 207-8
Irrationality:
  and history—298-9
  concept of, applied to society—280-2

James, William—170-1
Judaism—85

Kampffmeyer, P.—27
Kant, Emmanuel—2, 40, 41, 43, 44, 45, 50, 118
Kautsky, Karl—239, 313
Knowledge:
  analytic and synthetic (Hegel)—59-60
  its object—117-118
  its origins—172-3
  and practice—28, 115-117, 117-120
Kolakowski, L.—30
Korsch, Karl—30
Kosík, Karel—30, 116

Labour:—155-6
  abstract—361, 366
  alienated—104-7, 339-41, 345, 353-6, 363-6
  as man's essence—49, 338-40
  concrete—361
  creative—214
  in general—348-9, 360
  in mass production—215-16, 218
  its positive aspect (Hegel)—48
  for bourgeois political economists—23-5, 104
  in Greek society—12, 13, 14, 16-17
  for Hegel—46-51
  in Renaissance—18-19
Laws:
  of creative process—209
  of social structure—286-7
  of socialism—300
  of structural change—286-7
Left, Hegelians—94, 96
Lenin, V.I.—4, 24, 27-9, 58-62, 134, 179, 180, 183-6, 204, 205, 206, 212-13, 237, 238, 239-40, 246, 248, 252, 255-6, 264-5, 314, 326
Levels of praxis:—199-200, 230-232, 255-7
Line:
  political—255

Lloyd Morgan, C.—200
Lobachevski, N.I.—191
Love, human (Feuerbach)—81
Lukács, Georgy—30, 46, 47, 49-50, 241, 278-80

Machiavelli, N.—21, 312
Man:
  average—4-7
  and circumstance—123-5
  concept of—268-70
  and history—268
  as historical being—343, 350
  "practical"—8-9
  as practical being—18, 331, 334, 343
  as social being—342-3
  as theoretical being—15
Manetti, G.—18
Marxism:
  as ideology and science—243-7
  as philosophy of action—31
  as philosophy of our time—245
  as philosophy of praxis—137-41
  as philosophy of the proletariat—241-3
  and pragmatism—170-2
  as radical philosophical change—31
  as science—33
  and other social theories—27
Master and slave (Hegel)—53-5
Materialism, Historical—278-80, 281
Materials, preexisting, of ideology—248-50
Mathematics:
  and production—174, 175-6
Matter—116
Messianism:
  proletarian—234, 241
Method:
  Feuerbach—71-2
  Marx and Lenin—183-5
Mission:
  universal, historical, of proletariat—100-102, 234-7
Mondolfo, Rodolfo—74, 78
More, Thomas—19, 20

Natural Activity—4-5
Nature:
  Anthropological—111-112, 114
  in itself—113
  entological priority of—113, 119, 120
Nature, Human:

in general—346-9
Navel, Georges—220
N.E.P.—265
Noneconomic levels—280
Non recognition, of self—264, 366
Non-violence—316-18
Non-worker—105
Normativism:
  in art—224
Not-I (Fichte)—41

Object:
  of interpretation and transformation—125-6
  of recognition—118
  religious—74, 75, 77
  sensuous—74, 75
Objectification—352
  and alienation—108-9, 110-111
  artistic—208
Objectivism:
  of ordinary consciousness—6
  of praxis—301-2
Objectivity:
  I and II—352-3
Owen, Robert—165

Paganism—79
Party:
  Marxist-Leninist—32-3, 135-7, 253-6, 259
Pauperization:
  of the worker—354-6
Philosophy:
  and action—97-9
  of alienation—353
  German Idealist—25
  of history (Hegel)—273
  of man—349-50
  Neo Hegelian critique—93, 95
  and praxis—163, 166
  of praxis (Gramsci)—30, 32, 33
  and proletariat—100-102
  and its realization—97, 189
  fundamental problems—25-6, 30
Physics:
  and production—174-5
  quantum—176
Picasso, Pablo—208
Pico Della Mirandola—18
Plato—11-14, 16, 231
Plekhanov, G.—27
Plutarch—12, 16
Poiesis—1
Polis—11

Politics—7, 12-13, 160-1
Populism—28
Positivity (Hegel)—47
Possibility:
  aesthetic—207-8
"Practice":
  in everyday language—1, 4, 6-7
Practice:
  theoretical—161-2, 163
Pragmatism:—170-1
  of praxis—140
  concept of truth in—121
Praxis:
  bureaucratised—211-14
  as cognitive category—30
  creative—200-203
  as economic concept—24-5
  in Fichtean sense—41
  in Feuerbach—84-8
  its forms—156-61
  individual—149, 199, 269, 280, 287-90, 295-7
  reiterative or imitative—209-11, 215-18
  revolutionary—122-5, 178-86, 232-4, 264
  for social democratic theorists—26-8
  spontaneous and reflective—149
  nonintentional—259, 265-7, 271-3, 290
Process, Historical:
  as structural change—285
Process, Labour—157, 349
Production:
  in history and social life—109, 110, 128-9, 342
  liberation from—334-6
Progress:
  Rousseau's critique of—23
Proletariat—100-101, 102, 103, 130, 234-5, 241, 247-9
Purpose:
  of history—301-2

Rationality:
  of actual history—295-7
  of changes in social structure—283-6
  limitats of—278-80
  objective—278, 298
  of social structure—299
  and teleology of history—273-5
  universal and structural, of history—273-83
Reason—14, 80, 277
Reformation—43

Reformism—27, 235-6, 241, 314, 327
Relations:
  "human"—220-1, 323
  of production—271
Religion—52, 71, 77, 81-4
Revolution—100, 132, 133-4, 135-6
  essence of—315-16
  permanent—179-80
  theory and—178-81, 232-4
  and violence—312-13
Revolutions, Social, in history—28, 29, 44, 104, 264, 297, 313, 326
Ricardo, David—23, 181
Roads to Socialism:
  non-peaceful—170-1
  peaceful—325
Rosenkranz—47
Rousseau, J.J.—23
Ruge, Arnold—86, 87, 94
Rutkevich, M.N.—30

Sacchi, B.—19
Sacrifice (Hegel)—47
Saint-Simon, H.—26, 165
Sartre, J.P.—245, 269-70, 277, 320
Scarcity:
  Sartreian concept of—269-70
Schaff, Adam—30
Schelling, F.W.—40, 41, 44
Schopenhauer, A.—5
Science—159
  anthropological character of—114-115
  and industry—119
  "learned" and vulgar (Plato)—16
  and material production—173-8
  natural—172-3
  and technology—17, 18
Smith, Adam—23, 46-7, 49, 164, 181
Socialism:
  ethical—27
  scientific—127, 244, 247
Sociality—270-1, 342-3, 345
State, The,—212-13, 325
Stirner, Max—82, 88
Strauss, David—94
Structuralism:
  in explanation of history and social life—284-5
Structure, Social:—267, 283, 286
  complex—282
  rationality of change—283-6
Subjectivism—28, 254
  Fichtean—41
  in historical praxis—297-301

System, and Method—93-4

Taylor—218, 221
Taylorism—218
Teleology, historical—273-4
Theology (Feuerbach)—71
Thales—10
Theoreticism, absolute—88, 93
Theory:—164-6
  as knowledge—74, 118
  and politics—13, 14, 21, 22
  practice as basis of—172-3
  and religion—78-81
  and revolution—137-1, 178, 182-4
  as subjective activity (Feuerbach)—79-80
Thing in Itself (Kant)—40-1
Third World—323-4
Time:
  free—335
  freed from production—335
  of labour—335
Tools—52
Trade Unionism—241
Tran-Duc-Thao—219
Trotsky, Leon—212
Truth:
  criterion of—87-8, 121-2, 190-1
  and expressiveness—244
  objective—121
  pragmatist concept of—170-2

Utopianism—125

Vacuum, of consciousness—223
Vanguard, revolutionary—263-4
Violence:
  apologia for—319
  colonial—323-4
  as historical necessity—313-16
  as human attribute—305-6
  ideological or moral—317
  men and instruments of—324-5
  negation of its role—313-14
  origins of (Hegel)—56
  potential and actual—311-13
  in productive and artistic praxis—308-10
  Sartreian idea of—320-2
  in social praxis—308-10
Voltaire—276
Vörlander—27

Weitling, W.—178

World:
  as object of interpretation and
    transformation—149-51
  "practical"—4
  sensuous—119

Young Germany—98
Young Hegelians—97, 99, 249